HUNGARIAN REFUGEE #152
István B'Rácz

Columbia University Refugee Project - Hungary
1945-1956
CURPH#152

Edited by
Emöke Zsuzsánna B'Rácz

Burning Bush Press of Asheville

North Carolina

Copyright © 2021
Emöke Zsuzsánna B'Rácz
emokebracz.com

All rights reserved.
No part of this publication may be reproduced
or transmitted in any form or by any means
without prior permission.

ISBN: 9780965865739
Order @ malaprops.com
Printed in USA

Layout & Design by Kim Pitman
FireflyInx.com

INTRODUCTION

Following World War II, Hungary had to choose a government anew and that is where my story of my father begins

"I thought My Father Was God" is the title of an anthology (edited by Paul Auster), and I must admit I grew up with that kind of feeling toward a father whom I hardly knew.

My father, István B'Racz (Rácz Pista, among friends), was born in Turkeve, Hungary in 1923. He was educated at the local Jewish school because his mother knew that he would get the best education there. He was Calvinist. His sisters grew up Catholic. In Hungary at the time girls would follow the religion of the mother and boys would follow the religion of the father. Interestingly, this was never a problem for anyone in the family.

I don't know when he moved his parents and sisters to Budapest. We know that he went to the University of Politics and Economics (Közgazdasági Egyetem) in Budapest. He was involved in the Független Ifjuság (Independent Youth Party) and got elected in 1945 to represent them under the Kisgazda Party (Small Landowners' Party) in the Hungarian Parliament. To this day he is the youngest member ever elected to the Parliament.

October 23, 1991, he received the highest civilian award, the Officer's Cross, from Göncz Árpád, the Prime Minister, in a ceremony in the Parliament. He also received a Recognition letter in 1992 from Jozsef Antal, the new Prime Minister, as follows:

In the Name of Truth

In the spirit of the decision of the Parliament and the government of the Hungarian Republic, we recognize that you and your family bore unjust burdens, limitations and policing of your freedom as citizens.

March 31, 1950 - October 25, 1950 you were detained by the AVO, and from October 26, 1950 - September 16, 1953 in Recski Kényszermunkatáborban as a prisoner/laborer.

We know that you, your family and countless others suffered this in the name of Freedom for the citizens of Hungary. We believe that your actions will not be forgotten.

Budapest, December 1992

Antal József (Joseph Antal)
miniszterelnök (prime minister)

My father was always silent about what happened to him in the captured years and politically. When I asked he said, "I will not burden my children with that history." That was usually the end of that conversation. After his death in 1994, my mother handed me the "big Black book" that explained to me his political rise and life. I have read other memoirs about the era and found that all the authors were recounting their heroic actions. I read the big Black book again, and I was speechless. I heard in every word my father's voice and his unmitigated stand for the truth as he knew it and lived it. I always knew my parents were strong and special in their outlook in life, and never have I found more intellectually interesting company.

I have retyped the interview and shared the copy with Tamás Kabdebo who said "reorganize the Q an A segment but change not a single word of your father's." I have great respect for Tamás as a poet and a historian of that time period in Hungary.

The interview material from my father was recorded by Columbia University Refugee Project in 1957. He was subject #152 in the Vera and Donald Blinken Archives. There were no names to help me. #152 was the only subject interviewed who was born in Turkeve to a Catholic mother and a Calvinist father. Religion in my family was more part of the past history than reality in my childhood years. Stories I heard from my mother and my uncle Lajos about their wonderful experience in the Pozsonyi Uti templomban (in church) with pastor Albert Bereczky. He had a very strong young-adult program for the parishioners. My parents' friends were all part of that time and place. My uncle Lajos was my father's best friend. My mother, Margit, is my uncle Lajos's younger sister. They survived and weathered World War II and the following period all together.

My uncle Lajos, my father, and a dear friend, Pál Jonás, went underground evading the so-called draft to the German army. They were caught, tortured and sentenced to death. The truck taking them from Andrássi Ut 60 to the place for their execution came under fire by the "liberating" Russian air attack. They escaped and hid in the city. Life was never the same for them after that. My understanding of my father's political stand was that Hungary and her people deserved to be an independent Nation after 1000 years of oppression and subjugation to Anjous, Ottomans, Hapsburgs, Nazis and the Soviets.

My mother and I visited the Terror Ház in 2000, in Budapest. This is the museum for that historic period. We had to leave. We lost our breath in the torture room (in the basement) where I remembered the story…he was water-boarded and placed in a small hole in the wall as punishment. The accusation was that he was conspiring to overthrow the government, but there was no further hearing or judgment except the silent trip to Recsk, the Labor/death camp. There was no information about him for three and a half years. I asked where my father (Édesapám) was, and I was informed that he was recovering in a sanatorium in the mountains. This sounded quasi-romantic to a 5 year old, in a way, until in 7th grade when a man approached me as I was speaking to my best friend after church, and he asked if I was the "Senator's daughter". I went home and asked what was that about. I still did not get a proper explanation. The air was still filled with uncertainty and fear. Fear of "what" I never found out. I still carry some of that echo-of-fear stamped on my soul, but I get more and more understanding from his book about people and their fearful approach to life in that era. Understanding my parents' history and the time they lived in is making my life more complete. There is so much to behold and learn.

   I know he escaped the Soviet police state and house arrest on December 4,1956 by swimming across the Fertöd Lake to Austria and went on to Germany and France with other Hungarian Patriots. Eight years later President Kennedy and Premier Khrushchev agreed to reunite families separated since 1956. I was sixteen when we sailed by the Statue of Liberty on USS America. I asked him why he chose America and he said, " Because this is the country with the most potential to do good in the world."

Emöke Zsuzsánna B'Rácz Asheville NC emokebracz.com
Piroska B'Rácz Gibson (sister - artist) Asheville NC
István Péter B'Rácz (brother - composer) Hamden, Connecticut

Please listen to the poem Hungarian Childhood on Papyrus Nugator
istvanpeterbracz.bandcamp.com/album/papyrus-nugator

A MAGYAR KÖZTÁRSASÁG ELNÖKE

B. RÁCZ ISTVÁNNAK

A TÖBBPÁRTI DEMOKRÁCIA GONDOLATÁNAK ÁPOLÁSÁÉRT
ÉS AZ ESZME IRÁNTI HŰSÉGÉÉRT

A MAGYAR KÖZTÁRSASÁGI ÉRDEMREND TISZTIKERESZTJE

KITÜNTETÉST ADOMÁNYOZOM

KELT BUDAPESTEN, 1991. ÉVI OKTÓBER HÓ 23. NAPJÁN

Göncz Árpád

Prime Minister of Hungary Honors
István B'Rácz
In recognition of significant services toward the idea of multiParty Democracy
The Officers' Cross of the Order of Hungarian Republic
The award is given

FOREWORD

Nearly sixty years have passed since an event occurred which is now largely forgotten by Americans of a certain age but at the time seemed to threaten World War Three between the Western powers and what was then the Soviet Union. And since that event coincided with my 18th birthday and my registering for the military draft (it was compulsory then), the incident made a special impact on me: If war came, I was likely to have been caught up in it. While the Hungarian Revolution of 1956 may be largely forgotten by many in America, it is definitely not forgotten by the Hungarian people who lived through it, were exiled because of it, or lost friends or family members to the merciless Soviet invasion that extinguished it. Or by those who, like Emöke B'Rácz, are the children of the Hungarian expatriates of that time.

Emöke is the founder of one of America's best and most esteemed independent bookstores, Malaprop's, in Asheville, North Carolina. Emöke's father, the late István B'Rácz, was a leading intellectual and economist in his native Hungary and before the revolution had suffered arrest and imprisonment at the hands of the Communist regime there. Emöke is a poet and artist, and has memorialized the moment when, as a teenage girl, she witnessed her father's arrest:

> The knocking came at midnight in wintertime.
> The room was warm and at peace with the night.
> Two men brought in the cold under their hats,
> Grabbed most of the books and threw them into potato sacks
> My father was still and silent
> Like a falling leaf in the eye of the storm,
> The silence was broken by my mother sobbing
> As they dragged him through the door.

István B'Rácz, eventually freed from a labor camp of Recsk, was a witness to and participant in the revolution and, after its suppression, was one of approximately 200,000 Hungarian patriots who escaped and sought refuge in the United States and elsewhere in the West. The uprising was the first such to prevail, if only briefly, against communist tyranny and was a world-shaking event. Yet many younger people in this country have never even heard of it. Such is the whimsy of history and collective memory. Had it indeed ignited a war--and in a nuclear age that war might well have been the last war-- history and memory, had they survived, would have enshrined the Hungarian uprising and the holocaust it occasioned. But instead, its sixtieth anniversary seems certain to pass unremarked save by a relative few.

I am one of those American few. My 18th birthday fell on Friday, October 21, 1956. I wish I could recall some sense of what that date felt like, smelled like, looked like, but I cannot. October has always been my favorite month with its balmy Indian summer days contrasting with the chill of its autumn nights and the leaves of the hard-woods glowing yellow and crimson, its air sharp and crisp and clean. I must have been savoring all that. But despite its significance at the time, my mind seems to have discarded any true sense-memory. I have lost my draft card which, dog-eared and fading, reposed in my wallet for years until I knew I had safely aged out of that particular obligation. I wish now that I had preserved it, in case a glimpse of it might recall some detail of that then significant phase of my life.

But I did not. All I know is that on Sunday, October 23, two days after my birthday, students in Budapest began demonstrating against the repressions of the ruling Hungarian Communist government and the strictures of its masters in Soviet Moscow. At first the government, headed by Premier Imre Nagy, a Communist but also a reformer, hesitated as if uncertain whether the movement was a serious threat to national stability or might somehow be harnessed and controlled. But it was not long before Nagy seemed to embrace some of the principles of liberty and nationalism espoused by the demonstrators and the student movement began to attract the sympathies of elements of the wider population. Despite Nagy's seeming support, other enemies in the Hungarian government made the decision to stifle the uprising but found that they could not. The government was of course subject to the will of the Soviet leaders in the Kremlin. As the Hungarian movement grew, it became a struggle between growing numbers of students, workers and civilians and even elements of the Hungarian army against the dreaded AVH, the Hungarian security police. Vicious battles broke out in Budapest. Angry citizens broke into AVH headquarters and hunted down and lynched its despised agents.

Then on Sunday, November 4, when it was clear that the national government could not effectively resist the revolt, and that in fact the revolt had succeeded, the Soviet Union determined to crush it and invaded Hungary with Red Army troops, tanks, artillery and warplanes. They burst into Budapest and the Hungarians, young and old, men and women, workers and intellectuals, resisted Red Army troops in violent street battles. Children fought tanks with Molotov cocktails and nitroglycerine and other fighters resisted with rifles and submachine guns either captured from the AVH or handed over to them by sympathetic soldiers of the Hungarian army. Soviet aircraft bombed and strafed rebel positions. Soviet heavy guns shattered buildings. It was a scene almost unimaginable to those of us who had come to believe that the Iron Curtain had so thoroughly descended as to render armed resistance by the people of the Russian client states impossible. The spectacle of workers, supposedly the darlings of Marxism, attempting to overthrow a Marxist power, was electrifying to the rest of the world and a powerful lesson about the hollowness of Communist ideology.

The United States, through Radio Free Europe broadcasts and statements by political figures, had long advocated the rollback of Communist domination and the liberation of the occupied nations of the Soviet Bloc. As a result, many of the freedom fighters, in staging their revolt, had hoped their actions would cause the United States or the United Nations to intervene on their behalf. Indeed, when the Soviets invaded, the U.S. and other Western powers protested and demanded their withdrawal, and for a time it appeared that a conflict between East and West might come. The insurrectionists continued to fight on against great odds in the hope that the United Nations or the United States might step in.

But no action from outside was taken although the Hungarian patriots pleaded by radio for assistance. Instead the West dithered; simultaneously with the Hungarian revolt Egypt's leader Gamal A. Nasser had nationalized the Suez Canal and Britain and France had induced Israel to provoke a conflict with Egypt that would serve as a pretext for an Anglo-French invasion; fears of a major war were thus inflamed and the nerves of Western nations seemed to fail before the dual crises in Eastern Europe and the Middle East. And so, during November 1956, Soviet forces crushed the Hungarian revolution. Premier Nagy, captured by the Russians, was imprisoned, tried and later executed, as were others associated with the outbreak.

It seems to me an improbable yet also nearly inevitable fate that, given my lingering interest in the Hungarian experience of 1956, the time came when I would meet and come to know Emöke B'Rácz. I had returned to my native Western North Carolina from Washington, DC after twenty years as a lobbyist and technocrat, determined to become the writer I had always wished to be. I learned of Malaprop's Bookstore/Cafe and soon met Emöke. The relationship between bookseller and writer that began then has continued since, and of course over time I have come to know some of the story of her father and of herself as they lived the very same history with which I had been so long preoccupied from a seemingly unbridgeable distance.

Now Emöke, much to my surprise and pleasure, has asked me to introduce her father's recollections and observations of the Hungarian experience between 1945 and 1956 as gathered by the Columbia University Refugee

Project on Hungary. I do so with deep humility. I have read his words with respect, admiration and an awareness of my own inadequacy to do justice to his life and memory. As a writer I admire his ability to so concisely analyze competing political systems with a razor-sharp intelligence, as in the following passage:

"I never approved of communism, viewing it always as incapable of realization—as an asocial system... I have the feeling that communism as a system was based on the criticism of early capitalism and, with the passing of time, and with changes which occurred in the capitalist system, many forceful affirmations and statements of the Communist credo have likewise lost their application, usefulness, and ingredients of truth which they initially possessed.

Every person likes to construct his own life, and it is imperative that he is given an opportunity to do so. Leveling, equalization is necessary, but not to the point where every man possesses only one cup. Nor did communism achieve such results; there are social and class differences under communism just like everywhere else. The position of the leaders and of the good cadres is immeasurably better than the rest. There is a group of privileged few under both capitalism and communism; the difference is that the life of those who are not members of the group of the privileged few is incomparably more hopeless under communism than under capitalism. If capitalism oscillates to the detriment of the many, there is always room for slow but orderly and peaceful adjustment. If oscillation of an identical kind occurs under communism, a determined movement toward the caste-system is the result, and the only way for the masses is the way to prison. I value personal freedom above all else and for this reason I oppose communism in principle."

But he also invokes the personal, disorienting and Kafkaesque terror of an interrogation by the AVH, the Hungarian security police:

"They took me up for questioning and put me in a small room which was facing the room of my questioner. The small room had a sofa, a desk, and a chair. The window was protected by heavy iron bars. They gave me a large stack of paper and told me to write down the story of my life; they advised me to write down honestly and truthfully what I did against the peoples' democracy, with whom did I conspire, of what spy organizations am I a member, etc. Then they left me alone. While I was trying to think what I should do and how I should do it, my questioner came in and took me into his room. As I stepped into [his] room—there was a large, deep easy chair next to his desk—the first thing I notice is that a very close relative of mine is sitting in that chair. Her face is leaning slightly on her hand and her shoes, dress, in a word, everything she had on, I knew and recognized immediately.

At that instant, and later on as well, I had no doubt whatsoever in my mind that the person sitting in that chair was she. I wanted to go towards her and to tell her something, but they grabbed me, holding my mouth and hands tight, but permitting me to stay there for a second or two, giving me ample opportunity to view her to make certain that the person sitting there was really she and that no deception occurred and no attempt was made to mislead me. Having accomplished that, they took me back into the small room. There they again told me to begin writing my life's story if I wanted to get out of there. They also advised me that, should I refuse to write, the person whom I have just seen would be "well taken care of," and gave me a vivid description of what would happen to her."

INTERVIEWER: You do not consider it important or perhaps you do not wish to further identify the person you have seen?
ANSWER: She was my wife.

István B'Rácz's powerful, moving and insightful observations of one of the most memorable events of the late twentieth century are now, in this book, offered to the wider audience that they have always deserved.

Charles F. Price
Appalachian Author
Recipient of the Sir Walter Raleigh Literary Award

Author of
Season of Terror
Freedom's Altar
Hiawassee: novel of Civil War
Where the Water-Dogs Laughed
Cock's Spur
Nor the Battle to the Strong

Columbia University Refugee Project - Hungary
(CURPH)

"A" INTERVIEW GUIDE

Sections:		Page
(O)	Instructions and Forms	13
(R)	The Revolt of 1956	15
(W)	Personal Life and Work Experience	157
(S)	Social Problems and Education	219
(G)	Government, Party, Police	279
(C)	Communications	357
(I)	Ideology, Attitudes, and Opinions	369
(X)	Conclusion	458
	Notes from the Journal	464

Questions unanswered are excluded.

Interviewer's Remarks

As you may already know, this research project has been established for the purpose of learning about Hungary. What we are interested in is what has happened since the Second World War. How people reacted to what has happened. What did they like and what did they dislike, and why they did certain things.

This research, which is exclusively of a scientific character, is being conducted by Columbia University, one of the leading American universities. Owing to its scientific character, it does not propose either to justify or to refute any given thesis. It is independent from any political group or organization. It is not a government enterprise, not an emigre activity. Nor do secret military information fall within the sphere of our interest.

What we want is above all the truth. Most of us here tried to follow the events in Hungary, so that we know certain facts or at least we believe we know them. Therefore, I am convinced that you will have many interesting things to tell us. It goes without saying that you can talk of anything with us with the greatest frankness. In order to be able to judge things correctly, first we have to know the facts regardless of whether they are pleasant or unpleasant.

As you know, we do not care whether or not we know the names of the people we talk with. We do this partly for your sake, that is to dispel your possible worries in this respect, and partly in order not to have even a shadow of suspicion fall on ourselves. Also you are entirely free to refuse to answer any question to which you do not wish to reply for any reason. Please feel free to tell me if you wish to take a break or if you have any other observation to make.

I hope you won't mind if I take notes as we talk. This is necessary in order to retain exactly what I hear and thus have the full benefit of your experience for our work.

Bevezetö Megjegyzések

Mint talán már tudja, ez a mi tudományos kutató csoportunk azzal a céllal létesült, hogy Magyarországot minél jobban megismerje. Az érdekel bennünket, hogy mi történt a második világháboru óta. Hogyan reagáltak az emberek mindarra, ami történt, mi az ami tetszett nekik, mi az, ami nem, es hogy miért tettek bizonyos dolgokat.

Ezt a kutato munkát, amely kizárólag tudományos jellegü, Amerika egyik legtekintélyesebb egyeteme, a New-Yorki Columbia egyetem végzi, Tudományos jellegénél fogva nem kiván semmilyen elöre felállitott tételt sem igazolni, sem megcáfolni. Független minden politikai csoporttól vagy organizációtól. Nem állami kezdeményezés és nem emigrációs tevékenység. Titkos katonai informaciok sem esnek érdeklödési körébe.

Az igazságot akarjuk megismerni. Itt majdnem mindannyian igyekeztünk követni a magyarországi eseményeket, úgy hogy ismerünk bizonyos tényeket, vagy legalább is azt hisszük, hogy ismerjük öket. Éppen ezért meg vagyok gyözödve arról, hogy Önnek sok érdekes mondanivalója lesz számunkra. Azt talán fölösleges is mondanom, hogy bármiröl a legnagyobb nyiltsággal beszélhet velünk. Ahhoz, hogy helyesen itélhessük meg a dolgokat, elöször ismernünk kell a tényeket, függetlenül attól, hogy azok kellemesek-e, vagy kellemetlenek.

Amint tudja, nekünk mindegy, hogy ismerjük-e vagy sem az emberek nevét, akikkel beszélgetünk. Ezt részben az Önök kedvéért, illetve esetleges aggodalmaknak eloszlatására tesszük, részben pedig azért, hogy ránk még a gyanu árnyéka se hárulhasson. Ugyszintén, teljes szabadságában áll megtagadni a választ bármely, kérdésre, amelyre bármilyen oknál fogva nem óhajt válaszolni. Kérem, nyugodtan szóljon, ha egy kis szünetet kiván tartani, vagy bármi más észrevétele van.

Remélem, nem zavarja, hogy jegyezni fogom beszélgetésünket. Ez szükséges, hogy pontosan lerögzithessem a hallottakat, és igy az Ön tapasztalatait a legnagyobb mértékben értékesithessük tudományos kutatásunk számára. Mielött hozzákezdenénk, ha volna valami kérdése, igyekezni fogok tölem telhetöleg válaszolni.

THE REVOLT AND ITS ANTECEDENTS
Responses of Refugee #152: István B'Rácz June, 1957

1. ***What do you think we ought to know about events in Hungary?***

You should know of everything that transpired in Hungary during the ten years of Communist rule. You should know about the decisive changes that took place and shape there.

The free elections of 1945 revealed that only 17 percent of the voters endorsed the Communist Party. A sympathy gradually strengthened the Communists, especially in the ranks of the landless peasants and factory workers, who were never overly enthusiastic for Horthy, -- the middle classes have found their proper milieu under Horthy, they were prosperous.

This development of initial sympathy underwent a radical and drastic change in the course of time and became most evident among the peasants and workers. These two segments of the population, who initially welcomed Russians and Communists and sympathized with them for the actual changes they effected, particularly in the land reform, gradually saw the real aims of the new rulers. Total disillusionment characterizes the feelings of these masses.

In 1956, I witnessed the second burial of Rajk. In a small company of friends, we went out to the Kerepesi Cemetery of Budapest, where we saw young cadets from the Ludovika Military Academy lined up in stiff attention on either side of the long procession. They stood there, motionless, and we, who only recently came out of labor camps, looked at them with pity and said to ourselves: "There, this is a lost generation. They grew up in the Communist system; they have no ways of making comparisons. They are lost for Hungary. We are probably the last ones who still know reality."

This hypothesis of ours proved altogether wrong. The Revolution proved this very conclusively. There was a sudden, total change of attitude. You, gentlemen, here in the United States, have no idea, cannot even imagine, what Communism really is. I was at the University of Miami for three months. I have discussed communism with many students there. I have seen how American university students flirt (kacérkodnak) to a certain extent with socialism. They apparently are totally ignorant of the real situation both in the Soviet Union and in the satellite countries.

Communism not only did not improve the lot of the poor classes in Hungary, but it played on their naiveté, exploited and betrayed them. It was precisely these classes, whose liberation the Communists so eagerly proclaimed in the beginning, that turned against them. The remnants of the Horthy regime did not participate in the Revolution. The decisive force of the uprising was represented by the peasant youth of the universities, to the support of which the Hungarian youth from the factories also rallied.

You should know that the whole Hungarian nation wants to be freed from the oppressive grip of the Communists. You should know that we were and still are completely disappointed in the United States, in the United Nations, and that we feel that Hungary was sacrificed, was thrown to the wolves for the sake of saving the Suez Canal. Sixty-thousand (60,000) Hungarians have died in their attempt to regain their freedom, and because of the attitude of the United States and of the United Nations, they have died in vain. We cannot forget this so easily.

The trust of the Hungarian people in, and its attachment to, the United States and to the United Nations was deeply shattered.

We feel that a great deal could still be done for Hungary through the five-member U.N. investigating committee. We, who have only recently left Hungary, see and understand the Hungarian situation precisely. We are still in close contact with those who remained behind the Iron Curtain. We know that there still persists in Hungary a boundless expectancy, but, unfortunately, we know also how hopeless this expectation appears to be, if we look at it from the United States.

We are all too familiar with the barrage of Soviet and domestic Hungarian propaganda which charges that what happened in Hungary was not an uprising at all of all the people, but was the result of machinations of counter-revolutionaries and Fascists who have acted in unison with American imperialist spies.

In this connection I should like to simply state for the record that we, the emigrants, are in possession of a list of those who have either been departed or executed. About 60 percent of the people involved are young Hungarian workers.

You should, I think, know at least the outline of some of the more burning problems and questions that fired the revolutionaries, that gave them the impetus to do what they did and which kept them going even at a time when all seemed lost.

The foremost social, political, and economic question of the Revolution was welded together in the unanimous resolve of the people that Hungary's state of subjugation by the Soviet Union must be severed. Hungary wanted, above all else, national independence and individual freedom.

Another burning question was the agricultural question. I am sorry to say that the West, and the people of the United States in particular, do not understand this question at all, and I am afraid that the importance of this question to us Hungarians is not appreciated here.

In the United States, where there is so much land, where there is a better than ideal proportion between available agricultural land and the number of farming population desirous of cultivating such land, there is, of course, no agricultural problem.

In Hungary, all this is different. Hungary was a predominantly agricultural state before the Second World War, with the majority of the population earning their livelihood from working the soil. While there were several million farmers, the Hungarian arable land was traditionally consolidated into a few huge landed estates, controlled by the Church and a handful of private individuals. The situation was so oppressive that 1,200,000 landless agricultural day laborers saw themselves forced to leave their country and emigrate to the United States, Canada, and other places. All this emigration took place in less than a century.

The emigration did not solve the agrarian problem. Landless farm laborers continued to live under the steadily increasing pressures of population increase on the one hand, and economic oppression of the landed estates on the other. The domestic political struggles in Hungary between the two world wars revolved around this basic and central Hungarian problem.

Needless to say, they remained unsolved. It was only natural, therefore, that the seemingly benevolent and helping attitude of the Communists after 1945 evoked sympathetic responses from the agrarian masses.

The agrarian problem and other pressing sociological questions of Hungary were first raised by the so-called populist writers (Népi Irók). These writers analyzed every angle of these questions and described actual conditions on landed estates, small farms, and villages.

This sociography of such populist writers as Péter Veress, János Kodolány, István Sinka, and others, became the starting point of a nationwide discussion of social and economic questions, and mistakes, injustices, and unbearable conditions became widely known. It was in this atmosphere of social unrest and a thorough discussion of social injustices that the Hungarian youth grew up before and immediately after the Second World War. This youth possessed, at least the bare outlines, of a possible solution. They wanted a farm reform, of course, but they did not want collective farms (kolhozes), they wanted certain revisions and adjustments of the industry, but they never even dreamed of proposing an industrial policy that the Communists contemplated and later carried out.

In 1948 these young Hungarian intellectual forces were

mercilessly cut down by the Communists. Many intellectuals were imprisoned, others were interned, and still others were forced to give up their intellectual endeavors and to seek their livelihood as industrial laborers.

The ruthless Communist oppression, begun in 1948, continued until 1953. In 1953, Imre Nagy came to power and inaugurated a process of liberalization of every aspect of Hungarian life. Among the many things that Nagy proposed to do was the judicial review of the cases of incarcerated persons. As a result of this process, a substantial number of political prisoners were set free. These freed prisoners, for the most part young intellectuals, eagerly joined the Nagy forces and soon became interwoven into the fabric of the young intellectual leadership of Hungary. They were instrumental, for example, in establishing the Petőfi Circle. It was these people who later became the elite, the avant-garde of the Revolution. These people were agreed on what constituted the fundamental Hungarian questions and they spoke and wrote in a similar tone when proposing solutions to these foremost questions. Their reaction to whatever took place in Hungarian day-to-day politics was identical. It was this identity of views of the intellectual elite that explains why, in the turmoil of the Revolution, revolutionary pockets in various parts of Budapest and in the suburbs, while not organized, and not under a central command, gave all the appearances of an organized uprising; they were united in their aims and goals and methods.

These leaders were united in proclaiming that there would not be a restoration of Church lands or landed estates. (If there was a minority that opposed these views, it certainly did not dare come forward with its propositions.) They were also united on the questions of the future of Hungarian industrial plants: they did not propose restoration here either. (I encountered such views only abroad, after I left Hungary.) We were all agreed that certain phases of the industry ought to be de-nationalized and ownership and control returned to private hands. But we did not propose to de-nationalize key industries.

You should also know that the workers' councils were the product of the Revolution. They came into being as a result of practical revolutionary necessity. The unpopular and hated factory managers and other high officials of the pre-revolutionary factory management fled for their lives soon after the outbreak of the uprising. As a result, the factories stood there without direction. But the Revolution could not permit stoppages in certain industries (electricity, gas, bakeries) because their continued operation was essential to the success of the uprising. In these industries, therefore, the revolutionary workers themselves had to see to it that the production continued.

Thus, up until the time when Imre Nagy formed his government, the workers' councils performed a double function: a) they were protecting the industrial plants; b) they had a political role. In Budapest, this political role of the councils was considerable already during the first phase of the uprising. During the second phase of the Revolution, the Budapest councils represented the largest single political bloc and they had the greatest political power. It was during the second phase that the councils turned against the labor unions.

I already mentioned the name of Sándor Rácz. He was the president of the Budapest Central Workers' Council. We don't know what has become of him. He was a simple man. If it had not been for the Revolution, he would have continued as a first-class skilled worker that he was. He clearly saw what was happening and took the initiative. And we soon learned what a great leader he was.

The workers' councils were organized on the basis of democratic elections. The central leader of these councils, Sándor Rácz, clearly demonstrated his statesmanlike wisdom in critical situations. These people (Rácz and others) would have found solutions to difficult questions.

The members of the workers' councils clearly recognized that their immediate problem had to do with production, not with solving political questions. It was only because of inescapable necessities that they took upon their shoulders political questions as well. Discussion went on already regarding the reorganization of the labor unions. It was agreed that, once the labor unions are reorganized, the workers' councils would give up altogether their political role and retain the direction of production only.

To come back to a previous question for a moment, the question of reorganization of Hungarian agriculture and industry is extremely important, because these questions are some of the more important positive achievements of the revolution. Hungary, as reorganized and reconstituted by the victorious revolution, would not have had the appearance, nor the substance as the free world had imagined it would turn out.

The Hungarian people turned sharply and completely against the Russians. This, however, did not mean that the victorious Revolution would have reestablished capitalism. To the contrary. A free society would have been created with an economic policy and system where the workers' councils would have had an influential and decisive role.

During the Revolution about 65 percent of all the TSzCs's (Kolkhozes) disintegrated. Dobi himself admitted that only an insignificant number of TSzCs's could be salvaged. People vehemently opposed the establishment of the TSzCs's. Between 1950 and 1953, Rákosi, using the slogan "Communists go to the villages," sent thousands of Communists to the villages and farm districts, where they became presidents of the TSzCs's, and established themselves as absolute masters of the villages. These people were empowered to do whatever they pleased and made use of every conceivable method to force the independent farmers into the collectives. I myself was under constant police surveillance from 1953 to 1956. The Revolution was one of the most beautiful experiences of my life.

2. *When do you think the whole thing started?*

I should like first to discuss the Revolt. The Revolution has its antecedents. The Petőfi Circle was a closed, young intellectual group, which came into being shortly after Imre Nagy became premier in 1953. The Circle made it its policy to organize and conduct high-level discussions. The first meetings consisted of only a few participants. Later, when the Circle began giving clear expression to Hungarian problems, its meetings were very much attended and Hungarian writers also joined. These Hungarian writers also recognized the problems that faced the country.

The act of joining the Petőfi Circle represented a fateful decision on the part of the Hungarian writers, it represented a dividing line for them, requiring of them a decision to dedicate themselves either to the service of Rákosi or to the service of the Hungarian people.

I must say they made the right decision. They were with the Revolution. Only those less talented writers, for whom cooperation with Rákosi meant earning their bread, remained aloof.

The Irodalmi Circle and the Petőfi Circle prepared, conditioned, and transformed the Hungarian public opinion ever since 1953. The <u>Irodalmi Ujság</u> was in such a great demand and short supply, that a single copy of it ran to 20 forints.

The immediate cause of the rise of the events that directly led to the 1956 developments was the Rajk burial.

The Rákosi government had fallen and Rákosi himself lived a semi-secluded life, exerting his still tremendous power only indirectly. He used to summon to his office the leaders of the Petőfi Circle, of the Irodalmi Circle and of other organizations and tried to influence and persuade them to accepting his, Rákosi's, views. This was especially true after the Poznan developments.

At the time of the Poznan events, there were already two clearly recognizable factions within the Hungarian Communist Party.

The existence of two factions within the Party is the explanation of the Rajk burial also. The Rajk affair has long been the object of endless discussions, the Government always refusing to even as much as consider rehabilitation.

Immediately preceding the Rajk burial, an editorial composed by István Kovács, was already set to type, and ready for the printing presses, in the Szabad Nép building. The article began with these words: "We greet and welcome Rákosi's return." To counteract this subtle maneuver of the Rákosi forces within the Party, the anti-Rákosi faction hurriedly arranged for the official burial of Rajk. The burial, and the attendant ceremonies and the high tension of feelings that went with it, undermined Rákosi's position and made his return impossible. The burial, at the same time, offered a splendid opportunity for all consciously anti-Rákosi elements to assemble and to demonstrate their power.

Rákosi was progressively loosing his initially great popularity with the Hungarian people. He was very popular in 1945. Thereafter he began to be hated and detested, for personal, concrete reasons by some, because of the excesses in the Rákosi cult of personality by others.

The masses assembled in the cemetery. Münnich took the rostrum. His speech was vehement in tone and content; he demanded that the guilty ones be made responsible for their actions. He demanded to know why Rajk had to die. Kádár was actively supporting the same view.

During the preliminary investigation that preceded Rajk's public trial, Kádár played a peculiar role; Rákosi appointed him an emissary of the Party, directing him to visit Rajk in prison and there to persuade him to wholly admit his treachery for the sake of the Party, when on the witness stand in his public trial. In return, Rákosi promised, through Kádár, that Rajk's life would be spared. Everyone knows that the promise was not kept.

The personal, and political, conversation between these two political friends, both of whom opposed Rákosi for political and personal reasons, was secretly recorded on orders from Rákosi. When Kádár returned to Rákosi to report on his mission, his report also was secretly recorded. These two recordings were characterized by wide discrepancies and contradictions and conclusively showed what the true political views of Kádár were as well as his true relationship to the Rákosi faction within the Party. Both Rajk and Kádár were known for their anti-Russian, national Communist tendencies.

2 a Was there any "incubation" period before the outbreak? What events during the last few years contributed to it?

(i) *Stalin's death*
(ii) *Imre Nagy's Premiership, 1953-55*
(iii) *Reconciliation of Moscow with Tito*
(iv) *20th Congress of the Russian Communist Party*
(v) *Poznan events (June, 1956)*
(vi) *Replacement of Rákosi*
(vii) *Rajk funeral*
(viii) *Gomulka's return to power (October 19, 1956)*

This is an all-embracing question.

Let us consider them under separate heads.

Let us look at the economic sphere first. Without exception, every branch of the Hungarian economy operated on the basis of the norm system. The norm system was universally applied. The norms themselves were arbitrarily determined from above, and were based on the economic prognostication of the Party leaders, on what the Party desired to achieve economically, not on realistic capabilities of workers and equipment.

The living standard of the population was so low that every capable member of a family was perforce obliged to work, if it desired to maintain itself above surface. Family life, the end objective of normal people, was made impossible. The low living standard, and the resultant necessity that forced married women and mothers, too, to work in factories formed part of a long-range Communist plan, the end objective of which was the gradual disintegration and destruction of the family. The maintaining of an intolerably low living standard was continued, then, primarily out of ideological considerations. The destruction of normal family life was also fostered by placards proclaiming that whereas it was a duty of married women to give birth to children, bearing children constituted a glory for unwed girls. (Gyereket szülni anyáknak kötelesség, lányoknak dicsőség.)

The total earnings of a family were barely sufficient to cover the minimum food requirements and only very rarely was there some money left for the purchase of some clothing items.

Our economic misery was further aggravated by the regime's ill-advised and irresponsible policy of systematic large-scale industrial expansion, especially in the field of heavy industry. The classic example of the regime's irresponsibility in the economic sphere was its attempt to build a grandiose subway system in the city of Budapest. Plans were made, and construction work initiated on this pet-project of the Party, without prior engineering advice as to its physical feasibility. A tremendous amount of work and money was pumped into the subways until it became quite evident that soil conditions in Budapest would make its continuation impossible. It had to be abandoned. The cost of the experiment was staggering.

The Hungarian worker suffered a constant reduction of his purchasing power, while the speed under which he had to work kept on increasing. The Government used this convenient method -- drastic reduction of the workers' real wages -- to finance a disproportionate industrial expansion and to offset steadily rising costs of production that resulted from excessive centralization and from the colossal mismanagement.

(ii) Imre Nagy's Premiership, 1953-55

An individual did not have an aim, a goal, to live, and to work for, in Hungary; he did not have the possibility of saving. He had no influence over the education, over the future of his children. The fate, and the entire future of a child depended solely on the cadre of his father. There was an unacknowledged and undefined, and yet a very real and cruel and oppressive caste system in Hungary, whose high priests were such personages as the Party secretaries, members of the AVH organization, and others.

These people lived in their own make-believe world, completely isolated from the suffering masses. Members of the Party hierarchy occupied an exclusive, compact area of the Capital, the Rózsadomb section of Budapest, around which barbed wire barricades were erected. Heavily armed AVH personnel stood constant guard at strategic points of this enclosure, making sure that no unauthorized person would ever enter this Communist heaven.

Those living inside of this protected territory communicated only with one another and with the Russians. They did not know what went on the other side of the fence. They lost contact with the people, they did not understand their day-to-day problems and had no understanding for their desires and aspirations. They followed blindly the principles of their ideology, the dictates of the Party, on a dark road, without knowing where the road ultimately would lead, or where the end would lie.

I had once had an occasion -- during my stay at the AVH prison -- to enter into a discussion with an AVH major. The AVH had just finished beating me up in an underground interrogation chamber, when they suddenly changed their method of questioning. I was brought up to a plush reception room where I met the major. He proposed that we discuss economic problems, entirely off the record, as private citizens. Our talk led to the discussion of the state of Hungarian agriculture, to the analysis of the relative merits of small private landholdings versus socialized large estates. I asked him what the end of all this collectivization was supposed to be. My question visibly caught him off the guard, for he had no ready answer to my inquiry. He was thinking for a long while. At last he said: "At the end we shall ask for admission, as a member state, into the Soviet Union, and this decision of ours shall automatically solve all our outstanding problems and difficulties." This was his considered conclusion. And this shows how wide and deep the gap was between the aspirations of the people and the plans and policy of the governing circles.

(iii) *Reconciliation of Moscow with Tito*

To come back for a moment to the Government's policy of forcible and accelerated industrialization; the Government decided to completely transform Hungarian society and to establish those Marxian-Leninist prerequisites which, in their judgment, would bring about those material and social conditions where the roots of Communist ideology could be provided with a fertile soil. The proper element of Communist ideology, -- according to this theory -- is the <u>industrial proletariat</u>. In order to have proletariat of this sort, large-scale industrialization is absolutely essential. If this is not already available, it must be created. Thus the large-scale expansion, especially of the heavy industry.

The entire Hungarian economic life operated under a system of rigid, centralized, direction. In production an emphasis lay on quantity with no one paying attention at all to quality. This necessarily followed from the system of norms and premium-incentives. Wages were so low that no one could allow himself the luxury of disregarding the additional sums that the premiums represented. As a result, there evolved, in time, a gigantic conspiracy, where the workers produced a great amount of low-rate or worthless goods, the inspectors put their stamps of approval on them, and the commercial establishments accepted and passed them on to the consumer.

No one took conservation of material resources and of

manpower seriously. There resulted a tremendous waste. The Government, in its fervent zeal to expand the Hungarian industry, embarked upon the construction of a huge industrial complex at Mohács. The operation of this complex was planned to proceed with raw materials to be imported from Yugoslavia. The building of this enterprise was well under way, when difficulties of a political and ideological nature developed between Rákosi and Tito. The road to importation of raw material from the South was closed. The regime now decided to dismantle the entire Mohács complex and to rebuild it again at Dunapentele (Stalinváros).

This is an example how the Government embarked upon building one heavy industry after another, -- even though there was no need for it in Hungary, and even though we completely lacked both the necessary raw materials and fuels to run them, -- only in order to prove the correctness of what we knew were fallacious ideological and economic theories.

One of the results of this misguided planning and waste and economic mismanagement was the almost total lack of consumer goods and of necessary little luxuries like chocolate, candy, etc., on the one hand, and the total inability of people to buy any of these consumer items -- insofar as they occasionally became available in limited quantities -- on the other.

You may find it difficult to understand this, but the truth is that the lack of consumer goods, and the people's inability to avail themselves of them, assumed incalculable proportions. It turned out to be an existential problem for all Hungarians.

Individual Hungarians were acutely aware of all these problems, they recognized its true causes and magnitude, even though they had no way of expressing them. It remained for the Petőfi Circle to formulate and express these many-sided and deep-rooted grievances.

But while the Petőfi Circle undoubtedly performed a useful and magnificent job in this respect, we must constantly bear in mind that the Petőfi Circle only echoed and publicly proclaimed what actually were silenced protest-voices of many millions. The Petőfi Circle only gave a final resume of what every Hungarian knew from the beginning.

2 b.(i) What events followed Stalin's death:

I was interned at the time of Stalin's death at the interment camp of Recsk. (Recsk is situated about 5 kilometers from Parád, in Heves County, next to the Kékestetö.)

We were at Recsk. The news reached us two days after its occurrence, by way of civilians, who were employed at the camp, by way of newspaper-fragments that we found in the toilets and wastebaskets. It is characteristic for a camp, how well informed we were. We have developed a sixth sense that was capable of registering minute details and analyzing them and interpreting them.

The camp leadership made an attempt to conceal the news from us.

The effect of Stalin's death on us was twofold: (a.) Concessions were gradually introduced within the camp and (b.) cases of prisoners began to be taken under review; in June of 1953, some of the prisoners were freed outright, others were brought before court for trial, others were permitted to return to their homes to live under police supervision, etc.

2 b.(ii) What events during the last few years contributed to Imre Nagy's Premiership, 1953-55:

The contributing effect of Nagy's premiership was tremendous. Imre Nagy introduced a process of liberalization. The general atmosphere became more free, and people were voicing more freely their true opinions. Nagy introduced a new policy in the sphere of socialist legality, cases of many, heretofore held incommunicado, came under judicial review, and people began to speak about things and persons and problems that were untouchable in former times. Prior to coming of Nagy, utterances having to do with the Government's industrial policy, with the inferior quality of consumer and other goods, and with similar subjects were never tolerated. Such actions were anti-democratic manifestations and offenders were correspondingly punished.

Under the heading of socialist legality, the cases of all political prisoners were reviewed.

People felt the changing trend and under the impact of these concrete changes they came out from within their protective shells; engineers, for instance, who knew all along how some of the economic plans were faulty or wrong or unprofitable, came out and openly criticized them. This change was so remarkable that people openly discussed a variety of issues in public, on the trolley cars, and on streets.

In the period of 1948-1953, only Russian movies were available to the Hungarian public. Not only was one required to refrain from criticizing these inferior Russian films, even in the private company of friends, but also one was expected to pay high tribute in public to the supposedly excellent qualities of these products of Russian culture.

The question of religious education of children, especially after 1947, 1948, became extremely explosive. There was a formal agreement between the state and the Roman Catholic Church which formally stipulated the parents' right to have their children receive religious instruction on a voluntary basis. In the period 1948-1953, parents were required to sign a statement of consent, if they wished their children to receive religious instruction. Fathers signing such statements of consent, if they were Party members, were blackmailed into withdrawing them, or, failing this, they were intimidated in some other ways. If the signing father was not a Party member, he was simply thrown out of his job.

In this question, too, these were a notable change for the better after Nagy came to power.

Remarkable as all these changes were, the most striking, and the most widely felt changes occurred in the political sphere proper. Regarding political questions, everyone was permitted to freely express his views. The keeping of compulsory silence was no longer an obligation.

Criticism became free. In 1953 Tamás Aczél was able to formulate in writing, and to publish, what turned out to be the first criticism of the AVH and of the methods it employed.

There soon appeared a critical, sociological study, depicting the true life, and methods, and organization, and work of a collective farm. The work, written by István Márkus, (its title escapes me now) was a true-life sociological study of a village in the Dunántul Province of Hungary.

Approximately coinciding in time with the appearance of this study, there came the declaration of Imre Nagy that compulsory collectivization of farms would henceforth be abolished. These were tremendous changes. Up until that time collectivization was pursued by all sorts of forcible methods (tüzzel-vassal) and criticism of any kind of the collectives was most severely punished.

It was during this time (1953 and after) that it generally became known how ineffective, inefficient, and at times irrational were the agricultural production methods employed on the collective farms. It was these studies, made and published in this period, that permitted us to make real comparisons between private and collective agricultural enterprises. The collectives were more often than not mismanaged and they compared unfavorably to private holdings in every respect.

Some of this agricultural impotency I have seen myself; there was for example a peach orchard (60 holds/85 acres). The leadership of the collective decided to cut the trees because they simply did not know how to cultivate them.

The collectives were managed according to centralized directives. Every single detail was prescribed to them. And the directives had to be carried out. The trouble was that this centralized planning did not take into consideration local peculiarities of soil, climate, etc. The various farm activities were improperly and poorly executed, because on farms, too, workers performed their duties according to prescribed norms. The farm day consisted of 8-10 hours, in imitation of usages in effect in factories. Because the worker's pay was invariably tied to norm, farm laborers did not do a good job and farm production constantly decreased.

During the premiership of Nagy, much was written about the combine harvester machines. The harvesting by these machines left much to be desired. The machines left a high stubble (tarló) and the seed losses were tremendous. Immediately after the harvesting, the stubble-fields were ploughed, thereby eliminating the possibility of using them as grazing fields for animals or as flower-fields for agriculture (beekeeping).

All these questions came up for discussion; there were many critical voices uttered during meetings and lectures in the various industrial enterprises. While the main emphasis, at least in the beginning, centered around political and economic matters, the discussions also covered other important aspects of Hungarian life.

People soon embarked upon criticizing the organization, methods, and excesses of the AVH.

The AVH had a complex network that covered, and held under constant supervision, every individual and every manifestation of individual and organizational life in Hungary. There was the AVH proper, the secret police force, with all of its informers and agents provocateurs. And there was the all-embracing network of personnel bureaus. At the head of each and every personnel bureau there was an AVH member. These bureaus were responsible for collecting and recording of all sorts of information regarding every individual under their jurisdiction. All personal data, actions and utterances, views and opinions, political and religious beliefs and practices, -- in a word, whatever information could be obtained respecting a given individual -- was collected and entered on his cadre-sheet.

These confidential dossiers were distributed in many places during the Revolution. I have seen many a cadre-sheet in those days; an average sheet contained three-four hundred items of information, collected from various sources and covering every conceivable aspect of the individual's life.

In Communist Hungary a person's safety, job, opportunity, future, -- his very life, depended entirely on what sort of information his cadre-sheet contained and on what the particular mood of a personnel bureau's chief may have been at a given moment. If the personnel chief was in a benevolent mood, some poor fellow may have fared better. If he was a malicious, sadistic individual, he was entirely free to ruin a person's life.

These questions were also thoroughly aired during Nagy's premiership and the views presented cannot be said to have been sympathetic.

These, then, were the first fermenting mushrooms (erjesztö gombák). It is this period, and this milieu, that made the publication of the Irodalmi Ujság possible. The Petőfi Circle, too, began functioning in the very midst of these remarkable changes. The Imre Nagy Government must be fully credited with the opportunity it afforded to the Hungarian nation to unmask and to bring into full public view the grave errors and mistakes of the past.

2 b.(iii) *What events during the last few years contributed to Reconciliation of Moscow with Tito:*

The rapprochement between Tito and Moscow brought with it a noticeable result for Hungary. It made possible the temporary dismissal of Rákosi.

When the relations between Yugoslavia and the Soviet Union came to an impasse, the all-out crusade waged against Tito was carried out mainly under Hungary's leadership.

Tito was assigned all sorts of names -- he was dog chained among other things -- and was accused of all crimes under heaven. Those Hungarians who sympathized with Tito were summarily arrested. I have known many of them; they were brought to the same prison where I was incarcerated. The main offense of many of these people was the fact that they corresponded with relatives of theirs who happened to live in the Vojvodina Province -- a Hungarian-inhabited region of Yugoslavia -- because they wrote to and received letters from Yugoslavia, they were conveniently branded Yugoslav-Titoist spies and provocateurs.

The entire membership of the Hungarian-Yugoslav Cultural Society was thus jailed. Also, inhabitants of villages bordering on the Yugoslav frontier were summarily evacuated and trusted members of the Party were sent there in their stead. Nowhere else in the Communist orbit was the anti-Tito sentiment so high-pitched, nor the persecution of Tito sympathizers so severe and all-embracing as in Hungary. This entire campaign of agitation, personal attack on Tito, and political innuendo of the worst kind was personally led to Rákosi.

When Tito and Bulganin met in the Crimea, Gerő was also conveniently present. Tito and Bulganin came to an understanding that Rákosi must go. Tito made Rákosi's dismissal an absolute prerequisite to the normalization of the Soviet-Yugoslav relations.

While Rákosi had powerful backing in the Soviet Union, and even though he was well-liked and trusted by the Soviet leadership, the Soviet Union apparently was convinced that a Soviet-Yugoslav rapprochement was absolutely necessary and that, as a consequence, Rákosi and his accomplices, -- so thoroughly compromised during the anti-Tito campaign -- must be eliminated from positions of leadership.

The net result of all this for Hungary was the gradual melting and softening of the rigidly frozen air that characterized up until then both our public and private lives. The process in turn contributed in great measure to the formation, channeling, and crystallization of later events.

It was to Gerő's personal advantage that during the period of the anti-Tito campaign he held an economic assignment within the Hungarian Government, and therefore was not personally compromised. The Russians held Rákosi in high esteem and, while apparently Tito did not oppose the appointment of Gerő, long conferences and bickering preceded his now famous journey to Belgrade, on the eve of the Hungarian uprising.

2 b.(iv) *What events during the last few years contributed to 20th Congress of the Russian Communist Party*

Our history began with the Twentieth Congress. It was this Congress that affected the first all-embracing critique. The entire Russian-Communist history was up until then inextricably interwoven with the personality of Stalin. The Twentieth Congress represents the first occasion when this condition was brought to an end. The Congress acted joyfully on the anti-Stalin resolutions, and these resolutions of the Congress were enthusiastically received in turn. My knowledge of these events is only indirect -- those who have been in the Soviet Union at the time related to me how enthusiastically people received this good news. I also heard witnesses describe the jubilant mood of Russian officials in Budapest, both on the occasion of Stalin's death and when the news of the Twentieth Congress arrived.

Whatever transpired in Hungary after 1953, it did come about under the aegis of the Twentieth Congress. The leader of whatever movement after this time looked upon the Twentieth Congress as his bible. When encountering resistance or opposition or rebuke, they boldly cited the Twentieth Congress as their supreme authority, prudently pointing out that such things as they were engaged in were clearly permitted and desired. People felt free to express opinions and judgments that deviated from the official view of the Party and of the Government and at times embarked upon directly criticizing these very bodies.

Even in the Hungarian Parliament, a body of traditionally servile and subservient spirit, speeches of a mildly provocative nature could be heard; Parragi, an otherwise subservient and conciliatory individual, delivered a remarkable speech in 1954 on the question of Church and State. The entire program of the Nagy Government was based on the now fundamental premise that there are separate and distinct roads to socialism. The Nagy Government's policy was cemented on the thesis that, in the building of socialism in Hungary, policy may and ought to be based on the peculiar Hungarian characteristics, conditions, and circumstances. It was this kind of interpretation that prompted Imre Nagy to effect a substantial revision of Hungarian agricultural policy.

In a word, every movement and political undertaking in Hungary between the years 1953-1956 based its existence on, and was kept in existence by, the Twentieth Congress. Extremely important, it was the Twentieth Congress that permitted Hungarian writers to attack the many deficiencies and shortcomings of the regime from the left, a fact that secured them a quasi-cloak of legality and immunity.

2 b.(v) *What events during the last few years contributed to Poznan events (June, 1956)*

These events were extremely interesting; shortly after the news of the Poznan events reached Budapest, the Petőfi Circle met and many participating writers gave a positive evaluation.

Rákosi, seeing in these events an opportunity for his political revival, decided to try to stage a comeback. He marshaled the remnants of his power and influence and delivered an attack against the Petőfi Circle. But he was on the wrong side of the fence and his views were unfavorably received. From this time on, Rákosi's star gradually began to wane.

The Petőfi Circle speeches did not remain unopposed, however, and the Central Committee of the Party deprecated the opinions of Gábor Tánczos, Déry, and Tardos.

At about this time, a severe attack was leveled against the silenced Imre Nagy, who continued to reside in Budapest, and who became, without his conscious solicitation, the center of an opposition movement.

Nagy lived as an ordinary private citizen, frequenting various public places and speaking openly with people on the streets. His popularity had risen to enormous proportions. He became a pleasant figure of Budapest and everyone liked him. His professor-like figure was frequently seen in Pest, as he strolled by and kept lifting his hat in response to the innumerable greetings. Nagy supplied a pleasant contrast of a leader who was jovially mingling among the masses, and discussing and appreciating their problems, while those in power, the Communists, preferred to barricade themselves, and lived behind barbed-wire fortresses in the Rózsadomb section, secluded, separated from the people, without contact with the masses, problems, or reality.

Here, then, began the actual struggle. Both Imre Nagy and the Petőfi Circle and the writers were attacked by the Party. The sessions of the Central Committee became stormier and stormier. Rákosi delivered his last onslaught against the steadily increasing number of his critics. He went as far as to organize a <u>coup d'état</u>, just before the second funeral of Rajk; the article of István Kovács was already set to type and ready for the presses of the <u>Szabad Nép</u> which, under the title: "We Greet and Welcome Comrade Rákosi's Return" was meant to prepare and condition the public for the occasion. But this anti-Rákosi faction of the Central Committee got wind of these subtle maneuvers and set in motion its own counter-measure: it made hasty arrangements and preparations for the Rajk-funeral. The funeral, and the anti-Rákosi sentiment it provoked, took the very foundations from under Rákosi's feet and his coup d'état never had a chance.

I should like to digress here a little bit and say a few words about the Györfi Kollégium, an institution founded in 1943 and named after István Györfi. The acknowledged aim of this college was the education and training of intelligent, but poor peasant boys. The Györfi Kollégium had about 30-40 collegians on its roster. Many of these young people became members of the Communist Party after 1945. These people, following the ideology of Rajk, desired to organize and to bring into being a national communist Party. A number of them became exposed during the Rajk controversy and some, Ottó Tökés among others, who functioned as Rajk's secretary, suffered arrest and imprisonment. These were people with outstanding ability and training. One of them, Antal Gyenes -- who became the Minister of Forced Deliveries (Beszolgáltatásügyi) in the Nagy Cabinet during the uprising -- had the courage of distributing the cadre-sheets to all the employees of the Ministry. He took over the Ministry, issued a decree stopping all forced deliveries, and then dissolved the Ministry itself.

László Kardos was the first director of the Györfi Kollégium. Later he became the director of the National Center of Museums. Kardos and Gyenes were the spiritual leaders of the Györfi Kollégium. Both of them were ardent supporters of Imre Nagy, ever since 1953. András Hegedüs, Béla Szalai, and Gergely Szabó were also Györfi Kollégium alumni.

It was these people who later organized the Hungarian populist colleges (népi kollégiumok). They were instrumental in bringing into being the NÉKOSZ, as well as the Hungarian Collegiate Association (Magyar Kollégiumi Egyesület). The latter became integrated into the NÉKOSZ in 1948, and the NÉKOSZ itself was ordered dissolved in 1950 by Rákosi, because of its deviationist tendencies. The NÉKOSZ was accused of fostering and keeping alive Titoist and national communist ideologies.

The fact is that members of both the Györfi Kollégium and of the NÉKOSZ colleges were characterized by their national communist tendencies. Rajk was financing these institutions and the graduates of these colleges were appointed to very influential and well-paying jobs.

Because of the strategic positions they held, they were ideally suited to pave the way for Imre Nagy, and to establish a prestige for Nagy in the respective circles.

Shortly after the Poznan events the Györfi Kollégium organized and held a social event (a Party) to which all the alumni of the Györfi Kollégium as well as the alumni of various NÉKOSZ colleges were invited. Hegedüs and Béla Szalai were there and many others. László Kardos and Antal Gyenes, -- two leading figures of the Györfi Kollégium, who earned their livelihood as unskilled factory workers during the past few years, have meanwhile been appointed as assistant professors at the University.

Kardos and Gyenes approached Hegedüs and criticized his policies. They have pointed out to Hegedüs that Hungary's problem must be considered as a moral and humane problem, that Hungary must be freed from the clutches of the Soviet Union. Both Hegedüs and Szalai gave evasive answers and left the gathering shortly thereafter.

The Györfi-circle consisted of cultured and informed men. It was a pleasure to work with them. We represented similar, if not identical, views during the Revolution, and we were in general understanding regarding questions and methods to be worked on after the Revolution.

It was the Györfi-circle that formulated the thesis that the TSzCs cannot be maintained. Their negative attitude in this respect is not to be construed as an attempt to return to the old system; what they envisioned was a reorganization of Hungarian agriculture, free from compulsion and government regulation.

2 b.(vi) What events during the last few years contributed to Replacement of Rákosi

Rákosi's political power and influence was only broken

at the time of the Rajk funeral. Up until then a continuous struggle went on between Rákosi on the one hand, and the whole Hungarian public opinion on the other, with no one really knowing who the ultimate victor would be.

Rákosi's power was almost unlimited; at the beginning of Nagy's first premiership, Nagy, for instance, made his speech of introduction in Parliament, giving the main outlines of his program. The following day Rákosi delivered a speech on the radio, criticizing and correcting Nagy point by point. In this Nagy-Rákosi struggle Rákosi easily won. To be sure, Nagy was the Prime Minister of Hungary, but all the important positions were filled by Rákosi-men, on whose goodwill and cooperation the execution and implementation of the Nagy program depended. Nagy had a policy and he was anxious to carry it out, and the population would have liked to see the Nagy program executed, but all this desire was to no avail. Rákosi and his henchmen were in a position to sabotage it all. This Rákosi-Nagy struggle characterized the 1953-1955 period in Hungarian politics.

To give another example of Rákosi's methods; at the time the sociological study of István Márkus appeared, Rákosi summoned to his office Ernő Urbán, who was the first secretary of the League of Hungarian Writers at the time, gave him a stern lecture on correct Party behavior and demanded to know how such a work as Márkus's was permitted to be published.

Rákosi, as First Secretary of the Party, also took protocol precedence over the Prime Minister.

This Rákosi-Nagy struggle is the main reason and explanation for the almost complete ineffectiveness of Nagy's first government. People saw the struggle and they were fully aware that the real power centered in Rákosi's hands. They did not think that Nagy could hold his own for a longer period of time, and the changes that Nagy did bring about did not possess in the eyes of most people those marks of stability upon which a stable future could be built. People simply did not believe that the changes would last.

There was, for instance, Nagy's policy that farmers were free to leave the collectives. Nagy's policy declaration was discounted by an administrative order, issued by the Rákosi-clique, saying in effect that, while farmers were indeed free to leave the collectives, they may not take any farm implements with them, and must, before leaving the collective, assume full responsibility for, and pay in cash, their share of the collective's financial indebtedness. This sum may have amounted to anywhere from 25 to 50,000 forints. Besides assuming these financial burdens, farmers would have been required to purchase all sorts of farm machinery, horses, and other implements that are necessary for independent farming.

This explains why the extremely individualistic Hungarian farmers, faced with these insurmountable difficulties, continued to remain TSzCs-members, even after Nagy, at least theoretically, set them free.

This same situation applies to the small artisans' class. They, too, had a theoretical freedom to set up their own shops on the one hand, but were faced with insurmountable financial difficulties if they wanted to establish their own independent existences, on the other.

The fate of the small retail merchant was equally hopeless. Theoretically they were permitted again to operate. In practice, however, they could obtain a license only in places with limited marketing possibilities, they received an insufficient and irregular supply of goods and only infrequently were they supplied by the state with small quantities of consumer goods. As a result, the consumers were obliged to go to the state retail stores for most of their daily needs.

2 b.(vii) What events during the last few years followed the Rajk funeral?

I already spoke of the significance of the Rajk funeral. The funeral was staged and used by the anti-Rákosi faction of the

Party to undermine Rákosi's position, and to make his political comeback impossible. Rákosi was supported by Moscow. But there was a powerful opposition to Rákosi in the Hungarian Communist Party. Kádár and Münnich were personal enemies of Rákosi. Kádár, after his release from prison, was a very popular individual. Kádár made many speeches in the Angyalföld section of Budapest. These speeches, the airing of the Farkas-affair and the resultant demand that the responsible ones be called to account, tended to strengthen the already widespread anti-Rákosi sentiment of the masses. Antal Apró, for instance, while vacillating in the beginning, became a supporter of Kádár in the anti-Rákosi struggle, as soon as the relative strength of the opposing factions became known.

It was at this time of the funeral that Rákosi was accused for the first time in public as the one responsible for the murder of Rajk. Münnich went even further and spoke for the need of calling the responsible ones to account. The funeral presented an opportunity to the entire nation to express its sympathetic sentiment for Rajk, and to demonstrate by this stand its support for such staunch Rajk defenders as Kádár, Münnich, and the others. Hundreds of thousands came to the cemetery, with their very presence demonstrating against Rákosi.

The Rajk funeral represented, then, -- and it was so understood in all corners -- a gigantic and determined demand that Rákosi must go.

2 b.(viii) *What events followed Gomulka's return to power (October 19, 1956)*

I don't know if Gomulka's return to power contributed anything to the outbreak of the Hungarian uprising. I don't think so. The anti-Rákosi sentiment was so well on its way by October, that no change in its direction or ferocity could have been effected. We must note here, however, that the Petőfi Circle, as well as MEFESZ, started out with solidarity declarations for the Poles. The Polish events, however, must be viewed only as a circumstance that gave an opportunity to sending telegrams which expressed our solidarity on the one hand, and to discussing the formulation of the points of our own demands, on the other.

Thus the demonstration of October 22, originating from the College of Economics, formally was a solidarity demonstration, and it officially took place under the aegis of such a demonstration. But the 14 points were already formulated at that time and the already printed handbills were distributed in large quantities.

2 c. Looking back to events, was there any particular point at which you could have said: This is the real turning-point?

There were a number of important turning points; with 1945 an era came to a close. We had the beginnings of a brand-new world then, with the land reform and the many other changes. 1948 was another turning point. Rákosi calls it the year of the turning point in one of his books, where the beginnings of socialism have taken place. Actually, 1948 was the turning point of human wickedness and iniquity, the turning point of human arbitrariness, but without this turning point of 1948 there would have been no Hungarian Revolution in 1956. It is after 1948 that we learned what freedom really is. After 1948 every possibility of criticism ceased and every human life stopped. Prisons were filled to capacity. 1953 is another important turning point; Imre Nagy became Premier, the Petőfi Circle came into being, István Márkus published his book in that year. The Rajk funeral of 1956 was another such great turning point.

2 d. Before the Revolt took place, did you have any feeling that a big change was imminent? If so, when and what made you think so?

Yes, I did have such a feeling. It was something entirely subjective. I lived in a small village near Budapest. On October 22, I went to Budapest. I felt a compulsion to go to the College of Economics. The events that followed are known. Everyone lived in an air of expectancy. I met many people who have come from outlying districts of the country to the Capital. Many workers left their jobs, against standing orders, because they felt that something big was in the making. The demonstration was preceded by a tremendous national expectation and it proceeded to the accompaniment of a tremendous enthusiasm. At the statue of Bem, almost at the end of the demonstration there, running and breathless arrived Péter Veres, and announced that the League of Writers joins and affiliates itself with the youth.

2 e. What do you think was the part played by the writers in the events leading up to the Revolution?

The writers played a great and significant role. The activities of the Hungarian intellectual elite manifested themselves in the Petőfi Circle and in the Writers' Association (Irószövetség).

The Writers' Association was an exclusive Communist domain, where only reliable and faithful adherents to the Party line could gain admittance.

There were significant writers of national and international stature who were not members of the Writers' Association. I should like to mention in this connection such names as Áron Tamási, Lászlo Németh, István Sinka, and János Kodolányi. These writers were not Fascists, -- they were the leading representatives of the left-wing faction among Hungarian writers before the Second World War. They had great ability and wrote courageously about many sociological questions. They described the life of the non-privileged classes, of the poor, pointing out social injustices, unhealthy economic conditions, material and spiritual stagnation, and other characteristic features of pre-war Hungarian society.

These people either lived a life of forced literary inactivity after

1945, or were engaged in minor, or second-rate literary endeavors. Lászlo Németh restricted himself to translations; Kodolányi led a meager sort of existence by editing a small provincial paper, the <u>Balaton Akarat</u>.

These people may have been inactive, but they were by no means forgotten. Everyone in Hungary knew of them and people continued to keep them in high esteem. Révai did everything to win them over for the Communist cause; he journeyed innumerable times to Hódmezövásárhely to see Lászlo Németh -- the latter was engaged as a professor in the gymnasium of that city -- but all his efforts of persuasion remained unsuccessful. It was common knowledge that Lászlo Németh was not willing.

Another of the pre-war greats, Gyula Illyés, continued to write poetry. Again, everyone knew that Illyés was not accorded a treatment that he justly would have deserved.

Zoltán Kodály, the celebrated composer and collector of folk melodies remained one of the most determined and most outspoken opponents of the regime. He was assigned a beautiful home on the Kékestetö, but he refused to use it. The regime heaped every imaginable material favor on him, without any result.

These people, then, because of their past literary performance, renown, and wide prestige, continued to be significant members of the literary life of Hungary. Some of them, Lászlo Németh and Gyula Illyés among others, were admitted to membership of the Writers' Association after Imre Nagy became Premier.

Official recognition, fame and material reward continued to be Party-directed and ideologically-motivated; Ernő Urbán, for example, was a mediocre writer with very little talent. But he was a trusted and reliable follower of the Party-line. As a result, he became the chairman of the Writers' Association. It was he and people like him who received the prizes, the publicity, and the rewards. Others, the truly recognized cream of the crop, were on the edge of material despair. Sinka, for instance, was forced to rely on subsidies which Kodály so generously and continuously gave him.

As soon as Imre Nagy became Premier, a struggle began among the Hungarian writers. In this struggle the great majority of the young generation of Communist writers sided with the people.

There are critical times in the history of all nations, when literary personages must take a stand. We had such a critical time after 1953. And the Hungarian writers stood their ground and assumed responsible and correct attitudes in the crisis. They kept alive and fostered the spirit of criticism and they consistently worked to bring about the victory of the people's desires. To come to the young generation of Communist writers: István Márkus, Tamás Aczél, Tibor Mérai, Tibor Déry, István Sándor, and the poet Lászlo Benjámin were the outstanding representatives of this group.

They all began their literary careers in 1945. Most of them were members of the Communist Party as early as the late twenties, and they grew up in the illegal Communist movement. We collaborated with these people in 1943 and 1944, -- in the anti-Fascist movement -- up until the time of the execution of Bajcsy-Zsilinszky. In 1945, they all became full-fledged members of the then reorganized and reconstituted Communist Party, and devoted all their time and effort and talent to writing for Communist dailies and periodicals. They were talented from the literary point of view, and they were honest as human beings, who believed and had an ardent faith in communism.

These people were the front-fighters of the many-sided Party-polemics and Party-literature after 1947. But Rákosi decided to silence them.

This attempt at coercion on the part of Rákosi represented the beginning of a process of doubt that arose in the minds of many a young Communist writer -- a process that culminated in their total disillusionment.

They could not help noticing the striking differences that existed between their own lives and material and social circumstances on the one hand -- and the unbearable conditions of the masses on the other.

They, the writers, were given all the material advantages that the regime was capable of bestowing upon them. They had everything they desired. They were provided with cars, with money, with luxuries and leisure, and they were encouraged to travel to every corner of the country, to visit factories and kolkhozes (TSzCs), to talk to people and to discuss issues with them for the purpose of gathering concrete material for socialist novels, plays, and poetry.

These young Communist writers visited factories and villages and collectives, they lectured, and held discussions, and argued with the people. At first they could not understand the people, they could not account for what were obviously violent outbursts of denunciation and rejection of the regime. To them it was inconceivable that even Party members of the proletariat would assume a position, a view, that so strikingly resembled attitudes associated with reactionaries and Party-aliens.

This was the initial phase of the writers' disillusionment. They suspected that something was wrong somewhere.

In 1953, they openly admitted how firmly they believed until then in the infallibility of the Party. They have held the view that the basic doctrine, and the various official interpretations of that doctrine by Party congresses and Party leaders are to be considered sacred, that they are unimpeachable, that they do not admit of error or mistake. If there are errors and mistakes, if there is evil and injustice -- and they saw plenty of them with their own eyes -- all these shortcomings are the results of human fallibility and intellectual limitation, deficiencies that originate not from doctrine and official policy, but from impotency and short-sightedness of human administrators and executives.

By 1953, these Communist writers came to a conclusion; they declared that the causes of errors and mistakes are not in the human element, the roots of the evil must be sought in the Party, and the Party is in error, because it does not understand the people.

This was the first and decisive step. The struggle continued, within the Writers' Association, between the untalented group that faithfully represented Rákosi's views on the one hand and the open-minded and freewheeling rebels on the other.

I met many of these rebels at the end of November 1956. They were then engaged in the direction and advising of the revolutionary workers' councils. I spoke with Márkus, Déry, and others. It was these people who brought into being the central organization of the Budapest workers' councils. I had an interesting and characteristic conversation with Isvtán Márkus. He had taken his family across the border to safety, and himself returned to Budapest. I asked him why he did not leave the country. His answer: "You may do so, after all, you have spent five years in jail. But my situation is different. I always was a Communist, I always believed in communism, even though I frequently criticized actual conditions and personages. I must remain here. We Communists must never leave, we must take up the fight with Kádár so that everyone may see what a gross treachery was committed." Markus's family is now in Switzerland.

2 f. Was there any change in the "atmosphere" of Hungarian publications before October 1956?
If so, in what publications in particular?

This is an involved and complicated question. Let me try to take up the most important publications one after another. <u>Szabad Nép</u>: In the beginning, during the time of Nagy's premiership, <u>Szabad Nép</u> reported Nagy's activities, with no commentaries attached. The paper remained unchanged in every other respect.

When Sándor Novovácszky became Nagy's chief press officer, a corresponding change also occurred in the <u>Szabad Nép</u>'s redaction. Márton Horváth was dismissed from the chairmanship of the board of editors, and his place was taken by Miklós Gyimes. Gyimes was Nagy's man, and he changed the tone of the paper.

<u>Szabad Nép</u> underwent another significant change in 1954.

Rákosi's political importance increased, and the Rákosi political line was again co-represented in the direction of the paper. Szabad Nép after this worked under the strains of a Rákosi-Nagy compromise, it was neither hot nor cold.

The decisive change took place in connection with the Rajk funeral. Rákosi was bent on engineering a coup d'etat, and an article designed to support the maneuver was already set to type. The Rajk funeral prevented Rákosi from carrying out his scheme. After the funeral the entire editorial board of the paper was reshuffled. Unfortunately for Imre Nagy, he did not have an adequate group of newspapermen to replace the old guard.

The first order of business of the Revolution was the abolition of the Szabad Nép. The Szabad Nép headquarters was attacked by the insurgents in the first phase of the Revolution. Dudás used the building as the headquarters of his own forces. As a result, Szabad Nép ceased to be published during the Revolution and did not reappear ever since.

Szabad Föld: this was a weekly publication, written for the peasants, with an aim of paving the way for Socialist (collectivized) agriculture. Szabad Föld was started in 1945, under the editorship of Antal Gyenes. After the Rajk trial, Gyenes was replaced by Lajos Fehér. Still somewhat later, this publication became one of Rákosi's organs, through which Rákosi continually tried to frighten and intimidate the rural, village population. After the coming of Nagy, in 1955, Szabad Föld underwent another cycle, this time supporting the Nagy Government.

Irodalmi Ujság: this paper began to be interesting after 1953. Up until then it had an entirely different format and content.

After 1953, the Irodalmi Ujság became the official organ of the Petőfi Circle and of the Writers' Association. It firmly supported Imre Nagy and Rákosi-men had little possibility in participating in its direction or of contributing to its contents. When, for instance, the Central Committee of the Party deprecated the tone of the Irodalmi Ujság and condemned the stand this publication took during and after the Poznan events, this paper, while publishing the text of the Party resolution, was strong and independent enough not to add any commentaries to it.

This paper was in such a great demand, and in such a short supply, that regular subscription to it was out of the question.

The Irodalmi Ujság was a weekly, with a circulation of approximately 50,000 copies, 12,000 copies of which went to old subscribers. The rest was sold on streets. One had to order it, and have it reserved, days before the date of publication, and even then the price of it was at least 10 forints. Both the reduction of the Irodalmi Ujság and Imre Nagy made determined efforts to increase the circulation of the paper, but the bureaucracy, where the Rákosi-elements continued to dominate, made this impossible; the Central Association of Newspaper Publishers, the agency which controlled the distribution of newsprint, calling attention to the provisions of the Economic Plan, politely but firmly rejected the Irodalmi Ujság's pleas.

In contrast to this deplorable curtailment of the Irodalmi Ujság, Szabad Nép, the official organ of the Party, had a circulation of approximately 3,400,000 copies a day.

You must bear in mind that this figure by no means represents Irodalmi Ujság's popularity. Szabad Nép had a complete and thorough network of distribution, and it was sent everywhere, irrespective of whether people wanted to read this paper or not.

The Circle of Szabad Nép, an organization formed by ruthless and forceful methods, saw to it that everyone did buy this Communist newspaper. The fact that a person was, or was not, a subscriber, was carefully entered on his cadre-sheet.

There was also the institution of Szabad Nép Half-Hour, operating everywhere. This Szabad Nép Half-Hour took place every other day; someone read a few articles aloud to an assembled group, after which the participants were expected to make comments. And these comments had better be straight, according to the ever shifting and changing Party line, or else one was in real trouble. In order to be able to take a logical and consistent stand, when called upon, one had to regularly read this paper, even if he hated it more than his sins.

Needless to say, all factories, offices, farms, stores, and institutions of all kinds became automatic subscribers to the <u>Szabad Nép</u>. Factories were also regularly subscribing to the <u>Népszava</u>, while farms and collectives patronized the <u>Szabad Föld</u> (Free Soil).

How great this superimposed and forceful sale of unwanted propaganda was, I knew from the beginning, but I only realized in 1953 to what extent it failed to accomplish the purpose intended. When I was freed in 1953 and placed under police surveillance, I was permitted to work as an unskilled laborer. I went to work to a factory. People there felt themselves relatively free then and expressed their true opinions; the change of attitudes appeared to me of such magnitude and it certainly was so dramatic that I was quite confused. People freely and deliberately cursed the system, the regime, Rákosi, and the norms. I kept looking around, constantly preoccupied and depressed by the thought that the AVH would be there any moment. It took me about a month and a half until I again became my own self, became acclimatized and completely understood the situation.

The Communist reeducation program forced so mercilessly and systematically down people's throats, had exactly the opposite effect of what was desired and expected.

People saw the wide gap and contradictions between spoken or written words and reality, and they ceased believing there and then. And when opportunity presented itself, they gave expression to what they saw.

The system of distribution of Communist books was equally well organized; books of lasting value with long-established reputation, such as works of Jókai, Mikszáth, Gárdonyi, Herczeg, and of others, were nowhere to be found. Bookstores carried Soviet books only, students used Soviet notes on the universities.

After 1953, a small quantity of old Hungarian classical works reappeared again.

I was a great lover of books and I saw many a characteristic incident in bookstores. A lady would come in with a boy and say: "I should like to purchase a storybook." She would be presented with 20 or 30 Soviet publications. She would look at them and say: "I would like so much to have a Hungarian book." The storekeeper did not have any.

It was this craving for Hungarian books, and the intense hate associated with everything Russian that accounts for the burning of Russian and Hungarian Communist books during the Revolution. The hateful reaction to the twelve-year-old torture of Soviet culture sought and found an outlet.

Every industrial undertaking had a library and in the economic plan of each concern a library-plan was incorporated, -- a sum of money that had to be spent for books and other publications. But the company was not free to determine what books it will purchase, or how it will spend the library-fund. The usual procedure was that a representative of the factory visited a state bookstore, presented his library budget and the bookstore filled out an order to the tune of whatever amount of money the factory had available for the purpose.

Then there were the "culture half-hours". One was expected to attend these cultural meetings, to report on books one read, to make commentaries on others, and to show enthusiasm and admiration for Stalin. This was the Hungarian cultural policy in Hungary during Rákosi.

The other newspapers of Hungary were insignificant, because they were through-and-through Rákosi publications. The publishers of these were only able to sell them because of the tremendous apparatus they had and because, being government or Party supported, these publications could exert a tremendous pressure. No one really cared to read the Csillag, for instance, a paper edited by Urbán and company.

Antique bookstores were doing a thriving business, simply because it was these stores where books written and published before the Communist era could be found. All public libraries were thoroughly checked and all books that went counter to Communist ideology were taken out. The Hungarian youth, as a result, was completely shut off from the West and, for the most part, remains to this day ignorant of the great literary masterpieces and other works of the Western world. The Iron Curtain was felt everywhere, and people were fed the mediocre and uni-colored Hungarian and Russian literary products.

To say a few words now about the revolutionary press: let us take the Népszabadság first. The Népszabadság of the Revolution has nothing in common, save its name, with the Népszabadság of today. The Népszabadság actively supported the Revolution. It was the official organ of the reconstituted Communist Party. Its fate, and direction, was intimately connected to Kádár, and it continued to change as Kádár changed.

Magyar Függetlenség: this paper was edited by Dudás.

Dudás is of Transylvanian origin, an engineer by profession, -- a man who spent 9 years in jail in Rumania for his Communist convictions.

He crossed illegally the Hungarian-Rumanian border in 1941, joined the illegal Communist movement in Hungary, became a Rajk-supporter and spent some time in jail in Hungary, too, for his Communist activities.

Dudás underwent a drastic change in 1945; he vehemently opposed the Moscow-domination of the Hungarian Communist Party. His nationalistic stand brought him in direct conflict with the Hungarian Muscovites. Helpless, and unable to exert influence on the Party trend, he became completely disillusioned and he quit the Party in 1945. Here was a man who has suffered a great deal, spent a sizable portion of his life in Rumanian and Hungarian jails, and, when in 1945 a great career lay ahead of him, he quit the Party. He was a member of the Hungarian Peace

Delegation and, together with Domonkos Szentiványi and Gábor Faragó (the gendarme-field-marshall: csendöraltábornagy) visited Moscow towards the end of the war. These people represented Admiral Horthy, and it was they who signed the provisional armistice treaty between Hungary and Russia.

Dudás later joined the Small Landholders' Party and was an active member of the Parliament's judiciary committee. He continued to maintain contact with the Communists, especially through the instrumentality of Aladár Weisshaus -- the only Jew I have ever known to maintain anti-Semitic views.

Weisshaus conducted a series of well-received seminars among the factory workers of Csepel. He became extremely influential and highly respected among the workers.

Weisshaus was arrested in 1947, and Dudás followed his fate shortly thereafter. In 1948, he was brought to Kistarcsa, and still later he was transferred to Recsk. It was in Recsk that I met him. He did not stay there long, however. He was placed in a jail in Budapest, where he remained until 1953. With the coming of Nagy, he was freed (1953) and worked as an engineer until 1956. He enjoyed a tremendous popularity among the workers, who frequently invited him to hold seminars for them.

It is this great popularity, renown, and prestige of Dudás, -- qualities that were well established long before the Revolution -- that accounts for his phenomenal personal success during the uprising. He was the leader of the largest, and most powerful, organized group during the Revolution, commanding a force of 130,000 men in the Capital.

Western leftists often branded him a Fascist. In reality, he is neither a Communist nor a counter-revolutionary, his entire following consisted of factory workers.

Dudás was wounded after November 4. He remained in the Szabad Nép building for a while, transferring his headquarters to the School of Law building later. Still later his faithful workers sheltered him in a factory at Köbánya. Toward the end of

November, during the period of the passive resistance, Dudás still had a small-armed force in the Köbánya factory, which watched over his safety day and night.

He was eventually captured and was put in prison. A delegation of writers visited Kádár and asked him to guarantee the safety of Dudás. Kádár replied that he had no objection to Dudás whatsoever and expressed his desire to talk to him. Dudás subsequently visited Kádár in the Parliament building and, as soon as he entered, he was arrested. He was later executed.

Dudás was obsessed by a theory of his, and this obsession caused him to make a hasty, and ill-considered step during the uprising; he wanted to seize the Ministry of Foreign Affairs and to bring about a situation where the United Nations would recognize the revolutionists as a belligerent Party, i.e., he desired that the United Nations recognize that a state of belligerency existed in Hungary.

Because Imre Nagy did not see eye to eye in this with Dudás, the two men were not always on very friendly terms. Imre Nagy did not think that the recognition of the existence of a state of belligerency between Hungary and the Soviet Union by the United Nations would do any good.

Finally the two men arrived at a compromise; there was talk about Dudás becoming a member of the Nagy Cabinet, about Dudás and Maléter joining forces and organizing a unified revolutionary command.

These controversies had the nature of high-level political disputes and they are in no way to be construed as signifying differences between the rank and file of the revolutionists. The freedom fighters were in complete agreement.

To come back to the original question; the <u>Magyar Függetlenség</u> was one of the most influential newspapers of the Revolution. It was edited by Dudás, a widely respected man who at the same time commanded the strongest revolutionary force. Dudás's paper was not restricted to Budapest, organized attempts were made by his group to distribute it to the provinces as well.

Igazság -- the best paper of the Revolution -- was jointly edited by József Gáli and Gyula Obersovszki. Obersovszki was a newspaperman of long standing, Gáli was a playwright. Gáli was one of the most talented writers of the young generation.

The Igazság was a consequential, beautiful paper, a paper that was very hard to get during the entire crisis. Both Obersovszki and Gáli have been arrested and both are waiting execution under a death sentence.

Népszava. This paper used to be the official organ of the labor union. During the Revolution it became the organ of the Social Democratic Party. It was edited by György Faludi and others. Faludi was imprisoned at Recsk and I came to know him personally there. He is now editing the Irodalmi Ujság in London, England. Faludi is a very good poet, -- he wrote some beautiful poetry while in prison.

Kis Ujság. This was the organ of the Small Landholders' Party. The paper ceased functioning in 1948. During the Revolution it revived again. Béla Kovács and Dezsö Futó were its editors.

Szabad Szó. This was the official organ of the National Peasant Party. Its editor was Pál Szabó. The paper appeared probably only twice during the Revolution.

2 g. *Did any articles, poems, lectures particularly impress you? If so, which?*

Yes, there were a great many such items that impressed me. Márkus's book, for instance, Aczél's article in which he criticized the AVH, the evening debates of the Petőfi Circle, especially those pertaining to economics and politics.

3. *In your mind, then, what were the major factors leading to the Revolt?*

There were a great many factors, some of which I already

discussed in some detail. One could summarize these and say that the six-year Communist rule of terror, between 1948 and 1953, with its all-embracing exploitation and betrayal of our national interests in the economic, cultural, and political spheres as well as in international relations, inevitably led to the Revolt.

The people saw constantly the many clear-cut contradictions between official pronouncements, promises, and actual conditions in reality. People saw the endless Russian economic exploitation. Many people, some convinced Communists, some only opportunistic fellow-travelers, -- an attitude that one cannot condemn very well -- have seen through the years the many atrocities so contrary to human nature, the arrests, and the mysterious disappearances. We, too, disappeared without any trace. Our families were never notified. They learned of our whereabouts from a report by the Radio Free Europe. One of our group managed to escape to the West after a year and Radio Free Europe broadcast our names.

Personal freedom, and the security of one's person, were flagrantly violated. Then again, in the cultural life, we had to suffer spiritually because we were forced to express ourselves favorably and admiringly and enthusiastically when it came to lectures on Soviet achievements or personalities, even though only hate and scorn and rejection characterized our souls. Our living standard sank to a remarkable low, with practically no possibility left to us to satisfy our material wants and cultural needs. One was obliged to choose between a pair of shoes and a movie ticket.

In the sphere of health insurance, while the SzTK was well organized, one had to put up with a spiritless, bureaucratic machine where no individual attention was possible.

These are only a few examples of the innumerable grievances we had. All these little items tended to bring about a feeling of insecurity, impotency, and an attitude of determined rejection of the whole regime. This feeling and attitude grew, as time went on, until it reached enormous proportions. This repressed force found an outlet after 1953, when everyone was permitted to offer his views. Everyone used this opportunity, everyone criticized, and people constantly searched for mistakes. But this whole activity remained negative. The possibility of correcting the mistakes was not given us and the now gigantic stream of opposition transformed into a loud dissatisfaction. This dissatisfaction led us to the Revolution.

All this internal development in Hungary grew, and took shape, within the framework of the changing international factors affecting Hungary -- the death of Stalin and the Twentieth Congress in particular -- factors which inadvertently helped and assisted and accelerated the development and channeling of already existing phenomena.

In this connection the summit meeting in Geneva must also be considered as a contributing factor; the more conciliatory tone that resulted from the Geneva talks prompted the Soviet Union to grant certain concessions to the satellites and to give up or modify certain basic aspects of policy on which she previously insisted.

3 a. *Why do you think the Revolt occurred when it did -- not sooner and not later?*

This is an odd question. I should like to ask you a few similar questions: Why did the French Revolution break out when it did? Why did the First World War break out on the day when it did and not before or after?

The outbreak of the Revolt, and the precise moment of its occurrence must be explained in the light of the combination and composition of the various constellations which helped bring it about. Conditions and circumstances are different in Hungary and, say, in Poland. Poznan, for instance, is not the capital city of Poland. In Rumania, there was a heavy concentration of Soviet troops, also Rumania properly belongs geographically, culturally, and traditionally to the Balkan bloc, where the feeling and desire of belonging to the Western world is practically non-existent.

All these factors must be considered. If, -- and we are here on a hypothetical ground -- Piros, the Minister of the Interior, did not vacillate, if he had immediately granted, or if he had refused to grant to the end, the permit to hold the demonstration; if Gerő did not make that rude and provocative speech; if the Government and the Party had given in, and had granted the initial demands, promptly and fully, if the AVH had not killed that young and innocent girl, the initial crisis and the revolution may have been averted. This hypothesis appears quite plausible, and the initial demands of the Revolution seem to underline this sort of reasoning; the Revolution, in its first hours, desired no more than a reorganization of the Communist Party. No one even dreamed at that time of a possibility of re-establishing the submerged or disbanded coalition parties, let alone demand their reconstitution. We were operating within the framework we desired the dismissal of all Rákosi-elements and their replacement by Imre Nagy and by people like him. This was our basic demand, supported and reinforced by other, lesser demands, as embodied in the 14 points. If these points had been granted, I, who never was a Communist -- would have been satisfied also.

3 b. We have often heard about the efficient controls which the Soviets imposed in the countries they ruled. How come the whole system was allowed to collapse so easily?

The assumption that the regime collapsed so easily is fallacious. It did not; the Government of Imre Nagy remained under complete and direct control of the AVH up until October 26. The Nagy Government was held in captivity in the Akademia Street. It was this place where all the Communist functionaries assembled, Communist bodyguards and Russian tanks protected this Communist headquarters and sealed the entire Akademia Street. There were at least two Russians present when Nagy received visitors and attempted to talk with them. The Petőfi

Circle, and the Council of Hungarian Intellectuals (Magyar Értelmiség Tanácsa), under the leadership of Géza Losonczi, constantly organized deputations of all sorts, trying to maintain the contact with the Prime Minister, but this attempt was only partially successful.

It was only the victory of the Revolution, whose main outlines became apparent on the 27th, that permitted Nagy to free himself from the grip, to reshuffle his Cabinet, and to transfer his headquarters from the Akademia Street to the Parliament building.

In the Parliament building the possibility of conducting negotiations became greater and hundreds of deputations availed themselves of the opportunity to present their views and demands. The stand taken, and the demands presented, were, in the main, identical, -- underlining, of course, the identity and universality of problems and grievances and the necessity of their urgent solution.

The Nagy Government was held in captivity by the AVH. This explains the fact that the proclamation of martial law and the calling in of Russian troops were effected without Imre Nagy knowing anything of it at the time. When he later learned of these decisions, he did not oppose them in order not to thereby sever what little contact he was permitted to maintain with the revolutionists. This, by the way, is characteristic of Gerő's methods.

A careful analysis of the events clearly refutes the contention that the regime easily collapsed; the masses assembled at the radio building in order to be present when the 14 points of the MEFESZ are read in. This was supposed to be a peaceful demonstration and yet the 19-year-old girl was killed. The people there assembled were neither armed nor organized. In these first moments one can hardly speak of the AVH as having lost a decisive battle -- at that time most people were still very much afraid of the confidential house-informers. The disintegration began when parts of the Hungarian Army deserted the Government and went over to the revolutionists, when Maléter refused to shoot at the Kilián barracks and instead assumed command of the revolutionary group there. When the Ludovika regiment attacked the Russians. It was only after these events that the tide had turned and the AVH became isolated.

3 c. *What do you think was in the minds of the people who staged the demonstration of October 23?*

Formally, there was the desire to express solidarity for the Poles; actually, under the cover of this desire to express the Hungarian people's solidarity for the Poles, there burned the determination to simultaneously bring to expression the deep-rooted grievances of the Hungarian people. More specifically, the intellectual leadership used this occasion to voice its own demands against the Hungarian Government.

It demanded a cessation of the absolute rule of the Party; Gerő should resign, and the leadership of the Party on all levels should be re-determined by elections from bottom to top. Imre Nagy should be brought into the Party's Central Committee, he should be appointed Prime Minister and he should be permitted to resume his program along the lines of his 1953 policy declaration.

Hungary's economic independence was another of these demands; secret trade agreements between Hungary and the Soviet Union should be made public. These were known to have contained secret price lists whereby the Soviet Union was permitted to arbitrarily determine what products it would give to Hungary, what others she would receive, and at what price. These agreements were further known to have stipulated unfavorable transportation conditions and extravagant quality requirements.

There was the question of the uranium-ore; uranium mines in Hungary were under the exclusive jurisdiction of the Soviet Union. Hungary wanted to see her sovereignty --- political and economic -- reestablished in this sphere.

There was the symbolic question of the restoration of Hungary's traditional emblem, the Kossuth emblem.

There was the question of the Hungarian Army uniform. The outfitting of Hungarian soldiers with Soviet-type uniforms should cease and a uniform corresponding to Hungarian army traditions should be recreated.

There was the question of the freedom of expression. Freedom of expression of every kind, particularly the freedom of the press, was demanded.

Another demand wished to secure the recognition of the independence of the MEFESZ organization with the possibility given to them to publish a newspaper of their own.

These were some of the principal demands of the leaders of the Revolution. How did they hope to accomplish them? Their aim was to bring their stand to the attention of the general public, to publicize them in newspapers, on the radio, and by means of mass meetings. The principal aim of the demonstration was to exert a pressure on the Government and thereby to facilitate the acceptance of these demands by the Government. If the Government had decided to accept these demands, there would have been no revolution. There would have been a Polish-type solution. In Hungary everyone would have been satisfied with a solution based on the 14 points and the conditions thereby created would have been considered as a condition of almost perfect freedom.

Of course, Rákosi and the Russians knew that, once these concessions are granted, there would have been no limit to further demands later. The developments in Poland exemplified this very well. An evolutionary development would have been inevitable.

Neither those who organized the demonstration, nor the countless thousands who participated in it had prepared themselves for revolution. Not even an action against the AVH members was contemplated. That it did come to a revolution, that so much innocent blood was shed, is the sole responsibility of the AVH.

3 d. *How did it turn from a demonstration into a fight?*

The change in attitudes occurred at the radio building. A delegation with several members carried the demands of the demonstrators inside the building for the purpose of broadcasting them over the waves. One of the members of the delegation was a girl. The AVH at first used such devices as rubber truncheons and water hoses against the members of this delegation. When that failed, shots rang out and the girl was killed. The girl's body immediately became a symbol in everyone's eyes and the demonstrators, peaceful until then in tone and action, violently turned their wrath on the AVH.

At the Parliament building, also, the change in the attitude of the demonstrators occurred only after the news that fighting broke out in front of the radio building had reached there.

3 e. *Do you think different people had different purposes in mind on October 23?*

I don't think so. The reason for this becomes evident if you understand that at that moment the 14 points constituted the <u>non plus ultra</u> in everyone's mind. There were isolated instances of people, it is true, who have seen more in the demonstrations and who have read more into the demands than they actually represented, -- people who expected more from the Revolution than the spirit of the Revolution would bear -- people who saw near at hand the fulfillment of their personal desires and aspirations. These additions came later, however, and did not even exist on the first day. These personal aspirations and plans came only after the reestablishment of the political parties. To a starving man a small piece of bread represents the realization of a noble dream, worthier than most everything else in the world. Those who later did not stop here, who were not satisfied nor satiated with the outlines of the revolutionary program were people who, because of the very nature of their political status, could not and did not dare even dream about anything in the beginning.

3f. What people opposed the Revolt? Can you give me any examples from your own experience?

Opposing the revolt were members of the AVH, comprised Party secretaries and all those people who, either in the Party or in the government, held and enjoyed the fruits of responsible positions. To this we should add people of all categories who have committed some acts in the past and for which acts they expected to be punished after a successful revolution.

While the opposition came from many quarters in the beginning, only members of the AVH stood resolutely against the Revolution with arms in their hands. These people knew what fate to expect, they had nothing to lose and they had no other way out.

I must mention here that there were many people in the AVH ranks who were inducted and placed there against their own will for the duration of their military service. Many of these regular soldiers sided with the Revolution. This is precisely the reason why it was thought necessary to call in the Russians; after it became evident that the Hungarian Army would act as it did, and after the Communist leadership of the factories was eliminated from positions of control, the remaining force of the AVH die-hards simply was not sufficient in number or strength for the task.

The AVH consisted of two categories; the regular AVH force, forming an integral part, and under the command of, the Ministry of the Interior, and equipped with red identification books on the one hand, and the inductees, regular army personnel, under the overall jurisdiction of the Defense Ministry, but temporarily transferred to, and under the command of, AVH officers, with blue identification papers, on the other.

3 g. *What people were neutral?*

It is difficult to establish categories here. Individual people who remained neutral could be found among workers and among peasants for instance, but the great majority of the workers participated, and a few days after the outbreak of the revolt the revolutionary spirit reached even the outlying rural districts and villages, where the TSzCs-secretaries and others were dismissed.

The former middle class, as a class, was probably more neutral than the other classes, -- but one cannot state even this much in a categorical fashion -- after all many of these people were jailed and participated actively in the Revolution. One cannot set up social categories here.

There were people who were personally afraid or were cowards and therefore refrained from active participation.

The Revolution spread later to the entire country. There was practically no village or locality in Hungary where revolutionary councils had not been established, or where no change in personnel in industrial or agricultural establishments had taken place. Party and council secretaries and plant and TSzCs directors were everywhere dismissed and were replaced by people who were revolutionaries in spirit and outlook, if not in action.

It is undeniable that there were neutrals, but their number and strength was totally insignificant in relation to those who did participate. Also, neutrality was very difficult to maintain; one was under constant social pressure and had to take a stand one way or the other. A Budapest apartment building is a neighborhood group where everyone knows everybody else.

3 h. *What were the most popular slogans during the Revolt? as the Revolution progressed, were additional slogans formulated?*

Slogans there were in great numbers. The most popular and

the most persistent slogan was the demand that the Russians leave the country. There were others that were particular in nature or temporary in duration. Some demanded the ouster of the Rákosi forces, others demanded the return of Nagy. Still others demanded free elections and the re-establishment of political parties. There were slogans demanding that the AVH be disbanded. Others advocated strike (especially after the Gerő speech). Somewhat later in time came slogans demanding neutral status for Hungary and a withdrawal from the Warsaw Pact.

There were some slogans of local significance; one of these originated in Szombathely and soon became nationally accepted: it demanded religious instruction within the curriculum of schools, and a return of the church-schools to the Churches. Mindszenty made this demand his own when he delivered his radio address.

Other slogans had to do with the norm-system. Slogans in one form or another demanded the abolition of the norm-system. Another slogan, originating in the provinces, incorporated the demand that the compulsory deliveries be stopped. (To this day there is no compulsory delivery system in Hungary.) Other slogans demanded a return to the traditional flag and emblem. Still others demanded that the Army wear traditional uniforms. There was another, important slogan, declaring that we are not returning land or factory (this was already part of the 16-point MEFESZ memorandum). This last slogan was more defensive in nature; it proposed to prove that what went on was a Socialist revolution, not a counter-revolution.

A war of placards and of handbills began after November 4. This was the time when the Kádár-regime tried to take a few cautious steps. The revolutionists were no longer in possession of printing presses and their placards and handbills were mimeographed. Many a person was arrested and taken away by the Russians in those days, while reading these placards. The regime, at first, printed all its propaganda material, but people simply refused even as much as to read printed messages. After some time the Kádár-placards were also mimeographed.

3 i. Do you think the Revolt was anti-Communist?

If Rákosi and the Russians are Communists, then the Revolution was anti-Communist. If what transpired in Hungary between 1948 and 1956 was communistic, then the Revolt was anti-Communist. Many Communists participated in it, the writers and the great majority of the Petőfi Circle were all Communists. These people were not anti-Communists, they condemned and fought against the slave-master relationship between Hungary and the Soviet Union.

The Revolution was all for good-neighbor-relations with the Soviet Union. But the Revolution negated and denied both the Moscow system and the Rákosi-type leadership. The Revolution's ideal was complete economic independence from Russia, and complete political independence from both East and West, symbolized in Hungary's neutrality.

The revolution opposed and fought against Russian Communist imperialism and against that group of men who represented this imperialism in Hungary.

3 j. What do you mean by anti-Communist?

I am not going to define the term, because it is not possible to do so. Opposition to the ideology did come from all quarters with causes varied and innumerable. I am only going to try to describe anti-Communist feeling and some of its causes as they pertained to Hungary. Take, for instance, the United States. People here are experts in selling all sorts of products. The television advertising may be quite misleading, and yet it is very effective. I, for example, was influenced by it so that I now smoke Viceroy cigarettes.

The Soviet Union, and Communists in general, have a similar method. They advertise not products but ideology. In the schools a constant and never-ceasing advertisement went on, within the school curriculum, where the Soviet Union, Stalin, and Rákosi continued to be mentioned, and described, and praised almost uninterruptedly.

This advertisement centered around the personality of Stalin. An attempt was made to instill heroic love and endless devotion to Stalin in the hearts of the very young. Stalin was endowed with telepathic powers, capable of rushing to the help of children and rescue them from danger, or want, or give them what they are wishing for.

Similarly, Rákosi, the Hungarian Stalin, was a superman character. He had an infallible intellect, and he was an expert in every sphere of life, beginning from the butterfly to the air plane. Not only were children taught to admire and to love him, Rákosi was equally able to gently superimpose his will on everybody he desired. All he had to do was to deliver a speech, let us say, at the Writers' Club, at a rally, or some other place, and the contents of his speech were immediately transformed into a program.

This was the basis of Hungarian school and adult education. And this education, instead of succeeding in saturating the Hungarian mind with communism, provoked an entirely opposite sort of reaction.

If the Hungarian Revolution was anti-Communist, then this attitude was but the consequence of Communist educational methods. This sort of advertising was forced upon everybody, but not even kindergarten pupils took it seriously. They knew it was not true. More than that, they knew that they must never reveal to anyone their disbelief, lest they cause trouble to their teachers or parents. Thus, while they did not believe a word of this propaganda, they gave the impression, at least outwardly, of being thoroughly indoctrinated. This latter fact tended to deceive the Communists themselves.

Revai declared in Parliament in 1947 that communism stands or falls in Hungary depending on whether or not it will be able to produce a succession of Communist generations.

If the Communists had succeeded in re-educating the young generation according to Communist principles, then there would never have been a revolution in Hungary. The reaction of the youth, so fully exposed for so long to Communist indoctrination, was truly amazing.

Now the Kádár-regime tries to convince the Hungarian public and the world that what happened in October-November was the work of reactionaries. They are trying to say that those many students, recipients of Russian scholarships and of material favors, young people who were especially selected and sent to Russia for a number of years to study, were reactionaries. We know this is a lie, but the fact remains that the most favored and the most supported group, students who had all they desired materially, turned completely against them.

The intellectuals, upset (csömör) from this constant and, in the eyes of most people silly (surfeit, nausea) propaganda, coupled with the readily apparent contradictions between it and reality, led people to first reject it and then to hate it, and to abhor it from the very depth of their hearts.

People, then, became anti-Communists not because they were American and imperialist spies, or reactionaries, but because they recognized Communist statements and pronouncements to be false. Because there was such a clear-cut contradiction between Communist ideology and actual life.

Communists did believe, at first, in the infallibility of their ideology. They rationalized the inconsistencies and concluded that the people, those in charge of putting ideology in practice, were the originators of mistakes. But they, too, came to see the light, and openly declared that the very foundations, the ideology as well as the system of its implementation, are the real roots of the evil. (I am only paraphrasing here Tibor Déry's thesis, as enunciated during one of the meetings of the Petőfi Circle.) Tibor Déry was a Communist of long standing. He entered the Party in 1919. He returned to Hungary in 1945. He believed then -- he related -- that communism could be brought about by means of a dictatorship of the proletariat. In 1953 he finally realized that he was mistaken. And he openly admitted his mistake. "Only one thing causes me intense pain -- said Déry -- that it is at such a colossal price of young life that I feel myself obligated to disassociate myself from communism."

For those who were not Communists, communism nevertheless did become an existential problem. One part of this group was interned and incarcerated. Others, the majority, accommodated themselves to the inevitable. They did not see a way out, even though they would have preferred to live under different circumstances. For this very reason many entered the ranks of the Party, in order to secure their daily bread, to be able to send their sons to the university, and to be able to more adequately provide for their families. They knew quite well how all depended on their cadre status. These people tried to establish cordial relations with those in charge of the cadres. This is why the various seminars were so well attended. This is why the <u>Szabad Nép</u> so easily managed to maintain such a wide circulation. A life, however, where a person constantly wears a mask, is a boring, stiff, and unnatural form of life. Not even on excursions and outings was one of these people permitted to take off his mask, and to offer his real views on Rákosi, for instance, because the Party secretary was also there, and listened to everything he had to say. Nor was a man safe, or free, to express his views at home; there, the confidential house informer (házbizalmi) registered all his movements. It was an inescapable, terrifying and agonizing thought supervision. Liberation from these controls was greeted with extraordinary joy.

It was the determined rejection of, and the helpless opposition to, all these factors and circumstances of life that drove people to the anti-Communist camp. They joined the Revolution to stamp out once and for all this limitless terror. The confidential house informers were no longer active during the Revolution. They remained home behind locked doors. The all-powerful Party secretaries no longer dominated the factories. The cadre sheets were distributed to all concerned. Only then did people see in full actuality the scope and extent of the regime's police methods.

3 l. Were there some reactionaries among the rebels?

Yes. It is undeniable that there were reactionaries among the rebels. The number, however, was insignificant.

In the Eighth Precinct (nyolcadik kerület), for example, people recognized a former Horthy-general. Similar phenomena appeared also in the provinces. There were instances when former gendarmes and chief notaries (föjegyzök), former head administrative officials of rural civil administrations, succeeded in occupying and seizing the power in some villages. I am personally convinced that the victorious revolution would have dealt quickly and easily with these anachronisms.

There was, for instance, the case of Count Almásy, a former great landowner and aristocrat, who visited Imre Nagy and demanded that his lands be returned.

Occurrences of this sort were extremely rare. No one took them seriously and most people were impelled to smile when hearing of these Don Quixote sort of fellows as they chased the windmills.

3 m. Suppose Soviet troops had not been brought in. What do you think would have happened in Hungary?

This is a hypothetical question. I can give you only what my personal impressions were regarding these matters, though the Revolution undeniably supplied the contours, the main outlines of things to come.

It is a generally known fact that Hungarian democratic parties were reconstituted almost immediately after the outbreak of the uprising. Acts of Party organization and planning were in full swing, in spite of the first Russian intervention. It is also universally conceded that by the 28th of October we defeated the Russians. Had there been no further Russian intervention, normal life would have been resumed by November 4 at the latest. People were already engaged in clearing up the ruins, employees of the Beszkárt (municipally operated transit system of Budapest) were already repairing the high-tension overhead electrical wires. Factories were all set to resume their regular operations. In a word, Hungary's internal life would have reverted to normal and production would have been resumed.

In the field of international relations, the foundation was already there; Hungary repudiated the Warsaw Pact and declared her complete disassociation from power bloc politics both with respect to the East and with respect to the West. Hungary henceforth was to be neutral. Within this framework, and in conformity with this new outlook, our political and economic relations with the Soviet Union would have been worked out.

In the internal political sphere the resumption of normal parliamentary life would have been the first order of business; universal, free, and secret elections would have been held. Everyone spoke of this election as imminent, even as the fighting went on. The organization and operation of the Presidential Council was chaotic and unsatisfactory. Equally important, the Hungarian Constitution, as well as the parliamentary rules and procedures were in dire need of revision. Needless to say, a new electoral law would have soon been enacted. These would have been some of the more pressing and immediate questions to be debated and acted upon by the new Parliament. The basic principle in this respect was the preservation of constitutionality and of constitutional continuity, a very important consideration to legal-minded Hungarians and a principle in which even Dobi concurred.

Other important questions of internal political and economic nature were equally pressing and in need of solution. One of the most far-reaching of these was the constitutional and legal determination of the status of the workers' councils. These councils were forced to perform a dual function during the Revolution; they combined the activities of the labor unions with a political function whereby they acted as elected spokesmen of a substantial part of the population.

It was generally agreed that the workers' councils would relinquish their political part and that they would restrict themselves to the economic sphere. The workers' councils were to assume the overall direction and planning work, the administration of production units on the local level, while a newly elected and reconstituted labor union leadership was to assume the regular functions of a labor union.

The national government was to be entrusted to a coalition cabinet, the composition of which was to correspond to the relative strength of the various parties in Parliament. From this it follows that the Cabinet of Imre Nagy would have been reshuffled until it corresponded to the relative strength of the parties. The various expert, non-political portfolios would have been filled by experts of the respective parties.

It would have been the task of this coalition government to create new political and economic foundations for the country within the framework of a neutral and democratic republic and in the spirit of complete political freedom.

While the political part of this new program would have been relatively easy to accomplish, on the economic sphere the situation was more complex. We were faced with an acute depression and a very low living standard, brought about by the extensive and abnormal policy of economic expansion. We would have been obliged, no doubt, to seek economic assistance and long-term loans from the United States and from other Western countries.

Retail trade and small industry would have been denationalized and these small undertakings would have received the whole-hearted support and encouragement of the government.

In agriculture, 65 percent of all the collectives have already collapsed in the wake of the Revolution. While voluntary farmers' associations would have been permitted to continue, the government would have encouraged all those farmers who preferred to till their own land by assisting them in the purchase of livestock, equipment, seed, and fertilizers. All this with a view to resuming agricultural operation as soon and as smoothly as possible.

The tractor and machine stations would have been so reorganized as to make them available to independent farmers as well.

The question of cultural policy would have assumed immense importance. Needless to say, we could not have erased traces of Communist influence in a matter of days. It would have been our aim to counterbalance these influences by consciously popularizing Western ideas and ways. You must realize that the natural quest of Hungarians for culture was arbitrarily and forcefully directed into Russian cultural channels to a point of complete one-sidedness and isolation, where Hungarians knew only of things Russian, and were completely ignorant of new discoveries, new literary and other artistic creations in the Western world.

Another of our great tasks would have been the working out of the principles of the essence of democracy; it would have been our obligation to form a government from individuals who would have regarded liberty as their highest goal and greatest treasure. Hungary's development in this respect came to a complete standstill in 1848. Nothing of the sort was done since that time.

Speaking on the economic sphere I would like to mention that Hungary could have become a very prosperous country if she based her economic existence on those resources and potentials that are freely available within her geographic boundaries. Light industry should have been developed with the emphasis on those branches whose support and operation was assured by the availability of domestic raw materials. I have in mind here the production of electrical appliances, railroad equipment, tools, textiles, and canning industry.

In agriculture our aim would have been to introduce intensive as opposed to extensive, cultivation methods and practices. Instead of cultivating the traditional varieties of grain, we would have concentrated on fodder culture (takarmány), on production of various seeds for which the uniqueness of Hungarian climate offered an excellent basis and which, incidentally, could be exported in tremendous quantities; these seeds cannot be produced anywhere else in the same quality. We would also have emphasized the establishment of orchards and the development of a large-scale fruit culture. Nut-bearing trees are especially adaptable to arid (szikes) sections of Hungarian land, and in this connection we have achieved significant results even before the Second World War; Hungary exported more than 300,000 kilograms of various kinds of nuts between the two world wars. Part of our agricultural program would have consisted in irrigation of arid lands, and transforming barren meadows into thriving orchards. All this would have been ideally suited to smaller farm units and, if intensive cultivation methods were employed, a raising of living standard, prosperity, and satisfaction would have been assured the Hungarian peasants.

4. *What did you do between October 23 and November 4?*

I participated in the Revolution between the period you asked me (October 23 - November 4). My participation was not confined to any one place, I was in contact with all revolutionary centers in Budapest and everywhere I went I did those things which were important or necessary under the then and there existing circumstances.

On October 23 I was part of the demonstration that marched to the statue of Bem. After that we went down Rákóczy Street to the Parliament Square. Not everyone took part in the demonstration at the Bem statue. I remained in front of the Parliament for a long time and went thereafter to the statue of Stalin. I was at the statue during the evening and night of October 23.

On the 24th and after, I was mainly in Buda. My residence was in Törökbálint and I selected a place which was in some proximity to my home. I was stationed at the Móricz Zsigmond körtér and the Széna-ter. János Szabó, the leader of the Széna-tér resistance group, was a very good acquaintance of mine.

I was also a member of the Presidential Council of the Petőfi Circle as well as a member of the Revolutionary Committee of Hungarian Intellectuals. This latter group operated under the leadership of György Ádám and it was engaged, among other things, in the procurement of arms and in the distribution of these arms among the university students. Sándor Herpai, a high-ranking officer of the Budapest regular police force, fully cooperated with our group and provided the students with those arms and national guard (nemzetöri) identification papers.

4 a. Did you see any fighting between Hungarians, Russian troops, ÁVOs, or police? If so, whom, when, where?

During the first phase of the Revolution I was on the Széna-tér, which is one of the most interesting parts of Buda, -- a sector where the most serious and most decisive things took place. We were engaged in the sealing off of street entrances to the square with barricades and in building our actual defense line.

An especially savage battle took place on the Széna-tér during the afternoon of the 24th of October, with approximately 40-45 Russian tanks participating. Alongside of the tanks, members of the AVH forces from the Vörös Hadsereg Street AVH barracks also participated.

The freedom fighters were about 300 to 400 men strong. Their equipment was very meager and deficient. They used an overturned railway wagon and the surrounding houses as their cover. The Russians concentrated their fire on these buildings for the entire duration of the fight, which lasted uninterruptedly for three hours.

The Russians and the AVH-men advanced from the Széll Kálmán Square, but they were not able to break through the barricades we erected just a few hours before their arrival.

Our casualties were heavy, amounting to some 15-20 dead and many more wounded.

The insurgents fought with simple infantry rifles and a few machine pistols of the type used by the Hungarian Army. We later had a few machine guns, which we managed to capture from our enemies. We also had a few trucks and a car -- equipment we used mainly for the transportation of our wounded. We also had a Russian armored car. This was about one-and-a-half tons large and was equipped with a machine gun. This armored car came to our possession as a result of the exploits of a young man, Endre Cserbaköi, one of the sub-leaders of the Széna-tér group, who captured it from the Russians. In the first phase of the Revolution this armored car constituted our most important weapon.

On October 25 the AVH succeeded in capturing a small segment of our force, about 30 to 40 men. These people were taken to the Petőfi Akadémia (a military installation) and there were locked up. At that time (October 24) the amnesty proclamation was already in operation and Imre Nagy himself enjoyed a relatively greater freedom. It was under these circumstances that the Revolutionary Council of Hungarian Intellectuals succeeded in intervening on their behalf. Imre Nagy freed them. The Széna-tér group was freed, then, on the 24th, the day of their capture, and they all returned to their former units.

The following day, on the 26th, the same group succeeded in capturing the Petőfi Akadémia. They were greatly assisted in this by the enlisted men stationed in that installation, who, as a group, sided with the insurgents and came over to their side. As a result of this exploit, a revolutionary council was immediately organized in the Petőfi Akadémia, with Endre Cserbaköi becoming the leader of the council.

Part of the activity of the Széna-tér group was the seizure and confiscation, in the name of the Revolution, of the villas of Rákosi, Gerő, Hegedüs, Szalai, and others in the Rózsadomb section of the city. They found an immense amount of food, clothing, and luxurious installations in these houses. Rákosi's villa was also equipped with an atom-proof subterranean shelter.

We penetrated to the Rózsadomb by way of the Keleti Károly Street, and, while the Rákosi-clique no longer resided there, this exclusive sector was still heavily fortified and guarded by a strongly-armed AVH sentinel force, reinforced upon our arrival by other units from a nearby AVH barrack.

We went to the Rózsadomb on the 26th of October, led by János Szabó and Endre Cserbaköi. The AVH-men opened fire on us and a battle quickly developed, in the course of which we captured four machine guns and a large mass of lesser hand weapons. Some of the AVH were killed or captured, others retreated and fled.

This whole thing occurred in the before noon hours of the 26th. We left a small garrison on the Rózsadomb, the bulk of us returning and heading for the Petőfi Akadémia, the capture of which I already described.

On the Rózsadomb a minute inventory was kept of all the items found in these exclusive residences. Food of every variety and expensive clothing were found there. The residences were magnificently equipped with all the conceivable modern conveniences. While I have no personal knowledge of any papers or documents having been captured there, I should like to call your attention to the fact that certain papers were made public in France and also in Germany in this connection.

My situation in the Revolution was a special one; those of us who were members of the Petőfi Circle and of the Committee of Hungarian Intellectuals were also engaged in other aspects of the Revolution than actual fighting. Because we dealt with many questions of city-wide and national character, we were not confined to one place, nor did we remain in any one locality for long. As the fighting ceased in one locality, for instance, I would move to another. It was more the circumstances and events than I which determined where I was at any given moment.

October 26 and October 27 were days, for example, when we made it our task to convince the wavering Imre Nagy of the true nature of the Revolution. We have tried to persuade him to make the program of the Revolution his own. On the 26th the Government finally left its Akademia Street confinement and took up quarters in the Parliament building. The transfer represented a degree of change insofar as the tight control of the AVH over individual members of the Cabinet lessened somewhat.

It is true that the Parliament building continued to be watched by the AVH, and that the Parliament building itself was not without Communist guards. These guards, however, were under the jurisdiction of the Defense Department, not of the AVH.

Also on the 26th, the Cabinet itself was enlarged and reshuffled.

A great many delegations came to the Parliament building. All of them desired to see the Premier. The principal purpose of all these delegations was to try to make Imre Nagy understand that what went on in the country was not a counter-revolution, and to convince him that the program of the Revolution was not a counter-revolutionary program, but one that even Imre Nagy could easily accept.

Zoltán Tildy played a very forceful part in those days. He, for one, sympathized with the revolutionary ideals from the very beginning. He maintained that the Cabinet must never lose contact with the Revolution. He brought about the inclusion of Maléter into the Cabinet, securing his appointment as Assistant Defense Minister at first, and later as Minister of Defense. It was also Tildy who clearly recognized that the Government must not drift aimlessly (kullogni) behind the Revolution. The Government must, he said, accept, and make its own the demands and aims of the Revolution and must lead it through success and triumph.

Indeed, the Revolution was clearly heading toward chaos and anarchy and disorganization. Everyone joined it, worthy and worthless people alike. The AVH organization, thoroughly beaten and disorganized by then, was on the verge of collapse. On the 27, 28, and 29, one could no longer truthfully speak of an AVH organization, for there simply wasn't any. Many of them put on uniforms of the regular police force, escaped or submerged in some other way.

It was then (October 27 - 29) that the Calvin Square episode took place; a few AVH-men became isolated in the reformed church on the Calvin Square, they retreated to the church's steeple and the shooting began. It was on this occasion that AVH people were slain and posthumously hanged, a fact which, -- while I deprecate and condemn it as an extreme and cruel act, unworthy of the high ideals of the Revolution -- I also understand as a normal reaction of hate and wrath after 12 years of AVH terror.

This episode was not a pleasant or happy moment for the Revolution, and both the Petőfi Circle and the Revolutionary Council of Hungarian Intellectuals protested against it and condemned the action.

On the 28th, Pál Jónás, Gábor Tánczos, and a Catholic priest whose name escapes my memory, visited Cardinal Mindszenty as a delegation and asked him to take a public stand against the repetition of similar atrocities. Mindszenty immediately responded and publicly condemned the atrocities.

These, then, were the events which took place between October 27 - 29. Our activities and tasks were political, not military, in that period. On the 29th, the reconstitution of the political parties was made public. On the morning of the same day a nine-member executive committee of the Small Landholders' Party was called into being. More specifically, 120 leading exponents of the Small Landholders' Party assembled in the Party's Zárda Street headquarters, and these 120 elected the nine-member executive committee. The nine-member executive committee, in turn, immediately conducted discussions with János Szabó, the leader of the Széna-tér resistance group who, as it later turned out, himself was a Small Landholders' Party adherent.

The other parties, too, were in the process of formation; Sándor Kiss organized the Peasants' League (the league used to be a peasants' labor union between 1945 and 1947).

The National Peasant Party also came into being under the new name of Petőfi Party. Ferenc Farkas and some other former members of this Party constituted the provisional leadership. The

Petőfi Party elected a consultative body, with László Németh, János Kodolányi, Péter Veres, Gyula Illyés, and other noted populist writers as members.

The Social Democratic Party was the last in time of all the parties to reconstitute itself. Anna Kéthly, Gyula Kelemen, József Fischer, József Kömüves, András Révész, and others were its recognized leaders.

Once the parties re-emerged, some of their respective members took up their parts assigned to them in the Cabinet; Zoltán Tildy, Kovács, and Istvan Szabó represented the Small Landholders' Party, Ferenc Farkas and Istvan Bibó represented the Petőfi (Peasant) Party, Anna Kéthly, Gyula Kelemen, and József Kömüves were the Social Democratic Party representatives.

István Bibö of the Petőfi Party should here be mentioned. Bibö, on November 4, worked out a common platform to be adopted by all non-Communist parties, in an effort to consolidate all the anti-Communist parties in those critical days. We may have an opportunity to discuss this later.

October 29th was a decisive date for the Revolution. The Government, on that day, accepted, and made its own, all the demands of the Revolution, made determined efforts to consolidate the situation and decided, in principle, to immediately start negotiations with the Russians.

Under this new setup Maléter became the Defense Minister and organized the National Guard (Nemzetörség). Béla Király became the commander of this new force. Maléter is a graduate of the pre-war Ludovika Akedemia (the Hungarian West Point / Interviewer's note). He served in the Hungarian Army under Horthy. In 1944 he sided with those officers of the Hungarian Army who decided to get Hungary out of the axis block. He later entered the Communist Party. So did Király, as a matter of fact. This was a compulsory act for all higher ranking army officers. Király was relatively unknown -- I certainly never heard of him -- during the Revolution. Maléter, on the other hand, played a very interesting part in it; he received an order from Károly Janzza, then Minister of Defense, to proceed with his armored unit to the Kilian Barracks and to liquidate a "mob violence" there. The unit which Maléter commanded was an all-officer detachment. Maléter proceeded as ordered and, recognizing on his arrival the true nature of this "mob violence", instead of shooting at the "mob", he himself went over to their side with his entire group. The Kilian Barracks Revolutionary Council promptly elected Maléter as the barracks' military commander.

Maléter visited several times Imre Nagy in those hectic days as the leader of the Kilian delegation. It was on one of these occasions that he met Tildy, who immediately recognized his human and leadership qualities. There was, according to Tildy, no better qualified man than Maléter for the defense job. Dudás was unsuitable because he was not a military man and because his politics was entirely unacceptable to the Government. János Szabó, another man under consideration, did an excellent job on the Széna-tér, but would not have made a good Defense Minister. As a result, Maléter was nominated for the post.

As soon as the Coalition Cabinet began functioning, Tildy advanced his proposal that the Government should immediately enter into direct negotiations with responsible Soviet leaders with a view to bringing about the withdrawal of Soviet forces from Hungary. Tildy's proposal was accepted by the Cabinet, and since the Russians, too, appeared quite willing, the negotiations soon began.

The negotiations did go on and, outwardly at least, the Russians appeared sincere and cooperative. I suspected their sincerity then, and I am fully convinced now that the Russians never really took these negotiations seriously. Moscow entered into these negotiations because she saw a tactical advantage in them; the apparent willingness of the Russians to withdraw their troops from the city permitted them to withdraw a compromised, unreliable, and beaten force, the continued garrisoning of which in Budapest would have undoubtedly been more of a disadvantage than of an advantage to Russia. Unfortunately, the real Russian aim -- so clear today -- was not to withdraw, but to replace the beaten Budapest garrison. It is because of this imperative need to bring in fresh forces that the Russians entered into the troop withdrawal discussions in the first place. It is tragic that the Hungarian Government was not well informed about the Russian troop movements and that when it did receive the necessary information, it was much too late to effectively handle the changed situation. It must be quite obvious to everyone today that the fresh Russian troops in all probability received their order to enter Hungary even before the withdrawal negotiations got under way. This contention is further underlined by the actual reports the Hungarian Government did receive from various sources in the County of Szabolcs, shortly after the Russian forces crossed the Hungarian border, reports which, for some unknown reason, the Government did not take seriously at the time.

On October 29, Mikoyán visited Budapest and, among other of his conferences, met Tildy as well in a private apartment. The meeting took place in private quarters to lend an air of unofficial, private atmosphere to the discussions, so that both men could freely exchange views on all aspects of the situation.

During the conversation, Mikoyán promised Tildy that the Russian troops would definitely be withdrawn from Budapest by October 31 at the latest and that the evacuation of Russian troops from the rest of the country would also take place soon after that date.

Meanwhile, discussions of general aspects of the evacuation continued between Maléter and Ferenc Erdel, leaders of the Hungarian delegation on the one hand, and the Soviet delegation on the other. These delegations continued until the 2nd of November.

All these discussions were based on the promises which Mikoyán gave Tildy and on other verbal agreements these two men concluded.

On the afternoon of November 3, the mixed Hungarian-Russian delegations concluded their discussions, having reached an understanding regarding the main aspects of the troop evacuation. Further discussions and the working out of technical details of this operation were entrusted to a delegation of technical experts. These experts conducted their meetings at Tököl. It was at Tököl, where Maléter came as the leader of the Hungarian delegation, that the Russians arrested him.

On November 3, there were already significant new Soviet forces between the Danube and the Tisza Rivers -- a fact which Imre Nagy took cognizance of in his foreign policy declaration of that same day.

In the early dawn of November 4, the second Russian invasion of Hungary began. This time the Russians came not only with tanks, they also had an infantry of a considerable size.

Now to say a few words about desertion of Russian solders; one of the first of the numerous instances of such desertion took place just before the battle on the Parliament Square. In the vicinity of the Parliament building, in the Kossuth Lajos Street, a dispute occurred between some Russian tank soldiers and Hungarian freedom fighters. Russian-speaking Hungarians managed to establish friendly contacts with a group of Russian tank-solders who, after learning of the true nature of the uprising, deserted their forces and joined the Revolution. Five Russian tanks were involved in this incident. The Russians drove their tanks, with Hungarians riding on them, to the Parliament Square. A large mass of people were already assembled there. On the roof of the Defense Ministry building located in the immediate vicinity of the Parliament Square, AVH forces were stationed. Suddenly the AVH group opened its fire on the crowd assembled below. The Russians, not knowing what it was all about, took up the fight and returned the fire. The crowd stood helplessly between the two fires, taking heavy punishment from the AVH machine guns. I did not witness the actual fight, I only arrived about one hour after its termination. Many people were killed and many more wounded. Blood was literally flowing in streams down the gutter. This whole thing took place during the first phase of the Revolution. The assembled crowd was a peaceful group, intending only to demonstrate in the Parliament Square. The five Russian tanks, of course, came to the assistance of the crowd. What I saw there was a horrible picture.

Russians deserted their units in other sectors of Budapest also. There was, for example, a small Russian unit fighting in the Kilian Barracks. Such desertions usually occurred in small units, i.e., platoons or, which was even more often the case, individual Russian soldiers deserted their units and sided with the rebels. In Győr, for instance, the Revolution succeeded completely without shedding of blood simply because the Russian commander there refused to combat the insurgents. He even delivered a speech to that effect in the Győr radio.

The Russians stationed at Győr had many contacts with the Hungarian population and they had a clearer understanding of the Hungarian situation than did those Russian soldiers who participated in the first invasion of the city of Budapest.

This uncertainty about the attitude and the allegiance of some of the Russian troops and the outright refusal of others to fight the insurrection contributed in great measure to the apparently conciliatory stand the Russian Government took during the Mikoyán-Tildy talks and during subsequent negotiations. The Russians clearly saw the need to replace their old troops and they searched for a graceful and yet effective way to do it.

The fresh Russian troops of the second phase (October 4 and after) were provided with varying orientation instructions; some of them were constantly searching for the Americans. They were told that the American imperialists had attacked the peace-loving and defenseless Hungarian workers. Others were vainly trying to find the sea and the Suez Canal in Budapest. These fresh forces were clearly misinformed. They knew nothing of the Hungarian situation. They were a much stronger force than the previous wave, made up of both tanks and sizeable infantry. They were able to decisively execute their operations.

In the early hours of November 4 they encircled the Parliament building, the Ministries of Defense and of the Interior, and they occupied all the bridges. They also seized the various plazas of Pest and used their heavy artillery to bombard strategic sections of the city's interior. The whole operation, both in respect of weapons employed and in strategy followed, as well as in respect of battle tactics, had the earmarks of a carefully laid-out general staff plan, the aim of which soon became clear to us all.

The Russians first determined the exact geographical location of the more important resistance centers in Budapest, Pesterzsébet, Ujpest, Óbuda, the Schmidt-castle (Schmidt kastély), and other places. They then trained their heavy artillery on these locations and opened up a devastating barrage of fire. The softening action of the artillery was followed up by the deployment of tanks and infantry units, working in close cooperation.

As a result of this precise and overpowering assault, the Hungarians' fight for freedom was completely beaten by November 4 and 5.

That the by then hopeless struggle was still continued can only be explained by the fact that the insurgents literally fought for time. They wanted to provoke the dispatch of a United Nations delegation to Hungary and they wanted to ensure that the struggle continued at least until the United Nations delegation arrived. The odds against them were disproportionately great and the insurgents saw themselves forced to change their battle tactics. In this the Petőfi Circle and the Central Budapest Workers' Council actively participated. By this time, regular contacts have been established between the various resistance pockets. It was agreed and decided that the insurgents split up their forces into smaller units and henceforth conduct a guerilla-type warfare.

Everyone saw the end, the inevitable, and the fight was

continued only to give time and opportunity for the United Nations delegation to arrive in Hungary. The United Nations delegation was expected to take a firm hand and to contribute to the prevention of retorsions and executions which everybody recognized as the inevitable consequence, should the United Nations intervention fail to materialize.

This condition continued until November 12. It is during this period -- November 4 - 12 -- that the freedom fighters suffered their heaviest casualties. November 12 introduces that period the various fighting groups were forced out of the Capital. The forces of Dudás are practically annihilated. The Corvin, Kilian, and other groups retreat first to the Pesthidegkút area, and later to the Dunantul province. The struggle, occasional and sporadic, continues and the almost endless exodus to the West begins. Freedom fighters fought their way to the Austro-Hungarian border and crossed the frontier with arms in their hands.

In Budapest, the Russians were the absolute masters of the city. Russian troops combined with the newly-organized Kádár-units -- the latter were made up of AVH-members and loyal Communists -- to enforce and maintain a terror-laden order and peace. This combined force also continued liquidating remnants of the by-then isolated but still resisting revolutionary pockets. The Russians assumed the role of the wielder of the big stick in these operations, leaving the Kádár-forces to perform the distasteful and bloody job of liquidation. The Kádár-forces visited hospitals and forcefully removed all the wounded revolutionary fighters.

Coupled with the physical aspects of fighting, the propaganda campaign was also continued. In the second part of November, the leaflet and placard war reached its height; printing presses were no longer available to the revolutionaries, and stencil machines from various offices and factories were used instead. The streets of Budapest were flooded with revolutionary leaflets; in these leaflets the population was asked to continue resisting and to maintain the strike.

During this period, the Revolutionary Workers' Councils represented the principal power in Hungary. The leader of the revolutionary councils' central Budapest organization was Sándor Rácz, a 30-35-year-old tool and diemaker. In this central council both the Writers' Association and the Revolutionary Council of Hungarian Intellectuals were well represented.

It was also during this period that Kádár tried to cement and consolidate his power. He did not, as yet, decide to do away entirely with the revolutionary councils. He actually conducted negotiations with the leaders of the revolutionary organ, but the understanding reached was not honored by the Russians. The Kádár-group also tried to win the cooperation of the leaders of the democratic parties. Kádár proposed the formation of a coalition cabinet, with the lion's share of power to rest with the Party of Workers and Peasants (Communist). The maneuver did not succeed because Kádár refused to recognize the Social Democratic Party as a separate and distinct entity. The Small Landholders' Party and the Peasants (Petőfi) Party previously concluded a mutual agreement with the Social Democratic Party not to enter a coalition with the Communists except <u>en bloc</u>. Now, faced with the Kádár-proposal of a coalition without the Social Democrats, they flatly refused their cooperation.

This intra-Party mutual agreement was negotiated and signed between November 20 and November 22, stipulating that neither Party shall ever enter the coalition, nor will discuss any matter with the Communists on an individual basis. The three parties agreed, in other words, to always act in concert. Since neither Kádár nor the Russians were prepared to recognize an independent Social Democratic Party -- they said, in effect, that such a recognition would result in the splitting up and in the destruction of the unity of the Hungarian workers' movement -- the coalition never came into being.

Kádár continued to threaten both the parties and the nation, saying that, if he should not succeed in consolidating the situation, Russian military dictatorship would be bound to follow. The threat did not carry any weight, however, for everyone knew that such Russian military dictatorship was already an actuality. It was not Kádár who commanded in Hungary.

After November 20, for instance, András Sándor, a young Communist writer and one of the leaders of the Stalinváros radio station during the Revolution, was arrested. Sándor was accused of having directed the Stalinváros battle against the second Russian wave. A delegation of the Hungarian Writers' Association visited Kádár on Sándor's behalf. The delegation, with Sándor's wife as one of its members, heard Kádár solemnly pledge that the accused writer would immediately be set free. Actually, Kádár could not have acted differently, since the accusation, -- direction of and participation in the struggle against the Russians -- was not a punishable activity at the time. At any rate, Kádár did issue the necessary orders for Sándor's release. However, when the order was presented at the prison, the Russian commander refused to honor it or to abide by it, and András Sándor was not set free. He was, by the way, sentenced just a few days ago.

This is what Kádár's promise and executive power amounted to. Hungary was, in effect, ruled by a Russian military dictatorship. This dictatorship became all-embracing in scope and its activities were characterized by a constant intensification; the Russians, soon after Kádár's position became more or less stabilized, demanded a thorough and merciless liquidation of the Revolution.

Kádár's political attitude and behavior underwent two abrupt and highly significant changes during October-November, 1956; on October 30, in a speech, he frankly admitted that the Hungarian Communist Party was in a process of rapid disintegration. On November 1, he went one step further and announced the formation of a new Communist Party, the Hungarian Socialist Workers' Party, which, while proclaiming a platform of defense of socialist achievements and of fighting any counter-revolutionary moves, it firmly approved the Nagy-government's program in all respects, including Nagy's demand for a complete withdrawal of Soviet forces from Hungary.

Kádár spoke on this occasion (November 1) of his firm determination that Hungary must not be dependent any longer. And yet, two days later, he became a Russian stooge who readily organized a counter-government and repudiated Nagy and Nagy's program in its entirety.

The apparent contradiction of Kádár's attitudes is traceable to his compromised political past, a fact which the Russians fully exploited to their own advantage; on November 2, in the evening, a Russian car stopped in front of Kádár's private residence and Russian individuals (apparently MVD-men) took Kádár, Münnich, Marosán, and Rónai to an unknown location. On November 3, in the afternoon, Kádár and the others reemerged in the city of Szolnok, began negotiations for the formation of a new government, announcing its composition and program on November 4.

The role of Münnich, and his change of heart, is easily explained by his age and by his almost complete lack of will-power. Marosán and Rónai were people of no consequence, -- individuals whom no one ever took seriously. Kádár's situation was different; he was a man of deep-rooted anti-Russian feelings, a national Communist and Rajk-supporter of long standing, one who suffered long imprisonment and both inhuman and degrading tortures. He could not have reversed himself so completely as he did of his own free will. As a matter of fact, we know that he did not. A former high official of the Ministry of the Interior, whose name I am not free to disclose at this time (the man is awaiting sentence in a prison in Hungary), reliably informed us on November 4 that the two recordings of Kádár, made without his knowledge at the time of the pre-trial investigation of Rajk, came into the hands of the Russian MVD. Our informer has a direct knowledge of the record's contents. Rajk and Kádár always were considered the internal enemies and the greatest antagonists of the Rákosi-Gerő clique within the Party. These records provided an unmistakable evidence of Kádár's disloyalty both to the then Hungarian Communist leadership as well as to the policies of the KPSU. The records proved beyond doubt how both Rajk and Kádár desired to establish a Titoist Hungary. Rákosi and Gábor Péter transmitted these recordings to the Russians long before the outbreak of the Hungarian Revolution. The Russians kept the records and decided to use them against Kádár in the night of November 2-3. Kádár, a virtual prisoner of the MVD, and confronted with irrefutable evidence on November 2-3, when at the mercy of the Russian secret Police, apparently did not see any other acceptable alternative but to abide by the Russians' wishes: to form a new, puppet Government.

Kádár reversed himself again on November 25. From the time of the Szolnok proclamation up until November 25, Kádár never spoke of calling people to account for the part they played in the Revolution. He did speak a great deal about counter-revolutionaries and about misled young people who have innocently and inadvertently participated in a popular uprising, the true nature of which they did not know and did not understand.

On November 25, Kádár delivered a speech in which he identified the events of October 23 - November 4 as a Fascist and American-imperialist counter-revolution, and in which he for the first time posed the question of responsibility and of calling to account those responsible.

The speech signaled the beginning of the renewed terror in Hungary. People were to be punished for their revolutionary acts. The other political parties, which until then hoped in the possibility of some compromise solution, suddenly retreated. Immediately after November 25, the mass exodus to Austria reached its peak. The system of border patrols was not yet organized and only occasional Russian units hindered the refugees' flight.

November 25 introduces a new era, in which those forces which gave a positive evaluation to the Revolution submerge and continue their activities illegally. Sandor Rácz and Mihály Báli vanish from the scene. The AVH prohibits an announced meeting of the workers' councils' central organization, which planned to meet in the Budapest Sport Pavilion, and the mass deportations begin.

It is significant and characteristic for this period that Colonel Mátyás, the AVH commander of the Fö-utcai prison, restricts himself to the signing of the arrest orders, while the actual interrogation of the prisoners and decisions of their future fate is completely in the hands of the Russians. Equally significant, the Russian commander of Budapest is the virtual master of the city, to whom Kádár dutifully and regularly submits his reports.

4 b. Did you see any instances where Hungarian troops deserted their units or defied their orders?

There were many such instances. I personally was not an eyewitness to any of them, but a few instances are generally known, such as Malétér and his role at the Kilian barracks. The Defense Minister and the Division Commander gave direct orders to Malétér to go out there and to quell the revolt. Malétér proceeded to the barracks, went over to the side of the revolutionaries, and soon thereafter was elected commander of the Kilian forces.

Equally well known is the fact that the National Guard forces, made up of university students, were commanded by young army officers.

A significant portion of the Hungarian army, excepting the high-ranking army officers, sided at one time or another, some sooner some later, with the Revolution.

The Defense Minister of the present regime, trying to defend the reliability and the effectiveness of the Hungarian army, declared not so long ago that the army could have successfully combated the Revolution. He could cite only one example, however, where an army unit did go against the Revolution.

In the night of October 23, the revolutionaries did not have a single piece of weapon at their disposal. The fact that they did possess a considerable supply of them later, clearly testifies to the fact that there were army formations which either gave their own weapons to the revolutionaries, or opened their warehouses to them, or transported weapons from warehouses and arsenals to resistance centers.

The regime's one and only loyal military formation was the AVH, whose members were so thoroughly compromised that they really did not have any alternative or choice.

The fact that the Revolution, in its first phase, succeeded and became victorious, is attributable in no uncertain measure to the circumstance that the Hungarian army sided with the insurrection. At this very moment, numerous members of the frontier guard and of the regular army are tried by military tribunals. The fact of these trials, and the number of accused military figures, provides us with still another possibility of measuring the extent of military participation on the side of the Revolution.

4 c. Did you witness any mob violence?
If so how did you feel about it at the time?

I have seen only one instance of mob violence. It happened on the Szent István körút, on the Marx Square. The people seized an AVH first lieutenant. The lieutenant walked in civilian clothes and somebody recognized him. I arrived a few minutes after the seizure. The Lieutenant received a savage and merciless beating right there on the spot. Soon a national guard unit arrived, took the prisoner out of the mob's hands, and took him, as far as I could ascertain, to an assembly place for AVH prisoners to be tried later.

As to how I felt about it, I never did like mob violence. We were fighting already in 1945 against widespread Communist mob violence. But this time the people had positive reasons for their actions, whose underlying causes were both determined, real, and deep. The fame and renown which these AVH-men achieved for themselves at the Andrássy-út prison was based on such acts of brutality and inhumanity which are beyond the ordinary person's imagination. The AVH was a state within the state. Not even the ministries knew what the AVH was doing. Only the topmost leaders of the Party, Rákosi for instance, was kept informed of the AVH's activities.

If someone was unfortunate enough to become one of the AVH's victims, such person was no longer his own master; he became a slave of his capricious torturers and interrogators. Cooperatives, villages kulaks, better Social Democrats, Rajkists, -- all these and many others experienced on their own skin the bestiality of the AVH. Even the regular police force was afraid of the AVH. Not even they had any means of defending themselves against the AVH's encroachments and treachery.

All these facts and circumstances were ideally suited for the instillment of intense fear and of unlimited hate in the hearts of many, so that whenever an AVH-man was beaten or slain, it was never just the result of mob psychology and/or mob violence, there always were positive, concrete reasons behind it.

The attitude and aim of the Revolution was to disarm these people (the AVH) and to bring them to justice in regular courts. Whenever decisions to lynch some of them were made, such decisions always had a concrete reason. A series of efforts were made to halt these irregularities by the Cabinet, by Mindszenty, by Béla Kovács, by the workers' councils, by the Petőfi Circle, and by other revolutionary organizations. The population was admonished and warned both on the radio and by other means to refrain from these illegal lynching procedures. Constant reference was made to the normal, legal possibilities available in this connection.

6. I should like to ask you something about the action you saw. Did you fight alone or belong to a group?

I did not strictly belong to any one group. The very nature of any assignment placed upon me the necessity to be at different sections of the city. I was at the Széna-tér several times, I was also a couple of times at the Móricz Zsigmond kőrtér. All this until November 4. After November 4, a determined effort was made to adopt guerilla warfare tactics, after we recognized that regular fighting methods could not be applied against the overpowering might of the second invasion. The procedure adopted was to split up into smaller groups, to take cover in a house and to proceed from this base to a preferably distant location, there to engage in battle with the Russians and, upon inflicting damage and confusion, to suddenly retract to the base again. It was our endeavor to bring about a unified and identical point of view in this respect among the writers, the leading members of the Petőfi Circle, and the leaders of the guerilla groups. Having this aim in mind, we visited all the universities and discussed this new fighting procedure with leaders there. It was in this capacity of a liaison officer that I visited the Kilian Barracks, the resistance groups at the Korvin-tér, at the Széna-tér, and at the Statisztika tér, to which latter place the forces of János Szabó retreated. They later left the city altogether and assumed new positions at Pesthidegkút.

Unfortunately, I cannot fix the exact time of these events, the situation was rather confused and fluid, where day and night flowed together and became quite indistinct.

6 a. What was the origin of the group? Did it grow out of any existing group (army, students, workers)?

Let me describe to you the emergence of one group, the one which operated on the Móricz körtér. The heaviest fights took place there on November 5 and 6, when the whole plaza was destroyed. But let us go back to the formation of the group.

At the beginning of the first phase of the Revolution, the news spread that the Russians are on their way to invade the city. They were reported to be proceeding from the direction of Budaörs. Immense masses of people stood or walked on the streets. When the news that the Russians are coming reached the plaza, people began to build the barricades. I, too, joined them and became one of a chain, handing pieces of stone to those engaged in the erecting of the walls. While we built the barricades, I could observe only five or six men who were actually carrying arms. In the immediate vicinity there was a school building and the school janitor was also in our group. The barricades extended from house to house and we left only a narrow pedestrian path open. The janitor told us that he left the school building open and that we may use it if the need should arise.

One man in the crowd worked especially hard and made skillful and smart arrangements as the barricades were built. The others saw that everything he did was right, and whatever he said made good sense, and therefore they did whatever this man told them to do. He became the leader, the commander. He told me also to go into one of the houses. We escorted the women to safe places. The Russians arrived in about three or four hours. They came from three different directions, proceeding from the outskirts of the city. They stopped in front of the barricades and began to shoot. They were too far away, out of our range, so we could not return the fire. The Russians did not have an infantry.

At the instruction of the "commander", three or four smaller groups left the buildings which served as our cover, and using various side streets, tried to reach a position where they could attack the Russians from the side. The strategy was to try to disturb the Russian formation at various points from the side. The attempt was highly successful and the Russians retreated in about two hours.

This was not a big thing really. Altogether there were only two-three wounded in all. The barricades were built well and they served an excellent purpose. The Russians could not proceed past them. The city here had large and wide avenues, there was no possibility for us for an intensive attack.

You are asking me, who the "commander" was. I don't really know. No one in the group seemed to have known him personally. He issued his orders in an intelligent and sympathetic manner and everyone listened to him and obeyed him. Nobody contradicted him and there was no one who would not obey. The Russians left us and I, too, took leave of the group. The whole thing took place in the early afternoon hours. There were men, women, and children. After the battle was over, the superfluous people left the place. This one man took upon himself the responsibility to both build the defense line and to actually direct the defensive operations. There were a few people who disagreed with him at the time we built the barricades. Others disagreed with him as to what the type and location of the barricades should be. He had a winning personality and he patiently explained why things should be done exactly this way and why the counter-proposals would be disastrous. The others listened and understood him and his plan, and accepted both the plan and the man.

In other localities, things were sightly different. At the Széna-tér, for instance, Uncle Szabó (Interviewer's note: reference here is made to János Szabó, the Széna-tér commander) used to call a small citizens' meeting (népgyülés). His men assembled and Uncle Szabó laid bare and explained the situation and told of his plan to meet it. There was hardly any contradiction or dispute, for everyone knew the general situation quite well. A citizens' meeting was called on November 12, or November 13, the last meeting of the Szabó group, when it was decided to abandon Budapest and to go to Pesthidegkút. The procedure was similar to previous meetings, except that on this one Uncle Szabó himself had to be convinced that his ideas were not acceptable. Uncle Szabó wanted to remain in Budapest, come what may, until the United Nations intervention arrived. But the probability of such intervention dwindled, until, on November 12 - 13, it became quite hopeless. The Budapest buildings, all agreed, afforded no protection against Russian artillery barrage and against Russian infantry troops.

6 b. Who joined it? Was anybody recruited? Was anybody allowed to join? Who decided who could join?

More often than not this did not amount to a question at all. If someone proceeded to the Kilian Barracks, for example, and said there that he wanted to fight, he was given every opportunity to do so. Or, if a man wanted to fight, he simply went to the Széna-tér, stopped at one of the corners, and fought. Nobody questioned him, nor did anyone hamper him in any way.

On the other hand, the Széna-tér group, under the direction of Cserbaköi, executed one of their own members, after it became evident that he was an AVH-man. This, however, took place after November 4. Up until then, those who wanted to fight did so, those who did not, refrained.

Generally speaking, there was no recruiting. There was no time for this. And there was no organization, nor was there personnel available for this purpose. I know, for instance, that trucks were sent out to the neighboring villages, and any person who desired to come into the city was offered a ride. But there was no organized recruiting.

6c. What later became of your group members?

Not all the groups had the same fate. Those fighting on the Korvin-tér were forced to abandon the plaza around November 6 or November 7. They moved first from the Korvin-kör to the Ninth Precinct and fought there for a while, then later retreated to Óbuda and, retaining their weapons, they proceeded towards the West. They crossed the Austrian border between November 20 and November 26.

The Széna-tér forces retreated on November 12-13 to Pesthidegkút. There they remained, as a closed and organized unit, for four-five days, when some of them hid their weapons and, under the leadership of Cserbaköi, returned to Budapest. János Szabó and three of his comrades were betrayed by someone and were seized by the Communists in a week-end house. I have not witnessed the seizure myself, but I have it from an eyewitness who is now living in Europe. My informer was a close friend and co-fighter of Szabó. Szabó and others sent him to Budapest to settle some pending family business, both his own and of some others. He was to return and to join Szabó at the week-end house and the entire group was then to proceed to Austria. As he was returning and reached the vicinity of the week-end house, he was witnessing, from a safe distance, the last stages of his comrades' seizure. Russian and officers detachments of the Kádár-regime were kicking and throwing and hurling Szabó and his friends to a waiting military truck. Cserbaköi, too, fell into Communist hands and became their prisoner in Budapest in the early days of December. A few members of the Szabó-group did manage to flee to safety and crossed the Austro-Hungarian border in the last days of November.

The Pozsár-Perger group. These two commanded a group of university students who studied at the Budapest Institute of Technology (Müegyetem) and at the Péter Pázmány University of Budapest. The Pozsár-Perger group fought principally at the Calvin and Baross streets during the first phase of the Revolution. After November 4 they continued the struggle for a while, conducting a guerilla-type warfare. Later some of the members of this group concealed, hid, or threw away their weapons and returned to their homes. Pozsár and Perger were also engaged in the manufacture and distribution of Russian-language leaflets, until both of them were arrested sometime after December 4. Both Pozsár and Perger have since been sentenced.

The Dudás-group. Dudás maintained himself in the <u>Szabad</u>

Nép building during the entire period. I saw him there, for the last time, on November 4. I took Franz Germani, the Budapest correspondent of the German periodical Der Spiegel to Dudás's headquarters. I met Mr. Germani in the morning hours of November 4 at the Deák-tér Church. He approached me, and I willingly took him to Dudás's headquarters. Unfortunately, we could not talk to Dudás, he was wounded shortly before our arrival. We saw his assistant instead, a first lieutenant of the Hungarian army. The Russians were reported as proceeding from the direction of the Keleti Railway Station and the entire Dudás force was in a state of general alarm. We remained there for only one hour and just managed to leave the scene before the arrival of the Russians.

This day (November 4) witnessed the greatest single attack which was ever undertaken against the forces of Dudás. They stood their ground and defended the Szabad Nép building till late in the evening, suffering very many casualties. They then gave up the building and retreated.

This was one of the most formidable and most significant forces of the Revolution. Against this force the Russians proceeded most savagely and with resolute determination. As a result, it was this group whose members scattered and dispersed almost completely.

After November 4, the Dudás-force disintegrated into smaller units. Dudás himself remained for another four days in one of the buildings of the Péter Pázmany University. Then some of his faithful worker-followers removed him to Köbánya, placed him in a factory there, and watched over his safety day and night. The majority of the Dudás-group consisted of factory workers of Köbánya, and these people continued to defend their leader, so that the Russians were never able to take the Dudás factory, nor to liquidate the remaining portion of his group. It was Kádár who, plotting for the arrest of Dudás, brought about his seizure. Kádár invited his adversary to a conference in the Parliament building. Dudás, in good faith, accepted the invitation, and, as soon as he entered the Parliament building, he was seized and arrested. The first lieutenant, Dudás's deputy, was also arrested and sentenced. Two other important Dudás assistants are now in Canada.

6 d. *What sort of supplies and arms did the group have? Where from?*

The revolutionaries had hand weapons, -- machine guns were rather rare. Dudás had a few smaller arms, such as machine pistols, and especially rifles were available in great quantities (számtalan volt). The most important and the most effective anti-tank weapon was the so-called Molotov-cocktail.

What weapons we possessed we got from Hungarian army arsenals and warehouses, an operation facilitated and made possible by the Hungarian army itself. The initiative in this connection came from citizens of Budapest, particularly from people who were only recently discharged from the army. These people gave us the clues and tips as to the location of military warehouses, etc. I know of no instance where the army would have refused to open to us its warehouse or would have refused in any way its cooperation. As a matter of fact, in most instances the army itself undertook to transport both the available weapons and ammunition to prearranged localities at predetermined intervals.

The victory of the Revolution, in its first phase, is due to the Molotov-cocktails. Rifles served only for personal protection, at times when, after the tanks were ignited, one was obliged to take up the struggle with the tank's personnel.

But even more important than all this was the fact that the Hungarian army did not use its own might and weapons against the Revolution. The army held the key. While they did not support us en masse, actively, they did not turn against us either, and supplied us with weapons we needed. The army continued to be beyond the reach of either the AVH or of the Rákosi-clique, and individual soldiers either became active participants on our side or quit the army and went home.

Between Törökbálint and Diósd is a sizable and important army arsenal, from which we received immense quantities of ammunition and weapons. It was precisely this fact which made the Móricz Zsigmond area so important. The supplying of the Revolution with both arms and ammunition took place on this route. This is why the Russians fought with such savagery and determination against this area.

6 e. How was the group organized? Was there any discipline?

There definitely was discipline. And for two reasons: first, there was a danger, felt both by individuals and groups, which made disciplined behavior an imperative necessity. Second, leaders of fighting revolutionary groups were absolutely recognized and respected by all members of the group. These leaders were elected in many instances by the group members and enjoyed the unqualified trust, confidence, and esteem of every member of the group.

I never did like military discipline, but this was a voluntary discipline, and relationship into which everyone entered entirely of his own free volition. Because we lived so long under a dictatorship, and because we were subjected for so long to an involuntary and oppressive discipline of the Party, we were extremely careful and we made doubly sure to elect only those whom we considered to be our real leaders to positions of leadership.

While an immense danger and the prospect of peril faced each and every one of us, and our nation as a whole, and though we were in the middle of a savage war, we made sure that democratic processes were strictly observed and followed even within semi-military organizations. In the Kilian Barracks regular meetings were held and matters of principle were thoroughly aired and discussed before any decisions were reached. On one occasion

Malétér, the commander, was voted down in connection with an organizational question, and Malétér was obliged to give up his view and to abide by the majority's wishes.

This same may be said of the Széna-tér group. Szabó, who wished to remain in the city even after November 12, was obliged to comply with the majority's wishes and to withdraw his troops from the capital. People, even in the most difficult and perilous situations, continued to search for ways and means of just, equitable, and democratic solutions.

When the man who joined the Széna-tér group after November 4, the individual who was later executed as a spy (see also Section R, Q. 6 c), the act of execution was preceded by a thorough discussion of his case. Cserbaköi, his accuser, proved beyond doubt on a meeting attended by all, that the man was an AVH-spy. He was sent there either to report on the group's activities or to try to soft-pedal and pervert the group's members. At any rate, his case was discussed in a democratic manner. Everyone could speak his mind, and everyone could justify and give reasons for his stand.

We, too, during one of our visits, while in no way members of the group, were permitted to fully explain in public our views on whether the Széna-tér group should remain in the city or whether it should rather retreat. We took the stand, incidentally, (November 12) that the situation was hopeless, and that they should therefore leave the city.

6f. *Was there any leader? If so, what was his background, politics, military experience? How did he become the leader?*

Yes, there were leaders. Let me try to describe some of them to you.

János Szabó, leader of the Széna-tér group, was about 55-60 years old. He was a laborer, a transport worker (fizikai szállitómunkás) by profession. He must have been a soldier, but if he was, he certainly did not have a higher rank than that of a sergeant. He became a leader of his group because at that time, and under those circumstances, he possessed the clearest vision of them all and he recognized most fully what was going on and what to do about it. He was a very competent and skillful organizer. He cared for his men and was anxious to be of service to them. He was competent and he had the ability to do the right things at the right moment. He was the father of his young adherents. He scolded them and he praised them as the circumstances demanded, and as their good or bad behavior warranted it. He was recognized and respected by all, both as a man and as a leader. To be that kind of a leader one obviously must possess undeniable leadership qualities. And Uncle Szabó possessed just that. He fervently believed in what he was doing, and he had the ability to put in apt and convincing words the essence of his beliefs.

Dudás was a mechanical engineer, about 40-45 years old, an illegal (underground) Communist worker of long standing. I am not familiar with his military qualifications. He was Transylvanian by origin, entering Hungary illegally in 1941. He was arrested shortly after his arrival and spent one and a half years in Hungarian prisons during the Horthy-regime. He was one of the members of the Hungarian armistice delegation and, with Horthy's acquiescence, he visited Moscow together with Domonkos Szentiványi and Gábor Faragó towards the end of the Second World War and helped conclude the Hungarian-Russian provisional armistice agreement.

Soon after his arrival in Hungary in 1941, he joined the ranks of the Hungarian Communists (he had been a Communist in Transylvania for a very long time and spent nine years of his life in jails there), became a Rajk-supporter, and participated actively in the underground work of the Party until he was arrested.

He vehemently opposed the Moscow line and the Rákosi group's tendencies and, after Rákosi's triumphant return he became both disappointed and disillusioned. He quit the Party in 1945, later entering the ranks of the Small Landholders as a parliamentary delegate (Representative) and actively participated in the judiciary committee.

Through a Small Landholders' Party he continued to maintain his contacts with the anti-Rákosi faction of the Communist Party. He was a close friend and cooperator of Aladár Weisshaus. Weisshaus was arrested in 1947, and Dudás himself returned to jail in 1948. He spent some time at Kistarcsa, was later transferred to Recsk, and still later was taken to a Budapest prison.

I became closely acquainted with him at Recsk and came to know and learn his human qualities there. He was a leader there of a small work-group. Dudás was an extremely friendly fellow, the most helpful and comradely of friends, who took very good care of his men in the toughest and most difficult situations. He had the capacity to say a few warm, sincere, and suitable words to everyone in the right moment. The inmates of Recsk were enthusiastic about him and everybody admired him.

Dudás had long-established and friendly relations in Hungarian workers' circles. He was a friend of Aladár Weisshaus, the anti-Semitic Jew, who conducted well-attended seminars among workers, peasants, and intellectuals. Dudás himself was very well acquainted with these people, and he continued to maintain his good relations with the Weisshausists.

The Weisshausists, needless to say, were oppressed and persecuted after 1947 and both Weisshaus and Dudás were imprisoned. But Dudás was freed in 1954 and he found ready contacts among the Weisshausists. It was these people who formed the nucleus of his revolutionary army. Others, too, rallied to his support, so that Dudás had under him ca. 130,000 armed men during the Revolution.

His situation was the easiest and smoothest one of all the revolutionary leaders. He had an absolute prestige among his followers and every command of his was immediately carried out without a sound. He had attractive, warm, and winning personality traits, one of which was that he always took care of his own needs last, only after the needs of everybody else were completely satiated. This contributed a great deal to his prestige and explains to some extent his unparalleled personal triumph.

The Pergel-Pozsár group was made up exclusively of university students. I don't know very much of either Pergel or Pozsár because I did not know them that well. They were young people, active in university circles, notably in the Budapest Institute of Technology, in the Economic and Law colleges. They participated in the early demonstrations, in the organization of the MEFESZ, and in the formulation of the MEFESZ points. These activities of theirs made them both suitable and qualified leaders.

I must note here that as far as the university students were concerned, their group was not as close-knit as was the Dudás or Szabó group. Their situation was characterized by a more pronounced fluidity and they were molded by more than just the influence of their nominal leaders. Their status was also different from that of the other groups. The Revolutionary Council of Hungarian Intellectuals succeeded in establishing a friendly contact early in the Revolution with Sándor Herpay, a high-ranking officer of the regular Budapest police force. Herpay's cooperation made it possible for university students to legally possess and carry arms with them. They became a part of the National Guard.

The role of Perger and of Pozsár became more pronounced and more evident only after November 4.

6 g. *From your experience, what sort of person showed the most initiative for leadership?*

The question of leadership was inextricably interwoven with human qualities. The entire atmosphere of the Revolution was such that it brought the ideal and desirable human characteristics to the fore. The good and the beautiful human qualities only were supported and these were permitted to fully assert themselves.

Let me give you an example. It happened in the first days of the Revolution. We were standing in line in front of a Közért store. Stores opened only occasionally in those days, and a friend of mine and I joined the waiting crowd. The store distributed butter, milk, and other things, and suddenly I realized that I had no container with me. I remarked how annoying it was to stand there without a jug, when my small child certainly could use some milk. Behind me was standing a lady. She immediately offered to give me one of her two jugs, explaining that I need not even bother returning it. I have never seen her before or after. To you this little episode may seem dry and pointless, but never in my life have I experienced or seen anything like it. The people standing in line there were nice and pleasant and understanding. Shortly thereafter the storekeeper came out and explained that he alone was on duty and asked the crowd to file into the store in groups of five at a time. Quietly and calmly, and in a disciplined fashion, proceeded the distribution of what food there was.

This, then, was the atmosphere of the Revolution, and good human qualities triumphed in minute little chores just as well as in national undertakings. To positions of leadership came not ambitious and careerist-minded people, but individuals who were fit and suitable to work and lead and operate in, and in conformity with, this revolutionary atmosphere.

6 h. How were decisions made in your unit?

Decisions were always made in a democratic spirit. Citizens' meetings were most widely employed. Everyone was permitted to express his opinion and the decision of the majority was always accepted as binding by all. This, I realize, may not be especially revealing either to you or to Americans in general. But in Hungary it represented a tremendous change. We missed this procedure very much in the past decade and the people, having once again recaptured it, clung to it tenaciously.

There were situations when a decision had to be made as to who is to be included as member of a certain delegation. The revolutionary council proposed one or two people. Individuals stood up and made their own nominations. Finally a vote was taken. Those who approved of a man raised their hands. Then those who disapproved of him raised <u>their</u> hands. If necessary, hands were actually counted. Thus, some 350-400 people decided who those six individuals should be who will represent them. There were, of course, always some who were better known than others, and these had a better chance of being elected. The innocent childhood of the democracy was this, an innocence which, in practice, perhaps never existed and does not exist anywhere.

It was quite natural and understandable that this state of mind and practice developed, especially in the first phase of the Revolution, when the battle raged between the people and their government; the people's main strength lay in their unanimity of goal and purpose, and they invoked their main weapon, the power of the unanimous masses, and they used effectively the only means of mass expression available to them, namely the resolutions and the delegations.

6i. *Did you discuss plans or exchange information with anyone?*

During the first phase of the Revolution, there was practically no contact between the various groups and discussions of plans, or exchange of information did not take place. Actual contact was only created later, after the victory of the Revolution. Groups physically close to one another did maintain a sort of practical relationship in that they supplemented one another's weapon or munition needs and the like, but there was never any attempt to consolidate plans or discuss policy among the various groups.

During the second phase of the Revolution, determined attempts were made to bring about some sort of a unity, but even then centralization was neither intended nor desired. I, myself, too, was engaged in such a synchronizing operation. Dudás, for instance, visited the Széna-tér on October 26, spoke to the men there and told them of his ideas and plans. But this was about all. I don't know of any other such instance. Central synchronizing organs did not exist at all. I wish we had them. This is why we tried to bring about some sort of a centralization after November 4.

7. Among the various revolutionary groups, who had the greatest authority? Why?

Undoubtedly the Kilian, the Korvin-köz, the Széna-tér, and the Dudás groups had the greatest prestige and the greatest authority. There were several reasons for this: these were the largest groups and the leaders of these groups, because of their personal character and because of their success in battle, became both recognized and respected. Dudás, besides being the commander of the largest single group, also edited and published a national newspaper. Both the Kilian and the Korvin-köz groups published a mimeographed newspaper of their own.

Dudás's paper, the Magyar Függetlenség, was widely distributed, in the city first, later also in the provinces. The distribution in the provinces was not organized in any way; whenever a truck or car left for Szeged or Debrecen or some other city, it carried a large number of Magyar Függetlenség with it.

7 a. Were there any conflicts or disagreements among the rebels? If so, detail.

I do not know of any conflicts or disagreements, except the one which flared up when Dudás published his foreign policy plan. There was then a disagreement between Dudás and the Nagy Cabinet. Dudás wanted the Nagy Government to turn to the United Nations and have the United Nations recognize the Revolution as a belligerent Party. Dudás was bent on attacking and occupying the Ministry of Foreign Affairs in this connection. Imre Nagy opposed this whole scheme and Dudás was actually held a prisoner during one night a few days before November 4. I believe it was on November 2.

There was also the incident in the Kilian Barracks, when Maléter was voted down. The vote taken concerned a small matter of organizational nature. Maléter abided by the majority vote and continued as commander of the Kilian. (I know of this only through others, who related the incident to me.)

7 b. How did students and workers get along during the Revolution?

I don't think the fact that someone was a student, some other a worker, did carry any weight with it. It did not matter and it was of no moment. János Szabó, for instance, was a worker, and yet he was a leader of army officers, university students, university graduates, and of course of many workers.

Social background and belonging to this category or that was definitely not a problem. This question in Hungary, even before the Revolution, ceased to be an explosive one and classes did not represent the extremes they do elsewhere in Europe or even here in the States.

Many a university graduate, because of his bad cadre status, became a worker. And many a worker held leading, responsible positions. Also, the majority of university students were of worker or peasant stock and they did not consider their state of being students to be constituting a special rank. This was no longer a problem in Hungary.

Cooperation between the various groups was completely natural, and it worked out very well.

7 c. *Did you have any contact with any of the following: workers' groups; army units; student organizations?*

Yes, I had innumerable contacts with all of these.

7 d. *Did you have any contact with any of the following: intellectuals; clergy; peasants; revolutionary council.*

I was a member of the Presidential Council of the Petőfi Circle. I was also a member of the Hungarian Revolutionary Council. In this latter group Catholic priests and Protestant ministers were also to be found. Later on I also became a member of the steering committee (intézobizottság) of the Small Landholders' Party. I was also active in the newly-organized Peasant union (Parasztszövetség). For the rest, I was engaged in the reorganization of the Small Landholders' Party in the provinces and I also lived in a provincial village.

8. *How did Soviet troops behave during the whole crisis?*

The behavior of the Russian troops may be said to have varied according to the widest scale.

8 a. *Were there any differences of behavior among them?*

After the events of October 23, the Russians first of all occupied the Parliament building, the buildings of the Defense Ministry and of the Ministry of the Interior, and all the Danube bridges. The Russians took their prisoners to the Defense Ministry. At times there were as many as 3,000 prisoners there.

There were heavy fights in the immediate vicinity of the Defense Ministry. People mistakenly thought the AVH headquarters to be situated on the Jászai Mari Square. There were many casualties. Revolutionaries usually entered the nearest building, called up the ambulance, and the wounded were taken away.

Another incident took place on the Néphadsereg út, the Russians were firing in the direction of the Defense Ministry. A pedestrian, who was not even a freedom fighter, fell wounded and bleeding profusely. Revolutionaries pulled in the wounded man under the gateway of house No. 6. The ambulance arrived and, as soon as the white-coated doctor stepped out of the car, the Russians, standing only 200-300 meters away, began firing and killed the doctor. The wounded man continued to bleed. Another ambulance was called and, as soon as the doctor stepped out of he, too, was killed by the Russians. The wounded man died in the meantime. The Russians did not fire except when the ambulance arrived.

Take another example: in Győr, the Russian commander refused to shoot even after ordered to do so by his superiors. He was quickly replaced and was later taken away.

In the Kilian Barracks there was a small Russian detachment, about 30-40 people, who deserted their units and came over to our side in the early hours of the Revolution. They stood their ground to the bitter end, giving their lives for Hungary's freedom.

8 b. *What about Russian students in Budapest?*

> I have no knowledge of Russian students studying in Budapest.

8 c. *What about Chinese and other foreign students?*

> There were a few foreign scholarship students from Korea, North Vietnam, and other places, who studied at Budapest University. Eight to ten took active part in the Revolution, and a couple of them even crossed the Austrian border. I was asked by the Attache of the North Vietnamese Legation in Paris what I knew of North Vietnamese students and of the role they played in

Hungary. The majority of these students studied at the Budapest Institute of Technology and they participated in the Revolution there. Others, a smaller group, joined the Kilian forces.

These foreign students returned to the student hostels after the victory of the Revolution and remained there till the middle of November. AVH-men interrogated them and informed them that they would be recalled by their own governments within a few days. Those who left Hungary and went over to Austria did so because they feared that they would be called to account by their own governments. These were North Vietnamese and North Korean students. I had a long conversation with them in Vienna.

If you are interested in more details, the North Vietnamese Legation in Paris would be the most logical source.

These students held a well-attended press conference in Vienna, in the beginning of February. There are detailed reports in the Vienna newspapers.

8 e. *Do you know of any defections by Russians during the Revolt?*

There were Russian groups at the Kilian and elsewhere. Five Russian tanks defected during the battle at the Parliament building. There were many individual Russian soldiers who defected here and there.

8 f. *How much influence do you think Soviet authorities exerted in Budapest?*

It is obviously difficult to gauge the extent of the influence Soviet authorities exerted. As far as the Soviet military authorities are concerned, ordinary Russian soldiery was confined to its barracks before the Revolution. Higher Russian officers undoubtedly maintained some contacts with Hungarian officials, both military and civilian, but just how much influence they exerted I am not able to tell you.

Russian political influence and Russian economic involvement were immense; there were joint Russian-Hungarian undertakings and establishments, and Soviet Russia was the greatest single customer of many a Hungarian factory.

It is my firm belief that nothing occurred in Hungary which was not Russian-directed or which did not bear the seal of approval of the Russians. Hungary's position and status was similar to that of a colony, with Russia assuming the role of the mother country, except that instead of the office of the Inspector General, the Russians permitted the functioning of a quasi-formal government. This was the situation before the Revolution. During the Revolution those Russian troops which were engaged in combat against the Revolution were in no position to exert either political or economic pressure on us. On the other hand, various representatives of the Soviet Government frequently visited Budapest, with Mikoyan alone visiting our capital on four different occasions. The Russians considered it important to keep themselves informed of the Hungarian events and they no doubt tried to exert what influence they could both on the progress and direction of the events.

During the period of Imre Nagy's captivity in Akadémia utca, the Hungarian government was completely at the mercy of the Russians. Both Mikoyan and Susslov frequently appeared there.

After November 4, everything proceeded according to the dictates and wishes of the Russians. Kádár formed the Szolnok-government on Russian pressure. On numerous occasions Kádár freed certain Hungarian prisoners who were captured during the Revolution, that is to say, Kádár issued orders of release, which subordinate Russian officers, acting as prison commanders, simply ignored and refused to abide by.

The liquidation of the Revolution, both of individuals involved in it, and of institutions and changes which the Revolution had brought about, was undertaken on direct Russian pressure.

In the Pestkörnyéki prison, Colonel Mátyas, the AVH officer, limited himself to signing the arrest orders only. The actual interrogation and further fate of the prisoners was completely in the hands of the Russians.

The mere fact that Russian military tribunals were sitting in judgment over Hungarian citizens and sentenced them clearly indicates both the scope and extent of Russian influence in Hungary. Only the Imperial Bloody Assizes (Császári Vértörvényszék) have ever undertaken a similar step against Hungarian sovereignty. Such a Russian military tribunal sentenced 40 individuals in the city of Debrecen alone. Another Russian military tribunal operated in the city of Kecskemét. (I gained information concerning the Kecskemét tribunal by mail, forwarded to me by confidential informants in Hungary.)

A very close friend of mine was arrested in Budapest on November 8, 1956. We were imprisoned together at Recsk before the Revolution. He was active during the Revolution in Christian Democratic circles. His arrest occurred during the deportation days. People were simply picked up from the streets. He, too, was arrested while walking on the streets of Budapest. They found a Russian-language leaflet in his briefcase. He was brought to the Defense Ministry building first and was transferred later to Debrecen, where he was sentenced by a Russian military tribunal. I don't know what the sentence was, nor am I at liberty to disclose his name at this time.

Russian military tribunals operated on the supposition that Hungarian citizens tried and sentenced by them committed crimes against the Russian armed forces. These Russian acts flagrantly violated Hungarian sovereignty and also constituted a clear violation of the Hungarian Constitution. As far as I know, the Warsaw Pact delegates no such sovereign rights to Russia.

We have given wide publicity to these Russian acts in Europe and, presumably as a result of our action, the tribunals ceased functioning. They do not operate any longer. However, if the Russians would have had a legal right to proceed, I doubt it very much if they would have stopped.

9. During the Revolt, how did you find out about the course of events?

There were various means at our disposal. First of all, there was the radio. Broadcasting stations, especially in the provinces, were in the service, and at the disposal of, the Revolution. In Budapest, the telephone, aside from minor obstacles, caused by damage, functioned satisfactorily. To clarify a point, I must mention here that the Communist regime maintained 16,000 automatic telephone monitors at strategic centers of the city. These monitoring devices were dismounted by workers of the telephone factory during the first days of the Revolution. Telephoning after that time became natural again. You must note here also that bakeries, stores, and employees of telephone centers continued to work throughout the Revolution.

After November 4, telephoning became increasingly difficult and dangerous again, because the monitoring devices were gradually placed back into operation.

9 a. What part did the newspapers play? Did you read any? If yes, which?

Everybody read newspapers during the Revolution. This was one of the advantages of the regime; everybody was forced to read. People were forced to become subscribers to newspapers, to read them, and to comment on what they read. Reading became a second nature with most people, and this brought tangible results during the Revolution.

I read practically all of them; <u>Magyar Függetlenség</u>, <u>Igazság</u>, <u>Népszabadság</u>, <u>Népakarat</u>, (this was the best of them all, edited by József Gáli and Obersovszky), <u>Magyar Nemzet</u>, <u>Kis Ujság</u>, <u>Szabad</u>

Szó, and others.

Everyone was very eager to read, for the newspapers wrote the truth, not as formerly. This probably explains the great popularity these newspapers enjoyed. Because of the great demand, newspapers were extremely hard to get. To obtain a newspaper represented a great feat.

9 b. What did you learn by word-of-mouth? From whom?

Let me give you an example; the Petőfi Circle met in the afternoon of November 3. The Chairman informed us that an agreement has been reached with the Russians and that the Russians will evacuate the country. This was at the time when Maléter still conducted his negotiations with the Russians at Tököl.

Information of a confidential nature we gave and received by word of mouth even during the first phase of the Revolution, but especially during the second. Transmission of information by word-of-mouth was actually safer and this procedure was used when transmitting information of conspiratorial nature.

A tremendous amount of food was brought to Budapest by peasants from the provinces. These people told us of the events which took place in their localities. It was through these people, for instance, that the re-establishment of Small Landholders' Party contacts with the provinces again got under way and developed.

9 c. Did you listen to the radio? Domestic or foreign? What stations? What news did you hear in this way?

We did listen to the radio, during the first phase of the Revolution -- if and when we had time to do it. We listened primarily to Hungarian and secondarily to foreign broadcasting stations. Of the foreign stations I listened to Free Europe, BBC, to the Voice of America, and to Radio Paris. Radio Paris and the

BBC were the most objective.

9 d. During the Revolution, which media were more important for you in getting the facts, and which were less important?

This is a very unfortunate wording. The question does not make sense. It always depended on the nature of the thing. From the viewpoint of reliability the telephone was quite acceptable during the first phase of the Revolution. One did not have to conspire or speak in terms of coded messages. We called up Imre Nagy and did not pay any attention to the AVH. We knew that the 16,000 monitoring devices were out of commission. Then, again, there were other, concrete battle tasks, which demanded immediate consideration and attention. If such was the case, we stopped at any street corner and discussed the issues and made our decisions.

The second phase of the Revolution was different. Ours was more or less a conspiratorial status again, and we had to act accordingly -- even though the telephone service was relatively reliable even then. The installation of the monitors proceeded only slowly, because the workers went on strike. As late as December, the apparatus for censuring letters was not yet functioning. This is no longer the case today.

10. What was the fate, during the Revolt, of the old Government and Party institutions? How did they function? Can you give me some examples from your own experience?

We, the leaders of the Independent Small Landholders' Party, moved in, and re-occupied our old Party headquarters building at No. 1 Semmelweiss Street on October 29. Our building served as a Russian culture home before the Revolution.

Immediately after we took possession of our building, we informed (by telephone) József Halász, the Under Secretary of State in the office of the Prime Minister (miniszterelnöksegi államtitkár), bringing to his attention our action, asking him for acknowledgment and approval. Halász, who later vanished from the Budapest scene, immediately ordered the custodian of the building to stand with his crew at our disposal and to facilitate our using of the adjoining garage.

Members of the Cabinet stayed at the Communist Party headquarters building in the Akadémia utca from October 23 to October 26. On the 26th, the Cabinet was enlarged and the members of the Cabinet left the building. Members of the previous Cabinet continued to live in the city, except for those who fled. They were frequently seen on streets, the only change being that they now walked on their own feet and no longer traveled by car. I have met quite a few of them myself. Their persons were in absolutely no danger.

Employees of what used to be the Hungarian-Soviet Cultural Association (Interviewer's note: elsewhere identified as Russian Cultural Home), all former AVH-men, vanished from our No. 1 Semmelweiss-street Party headquarters. We gave them their work-books and their pay for November, and they departed. Zoltán Száray, my friend, did all this. I reproached him for this, but he remained firm and adamant and declared that these people will sooner or later be brought to court, and, if guilty, will be punished, but that their pay was an entirely different matter, they have a right to that.

This method, by the way, was characteristic of the procedure whereby human beings were treated throughout the Revolution.

In the office of the Attorney General (legfelsöbb ügyészség) a revolutionary council was quickly organized. This council decided to literally prevent the entrance of György Non, the former Supreme Prosecutor (legfőbb ügyész) into the building. Non continued coming to "his office" in the first few days as if nothing had happened.

Let me tell you a few words about this man. György Non, Hungary's Supreme Prosecutor, was Rákosi's confidence-man and one of the members of Rákosi's inner circle. In his youth he studied to become a Catholic priest. In 1942, he was put in the Margit-körút military prison for his illegal Communist activities. In 1945, after the liberation, he became the president of the MADISZ (Magyar Dolgozó Ifjúság Szövetsége). He was one of my greatest enemies. The fact that both the youth organization I led and I were persecuted and ruined, and that my fate after 1948 turned out to be as miserable as it did, is due largely to him.

We endeavored to form a youth association after 1945, but we failed completely, largely because of the Communist youths' bullying tactics and violence and conspiratorial machinations. We simply did not have a chance within the framework of the MADISZ. As a result, the Small Landholder, Social Democrat, and Peasant Party youth severed their relationship with MADISZ and formed their own, separate, youth organizations.

At the beginning of 1948, the various independent youth organizations were completely destroyed, their leaders were incarcerated, and the youth of Hungary was forced into one, unitary Communist camp. All this came to pass thanks to György Non.

Towards the end of 1948, Non becomes Minister of Popular Education (népmüvelési miniszter). The establishment of factory cultural groups and the organization of the seminar system are closely associated with his name, these novel creations were his brainchildren.

After 1953, in accordance with the new path and spirit of the Twentieth Congress, Communists everywhere clamored for the re-establishment of Communist legality. Hungarian Communists were no exception in this respect. Rákosi, fearful of dangerous and harmful revelations which might undermine his own political future, was very much interested in putting into the office of the Supreme Prosecutor a man whom he could trust. György Non was his choice. Thus Non, without any qualifications for the post, -- he did not even finish his university training -- became Hungary's Supreme Prosecutor. But qualification was only of secondary importance, the main thing was Non's political reliability and his slave-like fidelity to his master and benefactor. The important consideration from Rákosi's point of view was the establishment, at least formally, of a machinery that was to deal with the burning question of legality, and with the review of the cases of political offenders to be undertaken by a man who made sure that no Rákosi-incriminating evidence would ever see the light of day. And Non remained faithful to his master to the bitter end. He continued in office even after October 23, until the revolutionary council formed by his subordinates finally decided to lock him out.

At the time of the formation of the Hungarian Socialist Workers' Party, Kádár and his associates passed a resolution barring from membership those individuals whom they considered to have been Stalinists. High on the list of former Stalinists was the name of György Non. And yet he occupies an important position again.

The fate of county and of city councils always depended on what was going on in the provinces. The intensity of revolutionary waves differed from place to place. It could truthfully be stated that in the provinces these officials had fewer sleepless nights than those in Budapest. At worst, they were arrested and were locked up. I did not hear of more extreme procedures. Take the case of Béla Jonás, presiding judge of a people's court (nép-birósági tanácselnök); he committed suicide on November 3. He was unable to wait till November 4, when all would have been well for him again. Generally speaking, the Revolution was not brought about anywhere with the purpose of eliminating these officials. If liquidation of officials did take place in a few isolated instances, there were always very grave reasons for such action. Such officials must have given very grave cause if the insurgents actually lynched them. Such lynchings occurred in Pécs and Miskolc only, and the officials lynched were known to have ordered firing at innocent and defenseless people.

The Party of Hungarian Workers (Magyar Dolgozók Pártja), created in 1948, was the result of the forced unification of the Social Democratic and Communist parties. This new Party was essentially Communist, with a few Social Democrats also in it. This Party had a tremendous network, operating with a monthly budget of several millions. The Party had a current running account with the Hungarian National Bank. In many cases the Party had parallel organization. If, for example, there were more than 20 members in a given factory, then a Party secretary was assigned to them.

During the Revolution, the various Party organizations collapsed and disintegrated with surprising rapidity. It became evidently clear then that it was the fear from the AVH, and the necessity to hold one's job, and to earn some livelihood, rather than ideological conviction, that held these people together. Many a Party member ripped to pieces and burnt his Party book at the first sight of freedom. These people lived in a constant fear and their reaction, when free again, was tremendous.

On October 27, the Imre Nagy government is enlarged, is moved to the Parliament building, and is freed from AVH supervision. Kádár is experimenting for a while with the thought of maintaining the Party. Within a few days he recognizes the hopelessness and the futility of his efforts. Thereupon he proclaims the forming of a new Party, the Hungarian Socialist Workers' Party. He reads his proclamation on the radio on the 31st, and on this occasion, he gives a positive evaluation to the Revolution and renders splendid criticism of both Stalin and Rákosi, laying bare their sins and mistakes.

The Hungarian Communist Party (of the pre-revolutionary era), founded and maintained with tremendous effort, and at unbelievable cost, did not prove to be a strong and lasting organization, underlining again the old dictum that brute force and coercion cannot hold people together for long.

Party secretaries and personnel section chiefs rallied to the support of Kádár in the newly-founded Party. It is these people who make up the rank and file of the Kádár force in Budapest after November 4, and it is they who execute Kádár's first orders of revenge. (Megtorló rendelkezések.)

10 a. In substance, what institutions collapsed and what institutions (and controls) remained intact?

Collapsed the Party, the government, and the entire administrative apparatus. City, county, district, and village councils were reorganized and were known as revolutionary committees (bizottság). The old leadership and administrative set-up of industrial enterprises collapsed, too. Their functions were taken over by revolutionary workers' councils.

Collapsed the AVH. Collapsed the Hungarian-Soviet Cultural Society. This latter was the largest single social organization in Hungary. It had member organizations in every Hungarian village. The same fate befell the Society of Hungarian Veterans (Szabadságharcos Szövetség). The nucleus of this organization was the Society of Hungarian Partisans. This latter group had for its aim the military education and training of Hungarian youth. It conducted training sessions on Sundays before the Revolution. The Revolution benefitted greatly from this activity, because the young people knew how to handle the weapons.

These were the institutions which the Revolution necessarily destroyed, either because of their aims or because of their past performance and actions. Many of these institutions were abolished and dissolved, others were transformed by the Revolution and continued functioning in their new form. Many of the organizations appointed revolutionary committees, a new slate took over their direction, and the organization continued on existing. Hundreds of organizations were so affected, all the way down to the philatelist societies.

The general aim of the insurgents may be stated to have been an attempt to get rid of the Stalinist elements, to have these replaced by democratically-minded people who were loyal to the Revolution.

As far as the army was concerned, it was sufficient to replace a few people who occupied more important positions. The army caused the greatest surprise to both Rákosi and to the Russians.

10 b. What happened to the Party? The local (primary) organizations? The Party offices? Their personnel?

Party buildings -- and there were one or two well-equipped and well-furnished houses in every village -- were returned to serve as dwellings again. There was a tremendous housing shortage in Hungary. In Budapest there were innumerable examples where people, bombed out of their dwellings, simply moved into empty buildings. Whatever valuables were found in a Party building were recorded in an inventory by the revolutionary councils and were locked and sealed. In Budapest, the building of the Hungarian-Soviet Cultural Society was robbed and pillaged by the very employees of the Society. There was fighting around the building, the Russians bombarded the building and set it afire. Thereupon the employees undertook to "save whatever could be hauled through the doors".

The newly-formed parties received back their old buildings. The Small Landholders' Party, too, got back its old property, the building at Semmelweiss-utca 1. Ferenc Erdei, a member of the old government, signed the necessary transfer papers on October 30.

10 c. What happened to the Party? The uniformed (blue) police?

The blue police served well, in essence, during the Revolution. There was a world of a difference between this force and the AVH. They, too, used to be supervised by the AVH, and the blue police did not take kindly to this interference. There were blue police units which remained intact as a unit. They moved around freely and unmolested. AVH members in numerous instances put on blue police uniforms.

There was a fine cooperation between the blue police and the university students. The students received many weapons from the police force. Sándor Kopácsy, a lieutenant-colonel of the Budapest blue police force, consenting to the organization of the National Guard (Nemzetörség), armed a great number of the students.

The National Guard was so organized that a group of students, under the direction of a police officer, assumed the duties of maintaining peace and order. The police, as such, did not take part in the Revolution.

10 d. What happened the AVH?

The AVH fell to pieces completely. The government threw the AVH into battle to fight on the side of the Russians in the first phase of the Revolution. The fact that the AVH began the actual shooting and slew the first victims of the Revolution would have sealed the fate of this group even if they did not have the bad and dreaded fame. All the dirty jobs which Rákosi and his cohorts wanted done were entrusted to the AVH. No other group was reliable and trustworthy enough.

In 1950-1951, AVH-men were sent out into the villages and were entrusted with the organization of the TSzCs cooperatives. It was their job then to liquidate the independent farmers. These people would descend on a village, would enter the house of a farmer and would ask him in a "friendly" tone why he did not want to join the TSzCs. They would continue asking why does the peasant excite the other peasant and why does he agitate against the TSzCs. This "friendly" visit was sufficient enough. The following day the intimidated peasant ran helter-skelter and signed up voluntarily as a member. Or, if he did not give in so easily, the AVH had ready-made trumped-up charges against him.

It was these people who descended upon the peasants with the bailiff (végrehajtó) and took away the last of the peasant's animals in lieu of back taxes. If some of the peasants did manage to pay the taxes, new taxes were quickly invented and the unfortunate soul had no way of escaping his fate.

All these activities did not make the AVH sympathetic in the eyes of the people. In the factories, the AVH held equally tight controls over the people. Such offences as plant sabotage, instigation against production and against the norm fell under their jurisdiction. And they did not treat their victims with gloves on their hands. Even the most loyal of Communists were taken aback when a harmless enough person was imprisoned just because of a mild slip of the tongue.

During the Revolution, the AVH disguised themselves as physicians and as attendants and supplied ammunition with Red Cross ambulances to sealed-off AVH units. All these activities of theirs justified and made it necessary that the Revolution turn against them. Already the first revolutionary slogans were directed against them and the antipathy and wrath of the population not only did not subside, but it became more and more intense as the days went by.

There were in this detestation and hate of the AVH many other things too; take, for instance, the times when, because of the great capital investments made by the government, the people were not making enough money to provide the minimum food requirements for their families. The AVHs lived in great luxury and they did not even try to keep their good fortune a secret. This, too, turned the people against them. They acted as kings then (kiskirályok voltak).

There were innumerable instances where young people were jailed simply because they called to order (rendreutasitottak) an AVH member at dance parties, where the AVH man did not know or did not want to behave.

During the first days of the Revolution, the AVH was completely beaten and destroyed. At the time of the victory of the Revolution, there were no more AVH units. Many of them donned blue uniforms and tried to save their skins as individuals. In the provinces, most AVH units were arrested. On November 1 or 2, a government proclamation was issued in Budapest, ordering all AVH members to report to the Markó-utca, so that their background could individually be investigated. Those who have not committed crimes, -- went on the declaration -- would not be held responsible just because they were members of the AVH. Many an AVH-man went to the Markó-utca and reported.

The AVH, or at least many of them, put all their trust in the Russians and hoped in a Russian victory. These people resisted and fought to the end. They were annihilated.

Even if we do not approve of lynching, we can understand the attitude of the people and we can understand the reasoning behind their actions.

The high-ranking officers of the AVH fled during the first days of the Revolution to the Akadémia-utca, and from there they proceeded, together with Hegedús, Gerő, and Lászlo Piros, and under heavy Russian cover left the country.

10 e. *What happened to the courts?*

Béla Jankó was scared to death and took his own life on November 3. I don't know of any other case where a member of the courts would have acted so wisely. I don't know of any instance where court members would have been held responsible for their past actions.

A revolutionary committee came into being in the Ministry of Justice, which discussed the question of the courts and dealt with the problem of a reorganization of the judiciary system.

10 f. What happened to the army?

Army units were among the first organized groups which went over to the Revolution. Troops stationed in various localities, even if they did not fight, they at least remained neutral. The Rákosi-group made an attempt to bring up troops to Budapest from Székesfehérvár. These troops never arrived, because they did not want to side with the Russians against the population.

The most particular instance in this respect is the case of Maléter, who, having been ordered by the Minister of Defense, proceeded at the head of an armored unit to quell the uprising at the Kilian Barracks. He arrived and he went over with his entire unit to the side of the insurgents. Two days later he was elected commander of the Kilian force.

The Üllöi-úti Ludovika Akademia (an officer-training school) -- it functions under a different name now, but I cannot recall its present name -- is another instance; the entire school sided with the Revolution in the first days of the uprising.

The Petőfi Akademia (an officer-training school located at Pesthidegkút) cadets were at first engaged in battle against János Szabó at the Széna-tér. Within 24 hours, they, too, went over, and became the main bulwark of the Széna-tér force.

The attitude of the army and of the blue police force, and the position these groups took, became decisive for the Revolution. These troops were supposed to supply the infantry units to the Russian tanks, -- a combination which in all probability would have been quite effective. If the Hungarian army had sided with the Russians, then the Revolution most certainly would have been beaten at the very outset. Their neutrality and their cooperation, their readiness to give us arms and ammunition, the fact that officers came over to us and gave us valuable expert advice, -- all these things contributed a great deal to our victory over the Russians.

10 g. What happened to the central government, ministries?

During that period of the Revolution when it again became possible to move around and to communicate -- the period after October 27, -- in every ministry revolutionary committees were set up, patterned after other similar committees, as organized throughout the country. Ministry officials, especially lesser officials, were never too fanatic about the regime. They remained silent and they suffered because their job was their bread. At this moment all these people, with the exception of the compromised few, took new lease on life and elected trustworthy people, usually a former political prisoner, to head the committee.

All governmental bureaus were operating. This is not to say that people actually worked, but they were there, at least a substantial number of them, to receive their pay, etc. There of course were no contacts between the ministries and the factories, because the factories did not operate. As a result, there really was not anything to be done in the offices. What work had to be accomplished in the factories was done by the revolutionary workers' councils. Conversely, in the ministries, the ministerial revolutionary committees were the only groups who did anything at all. These groups were engaged in planning activity, discussing the new constitutional principles and new ways and means to implement the expected new setup.

There were a number of ministries and a great number of governmental bureaus, which were outright superfluous. Ministerial officials were well aware of this, and they just did not know what they were supposed to do. One of the ministers, Antal Gyenes, newly-appointed head of the Ministry of Forced Deliveries (Beszolgáltatásügyi) issued his first and only decree, abolishing the forced delivery system. His next act was similarly dramatic; he abolished the Forced Delivery Ministry itself. Question:Why was it necessary for white-collar workers to go into their offices?) Food brought up to the capital during the Revolution was channeled to various centers and it was distributed free of charge from these centers. Ministries were such centers.

Budapest continued to have its regular means of food distribution, and state stores continued in operation. State stores alone could not have supplied the population with food. Stores continued to handle such items as bread, milk, and sugar. Even with this dual supply of food, we just about managed.

10 h. What happened to the local "councils"?

Local councils were all replaced by revolutionary councils. These councils became the directing force in the life of the villages. The changeover from the councils to the revolutionary councils was relatively more peaceful in the provinces than in the capital. In many instances it took place to the accompaniment of a village celebration with steers being slaughtered and roasted for the occasion. There were no superior authorities and the revolutionary village councils were able to act independently, at least in the first days.

Schools continued to operate in many localities and the peasants performed their regular work in the fields, taking care of the important autumn-tasks.

An extremely interesting phenomenon was the disintegration of the TSzCs cooperatives; about 65 percent of these cooperatives disbanded. The forceful deliveries ceased and people everywhere in the villages slaughtered their pigs, fearful that the Russians might return and take their animals from them. (Slaughtering was strictly regulated before the Revolution and those who did receive a permit were legally bound to deliver a fixed amount of lard to the state.)

The change-over was expected and appreciated by the peasants more than by any other group. But the peasant masses are an individualistic lot, very difficult to organize, a group requiring a long time to develop its views and to decide to act. The process of TSzCs disintegration, for instance, while originating during the first days of the Revolution, has reached its height only much later, during the Kádár-era, when Kádár and his associates made determined efforts to stop it.

10 i. *What happened to the churches?*

Religious instruction became free and was made part of the school curriculum. Before the Revolution, such instruction was given only outside the school curriculum, under the supervision of the principal, if both parents expressed their desire for such instruction in writing.

In 1948, an agreement reached between the Churches and the state regulated the Church-state relationships. Church leaders who opposed these agreements were simply eliminated. The fate of Cardinal Mindszenty, of László Ravasz and of Lajos Ordass are well known and I need not repeat them here. Their places were taken by other men -- Lászlo Dezséry became the Lutheran-Evangelical Bishop, Albert Bereczky succeeded Ravasz -- men who were more subservient than their predecessors.

The position of the Catholic Church was more complicated. The government could not replace Mindszenty without the agreement of the Pope, and such agreement was out of the question. To remedy this situation, the government organized the National Peace Committee of Catholic Priests (Katolikus Papok Országes Békebizottsága) and appointed Richard Horváth chairman of this group. This renegade priest delivered innumerable speeches in the Hungarian Parliament, praising Rákosi to the point of tastelessness.

Richard Horváth and the other leaders of the National Peace Committee were paid agents of the AVH. They were the executors of the process of purification (tisztogatási folyamat) and caused many priests to be arrested, fired, or pensioned.

After the ascendancy of Imre Nagy in 1953, the criticizing mood as exemplified by the Twentieth Congress, asserted itself also within the Hungarian Churches. At meetings and congregations of priests, more and more criticizing speeches were made. These speakers denounced the religious leaders, spoke of the injustices affecting the clergy, and went as far as to propose disciplinary action within the Church against the clerical offenders.

The outbreak of the Revolution has found groups within the Churches who sharply criticized and challenged the top leadership of the Churches. Bereczky and Dezséry were forced to resign from their respective positions and Horváth was excommunicated.

Zoltán Tildy expressed to a visiting Catholic delegation his desire to see Mindszenty return and assume his former duties and functions. Thus encouraged, a group of soldiers freed Mindszenty from his house arrest and brought him to Budapest.

Ravasz was elected Bishop of the Reformed Church. Soon after his re-election, he spoke on the radio, expressing himself in favor of legality, and urging his adherents to refrain from lynching of AVH members. These, he said, should be brought to court and be tried, shedding thereby some light on the lawlessness of the regime.

László Dezséry, an ambitious young man, but devoid of talent, resigned as Evangelical-Lutheran Bishop and László Ordass, only recently released from prison, was re-elected Lutheran Bishop again. Ordass was well-known throughout Europe, and his release from jail and re-election as bishop was warmly greeted everywhere.

The Churches performed their work in complete independence from the state during the Revolution. After the defeat of the Revolution, the pre-revolutionary conditions were again re-established.

The National Peace-Committee of Catholic Priests was again re-established, and Richard Horváth, in one of his declarations, condemned Cardinal Mindszenty's counter-revolutionary activities. Dezséry and Bereczky are Protestant bishops again. Formally, at least, everything is as before the Revolution. In reality, Kádár was unable to recreate the pre-revolutionary conditions. A slight improvement is noticeable; the government does not dare touch the explosive Church question, just as the system of forced deliveries was never re-introduced. The Peace Committee of Catholic Priests is an association of a group of Catholic priests. There is no connection, official or otherwise between it and the Catholic hierarchy. It is the duty of the Peace Committee to point out counter-revolutionary activities and to accuse those who abuse their authority. The Committee has a dual function: its members serve as agents provocateurs and as AVH informers. They organize meetings, they pass resolutions, and they take a public stand on issues and on personalities. They were, for instance, responsible for the imprisonment of Janos Petery, the Bishop of Vác. They kept on talking about the Bishop and denounced him until he was finally put in jail. The Committee accuses a person, the AVH steps into the matter, there is the usual investigation and the usual result.

Take István Balogh, for example, a typical peace priest; he was an Under Secretary in the Debrecen Cabinet. He was the founder of the Balogh Party and had 14 or 15 representatives in Parliament after the 1947 elections. Balogh was the fattest (legkövérebb) man in Hungary. He liked beautiful paintings, beautiful women, and good drinks. He was later appointed Commissioner of Abandoned Goods (Elhagyott Javak Kormány-biztosa), he stole vast amounts, but he never could be proven guilty. Balogh and Parragi and Dobi assisted the regime to the best of their abilities. On appropriate occasions they stood up in Parliament, or in popular assemblies, and praised Rákosi. Their services were appreciated and they were never brought to account for their previous wrong-doings. Rákosi needed such men, because they were admirably suited to do certain things which Rákosi, as a Communist, could not have done himself successfully. It would have been bad politics for him even to attempt to do so.

In the Reformed and Evangelical Churches there are no such "peace" organizations; there was no need to organize such extra-church associations there, because the purpose for which the "Catholic" association was formed, outside of the Catholic Church proper, was easily accomplished within the Lutheran and Calvinist Churches.

The Catholic Church was different. It was much strengthened in numbers and superior in organization. While the regime was free to arrest priests and bishops of the Catholic Church, it could never hope to replace them with its own men. Moreover, in important matters of church-state relations, the Pope's approval was absolutely necessary.

In contrast to this, respecting the Lutherans, the Communists succeeded in placing Ernő Mihályfi, one of Rákosi's ministers, in the position of supreme lay supervisor (egyeremes világi felügyelet) of the Evangelical-Lutheran Church. The same may be said of the Reformed Church. To give you just one example, Jozsef Darvas became the lay chairman of the Debrecen diocese of the reformed Church.

10 j. Which organizations did the rebels use to further their own ends?

The Revolution operated through the revolutionary councils, the revolutionary workers' councils, the Association of Hungarian writers, the Petőfi Circle, and the Revolutionary Council of Hungarian Intellectuals.

10 k. What new kinds of organizations emerged during the Revolt?

The revolutionary councils, the revolutionary workers' councils, and the Revolutionary Council of Hungarian Intellectuals were new organizations. The latter group embraced such people as newspapermen, artists, professors, actors, researchers (kutatok), and university students. The Association of Hungarian Writers and the Petőfi Circle were also integral parts of this council, though they also operated as separate and distinct entities.

Professor György Ádám was the chairman of the Revolutionary

Council of Hungarian Intellectuals, and the various member-associations sent their delegates to it. The various Churches were also represented. It was this council of intellectuals which directed the political and ideological battle of the Revolution. It was this council which set the pace and took the stand in questions of principle. It was this council which set in motion its resources to free Nagy from the clutches of the AVH in the Akadémia-utca. The council opposed most energetically instances of lawlessness and of lynchings. The council continued to act even after November 4. In collaboration with the democratic parties, the council attempted to effect a compromise solution and to block attempts of some Communists to call to account revolutionaries. In this the council did not succeed.

Also after November 4, an action was inaugurated within the framework of the council which led to the centralization of the revolutionary workers' councils. Representatives of the council visited factories and other enterprises with a view to create a uniform stand among the workers. The demonstration of women on December 4 was also organized by the council. Professor György Ádám was arrested in the middle of December, and with his arrest the Revolutionary Council of Hungarian Intellectuals also came to an end.

10 l. What was the background of the Workers' Councils? What did they do? Who ran them?

The workers' councils came into being during the first phase of the Revolution: at the time when the program of the Revolution called for the ousting of Stalinist and Rákosi elements.

The direction of the industrial enterprises was taken over by the workers' councils. Their aim then was solely the direction of industrial production. It was the necessity of the hour, and the subsequent turn of events, which did force them to assume roles and responsibilities far greater than direction of production.

They were forced to assume a political role also, and parallel with this they took upon their shoulders the added duty of defending the economic interests of the workers. (The labor unions remained even during the Revolution Rákosi-creatures). There was also the added task of organizing and maintaining of a defense group, which members were entrusted with the defense of the factories from both the AVH and the Russians. This latter task was a very important function, since a great many of the workers actively participated in the Revolution.

After the unfolding of the first phase of the Revolution, when the Russians withdrew their forces, the workers returned to their factories and organized the workers' councils, -- organizations which Imre Nagy recognized as corporations directing the operations of the factories (üzemeket vezető testületek).

The main object of the workers' councils at the termination of the first phase of the Revolution was the reorganization of the labor unions. The councils wanted a new labor union leadership, to be elected by the rank and file, and to which the representation of the political and economic interests of the workers could be entrusted, with the councils retaining only the role of directing the industrial production.

Circumstances forced the councils to assume political roles also. They did take a definite political stand when declaring themselves against the return of factories to their former owners. With respect to the question of the future proprietorship of industrial enterprises, the councils proposed a combination of state ownership for some and of workers' joint stock companies (munkás részvénytársaság) for others. At no time was there any question of returning to the pre-World War conditions.

After November 4, the workers continued to strike, the election of a new labor union leadership became an impossibility, and the workers' councils were obliged to continue to play an active role in politics. After November 4, the workers' councils alone were capable of advancing demands against the government and, to do their job more effectively, the Central Workers' Council was established.

The workers' councils turned to the Hungarian writers for help and advice. This step appeared quite natural, especially after the writers expressed their opposition to lawlessness (törvénytelenség) and to the norm-system. The industrial workers looked upon the writers as their advisors and the writers were ready to accept this task. Very often a reputable writer would visit a factory and the workers would stand around him with both confidence and love.

It was the writers, for instance, who proposed the organization of the Central Workers' Council. Only such a Central Workers' Council will be able to create an actual authority in Budapest, argued the writers. And indeed, throughout November, the workers' councils represented the only power and authority in Hungary. They relied on such devices as strikes and resolutions, and Kádár did not dare touch them. As a matter of fact, Kádár, as late as December 1956, conducted constant negotiations with them. Meanwhile, the AVH was sufficiently reorganized and a network of informers was again built into the factories.

As soon as the reorganization was accomplished, Kádár changed his tactics and began opposing the workers' councils. He first limited the scope of the councils' authority and later abolished them entirely. By that time, leaders of resistance groups are simply kidnapped and Sándor Rácz, as well as his deputy, simply vanish from the scene. In the factories, mixed Hungarian-Russian troops are stationed and AVH-troops and Russian soldiers stand with machine guns behind the workers.

The first revolutionary workers' councils were organized in Csepel and in the Ganz works. They were patterned after the Revolutionary Committee of Hungarian Intellectuals. Revolutionary councils were organized in non-productive establishments, while their counterparts in factories and stores were called revolutionary workers' councils. Many Hungarians were thoroughly familiar with the economic structure of

Yugoslavia, but the Hungarian revolutionary councils and revolutionary workers' councils were not conscious copies of the Yugoslav model; the Yugoslav system was left behind, and was far surpassed, at the very beginning of the Revolution, as evidenced by the 16 points.

11. Now that it's all over, have you had any further thoughts about it?

Yes, I think very much about the Revolution. Subjectively considered, the Revolution was the greatest and fullest experience of my life. I was, on a number of occasions, in important situations where I could observe significant historical events between 1944 and 1947. But in all my experiences I have never seen an event more beautiful and more interesting than the Revolution. I came to know only later that the Revolution was regarded as such not only in Hungary, but throughout the world.

11 a. What do you think, was it a useful thing or not?

I have the feeling that the Revolution was unavoidable (kikerülhetetlen volt). Its usefulness is a question of secondary importance. To that question I answer with a yes and a no. In a certain respect the Revolution was useful; it answered decisively many a burning question which existed in Hungary and troubled the lives of most Hungarians, -- questions which could not have been answered any other way. On the other hand, 50,000 Hungarians died in the Revolution and yet the situation is not much better now than it was before. I really do not know if the balance is a positive or a negative one. One thing is certain: no matter how the situation in the world, and in Hungary, may develop, the results and achievements of the Revolution will continue to be cited and used as primary sources (eredményeire nagyon sokáig kútforrásként fognak hivatkozni). Also, if a revolution is at all endowed with the power of creating rights and legal claims (ha van a forradalomnak jogteremtö ereje), then the Hungarian revolution undoubtedly bestowed upon Hungary the right to independent and democratic existence.

11 b. Do you think it could have succeeded?

Yes, the Revolution could have won. It had all the means and prerequisites to success. The fact that it was unsuccessful is traceable, besides the Suez events, to the attitude of, and the stand taken by, the United Nations and the United States who, to a certain extent, are responsible for what happened.

I do not believe that the Hungarian events under any circumstances could have led to the third World War. The Russians were in no way prepared for such an adventure. If the West is afraid of a world war, the Russians are at least equally scared. It is my firm conviction that a determined stand taken by the United Nations would have been sufficient to stop the shedding of blood. If Hammarskjold had decided to land on the Budapest airfield, I do not think Kádár would have dared to endanger his life or stop him in his activities.

The frequent visits of Mikoyan and of Suslov, and their contradictory statements, intentions, and advice fully attest that the Soviet Government did not know what to do with the Hungarian Revolution. I am fully convinced that the Soviet Government would have been more than prepared to agree to a compromise solution, possibly on the Polish model, possibly to even much more than that, in order to secure to itself a graceful way out of a disagreeable situation. After the Suez events, of course, the military intervention of Russia became a natural stand. While an effective Western stand prior to the Russian intervention could have secured Hungarian independence, acceptable compromise solutions could have been effected even after November 4. The very fact alone that for a long period after

November 4, the various Hungarian democratic parties not only were not attacked by either the Russians or by the Hungarian authorities, but were actually the recipients of a number of compromise overtures, would in itself underline my above contention. Both Kádár and the Russians did everything to win these people over and to convince them that there was ample room for compromise and development, if they cooperated with the regime.

As far as the possibility of a third World War is concerned, which, it is contended, may have resulted as a consequence of a strong Western stand, I say that you have two opponents here (U.S. and Russia) facing one another. Both of them are fearful and the outcome of their struggle is determined by which of the two is more apprehensive.

I have the feeling that both the United Nations and the West have permitted a historical opportunity to slip out of their hands, an opportunity which may never again come their way.

11 c. Had you expected any help from the West? If yes, on what basis? In what force?

Yes, we of course did expect Western assistance. We expected the intervention of the United Nations. In the early morning of November 4, Imre Nagy appealed for direct help to the United Nations. Prior to that we already declared that we withdrew from the Warsaw Pact. We declared Hungary to be a neutral country and we asked that this neutrality be internationally recognized. More than that, after the second Russian attack on November 4, we continued the armed struggle until the middle of November only to give renewed opportunity to the West to intervene.

The attitude and stand the West took in connection with the Hungarian Revolution frightfully resembles the position taken by the Western world in 1939-1940 in connection with Poland

and the Baltic republics. In 1939-1940, the West sanctioned the Russian occupation of these countries and we now have the feeling that in the case of Hungary the same thing has happened.

I fear that the West, in line with its traditional method of searching for easy and comfortable solutions to difficult problems, has quieted its conscience by relying too readily on its wish and hope that Russia, after all, will collapse anyway. A policy of this kind, while extremely comfortable, is rather hopeless. And this is an extremely dangerous game; should the nations of the world one day be forced to conclude that the West supports only such trends and actions which directly serve its selfish purposes and abandons the little nations to their fate, a re-orientation of immeasurable magnitude will inevitably follow. This same thing holds true for the United Nations. The United Nations would have had a splendid opportunity to prove beyond doubt that it does intend to operate and abide by the lofty principles which are laid down in its Charter. Nowhere in the world was resistance against oppression and exploitation greater than in Hungary.

As to the form of Western assistance, we expected primarily political assistance and moral support. The Hungarian nation was convinced that a strong and determined stand taken by the U.N. would have been sufficient, and that such a stand, if taken, would have had its political results.

After November 4, individual pockets of freedom fighters appealed for direct help also, pleading for direct military assistance. Such requests were made only in the midst of pressing, extraordinary circumstances of the hour. In Dunapentele, for instance, heavy fights were going on, and the radio continued in operation, pleading for help to the last minute.

It is my conviction that political assistance by the U.N. would have been sufficient, especially if the United States applied its often repeated principle of carrying its fight to the brink of war. Dulles was preaching this principle time and again, and yet he remained strangely inactive when it came to applying it.

It is not a coincidence that Mikoyan sojourned in Budapest. His stay in the Hungarian capital seemed to show that the Soviet Union was ready to give recognition to the Hungarian facts. Then came the Suez events; England and France used the Hungarian situation to fish in the troubled waters of Egypt and to present the world with a fait accompli. The French-English violence gave a rare excuse to the Russians to act in a similar manner.

But even after November 4, the Russians were careful to instruct Kádár not to touch the democratic parties, -- a fact which shows that the Russians even then were still expecting a Western intervention.

It was wrong to adjourn and to postpone the U.N. session scheduled for November 6, and it was equally fatal to decide not to apply sanctions, especially when, after the mass deportations, it became clear that the Russians were guilty of genocide.

The Soviet Union feared war at least as much as did the West. It is true that the Soviet commanded the greatest land forces in the world at the time, but to what extent this force could be relied upon, especially after the Hungarian events, is rather questionable.

Sanctions could have been applied freely. The ideological and political accomplishments of the Revolution could have been safeguarded. The Revolution was painfully correct towards the Soviet Union. We emphasized again and again that we wanted to live in peace with the nations of the world, but that we wanted peace first of all with the Soviet Union.

The Hungarian Revolution and the stand taken to it clearly demonstrated that neither the United Nations nor the United States, nor the so-called Western world has any political blueprint, or even something remotely resembling a blueprint, for the solution of pressing European problems.

The United States did have a schema, it is true, that Titoism or Gomulkaism is to be assisted and supported. But what Hungary did, neither Tito nor Gomulka ever dreamed of doing. The Hungarian act was of an entirely different order, leaving Titoism and Gomulkaism hopelessly behind. For this the United States was not prepared. Characteristically, the United States decided to rather give up the whole Hungarian question than to deviate from its schema. Because they did not know what to do with the problem posed by the Hungarian Revolution, they did not do anything at all.

11 d. Why do you think it happened in Hungary, not in one of the other satellites?

It is difficult to try to support with concrete, objective facts any theory which one may advance in this connection. There are many, primarily subjective, facts which caused the Revolution to break out in Hungary, and not some place else; the Revolution may be explained by, and in the light of the centuries-old desire of Hungarians to live as a free and independent nation. History clearly proves that Hungarians always fought to free themselves from foreign interests and domination.

The attitude of Rákosi and of the Muscovite group contributed a great deal to the outbreak of the Revolution. These people served fully and perfectly their Russian masters, their performance in the field of political and economic exploitation reaching at times proportions over and above those actually demanded by Moscow.

Then you have the role of the Hungarian writers. Theirs was a special role. Hungary was fortunate in having an exceptionally capable and valuable group of writers ever since the termination of the first World War. These people kept their independence and integrity even vis-a-vis Rákosi. Or, if the writers happened to be communistically oriented, they, too, saw the clear-cut contradictions between Communist theory and practice.

Then you have the Rajk funeral. This was a unique occasion, and the opportunities it presented were fully utilized. It was at the funeral that loud and personal criticism was leveled against Rákosi for the first time. Last, but not least, is the geographical position of Hungary; of all the satellite countries, Hungary lies closest to free Europe.

11 e. What do you think of Imre Nagy?

Imre Nagy was a Communist. After the abortive 1919 period, he fled to Austria or Germany, going later to Moscow. He concerned himself primarily with agricultural problems and, as such, he did not have to closely associate himself with Rákosi. Nagy's role after 1945 was characterized by a straight and unswerving line. I consider him a very valuable and honorable man, who deserved the love and respect of his co-patriots. The Revolution, of course, went much further than Nagy's principles; Nagy wanted a return to the 1953 conditions. The Revolution demanded complete freedom and complete independence. Nagy wavered, and vacillated too long. In the first days of the Revolution, he, too, looked upon the Uprising as a counter-revolution. After November 1, he saw clearly what was going on and he accepted the fact that the Hungarian people made their final and clear-cut decisions on the questions affecting Hungary. On November 4, in the morning, he declared that the Hungarian Government opposed (szembefordul) Russia.

It is interesting to note that post-revolutionary Hungary continued to use and apply the agricultural policies of Nagy. Such principles as no forced deliveries, voluntariness of agricultural cooperatives, are still maintained. The regime did not as yet dare touch the peasants.

Imre Nagy was extremely popular even before the Revolution. His popularity was based on two factors: his own, personal qualities; he was a jovial, intelligent and cultured man. Also, the Hungarian people underwent a tremendous change in the last decade; when Parliament, on February 1, 1946, changed Hungary from a kingdom into a republic, the people, apathetic as they were, did not care what constitutional forms they were living under. By 1956, in contrast, everyone thought in terms of a republic. Thus Imre Nagy, the Communist leader, was able to command a wide-spread respect and popularity amongst the people because he represented, in the minds of most people, that democratic republic which Hungarians wished to bring about.

11 f. What other individuals were important?

Of the cabinet members, Tildy's position was the most eminent. Zoltán Tildy was not too popular either with the masses or with his own Small Landholders Party. He was the first president of the Hungarian republic. At the end of 1947, the Rákosi-forces interned him and kept him under surveillance until the end of 1955.

Tildy's political past was not very fortunate; his political start after the war was characterized by cooperation and identification with those elements of the Small Landholders Party (Dobi, Buttai, Mihályfi, Lajos Dinnyés, Sándor Barcs, György Parraghi) who were later responsible for the break-up of the Party and/or who actively assisted Rákosi in his endeavors.

Before the Revolution, Tildy spoke occasionally on the radio and wrote a few articles in the papers, extolling the advantages of cooperative farming (TSzCs). While he undoubtedly spoke the truth, his assertions were not well received and were not calculated to increase his popularity.

Imre Nagy asked Tildy to join his cabinet, hoping thereby to win the support of the Small Landholders Party. The Small Landholders themselves were undecided as to whether to support Tildy or not. The question was debated and eventually the Party's executive committee endorsed Tildy.

It is interesting to note that while the reborn Small Landholders Party officially began to function on October 30 (1956), Tildy was not a member of its executive committee, even though he served as minister of state in the Nagy cabinet ever since October 25.

Tildy was the man with the clearest vision and the only

member of the cabinet who had a definite program. We must do everything, he said, to stop the government from aimlessly walking (kullogni) after the Revolution. The government must stand at the head of the uprising. The government must not vacillate and must make all the demands of the Revolution its own. Having assumed the leadership of the Revolution, we must unite all forces, churches and other groups (testületeket) and with their cooperation we must reestablish weekday tranquility (vissza kell állitani a hétköznapok nyugalmát).

Tildy's role and task in the government was both immense and significant. Though he made innumerable mistakes before, he now acted flawlessly (hibátlanul). He considered the direction of the Revolution the last great political task of his life, and his popularity undoubtedly would have increased -- deservedly -- had the Revolution succeeded.

Of the actual revolutionary leaders, the most significant role was that of Dudás. He commanded the largest group of freedom fighters and he also published a daily newspaper, thereby exerting a political influence on public opinion also.

Another name of importance was that of Maléter. After his ingenious defense of the Kilian Barracks, Tildy decided to take him into the cabinet, where he assumed the direction of the Ministry of Defense.

I must also say a few words about the Church leaders. These leaders were extremely important insofar as they exerted a considerable influence on public opinion.

In 1948, Rákosi concluded an agreement with the Churches. One of the consequences of this agreement was the forceful removal and imprisonment of leading Church figures who opposed this agreement. The case of Mindszenty is well known. László Ravasz was forced to resign in 1948. Lajos Ordass was pushed out of the way by means of trumped-up charges of currency blackmarket dealings. New people were appointed to high Protestant Church positions, people who were more eager to see things from Rákosi's point of view. Needless to say, the new bishops were not too popular. Their popularity suffered even more as the bishops, willingly or not, actually performed such tasks which, in the eyes of the population, were decidedly anti-Christian.

Going to church became more and more difficult. Churchgoers were watched and religious life was subjected to ridicule in public. Religious instruction of children became uncomfortable, since both parents were required to file a written authorization with the authorities, authorizations which everyone knew came into the hands of the AVH. The AVH has used these at its discretion, often very successfully, to blackmail the parents.

The older generation remained adamant and continued loyal to its religious convictions. There developed an interesting process in the decade of 1948 - 1956; the practice of one's religion was subjected to many restrictions, more veiled than open, at the same time, as a result of these restrictions, people craved to go to church and their desire for religion and religious experience increased.

On October 31 (1956), Tildy received a delegation of workers and told them it would be a good thing (jó lenne) if Mindszenty came back to Esztergom. (Tildy actually went to Esztergom sometime later in the company of Maléter). The following day (November 1) Tildy received in audience Endre Hamvas, the (Catholic) Bishop of Csanád.

Tildy clearly recognized the tremendous influence the Churches exerted on the Hungarian population. He set in motion a process (teret engedett olyan folyamatnak) whereby both Ravasz and Ordass were rehabilitated. Tildy wanted the Revolution to proceed within the existing legal framework, he desired an early resumption of production and a consolidation of all the forces of the people.

Church leaders quickly responded to Tildy's bidding, made their stand public, and helped immeasurably in steering the Revolution clear of excesses.

Political parties; the Independent Small Landholders' Party was destroyed after 1947 with the assistance of such Small Landholders' Party members as Dobi and company. Only 15 Party members remained in the Parliament and these received monthly support monies from the regime to the tune of 100,000 forints per month. These fifteen supported actively the establishing of the dictatorship of the proletariat and the maintaining of the new social order.

Béla Kovács, another Small Landholders' Party member, reappeared during the Revolution. He assumed the direction of the Ministry of Agriculture on October 25.

Kovács was a peasant from the Baranya district. In 1941, he was a leading member of the Peasant League (Parasztszövetség), becoming the secretary general of the Small Landholders' Party after the war. He was an extremely popular figure. Kovács and Tildy represented the opposite poles within the Small Landholders' Party, Tildy being the spokesman of the extreme-left faction.

In 1947, Kovács was the leading actor of a conspiracy trial. False and trumped-up charges were leveled against him, but, as he was a Member of Parliament, his prosecution was more difficult. Parliament had to be asked to extradite him and this did not go smoothly; Parliament held the extradition session in April 1947. There was a fierce debate and, when it came to voting, the Small Landholders' Party, representing the majority, voted down the extraditing resolution. That very evening the AVD kidnapped Kovács, and Parliament, subjected to extremely heavy pressure and treats, consented and voted for Kovács's extradition. Kovács was tried by a Russian military court, but was never sentenced. He was kept in various prisons, held as an accused person under preliminary investigation. In 1955, Kovács was set free, returned to his native village in Baranya and remained there until the Revolution.

Kovács issued a statement in Pécs (31 October) and in Budapest

(November 1, 1956), in which he gave a splendid review of the Hungarian question. He emphasized that the Hungarian nation in the past twelve years was subjected to a bitter and grueling, but useful lesson; that the reforms and achievements gained immediately after the Second World War and after are not to be given up, and that after the Revolution neither the land nor the factories are to be returned to their former owners.

The Small Landholders' Party itself was organized in 1930. The idea of a Small Landholders' Party was first advanced by István Nagyatádi Szabó himself a peasant and Member of Parliament who in 1926 committed suicide.

The Party-founding meeting took place in Békés, in 1930, attended by such people as Tildy, Ferenc Nagy, Gaal Gaston, István B. Szabó, and others. The Party platform, known as the Békési Program, called for a land reform. The land reform proposed at Békés, viewed today, appears extremely mild indeed. The Small Landholders' Party remained an opposition Party between the two world wars. It was a very loose Party which had neither a firm organization nor an active organizational life.

In the 1930s, Tibor Eckhárdt and Endre Bajcsy-Zsilinszky joined the Small Landholders' Party group and the Party grew into a large opposition Party. Unfortunately it had neither a clear-cut, stable ideology, nor a crystallized point of view, nor a firm tactical program. It continued to exist and to function as an opposition Party, merely for the sake of opposition.

During the Second World War, the anti-Fascist front was organized, with Endre Bajcsy-Zsilinszky as leader. This group was a combination of heterogenous forces, including the Communists and Social Democrats. It is important to note that this participation of the Small Landholders' Party in the anti-Fascist front served as its credential and ticket of entry to the post-war political arena. Endre Bajcsy-Zsilinszky was the personification of personal integrity. He remained a brave champion of his ideals, openly advocating in Parliament the severance of all connections to Hitler and to Berlin. We must steer clear of Berlin immediately and we must get out of the war, he said. He enjoyed a very wide popularity. In 1944, the Germans arrested him. He resisted the arresting Germans with a gun in his hand. His attitude and spirit continued very high even in jail. The Germans executed him on the 24th of December, 1944.

In 1945, the democratic parties were organized. Of the parties formed, the Independent Small Landholders' Party appeared to be the most determined anti-Communist stronghold. This explains its 53-percent majority in the first post-war elections. People voted for this Party not because they were Small Landholders' Party, nor because they favored its program, -- it did not have any, -- but because it seemed to best exemplify their own anti-Communist sentiments.

Gradually an organizational life emerged within the Small Landholders' Party. The Party had its own youth organization -- the Independent Youth Movement (Független Ifjúsági Mozgalom), the largest youth group in Hungary.

The Independent Small Landholders' Party of 1956 resembled closely the Small Landholders' Party of former times. The only striking difference was the change in its leadership personnel. There was a change of generations (generációs váltás). The 1956 leaders were essentially young people, recruited from former members of the Independent Youth Movement. These people were brought up, were nourished and educated by the populist writers (népi irók).

The populist writers; these people made the re-discovery of Hungary their goal and program. They conducted research into the economic and social life of the nation. They analyzed the causes of economic and social troubles and maladies. They trained the young generation in logical and methodical thinking. The populist writers also found eager and active support among the lower clergy of the villages, who looked upon the populist literature as a justification of their own views. The generations born after 1920 received their very intellectual bread from the populist writers. These young people joined the political forces in 1945; they created strong youth movements and endeavored to mould the future of Hungary both in theory and practice along the lines of principles enunciated by their mentors.

After 1947, the youth organizations were destroyed. Their leaders were incarcerated. But in 1956 these young people reappeared again from their obscurity and formulated and put forward their demands. These people represented a uniform and identical view and stand, because they all received identical training. They all viewed similarly Hungary's future and they all held similar reforms necessary. All agreed in the necessity of land reform and all wanted to maintain the means of production under the supervision of the workers.

In 1938, populist thought invaded even the KALOT (Catholic Youth Movement) organization. (Interviewer's note: the KALOT was an organization of rural Catholic youth, under the leadership of Father Kerkai, S.J. Father Kerkai advocated, among other things, at least a partial secularization of the Church domain.)

Béla Kovács sided as early as 1945 with those forces who in 1956 became the leaders of the Revolution. This explains his forceful declaration of Pécs.

Another important role was played by the Central Workers' Council. Its leaders, Sándor Rácz and Mihály Báli, were the product of the workers' councils themselves. Neither of them had any political past. The Budapest workers' councils elevated them to positions of political importance and personal prestige, a fact rather unique in Hungary.

Rácz and Báli wanted no more for the workers' councils than the right to economic and administrative supervision of the means of production. They assumed political leadership only as a practical and inescapable necessity.

The formation of a central workers' council was the writers' idea, and its organization proceeded on their inspiration. The writers wanted a single organization, strong enough to make demands on the government. The political wisdom of this decision (to form the central council) soon became evident; the Council came to represent the only political power in Hungary. After November 4, it was the Council which effectively kept alive the revolutionary demands. Around November 20, both Rácz and Báli were kidnapped. From November 4 to November 20 these two people were the most important political personalities in Hungary.

Béla Király -- I heard his name only after the formation of the Supreme Command of the Budapest National Guard. Király became the commander of this force, with Maléter as his deputy. Otherwise I am not familiar with his activities (nem ismerem az ügyét).

Of the writers the most important were Istvan Márkus and Tibor Déry. The workers' council was Márkus's brainchild. It was Márkus who formulated the October 28 declaration of the Revolutionary Council of Hungarian Intellectuals. It was Márkus who led the workers' council deputation. It was Márkus and Miklos Gyimes who organized and kept alive the struggle after November 4. Gyimes was editor of the Szabad Nép after 1945. He loses his position, but returns in 1953, sides with Imre Nagy and becomes editor first of the Szabad Föld, later of the Szabad Nép. In 1956, he is assistant press secretary in the office of the Prime Minister.) The workers' council asked the writers for help and advice. Márkus, Gyimes, Déry, Gyula Hay, and Tamás Aczél went from factory to factory and told the local councils what to do and how to act, how to lead and how to continue the struggle. They were engaged in the production of illegal newspapers and leaflets, in the organization of strikes and of demonstrations.

Note. I tell you these things freely, for the sake of truth, but I also ask, since some of these people are still in Hungary, that they not be compromised.

Tamás Aczél -- he was the first man in Hungary who publicly accused and denounced the AVH. I had no contacts with him before the Revolution. During the Revolution his attitude and behavior were exemplary.

György Lukács -- after 1919 he went to Austria, later to Germany, and still later to Moscow. Lukács is a materialist philosopher. He made an attempt to interpret social phenomena on the basis, and in the light of, Marxist-Leninist doctrine. His teaching and influence went beyond Hungary's boundaries and he had a European reputation. After 1948, he came into conflict with Rákosi. Between 1948 and 1956, Lukács is brushed aside, but the regime did not dare put him completely in cold storage. Révai stated often how Lukács still needed a great deal of development and that he must free himself from the West. The Revolutionary Council of Hungarian Intellectuals wanted Lukács to become a cabinet member. This is how he became Minister of Adult Education. Lukács sought asylum, together with Nagy, at the Yugoslav Legation. He, too, was interned in Rumania, returning to Hungary not too long ago. Lukács's position is rather insecure (labilis). He is alive because he is indispensable. Hungary has very few well-known professors as it is.

11 g. Could you rank the following groups according to the degree of their participation in the Revolt: Workers, Peasants, Intellectuals, Soldiers, Youth (students, young workers), Irresponsible elements, and Anyone else?

The demonstration of October 23, complete with the 16 MEFESZ points, was started by the students. The demonstration was to be a sympathy demonstration in support of the Poles. As the demonstration progressed, workers and the general population joined in. We may say then, that in the starting of the Revolution the students had the main role. As far as the carrying on of the actual struggle for freedom, and the playing of important roles in it is concerned, again, the pre-eminent role belongs to the students. Workers, however, also participated. I would group the participants in the following order: students, workers, intellectuals, soldiers, and peasants.

Irresponsible elements there were only during the second phase of the Revolution. To give you an example of the cleanness of the Revolution: on October 28, the League of Hungarian Writers conducted a collection for the families of those who have given their lives for the Revolution. The containers used for this collection were nowhere supervised.

To give you an example for the irresponsible category: on October 31, I saw a man carrying two typewriters in the street. That was stealing. Another example: Count Almásy demanded his estate back.

I placed the peasants last because of their active role was less than that of the other groups. But this generalization does not hold true universally. The peasants' role in Miskolc, Pécs, and Györ was very significant. The peasants took their full share in such activities as transporting food, reorganization of the political life of the villages (the dismissal and replacement of councils and the disarming and arrest of the AVH). Peasants were also active in the dissolution or reorganization of the TSzCs cooperatives.

This same may be said of the army; while the army as a whole did not participate in the Revolution, the aiding of parts of it with the Revolution and the passivity of all the others was in itself of immense importance.

11 h. *Did you expect the university students to play the part they did?*

Thus far, every revolution has always found the students in the midst of it, particularly the university students. I did not think there was going to be a revolution. Once it came about, the students were the most versatile and the most determined fighters in it.

12. When did you decide to leave Hungary?

I have decided to leave Hungary on several occasions. Between November 12 and December 4, I made such a decision five times. The decision was not easy. I am no longer a very young man, and the 5 years which I spent in jail had their effect. I have already spent three and a half years at Recsk. I had to choose between renewed incarceration and exile. And finally the thought of Recsk prevailed. I think quite often, though, that perhaps it would be better if I were home, among friends, no matter under what circumstances. I cannot help feeling ashamed, knowing that one of my best friends is sitting in jail, sentenced to fifteen years imprisonment, while I am out here, free, but unable to help him. I left Hungary on December 4, 1956.

12 a. What made you decide after all?

The thought of Recsk, the certainty of my renewed incarceration. I discussed my decision with a great many people. This is why I started out five-six times.

12 c. Did you think of doing anything other than leaving Hungary?

We were in the Revolution. My friends were sentenced to jail terms or were executed. If I had stayed at home -- something I was seriously considering -- I was thinking of engaging in illegal activity; after November 4 there was a military dictatorship in Hungary. There was no other possibility but illegality.
At the time I left Hungary, a comparatively late period, escapees were required to pay huge sums of money to those who helped them across the border. I came to Austria without paying a forint; the truck which I boarded was loaded with people who paid heavy sums for their passage. Fortunately, the driver and another man -- a former director --, the two were in charge of the truck -- knew

me personally and they realized that I had to flee. They let me ride with them free of charge.

Our trip proceeded smoothly until, somewhere between Györ and Mosonmagyaróvár, we encountered both Hungarian and Russian troops. The commander of the Hungarian tank unit, a lieutenant, stopped our vehicle and the Russians forced everyone down from the truck, taking away our identification papers. The Hungarian officer, obviously trying to help us, called out to the driver: "Let me see your trip ticket!" The driver did have a forged trip manifest, authorizing him to proceed to a nearby village, but only a few names were on it. The lieutenant, in a remarkable outburst of both ingenuity and humanity, proceeded to read the document, adding fictitious names to it as he came to the end of the line. We immediately grasped the situation, and one by one, the whole group climbed back on the truck. We were saved.

WORK EXPERIENCE AND ECONOMIC CONDITIONS

1. ***Now tell me about yourself. What did you do in Hungary?***

I was a student at the University of Political Economy (Közgazdasági Egyetem). I completed three years of study.

From 1945 to 1947 I was a Member of Parliament, representing the Independent Small Landholders' Party. During this period I was also the president of the Independent Youth Movement.

I was arrested in 1948, spent two years in various jails. In 1950, I was placed in the internment camp at Recsk, where I stayed until 1953. In September 1953, I was freed and was permitted to settle in a small village near Budapest, where I was placed under police surveillance. I was not permitted to leave the village and I was restricted to physical labor, to be performed within the confines of the village. I found such work in a brick factory and started working on October 1, 1953, continuing to earn my livelihood there to the outbreak of the Revolution.

In the factory I was a physical laborer in the beginning, and was appointed later to a supervisory position, directing the work of some 6-8 men.

While in Parliament, -- I was the youngest Member -- I was assigned the task of parliamentary reporter (jegyzö). I was a member of the cultural and agricultural committees. All this from 1945 to 1947.

In November 1945, the elections were held. A great amount of preparatory work had to be done prior to the elections. During this campaign, I traveled a great deal, visiting every part of Hungary, attending meetings and conferences. After the elections, the long and drawn-out wrestling with the Communists began. We have made determined efforts to stop the Communist drive to power, but our attempts were unsuccessful. Prior to the elections, up until November 4, 1945, a provisional parliament was holding its sessions in the city of Debrecen. The elections, held in November 1945, returned an exceptionally strong Small Landholders' Party to Parliament. We received 53 percent of the votes cast. The Social Democrats had some 18-20 percent, the Communists 17 percent. Ten-eleven percent were allotted the National Peasant Party, whereas the Bourgeois Democratic Party (Polgári Demokrata Párt) had one or two parliamentary members.

Immediately after November 4, 1945, a coalition government was formed with Zoltán Tildy as Prime Minister. The parties, with the exception of the Bourgeois Democratic Party, were all represented in the Cabinet in proportion of their parliamentary strength.

The Communists sought, and received, the Ministry of the Interior, the Economics Ministry (Gazdasági Minisztérium), and the position of Deputy Prime Minister. The distribution of the key ministries was as follows: Foreign Affairs-Small Landholders' Party; Defense-Small Landholders' Party; Industry-communists; Commerce-communist; Interior-communists; Agriculture-national peasant Party; Education-Small Landholders' Party; Information-Small Landholders' Party.

Prior to November 4 1945, there was a lively debate as to how to hold the elections; the Communists wanted a one-list representation (közös listát akartak). This was entirely unacceptable. Then they endeavored to at least have a common list with the Social Democrats. But even this was rejected (Peyer, Ban, and Szelig were running as representatives of a separate Party). Having failed in their attempt to establish a unified electoral list, the Communists proposed the formation of a coalition government after the elections. The Allied Control Commission of Hungary was completely Russian-dominated, Voroshilov politely dictating on important issues. We vainly approached Schonfeld, the United States Representative, he declined to "meddle" -- as he put it -- in the internal affairs of Hungary.

We were frequently in Voroshilov's offices. Our Cabinet

members were subjected to heavy Russian pressure there. We endeavored to minimize the Russian pressure (csökkenteni akartuk). At last it was agreed that the differences be resolved by conferences.

The 1945 Coalition Government came into being as a result of direct, but veiled Russian pressure, clothed in presentable garb, a procedure in which the United States and the other members of the Control Commission willingly assisted their Russian colleague.

A group of Small Landholders' Party -- ignorant as yet of the Yalta commitments -- visited Schonfeld and asked him what possibilities were there for Hungary's internal development, what precisely were the objective facts which the Small Landholders' Party, though a majority Party, must face and acknowledge? Schonfeld told us that we belonged to the Soviet orbit and that our policies must correspond to this basic fact (mi a szovjet övezetbe tartozunk és politikánk ennek meg kell hogy feleljen).

Having received this cold-water treatment, the Small Landholders' Party sentiments cooled down, and the idea of a coalition cabinet was accepted.

The Communists had only 17 percent of the votes, but their influence in the government was proportionately much greater; they held sway over the interior and economic ministries and, viewing realities as they were, we knew we must primarily look to them to obtain economic assistance for Hungary -- Russia being the only country willing to give us sizeable help.

The AVH organization was built as early as 1945. Gábor Péter was its founder and organizer. He selected his men in such a fashion that he could trust them unquestionably.

There was a long and drawn-out political struggle, centering around the many abuses of the police and of the AVH. The tendency of the Small Landholders' Party from the very beginning was to retain the Interior Ministry to itself. The realization of this tendency proved impossible because of Voroshilov's opposition. We succeeded in placing a Small Landholders' Party under

Secretary of State in the Interior Ministry, but in practice this man was completely ineffective. The Communists were able to retain for themselves all the power and authority by resorting to their conspiratorial tactics.

The Communists have, from the very beginning, used the Interior Ministry as their own exclusive domain. As early as the beginning of 1945, in the Szeged Cabinet, and later in the provisional Debrecen Cabinet under the leadership of Miklós Dálnoky, the Ministry of the Interior was already in the Communists' hands. As the fighting Russian troops advanced on Hungarian territory towards the end of the Second World War, Muscovite and local Communists followed in their footsteps and organized the local police forces in villages and towns.

The local police forces in the liberated parts were under exclusive Communist control from the outset. When it came to the formation of the post-election cabinet, the Small Landholders' Party were left cold by Schonfeld and by the other Western representatives and, at the same time, were told by Voroshilov that the proposal advanced by Rákosi represented the only possible basis for the formation of the government. Faced with this situation, we were forced to accept not only the coalition, but the Rákosi plan of distribution of cabinet posts also.

Hungary was swarmed by a large number of Russian troops, our country was in the midst of a serious economic crisis, atrocities were innumerable, the illegal operation of the NKVD reached incredible dimensions and notoriety. Our plan was to stop all this as soon as possible. The only way to do this, -- we thought -- was to abide by Voroshilov's demands, to accept Rákosi's proposal. The Small Landholders' Party took it for granted that the Russians would leave the country and that a later possibility of rectification still existed.

We were satisfied with the distribution of the cabinet portfolios, but the question of the Interior Ministry continued to be a vexed and exciting one; determined efforts were made for the preservation of legality, and Members of Parliament have attacked in innumerable interpellations the Minister of the Interior, laying bare the illegal machinations of the AVH.

The Russians withdraw their forces, it is true, shortly after the coalition was formed, but the Allied Control Commission remained. The Russians' political and economic influence continued to be intense, and the Russians were able to keep the Hungarian nation in a state of complete insecurity. The Communists, under the leadership of Rajk, organized the three-Party leftist bloc (baloldali blokk) to counterbalance the Small Landholders' Party majority. The Russians used the age-old motto of <u>divide et impera</u>, inciting and supporting one group of Hungarians against the other.

The structure of the Small Landholders' Party was not a very fortunate one. Outwardly, it is true, it gave the appearance of a determined anti-Soviet sentiment, but it lacked unity, both organizational and ideological. There were numerous parties within the Party, each group fighting for its own point of view.

The Small Landholders' Party regarded the politically compromised elements of the Horthy-regime as untouchables, abandoning them to their fate. But not so the Communists; Révai came forward and not only defended the Nyilas fellow-travelers, but opened gates of the Communist Party to them.

The Communists, operating through their "built-in" (beépitett) agents, skillfully placed one Small Landholders' Party group against the other. Soon the groups were fighting one another and the salami politics (szalámipolitika) turned out to be eminently successful. Sulyok and twenty other Representatives suffered expulsion from the Small Landholders' Party. Later Pfeiffer and twenty other of his colleagues met the same fate.

Still later the Communists assaulted the main bloc of the Small Landholders' Party, attacking Ferenc Nagy and Béla Kovács, and depriving another group of 20-25 Members of their mandates. Sulyok organized another group, the Hungarian Freedom Party, and Pfeiffer formed the Hungarian Independence Party. Both of these groups ran for re-election in 1947 and achieved significant results. But both groups were crushed to pieces shortly thereafter.

In 1945, Hungary still retained its old state form (államforma). On February 1, 1946, a new constitution was adopted and Hungary became a republic. Under this new constitution, every Party, save the Fascist, was permitted to operate.

The parliamentary rules and procedures under which we operated during 1945-47 were entirely satisfactory and they corresponded to the requirements of the times. They were on a European level. The liquidation of the parties was not the result of faulty rules, it took place by means of back-door tactics. (A felszámolás hátsó kapukon történt). The Ministry of the Interior had a lion's share in this; the AVH, after 1947, while nominally under the control of the Cabinet, in reality received its orders and reported to none other but Rákosi and the Russians.

Economically, too, we were under complete Russian domination. Old German interests, real and imaginary, became Russian property under the terms of the peace treaty. Such concerns -- and there were a great many of them -- were completely Russian-dominated.

Politically our hands were tied. Voroshilov was the Chairman of the Control Commission and the Hungarian Government could do nothing at all without the prior approval of the Russians. Schonfeld did not help us in any way. Yalta, and the dreadful implications and hints as to its contents, became known only much later. Our fight was that of a determined but helpless blind man who fights, but does not know what, -- we did not know of Yalta, much less of what it represented, but the Russians were well aware of their opportunities under it.

Gábor Péter, a Russian citizen, created a dreaded renown for the AVH. The Communists continuously presented the nation with faits accomplis. The arrests and the fate of those arrested were most carefully planned and irrevocably sealed. The Small Landholders' Party fought a futile and hopeless Don Quixote sort of windmill battle against these encroachments.

The Leftist Bloc was organized, under the leadership of Rajk, to prevent the Small Landholders' Party from taking over the Interior Ministry. Even as it was facing this renewed threat, the Small Landholders' Party became disunited. The Communists used the situation to their own advantage; they attacked its vulnerable points and inflicted whatever damage they could.

Dobi and his colleagues, the left-wing of the Small Landholders' Party, were engaged in a constant fight within the Party with representatives of the right wing. Tildy, too, was with the left wing. As a matter of fact, it was Tildy who provoked this fight and, once started, he gave it his full support.

Our parliamentary rule provided that Members of Parliament could not be arrested except in cases where they committed felonies (murder, grand larceny, breaking and entering, rape, etc.). The State could ask that a Member's immunity be lifted if accused of embezzlement or of mismanagement of funds entrusted to him. This same held true if a Member was accused of abusing lawful authority. The rules on immunity (mentelmi jog) state explicitly that a Member of Parliament cannot be prosecuted on account of his political work.

If a law court or prosecutor's office asked that a Member's immunity be lifted, the papers relating to the accused Member's case were sent to the Parliamentary Committee on Immunity. The Committee on Immunity then made its recommendation to the full Parliament. This rule was valid until 1947. The Communists did pressure the Committee on Immunity even before 1947, but the Committee did not easily accede to their demands. ***Question:*** Could you give me an example where the immunity of a Member was actually lifted? ***Answer:*** Take the case of Ferenc Vidovics. He was a Small Landholders' Party member, a Representative of the County of Somogy, the prefect (föispán) of Somogy County, a good organizer and speaker, and extremely popular as a person. The Communists were unable to fight him in his native Somogy stronghold, but, bent on getting rid of him, they introduced false testimony against him, accusing him of bigamy and of having authored some pro-German articles. The evidence, though undoubtedly false, was presented and Vidovics's immunity was lifted.

There was the case of Károly Vértessy: Vértessy was accused of having been a member of the Prónay-corps and of having participated in the struggle against the Communists in 1919. Whether the accusations against Vértessy were true or false I do not know to this day. But his immunity was lifted.

There was the great conspiracy charge of 1947. The accusation was general in nature and the "conspiracy" did not have a leader at first. Later Béla Kovács and Ferenc Nagy were named as leaders and were accused of having formed a secret society for the purpose of overthrowing the republic and restoring the monarchy. The fate of Nagy is well know. The other accused, Kiss Sándor, László Vatai, Tibor Ham, and Béla Kovács were picked up by the NKVD. These people were arrested first and only later did the authorities request the lifting of their immunities. The immunity proceeding was slow, the Russians intervened and Parliament, barely representing the quorum, (csonka parliament), finally voted for the lifting of the group's immunities.

By the time of the second elections, in 1947, the parties of both Sulyok and Pfeiffer openly admitted their opposition status. Perhaps precisely because these parties were opposition parties, both of them were highly successful in the 1947 elections, (even though the Communists were guilty of many irregularities).

In 1947, and after, the Small Landholders' Party no longer had a leader. The Communists permitted both Sulyok and Pfeiffer to run for re-election because they hoped to thereby weaken the Small Landholders' Party. They supported, at the same time, the Dobi faction of the Small Landholders' Party. The Small Landholders' Party results in the 1947 elections were very miserable. Sulyok, Pfeiffer, and Barankovics's Christian People's Party (Keresztény Néppárt) received sizeable portions of the Small

Landholders' Party vote. The Small Landholders' Party, for all practical purposes, were completely beaten and destroyed. Later the Sulyok, Pfeiffer, and Barankovics forces were simply erased (kiradirozták), in spite of the elaborate rules of parliamentary game. After 1947, Members of Parliament were first arrested and only later came the request for the lifting of their immunities.

The fight also began against the right wing of the Social Democratic Party. Peyer was thrown out of the Social Democratic ranks. In the 1947 elections he and Bela Zsolt were running at the head of a new Party. Szakasits and Marosán were meanwhile fighting it out with Szelig.

The situation was similar in the National Peasant Party. There the leadership of the right-wing Imre Kovács was successfully challenged by the fellow-traveler Ferenc Erdei.

Question: What was your attitude regarding these baseless accusations of Members of Parliament? ***Answer:*** In the Vidovics case, Vidovics himself vehemently denied the charges. I did not believe the accusation myself. But it was extremely difficult to prove that the charges were without foundation. The produced evidence could not be proven false or forged and there was nothing we could do about it. The only thing one could do was to stay away from the proceedings. That is exactly what I did.

The great conspiracy charge against Kovács was different. It interested me more because I, too, was affected by it. What I want to say is that the same sort of method and tactics was employed in the Youth Movement also, with somewhat less success, I must add.

My situation was more stable there than Kovács's position in Parliament. There was a coalition body which embraced the major youth organizations. This was the Magyar Ifjúság Országos Tanácsa (National Council of Hungarian Youth). I was chairman of both this coalition group and of the Független Ifjúság (Independent Youth), while György Non, the chairman of the MADISZ, held the position of secretary general of the Magyar Ifjúság Országos Tanácsa.

In 1947, I was forced to resign my chairmanship of the Független Ifjúság. The Communists thereupon engineered a coup and brought all youth organizations under one leadership; the Egységes Ifjusági Szervezet was called into being. The KALOT, the KIE (the Hungarian YMCA) and the scout movement was stamped out even earlier.

As soon as I resigned as chairman of the Független Ifjuság, Zsigmond S. Nagy, in the name of the Fügetlen Ifjuság, accepted the Communists' bid and signed the Dobogóköi accord (egyezmény) in 1947, which abolished the various youth movements and created the Egységes Ifjusági Szervezet.

To come back to your question, which is a legitimate one, I must emphasize that you must view things in their proper perspective and analyze our attitude in the light of the milieu and circumstances which confronted us; Russian influence was overwhelming, the initiative, both in the political and economic spheres, was in the hands of the Communists. There was the pending question of the peace treaty. Up until the conclusion of the peace treaty we were living in a state of war. The Russians were able to do anything they pleased. The police force and the AVH were Communist dominated. In an atmosphere like that it would have been extremely difficult to justify politically a refusal by Parliament to lift the immunity of its accused members. You must understand the nature of the Small Landholders' Party, its impotency, its many mistakes and blunders which, in the final analysis, was the result of its very structure. Before the Second World War the Small Landholders' Party was no more than an election-day Party (választási párt), it never amounted to more than an opposition Party, a Party devoid of any organization, a group existing in the club-life of Parliament only, and nowhere else. It did not have a tradition (nem volt mozgalmi multja), it lacked experience, it had neither tactical principles nor a clear-cut program. It if had not been for Bajcsy-Zsilinszky, the Small Landholders' Party would have even lost its significance. Bajcsy-

Zsilinszky's participation in the Independence Movement during the war gave it its raison d'etre. In a word, the Party was not prepared for the task which awaited it after 1945.

But even assuming that our Party had all the qualities which it actually lacked, even then, while we could have postponed our fate, its coming, at a later date, would have been inevitable.

In the 1945 elections all those who did not have a political conviction deeper than opposition to the Russians voted for the Small Landholders' Party. Merchants and artisans voted Social Democratic. The Communists received the votes of Communists, of bureaucrats who worked under immediate Communist supervision, the Nyilas vote, the vote of Germanophiles and of rightists. For these latter groups voting with the Communists became an existential question.

The National Peasant Party was in no better shape. It was founded in the city of Makó, in 1938.

In the interbellum period the populist writers were the strongest, most talented and most effective intellectual force in Hungary. They discribed Hungary both economically and socially, pointing out the nation's maladies. Their unanimous conclusion: the necessity of a land reform. But the Horthy regime was based on a narrow, exclusive group. Behind the regime the Etelközi Szövetség (League of Etelköz), stood guard. These people ruled Hungary between the two wars. They jealously guarded their positions. They did have a guilty conscience, it is true, and, as a result, they permitted a degree of intellectual freedom. Books could be published and people were permitted to engage in academic discussions as long as they did not attack either the political or the economic status of the Etelközi Szövetség.

The populist writers were attacking the status quo and this brought them their popularity. The Interior Ministry was constantly after them, and the writers' attempt to form a political Party was thwarted. The populist writers finally succeeded in organizing the National Peasant Party. The Peasant Party did not have any significance between the wars. We knew it existed, but that was about all. It did acquire some importance after the Second World War, however, the Peasant Party had an extremely bad start in 1945. Many people will tell you that the Peasant Party was no more than a sister organization of the Communist Party. This is not true. It is true, however, that the Communists feared the Small Landholders' Party and the possibility of there emerging a single and strong agrarian Party in Hungary. To prevent this, they actively supported the Peasant Party.

The Allied Control Commission and other public bodies, including the Communist Party, gave all the support they could give to this rival agricultural Party. The Peasant Party was the recipient of money, cars, and of electioneering. Precisely because of this overwhelming assistance, the Peasant Party fared very badly in the 1945 elections. Many a person who would have liked to vote for them, gave his vote to the Small Landholders' Party.

The leadership of the Peasant Party (Péter Veress, chairman; Imre Kovács, secretary-general) tried very hard to correct these initial mistakes after 1945. They made an attempt to extricate themselves from the Russian tutelage and to assert their independence again.

I did not participate in the 1947 elections. The Small Landholders' Party suffered heavy losses in that election. But weakened as they were, the Small Landholders' Party could have still formed a coalition with the Balogh and Imre Kovács forces. Many former Small Landholders' Party representatives were in both these groups. There was such a plan after 1947 to secretly unite the Small Landholders' Party and Balogh parties. The united Party would have still been the largest single group and as such it could have effectively resisted the Communists and raised its voice in the affairs of the nation.

István Balogh, Imre Kovács, and a number of Small Landholders' Party, Dobi among others, actually met in the Független Ifjúság headquarters and agreed on a merger. They also worked out specific plans of action. Unfortunately the whole agreement was betrayed to Rákosi the very day it was reached, and Rákosi promptly shattered the whole deal. (The only person who could have betrayed this remarkable plan was Dobi, who was chairman of the Small Landholders' Party at the time.) This was the last attempt to save the country from falling completely under Russian domination. After this only smaller groups fought their losing battles.

Question: Could you tell me something of the Hungarian youth movements and of the role you played in them? **Answer:**

Sándor Kiss, Antal Gyenes, Béla Koss and I organized the Free Front of the Hungarian Youth (Magyar Ifjusag Szabadság Frontja) back in 1943.

We tumbled down (lebuktunk) in November 1944. The gendarmes arrested Sándor Kiss, Pál Jonás, János Horváth, and me. We were taken to the Margit körút prison and were subjected to a long investigation. Meanwhile the Germans encircled Budapest. We were later taken to the Márko-utca where we were under the supervision of the Gestapo. Still later they took us to the Pestvidéeki prison and finally to the basement of the Parliament building. In January 1945 we were handed over to the Nyilas authorities. We have passed from one Nyilas prison to another and these people treated us cruelly and in a barbaric fashion. They beat the Jews to death. We escaped on January 11 (1945).

Between 1942 and 1944, there developed in Hungary a solid youth front within which young people knew one another fairly well. These people became the leaders of the various youth movements. There was a fine cooperation among us, and we fought, in 1942-1943, at the University, for the creation of a unitary (egységes) youth movement. We were quite ready to cooperate with the various groups and factions.

We brought into being, in January 1945, the MADISZ organization. Sándor Kiss was chairman, Gyenes was secretary-general, Jonás became the leader of the university organization. Nyeste served as organizer. All parties were represented in the MADISZ.

The youth of the Communist front employed the same tactics within the MADISZ which the representatives of the Communist Party used in Parliament. Their aim was to secure for themselves the key positions and, using conspiratorial tactics, they endeavored to force their opinion and stand on all the others.

But this sort of thing did not work with us. We resisted and, in March 1945, the MADISZ disintegrated. The first to leave the MADISZ were the Social Democrats. Later we, too, abandoned it. I brought into being the Independent Youth Organization (Független Ifjusági Szervezet). Still later the Peasant Party also abandoned the MADISZ, so that only the Communists remained.

Up until the 1945 elections the various youth organizations operated as separate entities. After the formation of the coalition Cabinet, the government proposed that the youth organizations also form a coalition. As a result, the National Council of Hungarian Youth (Magyar Ifjuság Országos Tanácsa) was organized. This organization was to serve in a consultative capacity. It concerned itself with cultural problems and was to be the means of expressing the youths' stand in political questions. I was elected chairman of this organization, while György Non became its secretary-general. Non also retained his post as secretary-general of the MADISZ. Because there were so many profound changes in Hungary and because Hungary existed under an entirely new set of circumstances, political questions were extremely important for us and we devoted a great deal of time and effort in this direction.

Let me say now a few words about the Independent Youth Organization which was the youth affiliate of the Small Landholders' Party. Our organization consisted primarily of peasant youth. We had a sizeable membership in Budapest also, but that was not significant. The significance of our group in Budapest was felt at the universities rather than within the circles of the Budapest youth proper.

Young people born after 1920 were reared (intellectually)

by the populist writers. Their mode of thinking and their Weltanschauung thus molded, they naturally reacted very sensitively to problems of Hungary and particularly to problems affecting the Hungarian peasant class. Many of our youth actively participated in the execution of the land reform and our youth organizations played an important role in the social and cultural life of the villages.

Ours was a democratic movement, both in its organization and structure. We had our local organizations. Above these were the district and county organizations, with a centralized, national leadership. The central organization consisted of the chairman, the secretary-general, and the youth council. The council had 16-18 members, elected from among the most popular youth leaders, and it functioned as a policy-making (irányító) and controlling body. The council met once a month.

The Independent Youth Movement concerned itself primarily with cultural problems. We laid great stress on teaching our members in constructive and systematic thinking. We also instituted courses in rational agriculture, awarding certificates to many a student (arany- és ezüstkalászos tanfolyamok). We were concerned with all phases of agricultural problems.

The courses in agriculture were offered during the winter season; they started in November and terminated at the end of March. These were intensive courses, students lived together and studied together. One course ran for two years, the other for four years. Each terminated by a comprehensive examination. The two-year course resulted in the Ezüstkalász diploma, these who completed four years received the Aranykalász diploma.

Our aim with these winter courses was the propagation of methods and principles of intensive agriculture (belterjes mezögazdaság) on the Dutch and Danish models. Our problems were similar to those of Holland and Denmark: small territory, large population.

The land reform created small agricultural units (farms).

Our position was that the Hungarian farmers ought to engage themselves in the cultivation of such plants which assured them of a good income, a type of agriculture which affords them enough leisure to cultural activities also.

We wanted small agricultural machines, suitable for the cultivation of orchards and vineyards. We envisioned immense opportunities for our people in the fields of fruit growing and fruit packing industries; both our soil and our climate are perfectly suited for quality fruit growing.

Even more important, Hungary abounds in sodaic soil (szikes talaj) which, at the present, are barren wastelands, not at all adaptable for conventional agriculture. There were attempts to improve these lands and to use them for growing of wheat and corn. But the improvement so achieved is extremely costly, while the effect of the improvement is only temporary and in need of repeating every few years. Such sodaic (szikes) soil is ideally suited for the growing of nut-bearing fruit trees, without any need of special improvement. The possibilities of exporting such fruit (walnut, almonds, etc.) are limitless.

We also organized seminars which, unlike the arany - and ezüstkalászos courses, were not concerned with the attainment of technical skill in the field of agriculture. We conducted discussions here to find out, for instance, how would it be possible to reorganize Hungarian agriculture, how could we make it profitable, what would be the social and cultural consequences of such a reorientation, and how could we best meet them. We also discussed ways and means of defending Small Landholders' Party against the current of agricultural collectivization.

We also conducted political seminars for our members. Our aim was to acquaint them with the various civilizations of our age and to introduce them to the main political thought-currents of today. Even under Horthy, Hungarians received a rather one-sided view of these things, looking at the world through German and Italian eyeglasses. We analyzed the Marxian tenets as well as other important political thoughts, giving a thorough description of the American form of government. We tried to be objective in our discussions and to pinpoint faults as well as advantages of the several systems. Above all things our aim was to train ourselves in the principles of methodical learning and to develop a habit of political thinking.

We were also concerned with purely cultural problems. In this we followed in the footsteps of the populist writers; we wanted to acquaint ourselves with the ancient Hungarian culture, we wanted to learn and to know more of the artistic and literary products of this culture. It was our aim to absorb as much as possible of our native culture and, going one step further, to familiarize ourselves with the outstanding creations of European and other cultures.

In a word, we wanted to become truly European men by fully accepting our own cultural heritage and absorbing as much as we could of the super-national, European spirit. Our cultural ideal was Béla Bartók.

How did we finance our activities? We were a very large group (the largest in Hungary), numbering 600,000 members. Members paid a nominal due. During the inflation this was one kilogram of wheat per person. Later it was one forint per month per person. Other incomes we did not have. The agricultural courses did not bring us any money.

We did receive assistance from the Independent Small Landholders' Party. This assistance consisted of the Party placing at our disposal our headquarters building and providing us with administrative help.

The Independent Youth had its own weekly, edited by András Hamza. In 1945, this weekly served as the forum of the populist writers; such people as Lászlo Németh, Kodalányi, Sinka, Lörinc Szabó, Illyés, and Áron Tamási, unwilling to write for Communist publications, contributed a great deal to our paper.

The Independent Youth had a lively organizational life. We had various cultural groups, populist (népi), singing and dancing groups, we organized amateur dramatic groups and we had many clubs.

Politically we stood united against the Communists. Leading figures of our youth organization were attacked as early as 1946. These attacks were directed by the MADISZ first and later by the Hungarian Communist Party. It was because of these incessant attacks that the Communists succeeded within the short time of two years to bring about the Dobogóköi "Agreement". After Dobogókö, the Independent Youth ceases functioning and its members no longer participate in the Hungarian youth movement.

The unity of the Independent Youth was not the apparent unity of the Small Landholders' Party of 1945. Ours was a real unity. This explains the events of 1956. These young men, silenced between 1947-1956, reappear again before the Revolution. During the short time of the Independent Youth's existence, these young people participated in countless seminars, discussed diligently many political questions and developed a unitary (egységes) view and stand. There were no factions. To be sure, there were differences of opinion, but we all agreed on basic principles and proceeded from the same premises. This is how that unitary (egységes) stand and view developed which gave the Revolution its unity.

Equally important, the various youth leaders, Social Democratic, Kalot, Peasant Party and others, spent a long time in jails together; we had ample opportunity to get to know one another fairly well. We respected our differences and we continued to respect one another even though our differences continued.

Recsk, for instance, gave us an opportunity to prepare and analyze the balance sheet for 1945-47. We had ample time to discuss our mistakes, our aims -- what we would do, what our stand would be and how we would act if we ever had the opportunity again to freely operate in the body politic. This is why, though there were many political parties during the

Revolution, the revolutionary questions for all of us were identical.

The work of the Independent Youth Movement, the methodological manner of thinking and acting (modszeresség) a procedure also evident elsewhere, these were the forces of re-education which produced an entirely different Hungary; in the political life of Hungary a generational problem appeared. Those among the populist writers and politicians who accepted the validity of modern and up-to-date political currents were accepted by and became integral parts of the young generation. This new outlook did not as yet exist in 1945. But the young generation matured and developed and gradually invaded the political arena. This generation developed its program and this program became the program of the Revolution.

Young people within the Independent Youth Movement concerned themselves with a variety of problems. And the preoccupation with these problems brought up the question in the minds of many of giving up their traditional ways and becoming intellectuals. Most of them did not go past the fourth or maybe the sixth grade of elementary school. A great many of these peasant boys were extremely intelligent. Some of them completed secondary schools, others were university students.

The collegiate movement (kollégiumi mozgalom) had precisely this aim; to assist peasant boys to go to the universities. We in the Independent Youth Movement brought into being the Hungarian Collegiate Association (Magyar Kollégiumi Egyesület). Our aim was to establish, with the assistance of the general public and of the state, as many of these colleges and scholarships for deserving boys as possible. Between 1945-1947, there were about 40-45 such colleges.

These colleges were student hostels (közös diákszállások), where the students lead a fully autonomous life, elected their own directors and provided their own discipline. A college of this kind was a closed community (zárt közösség), having its own cultural program and life, which was both extremely intensive and productive.

The Communists, too, established their own colleges. These were the NÉKOSZ colleges. Rajk was the chairman of this national organization. After 1947, the NÉKOSZ organization swallowed up and absorbed the independent colleges. In 1949, Rákosi disbanded the NÉKOSZ in turn, accusing them of Rajkism (the Rajkists vehemently denied the charge that they were national communists. They were, in their opinion, the true Communists and it was Rákosi who deviated).

The important thing to remember is that the leadership and the members of the staff (törzsgárda) of the Petofi Circle all came from the Hungarian Collegiate Association and from the NÉKOSZ.

The great political opponent and adversary of the Independent Youth Movement was the MADISZ (Communist) organization. The Independent Youth Movement gained in significance from the large number of its members and from the remarkable unity among the members regarding the diagnosis and cure of the fundamental maladies affecting Hungary. The MADISZ was supported by the presence of the Russians and by the power of the Communist Party. The essential difference between them and us was money; the MADISZ had plenty of it available but our group was the more productive. The difference in principle between us was even more pronounced; the Independent Youth Movement was not a leftist, but an anti-Communist youth organization. We, too, approved of social reforms, but refused to call ourselves Socialist because the MADISZ had already appropriated that term for itself.

The SZIM (Social Democratic Youth Movement) operated strictly within the framework of the Social Democratic Party. The SZIM abided fully by both Party directives and Party discipline. Its role was that of a mediator between the Independent Youth Movement and the MADISZ, a role which was not too successful, I must say. By 1947, the SZIM, losing both independence and stature, actually came to serve as assistant of the MADISZ. Even before 1947, Communist influence within the SZIM was everywhere observable. A large number of Communists who found asylum in Social Democratic ranks before the Second World War remained within the Social Democratic Party even after 1945 and did their job for the cause there. (The Social Democrats made it their policy before the war to permit members of the outlawed Communist Party to submerge in their ranks and to operate within the Party and in the labor unions as a Communist faction.) As a result, the Communists had an inside view of everything and were very effective in interfering in the Social Democrats's affairs.

The Peasant Party youth was insignificant both in number and in every other respect. The duties and functions which it proposed to fulfill were already taken care of by the Independent Youth Movement. Because of this parallelism, the Peasant Party youths were unable to organize in many localities. All in all, there was a fine cooperation between them and us, we sponsored many joint actions, we divided our roles in the MTKT and we worked against the Communists.

The KILOT, the KIE, and the scout association worked in close harmony with us. They retained their separate identities, but in many localities they actually functioned within the framework of the Independent Youth Movement.

The scouts were the first group to be disbanded, at the end of 1946. The KALOT met its end in the beginning of 1947, and the KIE shortly thereafter. In the place of the scout movement, the Úttörö (Pioneer) group was organized in the first part of 1947. The úttörök embraced children between 6-14 years of age.

2. *Please tell me about the jobs you held in Hungary. Start with the first and enumerate them in order.*

I already told you of my position as a Member of Parliament and of my experiences in the Hungarian Youth Movement. Let me relate now the job I had after my release from Recsk.

I worked in a brick factory. I was hired as an unskilled laborer, later I became a loader. We loaded bricks into wagons in the freight yard. I was later transferred to the kiln. My job was to carry the clay into the kiln.

We produced bricks (6 x 10 centimeters in size) with the help of machines. The clay was let to dry in the sun. When hard, the clay was brought to the kiln and I placed them into the kiln. The quality of the finished product depended on how I placed the clay into the kiln. The kilns were large furnaces with fires burning in them from spring to fall. Their temperature was 70 to 80 degrees Celsius. I was later made a foreman of the kiln-shift consisting of 11 men.

2 c. How long did you have this position?

I worked in this factory from 1953 to 1956.

2 e. Tell me about the place (organization, company, form) you worked at.

The plant was an old concern, a private undertaking, its kilns were small, the plant's equipment was primitive, with some modernization. The original kilns were enlarged, we had a modern press and the plant was electrified. The undertaking was well over 12 years old (it started operating before 1945). We had an abundant supply of high-quality clay, it could well have been used for ceramics also. We produced bricks of high solidity. The plant was owned by one man. The plant's yearly capacity was 60 million bricks. Approximately 50 people were employed. There was a plant director and a production leader, one office worker and one stenographer. A large part of the administrative work was done by the leaders of the various work groups. There was only one general shift, those carrying the clay into the kilns worked in two shifts, and the burning in the kilns was done in three shifts.

2 f. What did it do? Was it a large organization? An efficient one?

The association of brick factories of Pest County was a large organization, but our factory, an integral part of this group, was one of the small members of the association. It was an efficient organization, due largely to the plant manager who was both an able organizer and an expert, a man who, because of his family background, could not aspire to higher positions.

3. How did you like this job?

I did not like this job at all. I didn't because I was forced to do it. I was a political prisoner at Recsk until 1953. When released, I continued to live under a strict police supervision and I was forbidden to engage in any kind of work but physical labor. I had the choice of working on a state farm or in this factory. Of these two I chose the factory because this was closer to my dwelling and because I made more money this way.

3 b. What did you dislike about it?

This was not my profession. For a man who, even in a job like that, is obliged to keep quiet, the job obviously cannot be too pleasant.

3 c. How did it compare with other jobs you had?

I think you can draw your own conclusion.

3 d. What were the working conditions?

Our work was seasonal in nature. During the winter months, we engaged in maintenance work. Working conditions were primitive. It was a hard physical labor. There were, it is true, some attempts at mechanizing certain phases of the production, but this transformation was neither perfect nor completed. Even after mechanization, there still remained a great many tasks where actual menial labor was indispensable (the mining of clay, where they did not always use explosives, the loading of the lorries was done by hand, and the miners were pushing these trucks by hand to the elevator). While the actual production of bricks for the most part was done by machines, the actual moving of the bricks (15 kilograms each) was done by hand.

The technical level of the plant was deficient and with all the good will and effort of the manager it remained rather simple and primitive.

We received work clothes. The miners were supplied with rubber boots and raincoats. Those working at the press were given shirts, overalls, and leather aprons. Those working at the kiln received underwear, work clothes and 1 ½ liters of salty mineral water daily, or 15 dekagrams of sour bonbons. Workers engaged in transportation were also given work clothes and protective overcoats.

There were locker rooms, one each for men and women, and showers were also available with free soap for those who worked at the kilns.

The place was very crowded. It was a small undertaking with a disproportionately high production plan (60 million bricks a year). Machines were everywhere, with little working room left to move around. Because of the immediate proximity to the clay mines, expansion was not possible.

The quality of the bricks varied. We could have produced superior quality bricks, we had excellent quality clay at our disposal, but the production plan was too high. We had monthly and daily production targets, both of which were beyond our capacity. The ideal technology of production, nicely worked out on paper, was never kept. In the mines the clay should have been cut to small pieces, so as to permit efficient and thorough grinding. This was never adhered to. Most of the machines were obsolete, spare parts did not arrive in time because of the centralized system of distribution. Because of the complicated administrative procedures involved, our orders were sometimes delayed for months. The grinders' throwers were worn. Another problem was the mixing, in a certain ratio, of coal dust with clay, an important prerequisite of good quality brick. One man would have been needed for this operation, but the factory plans did not permit this. As a result, the bricks deformed and lost much of their value. Also, we should have used brown coal in our kilns, which we only seldom received. The result was that the bricks either were not baked well enough, or else the bricks stuck to one another.

3 e. How did you go to work? How long did it take you?

I lived close to the factory. It took me about 20 minutes walking either way.

3 f. How many hours a day did you work?

When at the kilns, I worked 8 hours, in summer 10-10½ hours, on Saturdays till 12 noon.

3 g. How many days a week did you work?

I worked six days a week. If I worked 10½ hours a day, then I only worked till noon on Saturday.

3 h. Did you work overtime? If so, how were you paid for it?

Yes, I did work overtime. For the first two hours we received 25 percent more, for the next two hours 50 percent more, beyond that and for work on Sunday we received 100 percent more of our base pay.

3 i. Were there legal holidays? How many?

Yes, there were four legal and paid holidays (May 1, April 4, August 20, December 25).

3 j. Were there paid vacations? How long?

During the first two years of work, one got 7 days paid vacations. For each two years thereafter, one additional day was given. In no case did the total number of days go beyond 14-16 days. Those who worked at the kilns received an additional four days for health purposes.

3 k. Did this vary from job to job?

The basic administrative order provided for 7 days for the beginners. Thus you had 7 plus, or 7 plus 4 plus. Youths (under 18) received 14 days plus. Women received 6 weeks if they gave birth to a child. The management wanted that we all take our vacations during the winter.

3 l. Was there any punishment for lateness and absenteeism?

Yes, an intensive campaign was waged against both lateness and absenteeism. Violators were fined, the sum in each case being determined by the plant leadership. This practice was no longer adhered to in 1953. Instead of being punished, offenders were "educated"; their names were brought up during union meetings or production conferences and the persons themselves were derided and ridiculed. "You must improve your relationship to work" was a standard admonition. If someone was late, his relationship to work was bad. He was neglectful, he violated factory rules; he was politically unreliable. Almost anything could be fitted under the heading of "bad relationship to work". People were afraid of this, because this was connected with the system of cadres. Both the Party secretary and the factory leader were entitled to enter their observations on a person's cadre sheet. And the cadre sheet had a very great significance in a person's life.

3 m. Can you remember changes introduced in the norm system, and how where they carried out?

I can speak only of the period after 1953, the norms we had at Recsk were not normal. They were very tight and inhuman.

Generally speaking, the norms were based on empirical knowledge, on observations of the time-study people. Processes in part were measured in terms of time and the question of what separate motions constituted the entire work process was thoroughly analyzed. This was perfectly all right. But in the final analysis the norms were not based on experience so gained, but were brought about by dictates coming from above. Planners have seen, for instance, that a certain process is either too expensive, or that people were making too much money. Either of these called for immediate re-evaluation. The norm-man was sent out.

His was a confidential work, which was extremely unpopular. The norm-man was a good Party member, not a good and conscientious expert. He received an order, and carried that order out, disregarding every technical or human consideration.

There was usually a conspiracy among the workers when the norm-man appeared on the scene; workers performed their tasks slowly and in a complicated way. This, of course, did not help them in any way. The norm-man had an order to reduce the time-element, say, by 20 percent. He carried his order out irrespective of what the workers did or did not do.

An integral part of the norm system was the system of work

competition. Workers competed with one another to produce more and more on the principle that who produces more makes more money. The norm represented 100 percent. He who produces more received more pay according to a progressive scale.

This same principle was employed also on the collective farms; there was an initial norm at the start. People were anxious to overproduce in order to earn more money. When this overproduction became pretty general, i.e., most workers overproduced, the norm-man appeared on the scene and tightened the norm. This increased output became the new basis (100 percent) and for this increased output people received the original pay or even less than that.

There was the system of progressive incentives, known as premium. The premium represented a certain percentage of the base pay. In our factory, for instance, for 101-110 percent of production there was a 25 percent premium. For 110-120 percent of production there was 50 percent of premium. For 120-150 percent of production there was 75 percent of premium. For over 150 percent of production there was 90 percent of premium.

In practice this meant that if I had to load 400 bricks per hour (100 percent) and I loaded 600 instead, for the 400 I received sixteen forints, for the 600 twenty-four forints. The minimum living standard for menial laborers was fixed at 800-1000 forints. People earned 1400-1600 and even more forints. The truth was that 1000 forints were not sufficient for subsistence. As a result everyone strained himself and overproduced, to be able to satisfy his real minimum requirements. Subtle slogans were used to bring all this about; produce more, you live better (Termelj többet, jobban élsz), Overproduction is a patriotic duty (Többtermelés hazafiúi kötelesség), etc.

They were using a slightly modified Bedeaux system in Hungary. This system is usually applied to highly mechanized industry only. In Hungary it found application everywhere. In the brick factory, for instance, only two-three people worked who were paid by the hour. The gist of the Bedeaux system -- Produce more, earn more, produce less, earn less -- was essentially adhered to in Hungary; 80 percent production was paid in full. Those who produced less than 80 percent were gotten rid of at the first opportunity. Those who produced between 80-100 percent received proportionately less pay than the stated normal.

The norm system reacted to the changing political atmosphere. In 1953, when Nagy came to power, the norms were not slackened. The easing up came about by the fact that the norms were not interfered with (i.e., there was no tightening) and workers were permitted to simplify the work process. They were allowed, for instance, to lift six, instead of three, bricks at a time, even though a great many bricks broke in the process. After 1953, the plant leadership did not pay any attention to these things.

In 1954, 1955, in politics there was a return to Stalinism. Production costs were everywhere on the increase. As a result, there took place a national norm reorganization, involving a tightening of 10-15-20 percent.

There were two types of norms: national norms and local norms. In every branch of industry uniform production procedures were compiled. Every step of brick manufacturing, for example, was strictly prescribed. The time studies were based on this production manual; the processes involved were known, the time required to do them was measured and the national norms were fixed. Every undertaking was free, on the other hand, to utilize its own local norms. These norms were tighter than the national norms (this or that object may be closer in a given plant and thus a given production step may require less time and/or effort than somewhere else).

After 1953, the local norms were generally not used. National norms at this time are relatively bearable. At the end of 1954, and during 1955, the national norm is tightened 15-20 percent, there is a return to the local norms and the technical procedure as prescribed by the production manual is strictly observed; there is a tightening of the work discipline.

3 n. *What about the speed-up system?*

Speed-ups were carried out by such devices as work competitions, to the accompaniment of political slogans. Social production - so read the slogan - is very important. He who disapproves of this is a traitor, a Fascist, an American imperialist spy, a reactionary. He who is branded any one of these evil geniuses is a lost man. This was one of the tactics of those in control of production; political means were used to enforce accelerated production tempo.

Various meetings and conferences served the same purpose. So every week there was a union meeting and production conferences were held every other week. On these meetings people were forced to take a stand, to declare themselves in favor of Socialist production. Those who do not express their opinion are not with us - reasoned the Communists, and those who are not with us are against us. Negative reactions were thus registered on the Káder (Cadre) sheets. The practical result; just as the Lama of Tibet keeps on turning the prayer-wheel - these people, like parrots, automatically memorized and repeated Communist slogans.

3 o. *What benefits were connected with your job?*

The SzTK law provided that the SzTK contributions are fully paid by the employer. There was no deduction from one's pay for this purpose. Employers were required to report all employees for this purpose including part-time help. Anyone who worked was assured free medical care. The medical sector too, was nationalized and, with the exception of a few outstanding specialists, all Hungarian physicians were employees of the SzTK. These physicians were permitted to maintain a private practice, but only after they satisfied their SzTK obligations.

If a person required hospitalization, from 25-75 percent of his pay was withheld for medical purposes. While he was ill he did not receive pay, but assistance. This assistance was paid by the SzTK. The amount withheld depended on a person's marital status, number of children and how long he worked continuously.

Otherwise medical and surgical care as well as medicine were free. When purchasing medicine one only paid for the handling and administrative costs, the drugs themselves were free of charge.

As a general rule, a person on sick leave received 50 percent of his pay if he worked less than two years continuously prior to his becoming sick. If he worked longer than two years, he lost only 25 percent of his basic pay. In practice it worked out as follows: a man who worked more than two years and who earned 1,000 forints prior to his illness, now received 750 forints as assistance from the SzTK. From this pay 50 percent, that is 350 forints was withheld for hospital purposes. He received then 300 forints per month while in the hospital.

SzTK was a social and good system in principle. It shows that people were taken care of in times of distress. Its disadvantage was that the medical care became mechanized. The SzTK physicians were not only taking care of the hospitalized sick but also went out visiting the out-patients (those who were at home), and there were a great many out-patients. Besides, he was burdened with administrative work, such as reporting of the diagnosis, keeping the patient's personal record, etc. In practice the doctor had no time, his work became a routine. There were many false diagnoses, the true nature of the illness was often not recognized, the wrong medicine was prescribed, etc. There was also the psychological point of view; sick people are more sensitive and in need of greater patience. The doctors did not have time for this. They were cold and rigid in their relations, mechanical in their actions. Complaints were many and the antipathy growing.

A hospitalized or sick person received his assistance money for a full year merely on the recommendation of his physician. If the illness continued for more than a year, the person was subjected to a re-examination, his status was re-evaluated and he may have lost a certain percentage of his support money. There was a night watchman in our factory whose leg was amputated. He was very ill for a long time. From time to time he had to come in and work for six weeks and then he continued on sick leave again.

Let us consider the vacations; the question of workers' "resorts" was handled by the SzTK. There were factory resorts also, maintained by factory funds, but these, too, were under SzTK supervision. The cost to vacationers of these facilities was a mere trifle. There were vacations which were completely free of charge. Others ran from one to eight forints per day covering all expenses. If the whole family was vacationing, then usually the father only had to pay, say, eight forints. The other members went free.

Vacations, too, went according to the Plan. The Plan laid down the number of people to be sent to resorts. The factory management decided who these people would be. The emphasis was on good workers. The unions, the plant management and the Party made these decisions.

There were resorts reserved for the sick. The SzTK district physician was empowered to make recommendations in this respect. As a rule, this was a rather difficult question and very few people succeeded in obtaining such accommodations.

People usually went to resorts which were situated in Hungary. Some went to Yugoslavia, Czechoslovakia, Rumania or the Soviet Union. All this was decided from above, people being selected for this or that resort.

The principle of the SzTK and the workers' resorts is laudable, but in reality there were many abuses. Those who were in the Party or otherwise associated with the regime were the ones who reaped the benefits.

Free tickets; in consequence of the SzTK membership a person or family received once a year a 50 percent discount on the nation's railroads. This could be used on any occasion, and for whatever distance, within Hungary.

4. What about the people you worked with? What sort of people were they?

Those were primitive (simple people). Most of them were young, and middle aged, not older than fifty. Their educational level was four-six grades of elementary school, the younger ones usually had six years of schooling. From 1953-1956, a number of former (earlier) existences (Lecsuszott existenciak) joined us (a former officer of the police, a former civil servant, a former teacher and others), people who could not get employment elsewhere. There were about five-six of these.

This was a provincial brick factory. Its labor force came from the village and from the adjoining villages. All workers were of peasant stock, about fifty percent of them single. There were many young girls 18-20 years of age. During the summer a large number of students, 17-19 years of age, joined us too. About 35 percent of the labor force were women. They were assigned lighter duties, such as feeding the machines, etc.

4 b. How did people get along at work?

Everyone was comrade or colleague to everybody else. (Elvtárs vagy szaktárs). This sort of address assumes equality, but the assumption is fallacious. We did not have the great degree of dependence (függöség) so characteristic of France, but the inequalities were there, nevertheless, in disguised form; the Party secretary did not have to use abusive or vituperative language when speaking to his "equals" in order to show his absolute superiority. If you work as you do now - he would say - you are hindering production. It seems to me that you intend to sabotage here. A "friendly" remark like this was extremely consequential.

4 c. Did you meet any of your colleagues (fellow workers) privately, socially?

Yes, I met a few people. My situation was a special one. Everybody knew me in the village. I was a member of Parliament after 1945. I knew many people and even more people knew me. Besides, in a small village, everyone seems to know everything about everyone else. They knew of my stay at Recsk and that I was under police surveillance. I was released in 1953, at a time when criticism became open and people loudly denounced and cursed the regime. In the village life was not as complicated as in intellectual circles. There a worker, even though a member of the Party, did not hesitate to speak his mind.

People always wondered what my opinion was. This is why I got my relatively good assignment at the factory. They placed me to the kiln because the workers demanded that I be put there. The past ten years taught these people many things; they learned to read newspapers regularly and to read in between the lines and to find out instantly that the paper is not telling the truth. They came to me and asked me to confirm their doubts and suspicions. At first I was afraid to answer them, later I answered them with a yes or no, but we got to know each other well and we did discuss things at length.

During the Revolution I spent all my time in Budapest. These people elected me chairman of the workers' council even though I was not there.

4 d. Did you discuss politics with any of them?

During 1953, I refrained from discussing politics, but later on we did have intensive discussions with a small group. I discussed a great many questions with some of the older workers, with the plant mechanic and with the kiln loader.

From 1953 to 1956, our factory was a normal place. The Party secretary was an old man, and an honorable man. He always sought to ask my advice. I had no difficulty with him at all. We were not friends, to be sure, he asked questions of me and

I answered them. It was mostly younger people that I had to be careful with.

4 e. *Was there a difference at work between Party members and non-Party people?*

Of course. These best jobs were in the hands of Party members. Jobs which paid less were assigned to non-Party people. This was one of the incentives which was used as a means of recruiting new members. At the kiln, "the best paid job", I was the only one who was not a Party member.

People did not enter the Party because they believed in it. Joining to them became a question of bread. Some people just out of universities had to make up their minds when entering one of the industrial enterprises. Their chances of advancement were entirely different if they were Party members. If they refused to join up, be they engineers or soldiers or what have you, they were given a subordinate assignment irrespective of talent or learning. Party members had advantages also in receiving preferential treatment when it came to vacations, using other SzTK facilities, finding an apartment or sending their children to the university.

4 f. *How did the trade union operate?*

Our trade union was very weak. Brick manufacture is a seasonal enterprise with a great fluctuation and turnover in its personnel. Because there was no great stability in this respect, they did not pay much attention to the union. Union membership did not have any practical significance, no advantage came from it, save in the question of vacations. It was the union which recommended people to be sent to cheap vacation resorts.

Otherwise it would have been the job of the union to concern itself with questions of production. But there was no possibility to do that. The union did work in the cultural sphere; it conducted seminars where political questions and, occasionally, questions of productions were introduced and discussed. Outside of the Party it was here, in the union, that an attempt was made to get hold of non-Party members, and to saturate them with Communist ideology.

Between 1948-1953, all people who worked, save for some employed as factory sweepers, necessarily belonged to the union. After 1953, this changed somewhat; many people did not pay their dues and did not regularly attend union meetings. These meetings were held bi-weekly, revolving around a program worked out by the union leadership; there were several cultural groups, sports, library, the union organized celebrations on May 1, August 20, there was dancing and drinking.

The union was conducted by the chairman - secretary and the culture and sport referees. These were not paid positions, and were considered to be voluntary contributions for the development of society. The officers of the unions were elected (they were not real elections, however).

4 g. Did the union undergo any changes since 1945?

In 1945, the unions were in the hands of the Social Democrats. But even then there was a large number of Communists in the Social Democratic ranks, people who were accepted by the Social Democrats during the Horthy regime where Communists and Communist activity were illegal. These people remained even after 1945, and gradually took over the direction. In 1948, the two parties merged and were known as the Hungarian Workers' Party.

One of the reasons why the workers' council movement was originated was the widespread recognition of the great influence Stalinists and Rákosists played in the life of the labor union. One of the chief aims of the movement was to cleanse the unions of these elements, and to bring in new people and new spirit in the labor movement. The labor unions represented a tremendous network. In larger factories union leaders were among the best paid men in the industry.

4 h. Did you encounter the work of the "mediation committees"?

There were no mediation committees in our factory.

4 i. Was there a "shop triangle"? If so, how did it operate?

Yes, there was a shop triangle. It consisted of the plant director, Party secretary and the chairman of the labor union. Outwardly, the triangle did not perform any function at all. It did not have a legal basis. The triangle was a creature of the Party. In practice, however, the triangle represented the supreme leadership of the factory. All three members worked in the plant, they were in close contact with each other and represented the inner cabinet of the plant. They saw to it that technical directives were kept, they determined who worked where and what. They were the masters of hiring and firing. They decided whether a given offender would be prosecuted and to what extent. In a word they kept their own affairs well coordinated and while you could not feel their direct influence - they never acted in the open as members of the triangle - everyone knew that the three men were absolute masters of life and death.

4 j. Could a specialist get ahead even if he was not politically reliable?

It all depended on what kind of relationship the specialists had with the shop triangle. Generally speaking he could not go ahead if he was not reliable politically. The basic consideration in determining whether a man was suitable or not to perform a confidential task continued to be his Káder (Cadre) sheet. There were, of course, small and limited possibilities within a factory, if the individual was on friendly terms with the triangle.

4 k. Were any incompetent people advanced because of political connections?

This was a very general and widespread phenomenon in Hungary, especially under the rule of the Communists. Jobs were not tied to formal qualifications. "From everyone according to his ability" is a well known Communist slogan. In reality the good Káders were given absolute preference. Workers became factory directors. This widespread dilettantism very often had the gravest consequences. Factory directors accepted and pledged the performance of tasks which were far beyond the factory's capacity. Being ignorant of both production capacity and procedure, they not only pledged the performance of tasks which were hopelessly beyond their capabilities, but they refused to subsequently recognize their error and extorted through blood and sweat the execution of their exorbitant plans. This meant, of course, a reduction of the workers' real wages, because premium payments were largely eliminated. Another important result of this was the inferior quality of the finished product.

4 l. Did political officials interfere with operations? Were instructions handed down that ran counter to rational operations? If so, was it possible to remonstrate?

In the shop triangle, the Party secretary was one of the members. This meant in practice that he supervised the factory's work. Production ceased to be an economic task alone. It became permeated with politics. Whatever we did we did so for political reasons. We worked hard because of Stalin's birthday, we raised quotas and production targets because of lesser or bigger political considerations.

Since production sabotage fell within the immediate competence of the AVH, the role of the political supervisor took an enormous significance. The Party secretary never handed down direct instructions, he limited himself to making comments and observations. Such comments and observations never failed to have the force of a direct command, and their execution did not always tend to make a task of an individual worker or of a whole factory an easier one, or more rational.

To remonstrate against the Party secretary was extremely difficult indeed. If somebody did object to his proposal, such person was usually depicted as an enemy of the Peoples' Democracy, as a saboteur. Once a person was thus branded, the accusations did not fail to have a devastating effect on him. The accused was ruined for all practical purposes for, just as if you accused somebody here of homosexuality, he is considered as a moral outcast in his community, without having a chance or possibility of defending himself.

4 m. Did all this vary much between 1948 and 1956?

There was a change after 1953, in this respect. One could object, with a fair degree of immunity, to obviously wrong procedures. After the effect of the Twentieth Congress became felt in Hungary, a greater freedom of speech was permitted within the framework of legality. Party secretaries became more cautious and reserved. If differences of opinion did develop, the AVH was not called in automatically. This was a tremendous change. It was this development which resulted in the widespread discussion among the workers of the grave injustices perpetrated against them. The basic fallacy of the regime's industrial policy, the norm system, and many other grievances became the common objects of discussion. The very fact that people were allowed to talk about these things represented a tremendous change.

The various daily and periodical publications also discussed these questions, a circumstance which contributed a great deal to freer discussion among the people. The question of professional competence was one of the many topics considered. The very broaching of this question tended to cut the Party secretaries down to their true size. They were admonished to meddle only in those things and to talk only when they knew what they were talking about.

4 n. Who were the good Káder? What were the criteria for someone's being a Káder?

This is a difficult question. I am not familiar with the Communist principles on which the classification was based.

There was the category of peasant or worker origin. But here, too, were sub-categories; there were the poor peasants and the rich peasants. The kulaks were not good Káders. Regarding intellectuals, the criterion was the parents' relationship to, and the view of, the Communist Party. A person's relationship to his work in the Party, in the labor union, was another consideration.

Regarding peasants, three categories were recognized: a) poor peasants. This meant agricultural laborers and people of this category, who as a result of the land reform, received some land, usually five holds. b) Middle or working peasants; these were people who held land, about 10-20 holds, either as a result of the land reform or otherwise, who cultivated their own land and did not employ any agricultural day-laborers. c) Kulaks were people who held 20-25 or more holds of land, employed outsiders on their land and perhaps were engaged in other activities also.

4 p. Were there any secret sections or ÁVO informers in your place of work?
If so, what sort of people were they and what did they do? Can you give any examples?

There were no secret sections at my place of work. It was a very small establishment. These people were usually found in larger enterprises. The personnel-section head of the association of brick factories, for instance, was an AVH informer.

The personnel section employed a number of agents (these did not strictly belong to the AVH). These were well paid, comfortable positions. The agents' task was to make mood and tendency reports, to describe how a meeting was conducted, what the reactions were. They were to observe the behavior of people in key positions, to report on the way they handled and treated men, etc. These reports did not go to the Plant leadership but, through the personnel section were forwarded directly to the AVH.

Informers we had in our plant also. The chairman of the operating committee (üzemi bizottság) was one of them.

The operating committee was responsible for the promotion of production, for drawing in of workers into the direction of the plant. This committee was charged with the organization of production as well as with the promotion of productivity. The committee was to make certain that the best qualified experts occupied the key positions. It was this committee which negotiated the collective contracts with the factory. The contract in turn defined the work within the economic plan as well as the production goals. The committee further determined the type and amount of raw materials needed and what new machines, etc., would have to be acquired. The operating committee, on the other hand, pledged in the name of the workers that the norms would be satisfied and reached to such and such (in percentages) a degree, that such and such innovations (újitások) would be carried out, that the quality of the finished products would be raised, etc. The committee also concerned itself - in general terms only - with the question of wages insofar as the given norm system permitted this. The operating committee was an elected body and cooperated closely with the factory leadership and the labor union. In our factory the chairman of the operating committee and the secretary of the labor union was one and the same person.

Everyone knew that the chairman was an informer. He was rather an unpopular figure and one had to behave himself correctly (vonalasan kellet viselkedni) if in the chairman's proximity. The chairman, on his part, was trying to prove to everybody that this is the correct way, rather than the other, because the Party wants it this way.

This man reported on everyone. He was the strongest man in the factory after the Party secretary. Everybody was afraid of him. The chairman's role was probably greater than that of the Party secretary; the Party secretary acted through the chairman of the operating committee and his views, personal and official, were known in advance. The views of the chairman, on the other hand, became known only after the AVH arrived on the scene. I, of course, began working after 1953, at a time when even the AVH's power was somewhat limited.

5. *What possibilities were there for changing jobs?*

Labor laws, passed in 1950 and on, rendered the workers' possibilities of changing jobs more and more difficult. Before a worker could change jobs he had to secure the consent of the factory leadership. A worker did not have the right to terminate his employment, to quit a job, under any circumstance. If he did quit, his action was considered arbitrary (önkényesen) in which case he could secure employment with the aid of employment agencies only. These employment agencies invariably sent him to a mine or to some other hard physical labor.

Each factory had a Committee on Discipline (fegyelmi bizottság). This Committee was empowered to institute disciplinary action against any worker on the recommendation of either the labor union or of the Operating Committee. Such action took the form of a verbal or written rebuke, of a transfer within the factory to a lower paying job, or a dishonorable discharge (fegyelmi elbocsájtás). This latter carried with it all the consequences of arbitrary quitting, as explained above. Whatever form the punishment took, it was duly recorded into the worker's workbook as well as in his Káder sheet.

The punished worker had the right to appeal to the labor union's Committee on Conciliation (Szakszervezeti eggyeztetö bizottság) but the act of appeal did not invalidate the disciplinary Committee's action (ez nem volt halasztó hatályú). As a decision of this appellate body could be further appealed to the industry's Committee on Conciliation (iparági egyeztetö bizottság). The decision of this authority was final.

5 a. *Why did you change positions? Under what circumstances would you have changed your job?*

I did not have any possibility at all to change my job, as I have explained previously, I was living under police supervision. I was restricted to this village and there was no other place available.

Other people, not so restricted, changed, or would have changed, their jobs to better themselves economically. Also, people whose political past was compromised and who, as a result, lost their jobs and now worked as unskilled laborers, tried to better themselves by attempting to become skilled laborers. Such people wanted to change jobs in order to be near a school where they could take courses. Still others had tried to get back to their old fields, even if they had to work in a subordinate position.

5 b. *If you had been free to choose your work, what kind of job would you have picked for yourself? Why?*

Under such circumstances I would have gone back to my own field. This is natural and self-explanatory. Why? Because of monetary considerations and considerations of comfort and convenience.

5 c. Do you think you had a chance to be successful in Hungary?

I think I would have had a chance in Hungary. This, of course, is rather hypothetical. I was assuming that the trend originated by Imre Nagy would have continued. With him the process of rehabilitation got under way. Communists were rehabilitated first but other groups too, we hoped, would have been considered later. I got into my predicament unjustly, I sat in prison for five years without ever being tried in court, imprisoned simply on the strength of a Party decision. I assume that I might have gotten a chance to be rehabilitated later. The police supervision would have been lifted and I probably would have returned to the type of work and existence that would have been suitable and satisfactory. These, of course, are but hypotheses. If the Revolution had succeeded, I certainly would have had a variety of personal contacts and my future prospects would have been favorable.

5 d. In general, did you think people want to succeed or get ahead?

The question, I am afraid, is ambiguous. It all depends on what you mean by succeeding and getting ahead. If your meaning is making as much money as possible, then my answer is yes. If, on the other hand, success is to be equated with seeking governmental and/or social recognition, then I must answer in the negative. Indeed many people rejected the prestige and acclaim - which was theirs just for the asking - just in order to preserve their moral convictions. People did try very hard to secure themselves a more or less comfortable living, but they definitely did not seek or desire recognition.

There were writers who donated the proceeds of their Kossuth Prize - they were not allowed to refuse the acceptance of the distinction itself - to people who were less fortunate than themselves in order to thereby declare that they are in no way in agreement with the government.

The young generation, too, attempted to gravitate towards such fields, and to work their way into (beásni) such positions where they hoped this to be realizable without becoming Party members. This, of course, was a hard task. For leading positions Party membership, and the type of Party work one performed, was certainly not the least factor considered. Professional competence, while a factor, was only of secondary importance.

Scientists and artists excepted, - these formed a separate category - the leading positions everywhere were occupied not by the most able and most competent, but by the better Káders, by those whose fidelity to both Party and ideology left nothing to be desired.

5 e. Suppose you got the sort of living conditions you like -- what would you spend your money on, and what would you do with your leisure time?

I can only give you a hypothetical answer; books have been always one of my great passions. I spent a large amount of money on them. I enjoyed collecting books of exquisite types and binding. Money is of no importance if I get hold of a book of good typography. I also enjoy going to the theater, or to travel in a leisurely fashion, - something again which requires money. I would travel, if I could afford it, would inspect in every little detail everything from the great masterpieces of art to the way people lived and acted.

5 f. What were your ideas of this before you left Hungary?

I did not have any ideas about the above; I had neither time nor opportunity to concern myself with thoughts of this nature. It certainly was not my most important problem.

5 g. *If you had stayed in Hungary, would you have wanted your children to do the same kind of work as you did? Why?*

Naturally not. This is rather self-explanatory. Every man, I think, has within him the innate desire of creating for himself and for his offspring better opportunities. The work I did was neither pleasant nor good.

6. *How well off do you think you (your family) were since the war?*

It was fairly hard. My father was a poor peasant, possessing only a few acres of land. We lived not far away from Budapest. We were fruit growers, specializing in peaches. We sold a significant amount of peaches for export before the war and the inland marketing possibilities were equally very good. After the war the possibility both of exporting and of local marketing dropped markedly until, as a result of forced collectivization it vanished completely. Our income suffered a drastic reduction.

Between 1945 and 1947, we were not badly off. After my arrest my family lived under extremely reduced material circumstances and there was no improvement either after I got out in 1953, and began working in the brick factory. I was living with my wife after 1953, and we had not enough money for clothing, let alone for satisfying our cultural needs.

6 b. *What sort of things could you afford to buy, and what couldn't you afford?*

We could afford to buy food, primary necessities, to pay for rent, and to get the minimum amount of clothing. Whatever went beyond this was beyond our reach. Before we could buy a book, or a theater ticket, we had to hold a family consultation and juggle our budget around, giving up something else.

6 c. *Did you feel you personally (your family, household) were getting a fair income?*

According to Hungarian standards my income was not a bad one.

6 d. *Did you feel you were being exploited? If so, by whom? What do you mean by "exploited"?*

I was definitely exploited. I worked, for five years, against my will in a hard labor camp, without any compensation. Even after I was set free, I was obliged to spend my days in a factory, as a menial laborer, when I could have performed other jobs, at much higher pay and with far greater satisfaction. So I definitely think that I was exploited.

The state was the exploiter. Under the cover of socialist phraseology and slogans a state capitalism developed, a capitalism which pocketed unheard of sums as profit. The state reaped this profit not as a reward for risking its capital, but as a consequence of a deliberate state and social policy. The state justified this tremendous exploitation by its desire to develop a significant heavy industry. To bring about this heavy industry enormous investments were necessary. To solve the problem of financing these investments, a systematic lowering of the living standard was instituted and "peace loans" were forced upon us (10% of our gross income) to further rob us of our incomes.

Exploitation is when a worker does not receive compensation for his work. By compensation I mean value of his product less the necessary production costs.

7. *I should like to know more about how people made and spent money.*
   What was your wage (salary) in:

   (i)   1947? 800 forints per month
   (ii) 1952? no income;
   (iii) 1955? 1400-1500 forints per month.

7 a. How did your pay compare with that of people who had other types of work?

My income (of 1955) corresponded to that of an average skilled laborer. I was not a skilled laborer, but with my work at the kiln and the additional bonus I received as a compensation for the heat there, my income did amount to that much.

7 b. How did your pay compare with that of others who did the same kind of work?

I had the highest pay in the trade.

7 c. How many members of your family (household) were working? Why?

My wife was working also. She worked at a statistical concern (gépstatisztikai vállalatnál) making circa 1,000 forints per month. My father-in-law, we were living with him, received a pension of 400 forints.

My wife was working because my income alone did not suffice to keep us going. The employment of women was consciously fostered by the regime. Workers' wages were so calculated to be sufficient for the maintenance of one person only. If a household had several members, then as many members of the household as were capable had to go to work since one man's pay in no way covered the whole family's expenses.

9. *Let me just ask you a few things in addition to those on the form. What were dwelling conditions like?*

This was the greatest problem of them all. There were innumerable joint tenants (társbérlö); one apartment was shared by two or more families. Dwelling needs of individuals and families were strictly regulated. A married couple was allowed a room and a kitchen. If they had children, they could aspire to two rooms and a kitchen. In the case of a physician, a university professor, or a creative artist an additional room was assigned.

All apartments were rented out through the intermediary of the Housing Bureau (lakáshivatal). Recently married couples very often continued to live separately, others did not marry because of the severe housing problem. The Housing Bureau, when assigning available space, took into consideration the applicant's political reliability. Good Káders were given a preference.

From the point of view of plumbing and appliances, Budapest was a much better place than the provinces. Many of the apartment houses had central heating systems, and were equipped with bathrooms. In the provinces such things as running hot and cold water and bathing facilities were rather a rarity.

The best furnished places were the old apartments. Furniture was very expensive. One room furniture, mass-produced (typusbutor) was 8,000 to 10,000 forints and up. People were saving for many years to buy one room of furniture, or else were paying their debt month after month for years.

9 a. *On the average, how much time did you (your wife, your mother) spend waiting in queues? For what items?*

Consumer goods of the everyday variety were occasionally difficult to get. Such items as sugar, salt, flour, etc. A shipment would arrive to the local store and people would immediately swarm the place. The period 1953-1956, was relatively better.

Up until 1953, the distribution of food proceeded on the basis of coupons (élelmiszerjegyek). This, of course, necessitated long queues.

The case was not better even after 1953, regarding such items as lemons, rice and imported products generally or items which Hungary did not produce in sufficient quantities. One was obliged to stand in lines also when purchasing the Sunday meat on Saturday. Since no refrigeration facilities were available in private homes, such meat could not be bought earlier. Very often we also had to wait long when purchasing lard. In a word, the items for which we waited, sometimes in vain, varied from time to time, only the waiting in queues persisted. Once a person got into the store, he was limited to a certain quantity, i.e., a pound of rice, two pounds of meat, etc., depending on the available supply. These amounts were usually posted.

9 b. In general, did the availability of food vary a good deal? On what items in particular?

The availability of food varied a great deal. But the supply of clothing items also fluctuated. This was also true of stationary goods, particularly in the fall. Often enough many of these things were available but the planning was haphazard and the calculations faulty. Somewhere along the line a bureaucrat missed a number or two which then resulted in a general confusion.

9 c. How much of the household's income was spent in state stores, in peasant markets, on black markets, and what sort of things were bought in each?

Most items were purchased in state stores. There were hardly any other possibilities. The few private stores or artisans who still existed charged much higher prices. Their tax was high and they received their products at much higher prices from the warehouses than the state stores. Peasant markets there were none. Vegetables and fruit we produced in our own garden. We went to the black market for such items as rice, pepper, lemons, caraway seed (köménymag), etc. Prices there ran to 130-150 percent.

9 d. Did all this vary much from 1948 to 1956?

There was an improvement after 1953. The export shipments were reduced and the domestic supply became better. The improvement was particularly noticeable in food items. Also, after 1953, some of the factories devoted some of their production capacity to consumer goods. Coal shovels, for instance, appeared after 1953, for the first time again.

10. In general, how did you feel (what did you think) about the development of the Hungarian economy?

The organization of Hungary's economic life was based on a hypothesis or, to be more precise, on one of the doctrines of the Communist Party. According to this the state must have a significant heavy industry and continuous industrialization is a must. The degree of transformation of an agricultural state into an industrial state is at the same time the measure of socialist progress and achievement. In the Soviet Union this development is 30 years old and it certainly was not a fortunate one. In Hungary these changes were brought about within eight years, without capital, and the developments were based solely on a systematic lowering of the population's standard of living. The entire program was carried out by reducing the population to naked poverty.

After 1948, a series of large capital investments were effected, investments which represented a very large portion of our national income. Characteristic of the proposals of these investments is the iron works of Stálinváros. The huge undertaking was originally built in Mohács. The plan was to utilize iron ore from Yugoslavia and coal from the neighboring satellite countries. The huge structure was half way finished at Mohács when our relations with Yugoslavia were broken. Whereupon the plant was dismantled and was transferred to Stalinváros, there to operate on the basis of Russian ore and Polish coal. The truth is that there is not even a faint hope that this concern will be able to operate rationally and economically after the lapse of a few decades.

Take the underground railway (Budapest subway); this project was started around 1950, and it cost the state many millions each year. Having expended enormous sums, the project was abandoned in 1953. As it turned out, the sub-soil of Budapest was not suitable for the construction of a railway; the soil was too loose.

Take the construction of the main eastern canal (Keleti föcsatorna); this was started during 1948 or 1949. The canal runs through the Hortobágy Puszta and connects the Tisza and Maros Rivers. This project was of more value. While it drained the economy and made life more difficult, it at the same time turned the Hortobágy Puszta into arable land. Irrigation also improved the arid regions of Nagykunság.

The hydro-electric works (erőmű) of Tiszapolkány was also another ambitious project; a dam was built there on the Tisza for the production of electricity. Another large undertaking was the combine of Kazinc-Barczika, and one could go on enumerating the many lesser works which were constructed.

Of these, Tiszapolkány, Kazinc-Barczika and the quarry (kőbánya) of Recsk were constructed in their entirety by Hungarian prisoners, who were not paid a cent for their labors.

As a result of these enormous capital investments, the peace loans were raised to 10-15 percent, and the large-scale construction was financed partly by a lowering of the workers' wages and partly by the tightening of the norms. The capital which ought to have been used for the production of consumers' goods was all channeled into the heavy industry sector.

The agricultural economy was disrupted and an accelerated collectivization was forced upon the farmer. All this with the view of securing enough wheat for bread and fodder for the livestock.

The entire economic policy was mistaken and defective; Hungary had lost her mineral territories after the First World War. We did not have any of the important raw materials which, if available, could have justified the bringing into being of a heavy industry. All our raw materials had to be imported and, as a result, our industrial products were too expensive, incapable of competing with goods of other countries either in European or world markets.

The heavy industry thus created was not in the position of producing quality products because, hoping to reduce costs, the regime constantly tried to use raw materials available in Hungary as substitutes for imported raw materials. Also, transportation problems were notoriously unsolved, supplies were delayed, production targets, at the same time, had to be met in full. The result: a high percentage of scrap and rejects (selejt).

Imre Nagy recognized all this and, in his 1953 speech to the Parliament, gave an excellent analysis of our economic maladies. In outlining his policy he defined the reduction of the heavy industry and the intensification of agricultural production as his goal. There was to be a pronounced emphasis on those branches of the industry which could utilize our own agricultural products as raw materials.

10 a. Was it a healthy development?

No. It was not a healthy development.

10 b. Was anything wrong with it?

Our economic structure should have been adapted to the naturally existing conditions of the country. The Soviet Union was in a position to do what she did economically, because she had an abundant supply of raw materials, and she could erect factories on sites where the raw materials lay. We were in no position to duplicate this procedure. More than that, our whole economic structure was thus built and designed under pressure and at the instigation of the Soviet Union. The Soviet Union wanted to see a heavy industry in Hungary because she wanted to create a market for her surplus raw materials which she was able to sell at high prices. In contrast, uranium ore, the raw material we ourselves possessed in significant quantities and which we should have exploited ourselves, was handed over by our government to the Soviet Union. The Soviet Union had an exclusive concession in this field and Hungarian scientists, including the nuclear physicist, Professor Jánossy, were not even permitted to come near the scene. Jánossy was taken to the Soviet Union later and his fate is not known.

The situation was similar with regard to our bauxite resources. This aluminum ore was shipped out, partly in raw form, partly in the form of a semi-finished metal, to the Soviet Union and returned to Hungary as a finished product. The situation was very similar to that prevailing during the Austro-Hungarian monarchy; our raw materials were shipped out and we were obliged to purchase the expensive finished goods back again.

10 c1. What about the economic situation in Hungary before 1941?

The basic fact here is that after Trianon, Horthy and his entourage took over the power in Hungary, they used this power for their own personal economic benefit. Secure in their own little world they were foolish enough not to carry out the necessary reforms. This self-centered attitude characterizes the policies of the Horthy regime between the two wars.

To this basic fact we must add the equally important element of Hungary's actual position after the first World War; we were forced to pay reparations, our mineral resources were taken away from us, and the worldwide economic crisis affected Hungary much more than it did other countries.

After 1938, the war did bring about an economic upswing, but our economic situation in the inter-bellum period nevertheless must be considered as a negative one.

Our great economic problems were great indeed already after the First World War. But the greatest of these, the land reform and the adequate adjustment of our wage policies remained unsolved. Had they been solved adequately in time, perhaps our whole orientation might have been different and perhaps the post war events after 1945 would also have taken a different course and trend.

10 c2. And between 1941 and 1944?

In 1938, a general economic revival and prosperity set in and this continued well into the war years. We have supplied Germany with all kinds of goods, a great amount of industrial products came to us from there and, with these, also entered the German Mark. There was a total employment and unemployment was non-existent. During this time the Jews were gradually forced out of Hungary's industrial and business rank fields where, up until 1941, they had a considerable basis and influence. Many a person was able to secure for himself a good job during this period, capital became more freely available, primarily to those who were in the Horthy camp. This, we must bear in mind, was plain robbery; they took things away from one group and gave that to another group, which, in itself, is not an economic achievement but simply lifting of a less advantageously situated strata into a better position.

10 d. Do you think the changes in the economy after 1944 were an improvement or a deterioration? In what ways?

The period immediately after 1944, was, for Hungary, a period following a lost war. A lost war never did bring about an improvement in the economy. We were robbed by the Germans and, when they left, we were robbed by the Russians. If you add to this the damage caused by bombings and armies fighting on our soil, and the resultant dislocation and chaos, the result is economic disaster.

The land reform itself represented a great dislocation and chaos and loss in our agriculture but we had to view it as a social and human obligation and we carried it out.

Between 1945-1947 there was a decided improvement and progress, especially after August 1946, when our new currency, the forint, reached a high stability.

The currency reform and stabilization was carried out according to plans made by Béla Imrédy. Imrédy, the former prime minister and foremost currency expert, was incarcerated at the time. He prepared his blueprints at his leisure in jail and offered them to Rákosi in exchange for his life. He sent his plans to Rákosi and Rákosi used them but Imrédy was executed, nevertheless. Forint, the very name of the new monetary unit was Imrédy's idea. Imrédy gone, the Communist Party claimed credit in all the world for the excellent work.

After 1946, our export to the West was considerable. The small land holders achieved good results and the industrial and commercial undertakings, still privately owned, began an unprecedented expansion. The most interesting phenomenon in this post-war industrial expansion was the tendency of agricultural-industrial cooperation. Agriculture tended to abandon the traditional practice of producing cereals only and turned more and more to industrial crops; industry, in turn, gravitated automatically so to speak, to types of production where agricultural products were the raw materials.

The splendid development was cut to pieces by the Communists in 1948. What happened after 1948, should become increasingly evident to you from what I have said earlier during the interview.

10 e. Did you hear of any discussions in the government or Party about how much consumer goods to produce?

The argument of consumer goods versus heavy industry and capital goods was not a sharp and pronounced one between 1945-1948. The cabinet was practically unanimous then that our industry should primarily devote itself to the production of consumer goods. The argument began in 1947, during the debate on the first Three-Year Plan when the Communists tossed in the question of heavy industry, more specifically the tooling industry (szerszámgépipar). They proposed that Hungary should build up a heavy industry and pave the way for the production of tooling machines for export.

Even as these discussions went on during the Three-Year Plan debate, the MÁVAG was voted a large sum for investment purposes practically without a debate.

The debates centered around the pregnant question of Socialist versus bourgeois-democratic (polgári-demokrata) economics. Foremost among the opponents of Socialist economics was József Bognár who later became one of the most subservient servants of the regime.

It was this debate on theory which served as a basis of attack against the right-wing of the Social Democratic Party, leading ultimately to the elimination of the Social Democratic Party in June 1948, when the Hungarian Workers' Party (MDP) was created.

The economic policy of Imre Nagy in 1953 represented a sharp rejection of the entire concept of forceful industrialization. After

1953, the still unfinished larger projects (such as the Budapest subway) were simply abandoned. The production of consumer goods was emphasized and was carried out even in the machine tool industry.

10 f. What about the re-emergence of the private sector (maszek) in the last few years?

After 1953, very many people (farmers) left the agricultural kolhozes. This set the pattern and soon a number of small-scale service industries (ellátó kisipar) and artisan workshops (kisműhelyek) sprang up everywhere.

As the political struggle between Rákosi and Nagy fluctuated in this period, so appeared waves of contradictory orders, some favoring, some impeding the re-establishment of the private sector. Nagy said the farmers could leave the co-operatives, while Rákosi insisted that first they would have to pay in full and in cash their share of the co-operatives' debts. They were free to go and to become independent farmers again, but their livestock and implements could not be taken out. They not only had to pay but also had to re-invest in implements and livestock. Not very many were financially strong enough to do so.

This same thing happened to the small merchants. Yes, they did get their licenses and permits to operate again, but these licenses were issued for stores to be opened in the peripheries and outlying districts where it did not pay to open a store in the first place. Those who did choose independence, nonetheless, soon found out how utterly dependent they were on supplies from the government warehouses. They were given limited supplies from the government warehouses. They were given limited supplies and even that only once in a while. Whatever they received they sold at a higher price because they themselves received those goods at a higher price from the government, and the people, driven by necessity, all gravitated to the government stores where everything was cheaper.

The fate of the small artisans was not much brighter. They had a hard time trying to find raw materials. If and when they received a supply from the government, they, too, had to pay a higher price than their counterparts in government stores. Thus, if you wanted to patronize a private cobbler, and brought him your shoes for repair, you also had to bring with you a pair of soles.

This went on until the Revolution. The process of liberalization reached a critical point in 1955. Hegedüs did not at once try to erase all that Nagy brought about. 1953-1956 is pretty much a unit, the actual repression is beginning to be re-introduced only in 1956. Neither the people (individually) nor public opinion were prepared to acquiesce in and accept this retrogression and this, no doubt, contributed to the outbreak of the Revolution.

10 g. How were things in the last year before the revolt, materially -- better or worse? Explain.

Things were better in 1956, than in the period 1948-1953, but were worse than under Nagy.

Since Nagy eliminated from his program the large-scale industrilization and since projects already begun were abandoned, peace-loans were no longer compulsory. Neither did Hegedüs dare touch the norms. While the norms remained the same, factory leaders shut their eyes to the many rationalizations (simplification of processes) and so the norms remained loose.

In agriculture, forced deliveries continued to be the rule, but peasants were permitted to sell at the same time whatever surplus they might have had on the open (not regulated) agricultural markets.

There was a better supply of consumer goods and gradually people were able to buy a few items occasionally.

There was also a noticeable ray of sunlight in the political climate. People began to move around more freely and many of them changed their jobs. All this could be accomplished without the former red tape and without a careful scrutiny of the Káder sheets. After 1953, - though the old formalities remained - people were usually granted permission to change jobs whenever they applied for such a change. This resulted in more freedom and better income. Coupled with this, participation in political discussions also lost much of its dangers and terrors of former times.

11. Among the various complaints people had, how important do you think material conditions were?

They were very important, indeed. The fact is indisputable that the people were conscious of how useless and hopeless a life they were leading. There was not a ray of hope there. They earned just enough to buy what were really the bare necessities of life, only occasionally having some money left for something else.

There was in Hungary no possibility of saving for the sake of security (Teljes vagyonbizonytalanság uralkodott). People could not even aspire to purchase for themselves such things as a house, farm, etc., the possession of which represents the ultimate aim and goal in the lives of most individuals.

This created a certain discontentment. Opportunities of earning money were equally not within the free choice of the workers. He was transferred from one job to another without having any say-so in his own fate. This, too, nourished the discontentment. These were some of the economic problems of the average man and all his other grievances were rooted in this basic problem, he registered them (became aware of them) through, and because of, his economic troubles. It was through his material conditions that he saw the various injustices and peculiarities of the regime; he could not buy a book, or he could not buy what he wanted to buy. It was through this all that people saw how they were standing face to face with a state power, a colossus that declares the happiness and well-being of people to be its only aim, a colossus, however, whose visible actions distinctly negate and oppose its declared lofty aim.

We did not revolt earlier because it was not possible and because we were not sure ourselves. We were exposed to Communism for the first time only after 1948. We tasted it and we still waited for the results they promised. Later we saw how the building is cracking, how presumably sage and wise men do nothing about it, or can do nothing about it. Soon came the writers, the Petőfi Circle, people took on courage and became resolute and determined. Still later came the rehabilitation of Rajk. That, indeed, was an incredibly stupendous event.

People, when they are in a very difficult situation and are weak will suffer (türnek), but when they eat, they stretch (kinyujtóznak), their aims become higher and they are no longer prepared to suffer. A man who is writhed with pain and is laying on the ground is not a dangerous man. But if he thinks he is able to hit then things may happen. Revolutions happen in the spring.

11 a. How important were they for you?

I could repeat again what I said to the previous question. Economic interest is one of the greatest moving forces in a man's life. Well understood egotism is the driving force in economics (Helyesen felfogott önérdek a nemzetgazdaság mozgató ereje) said Adam Smith once.

Certainly economic affairs are more important than cultural affairs. I may forego the latter but I cannot go without bread.

11 b. What other complaints were more (equally) important?

The question does not sound right (Sántit egy kicsit a kérdés). All other complaints are stemming from economic problems. We had to keep quiet because of the AVH. We witnessed the elevation of a few men to positions of gods. These men, in their new capacities, were declared infallible and we had to do whatever they told us to do in spite of the fact that we say that they were wrong. There was the question of prisons; there were few families who did not have someone or another in prisons. There was the absence of consumer goods and innumerable smaller grievances.

11 c. For what groups of people in particular?

There were only three groups of people (peasants, workers, intellectuals) and people in every group had plenty to complain about. (I'm not speaking here of Party members and other privileged segments.)

The independent peasants were burdened with taxes, bailiffs (végrehajtó). The AVH and the TSzCs delegations constantly pressed them to enter the cooperatives. Those who were members of the cooperatives did not earn enough money to live by. They were forced to go and work someplace else during the winter.

The factory worker made 800-1400 forints per month. Both he and his wife were working to be able to feed their children. While they were working, the children were at home, alone, doing whatever they pleased. They could not buy enough food, let alone clothes. The men were drinking, in despair. Never before were there so many alcoholics in Hungary. Completely drunk, they would go home with their wives waiting for them already full of complaints; no potatoes, no shoes, etc.

The intellectuals; they were poorly paid. Every move of theirs was strictly checked and observed; their relationship to work, political checks, etc. There would be meetings, the seminars, the comments they were forced to make, the newspapers they were forced to read, the praising of Stalin and of others, all these did not tend to cheer up the intellectuals.

There was a slight chance for the better during 1953-56, but that was only a temporary relaxation -- a slightly more humane life -- not a real change.

Social Status, Education, Family, and Religion

EDUCATION

1. What schooling did you have in Hungary?

I have completed three years of study at the University.

1 a. When did you attend school? For how long?

I attended a Jewish elementary school in Turkeve (1930-1934); I spent the next four years at a high school, the Budapest Állami Váci-úti Polgári Iskola, (1934-1938); I spent the next four years (1938-1942) at the Budapest Vas-utcai gróf Széchenyi István college of commerce (felsökereskedelmi) taking my maturity examination (érettségi) in 1942. From 1942 to 1944 I attended the School of Economics of the József Nádor Technical and Economic University (József Nádor Müszaki és Gazdasági Egyetem Közgazdasági Kara). My studies were interrupted between 1944 and 1947. In 1947, I went back to the same university and studied for another year (1947-1948).

1 b. Did you attend public or parochial school?

I received my elementary school training at a denominational (Jewish) school. Thereafter I always attended public schools.

1 c. Did you attend school after 1945? If so, please describe it.

Yes. At the time I attended university it was still conducted according to the old system. The reorganization of the universities began only in the fall of 1948. After 1948, this school became a Marxist university. There was no structural change until 1948 and the professors were not replaced either.

1 d. Did you attend any evening school or special technical school?

No.

1 e. What made you choose this school (these schools)?

My parents did not enjoy good material circumstances. Sending me to school presented a great problem. My parents were simple people. My grade school teacher finally persuaded them of the advisability of sending me to higher schools. The four-year high school (polgári) appeared to them to be the most feasible and, at the same time, the cheapest one. Having reached good results there, it was again one of my high school instructors who convinced my parents of the need of my continuing my studies. He recommended commercial college because there no Latin background was necessary (I did not have a Latin background). Having graduated from the college of commerce (kereskedelmi), I made the personal decision of entering the Economics University; in this decision I was prompted by the unsettled economic conditions of Hungary. Questions which always interested me deeply, the land reform, the social status of peasants and workers, made me decide to study and acquaint myself more thoroughly with the problems of our country's economic life. This is why I decided to study economics.

2. Did you feel you had received (you were getting, you would get) as much schooling as you wanted?

Yes.

2 a. How much schooling did you want?

I wanted to finish my studies at the University, go earn a

Ph.D. degree. I contemplate continuing my studies even now.

2 c. *Do you think your life might have been different if you had had more schooling? If yes, in what ways?*

Viewing my career in Hungary, I believe I managed to get what I wanted to get. I was a Member of Parliament and the leader of the largest youth group in Hungary. After all, a man 22-23 years old cannot desire much more than that.

2 d. *What sort of student were you -- average, below average, above average?*

All in all, I was a superior student. Otherwise I could not very well have continued my studies. My parents made the immense sacrifice of letting me go. I had to take care of the rest. I did not have to pay tuition and I received all my textbooks free of charge.

2 e. *Did you have the same opportunity as everyone else to receive an education?*

This would be an overstatement. In studies, yes, there I did have equal opportunity. But those who enjoyed better economic circumstances acquired their education much more easily and with less effort than I did. There were clearly recognizable class barriers, and differentiations. I am not complaining here, merely stating facts.

4. *What do you think were the main objectives of education for Communism in the schools?*

There were certain clearly admitted pedagogical aims and goals; among these was the upbringing of a generation in Communist milieu; a generation with a Socialist Weltanschauung, the cementing of a generation whose thinking would be along Communist lines. Révai repeatedly stated that Communism in Hungary will stand or fall depending on the Communists' ability to produce a succession of Communist generations. Only then are we going to start on the road of Socialism. This was the gist of his speech in Parliament which he delivered as early as 1947, during the debate on the Ministry of Educational's budget.

4 a. *What was stressed -- efficiency, social justice, compliance, or something else?*

They tried first of all to give -- and this is my personal opinion now -- an ideological training from the Kindergarten on. They dealt a great deal with questions of social justice. On the level of the grade-school pupils they conducted seminars, and the teachers told a great many facts and tales about Stalin and about Rákosi to their pupils.

In the Úttörő (Pioneer) movement, in which all the students, save the intellectually very weak ones and the bad cadres participated, the Communists employed the educational principles employed by the scouts.

On the secondary-school and university levels the KISZ circles were highly emphasized. The continued good standing of holders of university scholarships depended solely on the work they performed in the KISZ. Once a week meetings and seminars were held.

Every university had Marxist chair (Faculty). Every school on all levels taught the Russian language. The teaching of the Russian language was used as an effective means of propagating the ideology and of exerting cultural influence. The ideological training was well organized and very thorough.

In the period 1948-1950, the ideology was stressed, even to the detriment of scholastic achievement. Scholastic results were considered secondary then. After 1954, scholastic competence was equally stressed.

The Communists made a careful selection of the student body. They were looking for good students whose cadre was good and did everything to promote these. With the help of carefully prepared statistics, they constantly analyzed and controlled the composition of the university student body, keeping the ratio of the undesirable well under ten percent.

4 b1. How effective do you feel was education for Communism in the schools?

The Revolution most effectively answered this question. It was the work of, and was carried primarily by, secondary-school and university students and by graduates of these Communist institutions. Think of the deputations that went to the radio building, think of the MEFESZ delegation.

4 b2. What about the teachers?

In 1945, the old teachers were still performing their tasks. Between 1945-1948, a large number of good cadres were quickly trained as teachers and were placed in strategic positions. Small cells of Communist teachers exercised control over the schools' faculties. With very few exceptions, only reliable Party people were employed as school administrators.

In the period 1948-1953, the Communists attempted to change the entire faculty of the universities. They succeeded in replacing the old personnel, but the standards suffered a great deal in the process. Before the war, the level of Hungarian universities was rated high. This was no longer the case after 1948-1953. All the well-known professors who enjoyed a European reputation were pensioned, or were assigned insignificant tasks, or else were fired outright.

In my university only two professors remained after 1948. The old faculty was replaced with new men, young men, among whom there were one or two brilliant people, but the majority were grey and obscure individuals. Their talents were good enough for secondary schools, but not for universities. The final result of this wholesale changeover was a substantial lowering of university standards.

4 c. How did school children feel about Communism?

The Communist school policy made the children remarkably mature. It was sad, indeed, to observe how already in elementary schools children learned the art of accommodating themselves to the extraordinary circumstances, they knew precisely what they were supposed to say, what they were permitted to say, and what they were never to say in school. The children did not go much for the ideological things. Their attitude was similar to our attitude to required readings. Rather than read the classics, we used the syllabus method and studied the outlines. Later we realized how good a reading we missed, but at the time we thought the required readings were outrageous. So were the children with the ideology. They did not pay much attention to the lectures (egyik fülön be, a másikon ki). Most students gave mechanical answers to questions on examinations, with no one taking the whole thing seriously, not even the smallest children. It was just like the compulsory Sunday Mass in older times; the pupils' main interest then was to be physically present, so his teacher could see him, but he neither knew nor did he pay much attention to what the priest was actually saying. Such was the case with the ideology too, from the first grade on to the universities. It was considered fashionable to oppose the teacher and to find plausible pretexts to avoid a lecture, and those who engaged in this sort of thing were looked up to. (Divat volt a közbeszólás, vagánység, ellenkezni és kibújni).

4 d. What did they like about it?

I don't know.

4 f. Do you think this has changed in the last ten years?

The aversion of students did not change. In other respects there were marked changes. After 1953, it was the students who first availed themselves of the opportunity of freedom to criticize. Since instructors were ever ready to discuss various problems, the criticizing mood developed markedly and the students eagerly used every opportunity to raise controversial questions.

In the fall of 1956 (before the Revolution), the compulsory study of the Russian language was abolished. Russian became an elective subject. Every student was permitted to freely choose his foreign languages. Very few students chose to continue studying Russian.

4 g. In what ways are youngsters today different from those in your days?

Youngsters of today are of course different from those in my days. Hard times tend to train and educate people better. Our lives were by no means free of difficulties and complications. Yet we lived a carefree life. I was completely free to do and to think as I pleased. I was free to declare myself an Atheist. This sort of freedom was not given to the youth of today. The absence of these material and intellectual freedoms made the youngsters a more serious lot, more thoughtful and deliberate in their ways, and more yearning at the same time.

A group of this youth, the 2000-member MEFESZ meeting, crafted the 16 points. If we read the points, we clearly discern in them the splendid presentation of the Hungarian people's main grievances. This document alone would fully attest to the remarkable maturity and foresight of our youth. It is a curious accident indeed, that the difference between 1848 and 1956 is a difference of working of the drafts only. I consider it remarkable that our youth was able to find during those problem-ridden days a formula designed to secure us both a national independence and human (individual) freedom.

I read a great deal about the era of Reformation in Hungary. I was astonished when I read of young Hungarians who became preachers, young men who have given their lives to a cause, to have gone to far-off universities in foreign lands to prepare themselves for this service. Those preachers had to overcome tremendous obstacles and reached their goals in a roundabout way.

The youth of today have also made unheard-of efforts to keep abreast of the more significant intellectual cross-currents, something which was absolutely necessary for the drafting of the 16 points.

Our youth did have a love of forbidden things, it felt the attraction of perilous undertakings.

4 h. Has education for Communism changed the attitude of children? If so, toward whom and what?

We have not seen much of them, and when we did see them, we could only register surface appearances. They all had a characteristic quality; they made every attempt to take lightly and almost jokingly serious questions. They took this attitude in order to be able to treat ideological questions in a light manner. This was their defense against their teachers and instructors.

I did not think much of this youth up until the Revolution. I looked upon their thoughtlessness and prodigality as a symptom of a radical change, as indicating a profound recklessness. It soon turned out that underneath the surface-appearances they were seriously thinking men. They did their serious thinking when completely alone, because they knew only too well that thinking in the open, in public, would not be conducive to their well-being. I never realized, for instance, that these young men, so superficial when in the open, were listening to the Western radios, were engaged in studying Western languages and were reading German, French, and English literature written before the Second World War.

This was a completely misunderstood generation. Both Communists and anti-Communists misjudged them. We considered them to be much too weak, lacking backbone and resolution and determination. The Communists, on the other hand, looked upon them as absolutely reliable. They believed that the Moscow stipends and scholarships will make this youth loyal, faithful, and docile Communists.

4 i. *At what age do you think it is most (least) effective?*

Generally speaking, all kinds of education is most effective in the early youth. Already the Ottoman Turks recognized this truth when they selected young children to be trained as janissaries. This very same method was tried by the Russians; they erected janissary schools for foreign students. The fact that the system did not prove successful must primarily be explained by the internal contradictions so plainly evident in the regime.

Students in the age brackets of 18-20 everywhere experience an instinct-like urge of acquiring all sorts of knowledge. They are craving for free access to all sorts of information. They would like to know everything, to learn of every secret. They are conscious of their capabilities and they seek out areas where to employ them. It was at this point that the Communist education collapsed. They very definitely pulled down the iron gates (rendkívül határozott sorompókat engedtek le) and set arbitrary limits beyond which the student could not hope to go. The youth looked upon this procedure as does the bull upon the red cloth. Those areas of enquiry which are beyond reach because shut off by human arbitrariness, the things about which one is not permitted to speak freely, are extremely interesting. Forbidden things have a curious gravitational power and their learning and mastery becomes the non plus ultra of a young man's desire.

Communist education would have been eminently successful if the educational processes and the access to all sorts of information had been free, if the internal contradictions of the regime had not been present, if the instructors could have proved clearly and beyond doubt that of all social and economic systems the Socialist system were unquestionably the best.

The gravest of all the mistakes of the system was the fact that it did not allow opportunities for free debate. Instead of free discussion, the system imposed laws and regulations upon the youth at a time when the youth was least receptive to arbitrary rules. The rigid exclusion of certain areas and problems from free discussion had a decidedly destructive impact on the Hungarian youth.

FAMILY AND FRIENDS:

5. *Now let's talk a bit about your family. What was your father before the Communist take-over?*

My father had two and a half holds of land which he cultivated. He was working in a factory besides this. His work in the factory was only seasonal and occurred in years when the agricultural economy did not prosper.

5 a. *Did your father change jobs after 1945?*

No, he did not. He received an additional two and a half holds of land as a result of the land reform and now he no longer worked in the factory.

5 b. *What did you think about his job?*

What could my opinion have been? My father was an upright, honest, and industrious man, who devoted himself to his family and led a sober life. It was not his fault, but the forces of circumstances, that he did not achieve a higher state in life.

5 c. How much schooling did he have?

He completed six years of elementary schooling.

5 d. Before 1945, were there any servants (maids) in your family? If so, until when? How do you feel about it?

We never had any servants.

5 e. Did your family (household) own any property? If so, what happened to it?

My parents had a house and five holds of land. I, too, had a house.

5 f. When you were a child, compared with most people, were you better off or worse off?

We were poor people. Compared to other people in the same social class we had a very good life. My parents were very understanding, they gave us all we needed.

5 g. When you were a child, how many people were there in your family (household)?

There were the five of us (three children).

5 h. What happened to these people?

All five members of the family are still alive.

5 i. As of 1956, did any relatives live with you? Why?

No, I married in the meantime and founded my own family.

5 j. When we speak of family, who really should be included in it?

Father, mother, and sisters and brothers constitute the family. This composition later changes and expands; my sister's husband and their children, my second sister's family and my wife's family became part of it. After the initial expansion, the family contracts again.

5 k. Did your social origin help you or hurt you in Hungary in the past ten years?

I cannot speak of any advantages resulting from my social origin. My class origin became an outright disadvantage in prison; it was very hard to prove that I was a reactionary.

6. Were you married when you were in Hungary?

Yes.

6 a. What kind of work did your wife (husband) do?

My wife worked on a Hollerit machine (she was an IBM bookkeeper in a statistical concern). She was employed in a supervisory capacity.

6 b. How long have you been married?
I am married since 1945.

6 c. How many children did you have?

The oldest girl is ten years old, the younger is eight.

8. Did you talk to your wife (husband) and children about political matters?

Yes, I talked to my wife about political matters.

8 a. What sort of things were said?

We discussed acute questions of the day.

8 b. Did this change in the course of time?

No.

9. Did you and your wife ever have trouble with your child(ren) over their education?

Yes, we had tremendous problems and troubles. There was a duality (kettősség) between the family life and the instruction given at school. Our children did not receive formal religious instruction, and in spite of this we had many troubles. The difficulty was ever present of explaining a truth which was true only in our family circle, but not in school. Our children knew precisely what they may and what they must not say in school.

10. Did any other authorities or persons exert any influence on your child(ren)?

Yes, the school did exert a great influence. They were taught in school that there were two types of people: those who were Socialists were exemplary and loyal persons; those who were not

Socialists did not possess any positive qualities. They were only second or third rate people.

11. *Generally speaking, did you (and your brothers and/or sisters) get along pretty well with your parents?*

Our relations were very good.

12 a. *What sort of things were said?*

We discussed important or timely issues of the day.

12 b. *Were there any changes in this in the course of time?*

No.

13. *Have you had any trouble with your parents over your education?*

I always was, and still am, in a very pleasant circumstance in this respect. My dear mother, though her education was rather rudimentary, was an extremely sensitive and thoughtful person. She always reacted very sensitively on her cultural level to whatever was beautiful or interesting. Through my mother, this point of view became an integral part of my own life too.

13 a. *What about the kind of work they wanted to do?*

I had complete freedom in this respect, limited only by our material resources.

13 b. *What about the friends they had?*
I don't remember any instance of parental interference in this connection. It is true that I did not make friends easily. I

always had only a very few friends. And even these few became my friends only after a long time, after I learned them thoroughly. My mother enjoyed company. My friends were coming to our home and I went to theirs. My mother was well acquainted with all my friends.

13 c. *What about politics?*

In our family I was the only intellectual in many generations. The consequence of this was that I enjoyed a great respect in the circle of both my immediate family and among the relatives. I got used to a situation where my advice and opinion were eagerly sought after, but, at the same time, I had to be very careful what I was saying because whatever I said was taken seriously and remembered.

13 d. *What about religion?*

My father was a Calvinist and my mother was Roman Catholic. My two sisters were Catholics and I am a Calvinist. Our family was religiously mixed. This fact meant two things: there was an internal, real religious tolerance within the family. My mother held that everyone is completely free to lead such religious life as he thinks best. My father was not a religious person. He went to church once or twice a year, paid his church taxes, and that was all.

My mother was a woman who led a much more sensitive and deeper spiritual life. She was very religious in her early youth. She was extremely sensitive. She craved the good and the beautiful. She disliked and detested the contradictions which all too often were rather apparent between what the priests were preaching and what they themselves practiced. She was very religious and God-fearing in her own way, and yet at the same time she gave us great freedom to determine our own relationship to this question.

I myself passed through various periods; I was a rationalist at one time, then an atheist, and still later a believer. This all took place during my adolescent years. At the time I was eighteen, the only authority I recognized was reason. Later I became acquainted with contradictions in the lives of religious people. Outwardly their lives were good and beautiful, but inwardly they did not pay any attention to religious principles. Still later I became a member of a youth organization and there made the acquaintance of an excellent Calvinist priest. It was due to his influence that from then on I again am a believer.

13 e. *What about sex education?*

I grew up with my two sisters. I was quite used to the company of girls. The family's life was very healthy from this point of view.

13 f. *Anything else?*

No.

14. *Can you describe your family life in the last few years?*

I married in 1945. In 1948 I was arrested. In 1953 I was set free again. All in all, I spent six years together with my wife, which is not too long a time. I was very satisfied with my marriage and with my family life.

14 a. *How close was your family?*

We lived a very fine family life. My wife was patient and understanding. She looked over my deficiencies and faults and impatience.

14 b. How typical do you think this was?

Our life was not typical.

14 c. What did you do with your leisure time?

I practically never had any leisure time. There was a great amount of work to be done. We lived in the province. There was always work around the house, in our large garden with the orchard trees. Besides, I had two daughters. They expropriated every bit of time I had.

14 d. What sort of things did you do together with your (wife, children, parents)?

We were very seldom home at the same time. Both my wife and I worked in two shifts. And these shifts quite often did not run parallel. We did not have much time together.

14 e. How much time did you spend together?

We were together on Saturdays and Sundays and on weekdays whenever circumstances permitted.

14 f. What sort of things would you have liked to do that you couldn't?

I could not travel abroad, for instance, I could not read those books which I wanted to read, or which would have interested me. I could not go to the theater or to concerts as often as I would have liked to. I was only able to bring my daughters to a few places, when I would have liked to show them much more.

14 g. Were you free to do what you wanted with your leisure time? If not, what controls or pressures were there on it?

I was under constant police supervision. I was not permitted to leave the village in which I lived. I was not permitted to go to the movies, to the theater, to a restaurant, or to any other place of assembly. I could not have a telephone. My correspondence was strictly checked. I was not permitted to have a radio capable of receiving foreign broadcasts. I had to be at home at 10 p.m. every day and could not leave the premises before 6. (This latter point was not strictly observed.) I had to report once a week to the police.

15. *Do you feel/think that since 1945 family ties have loosened or tightened?*

Family ties certainly loosened after 1945. This was an officially-supported tendency. In order to loosen family ties, the economic plan was so constituted that everybody had to work. People were kept in the shops even after the workday ended. Sports events, entertainments, common excursions and parties were held at the factory, not to mention the various meetings and seminars and production conferences. In a word, the place of work became the center of a man's life.

The regime encouraged childbirth outside the family. In the fifties, official placards proclaimed that giving birth to a child was the obligation of the mother, but it was glory in the case of an unwed girl.

The concept of an illegitimate child was abolished. The child's mother could claim any male at all as her child's father, without running the risk of ever being prosecuted. Since the illegitimate child did not bear the name of the mother, there was no such thing as an illegitimate child.

15 a. *Can family members trust each other?*

Yes and no. It always depended on the actual situation, on

the circumstances, and on the character of the family members. Generally speaking yes, but in numerous instances no.

Anti-democratic political attitude on the part of husband or wife was a recognized cause for divorce. If the husband was under police supervision, or in jail, or interned, the wife could divorce him automatically and keep all the husbands' belongings and estate. There were innumerable incidents when the wife actually took advantage of this opportunity. I knew a great many people at Kistarcsa (forced labor camp) who were thus divorced. The law worked the other way round, too, but it was generally the wives, not the husbands, who terminated the marital contracts.

15 b. Are they more dependent on each other than before?

They were absolutely dependent on each other. The family constituted a defensive and offensive alliance (véd- és daczszövetség), if the family members understood each other. This dependence was further underlined by an economic dependence; both husband and wife worked, many families in the wider sense lived together because of the bad housing conditions. I, too, lived with my in-laws. We lived together, the six of us.

15 c. Are children growing estranged from their parents or not?

Parent-child relationship did become more loose. Children enjoyed more independence and more freedom. The schools endeavored to artificially loosen the ties between parents and children. The parent no longer represented an absolute and unquestioned authority. In many instances, the teachers encouraged their students to bring about a situation at home where the parents would be forced to admit a standpoint contrary to that represented by the school or by themselves, and did all they could to make a success of this showdown. They, (the teachers), knew quite well what great moral force the family represented against Communism.

While all this is true, here again, the Revolution proved beyond doubt that the binding force of the family was far greater than that of the school.

15 d. Is this equally true of town and country?

By and large this is equally true of town and country, but there are qualitative differences, resulting primarily from the natural divergence of town and country. In the city the checking and supervising of children is a great deal more difficult than in the country, especially if both parents are working. While the parents work, the city children may do whatever they want to do. It is more the school and their friends, rather than their parents, who are responsible for their education.

In the country all this is different. Usually the grandparents live there too. And the grandparents have more time and patience. They could attend to the children with more loving care.

15 e. Have there been any changes in the ways of rearing children?

Yes, very definitely. Especially after 1948, when the old-type family life collapsed. Both parents were forced to go to work, the children were left in kindergartens, day nurseries, schools, or other institutions. Many a mother became despondent and impatient because of this situation, where they only saw their children for an hour or two a day. The child was still sleeping in the morning when the mother carried it to the day nursery. In the evening the child was brought home, was given supper, and was again put to bed to sleep. There was no way at all of educating these children.

15 f. Has there been any change in the attitude toward divorce? In the number of divorces?

Divorce statistics rose substantially in the cities after the Second World War. Innumerable people were taken prisoner and were kept in POW camps for eight years at times. The husband came home and, if the wife had not divorced him as yet, both he and the wife soon found out how greatly they changed and the only way out was divorce. Or, if the husband was put to prison after the war and later was freed, the situation was rather similar.

Then the circumstances of life, too, have undergone a tremendous change. Both husband and wife worked all day, in the evening they were both tired, after they were kept at their respective working places long after the actual work came to a close, at any rate the patience and understanding and forbearance toward one another was oftentimes totally lacking.

Divorce procedures were made relatively easy. Above all, a divorce was not an expensive affair, and so people reconciled themselves to it easier than if it had represented a financial burden.

I know of a number of instances where young people married, but, because of lack of housing facilities, they continued to live with their respective parents. After a while they either agreed to divorce outright or else took up residence with the in-laws and divorced shortly thereafter.

16. *Do you think relations between boys and girls have changed in Hungary in the last ten years?*

Relations between boys and girls became more free, and I suspect this change may have brought about salutary results. Absolute freedom, all the way down to sexual intercourse, certainly was not beneficial, but the co-education had certain advantages. There developed a healthy rivalry between boys and girls which often resulted in better scholastic achievement. The necessary sexual information (felvilágositás) could be given more smoothly in schools and was associated with less inhibition and less bizarre and unhealthy imagination. This is particularly true if it is realized that these problems affect both boys and girls at about the same time.

Under normal social conditions coeducation and conducting of common girl-boy programs is good and right. In Hungary, because of the regime's political tendencies, the results of this experiment were marred by rude excesses and immoralities. While the experiment was not a complete success, the new system had more advantages than disadvantages.

16 a. What about the age at which people marry? Was there a change in recent years?

The age at which young people marry dropped; young men marry at an earlier age now than before. This was brought about primarily by changes in their economic status, they becoming economically independent at an earlier age now than formerly. The marrying age now is 20-22-24, whereas formerly it was 26-30. There was no change in the marrying age of girls.

16 b. Have courtship and marriage patterns changed? What about the role of parents in this?

Yes, there were certain changes. Young men marry at a considerably younger age now. Before the Second World War the accepted marrying age for males was around 30. Now it is around 20. In the courtship, too, the process of liberalization was everywhere noticeable. The change, coming as it did as a result of changes affected in schools, was inevitable. It had its advantages and disadvantages. Young people were much more at ease when together, their relations were far less constrained than before, and their conversation as well as their social contacts lost much of their former stiffness and formality, to be replaced by easygoing, light, and, to a certain extent, more human and natural way. Young people were, in a word, free from social and ethical pressure or restraint. I recognize all the advantages of this liberalization, but the excessive libertinism (szabadosság) in which many indulged led, I must say, to the destruction of family life.

The Communists consciously fostered and encouraged this sort of development after 1948. In their efforts to break up the family, they not only sanctioned but advocated extra-marital sexual relationships. There were propaganda campaigns which openly proclaimed this sort of thing as the new, official version of conduct (asszonynak szülni kötelesség, leánynak szülni dicsőség). This false morality was by no means universally rejected. Many looked upon it as a justification of their own desires and actions. The campaign was definitely poisonous and destructive.

Parents and society were totally opposed to this new standard of morality. Parents strove to bring up their children according to the old and accepted moral code and, while they did all they could to enforce this code of living at home, they were powerless and did not dare to openly denounce the official innovations. The inevitable result was a curious duality of home and school, where parents and teachers desperately fought for hegemony over the children.

16 c. What do you think about it?

I am conservative in this respect. I subscribe to the old-world standards and I consider the family and social ideas of that old world (régebbi világ) as right and proper. The so-called ethical and honorable family life remains, in my judgment, the basis and foundation of a normal social life. I cannot accept, even in principle, the point of view represented by the Communists.

16 d. Was there more loose sexual behavior than there used to be? If so, why? What forms does it take?

Yes, very definitely. This loose sexual behavior was not, however, the rule. The official policy of the state did have the loosening of morals and of sexual behavior as its aim. But the society's reaction to these policies of the state was equally tremendous and far-reaching. The state's policy was rejected by the great majority of the people and the government's proposals never really had a chance of success. This would only have been possible had the old generation suddenly died out with the new Communist generation delivering a vast and devastating blow to the remnants of accepted standards and usages and customs. As it was, the old generation did not die out, and the Communists were not even able to indoctrinate the new generation.

When I speak of more loose social behavior, all I mean is that, such conduct having been officially sanctioned, boys and girls did have more opportunity to engage in irresponsible actions, and many of them did so act. These opportunities were available in schools, in mixed camps and other places where boys and girls worked together, played together, and lived together without any supervision. In the absence of supervision and of definite programs, they naturally filled the gap with activities of their own choosing.

This much about the youth. With the older population the situation was not much better. There the laxity of the divorce laws and the ease with which a divorce action could be accomplished certainly did not contribute to moral stability. Divorce had no ill consequences either financially or socially, and many people took advantage of it considering it an easy way out of their difficulties. The number of divorced women is about 67,000. The number of those women who are divorced in fact, though not legally, is even larger.

16 e. Was there any prostitution?

Prostitution was not officially permitted. It had been abolished in 1947. In Hungary, prior to 1947 there were officially sanctioned public houses of prostituting. My own belief is that prostitution flourished in Hungary, even after it had been abolished, no longer legally, but in secret, just as is the case in all countries in every part of the world.

16 f. In your opinion, were the Communists more strict or less strict about sexual matters than the authorities before? In what ways?

The Communists were decidedly less strict than the authorities before them in these matters. They abolished the legal and social concept of illegitimate child. There simply were no illegitimate children in Hungary. The mother of such a child was able to name whomsoever she pleased as the father of the newly born. The Communists, then, were far more eager than the previous regimes in destroying the legal and social obstacles which formerly tended to check unethical behavior.

The Communist ideology contains the entire free-love (szabad szerelem) complex. It was because of tactical considerations that they more or less accepted the institution of the family. They certainly did not support this institution, but did all they could to loosen its ties.

16 g. What do you think about birth control? How widespread do you think it is?

I don't have a precisely-formulated opinion on the question of birth-control. I am, of course, familiar with Malthus's arguments. But Malthus's prognostications have not become a reality, -- at least not up until now. Birth control was strictly prohibited in Hungary before the war. The prohibition did not actually entirely eliminate it, of course, and it was fairly widely practiced, especially among the poor of the villages where large crops of babies destroyed the already delicate economic balance. The women themselves or their incompetent neighbors performed usually these dangerous operations, which very often left the expectant mothers crippled or caused their death.

Birth control continued to be prohibited under Stalin. It was held then that the nation must develop quickly and that many workers were needed for the expanding economy. After 1953, the government, recognizing the futility of prohibiting laws and desire of avoiding the innumerable tragedies that resulted from the practice, permitted the formation of an AB Committee in Budapest, at the Rókus Hospital. This committee was empowered to permit an operation, either because of reasons of health or because of social considerations. Some physicians continued to handle abortion cases, but they were severely punished if apprehended.

In 1954 another law left it up to the parents whether to permit birth of a child or not.

Prophylactic devices were not used at all in Hungary. The devices that were available were extremely primitive and people did not use them for that reason.

16 h. Do you think the attitude toward illegitimate children has changed? Are there many?

There are simply no illegitimate children in Hungary. (I already explained why.) It is extremely difficult, if not impossible, to even guess what their number may be, because officially and legally there are none. The fact remains that there are many ladies who live alone with their son or daughter.

16 i. Do you think the status of women has changed in Hungary since the war? If so, can you give examples? Is it a good thing or a bad thing?

The status of women has definitely changed in Hungary, especially after 1948. After 1948 the employment of women rose to unprecedented heights. Women were simply forced into the factories as a result of the introduction of planned economy. Before the war the living wage (létminimum) of a family was calculated on the basis of the husband's earnings alone; after the war the living wage represented a subsistence-money for the working individual and no more. The wages of the husband alone were barely sufficient for the family's food supply, -- a very meager supply at that -- and the wife was obliged to go to work too. Adolescent children also joined their parents as soon as they could. This is the explanation of the phenomenal rise in the employment of women. The Communists were determined to "lift the fair sex to its status of complete equality." Men and women of the same educational background received precisely the same consideration and pay in whatever field of endeavor.

As to the second part of your question, I do not think it was a good thing. I reject it because it represents the first step towards the systematic destruction of healthy family life. There are, of course, girls who want to work and who do not intend to marry. The primary purpose and natural task of women remains, nevertheless, motherhood and the rearing of children. The leaders who direct Hungary's life did not leave any room for such development.

17. *Do you think the general state of morals has changed in Hungary in the last ten years?*

The general state of morals has certainly changed in the past decade. The level of morality has definitely sunk. This fact is undeniable. All we could do, at best, is to cite qualifying and extenuating circumstances to explain it. The level of morals was not high under Horthy either. That society, under Horthy, was a hypocritical one. They preached water and drank wine. Our society, after the Second World War, was a freer society. And because it was more free, we know much more about it; about its virtues and about its vices; we were able to freely discuss them and no one ever thought of hiding them. And the freedom that the postwar society enjoyed did have its effect. It was a healthy change. If it were possible to compare statistics of "good families" of the prewar and postwar periods, the latter would present a much more satisfying picture, I suspect.

There is, of course, a seeming contradiction in what I say. I said that the level of morality had definitely sunk after the war and, at the same time, I claim that the postwar society compares favorably to that of the prewar period.

The general state of morals did sink after the war. Because the society is more free now than formerly, those actions which formerly were rejected as immoral and were, therefore, concealed, -- those very same actions are performed today in the open, under the eyes of the public. Marital unfaithfulness and adultery were formerly branded as unforgivable sins against public morality. Some people no doubt did commit such sins, but in secret. If apprehended, they made the headlines and the scandal had no end in sight. Today, married men and women are certainly no different. They do commit adulteries, especially on vacation resort spas, but they do it in the open. People do know that this man and that woman (both married, but not to each other) live together as husband and wife for weeks. No one pays any attention to such incidents, they are no longer affairs.

Those who do live normal marital lives are much stronger today than before. They have strengthened and cleansed their inner lives. Communism was a touchstone to both their convictions and their determination to live by them; such families had no outside restrains or social convictions to keep them in check. Everybody was free to pick and choose husbands and wives at will, and it took both courage and determination of conviction to fight against the separating tendencies of the state. Resistance to temptation had a wider and deeper role than ever before.

From this it naturally follows that the amoral tendencies and pressures of the state touched not only upon the relationships of mother and father, but affected the very lives of the children as well. The parents' love towards one another and towards their children, and the children's love towards their parents represented that leaven which eventually neutralized and checked and invalidated the powerful tendencies of the Communist state.

The parents had to wage a battle against the schools. They had to listen patiently to the children when they related what took place in the schools or what they were taught there. Then they had to even more patiently explain to the children controversial points and to set them straight, if and when the need arose. In a word, parents spent much more time with their children after 1948 than ever before. In the school the children were exposed to a never-ending process of alienation and estrangement from their parents and each day the parents fought a battle to reconquer their children's trust and love and affection.

The children saw that their parents loved each other (husband and wife worked on two different shifts). The parents accepted the differing shift assignments so that one of them would always be home. The Sunday dinner, so irksome and such a nuisance before, now turned into a holiday feast with all the members of the family sitting together at the table. It was these little and seemingly unimportant things which strengthened the family against the anti-family policy of the state. These little pleasantries tied firmly together the several members of the family and taught them to love and to protect each other.

17 a. Can you give examples of low morals from your own experience?

I have seen youth camps where boys and girls slept together under the same tent, collegiums (student hostels) where there were no separate quarters for males and females.

There were, I must say, girls who refused to go to youth camps because they knew that society would look down upon them if they did it.

17 b. Is there much stealing? If so, by whom, and for what reasons?

This is a complex question. In Hungary it was considered a moral deed, so to speak, if a person refused to abide by, or refused to execute laws or did not do what regulations required him to do.

If somebody has stolen whatever thing from his fellow-worker, he was considered a thief and his action was accordingly branded morally wrong. The offender was looked down upon with contempt. If a person, on the other hand, "stole" wood from the factory so he could warm up his room, his taking the wood was not considered stealing by the public. A soldier in Hungary, for instance, never steals anything, he merely "procures" (szerez) what he needs. Most everybody acted similarly to the soldiers in this respect. The state waged a determined campaign against this system of procuring, but officials were never able to marshal public opinion against this system.

I could not have stolen anything, even if I had been disposed to do so, because people would have criticized me for it; knowing my past they looked up to me as some sort of a model (ideal). I personally never had any difficulty in understanding others who stole. I could fully justify their actions and accepted them as not morally wrong.

I knew an architectural technician who built himself a cozy little house entirely out of stolen goods. Everybody in the village knew this. And yet this man was praised by the village's inhabitants, -- myself included -- for his resourcefulness and perseverance, with no one ever voicing a protest.

Why did people steal? They were obviously in dire need of supplementing their meager incomes and there was ample opportunity everywhere to procure something. You have a planned economy in Hungary and all the planning was done in a centralized way. The central planning bureau planned the minutest little details of every operation. The allocation of materials was also centralized. This necessitated a bureaucracy of tremendous proportions. An incredible superficiality characterized the work proportions. All kinds of materials, raw and finished, were shipped around needlessly, in a rather complicated, roundabout way. Sizeable quantities were lost track of or were entirely forgotten in the process. Material, valued in the hundreds of thousands, was standing there rotting and disintegrating, for years. The people saw in this a clear evidence of carelessness and indolence, as practiced in high governmental agencies. Seeing this practice in high places, they themselves began to wonder. Many a man thought he was doing a good deed by "saving" at least some of the material and putting it to good worthwhile use.

Our factory received at one time a freight carload of tarred insulating paper so that they may cover the bricks and protect them from rain and snow. Just before a rainstorm the management sent out some men to cover the produced bricks. But the storm subsided and it did not rain. The paper, however, was left out in the open. Then came the loaders and began to load the bricks into the freight cars. Since they were not paid to take off the papers, and doing so would have involved additional labor, they simply threw them on the ground, together with broken bricks. Now who could accuse a man of stealing if, seeing the obvious waste and conscious of his own urgent need, he collected these papers, took them home, and used them as he saw fit? This is the way people viewed stealing. We must therefore sharply distinguish actual stealing from wage-supplementing (bérkiegészités). Stealing is hen a person steals personal belongings from another. The taking away or "procuring" of material which more or less does not belong to anybody (félig gazdátlan dolgok elvitele) is definitely not stealing.

Aside from these factors I just enumerated, stealing was also a conscious anti-Communist action.

17 c. Is there much bribery (graft, embezzlement)? If so, by whom, and for what reasons?

I cannot give you precise information on these because these actions took place at levels where I had no insight. Bribery, graft and embezzlement took place in governmental offices and in certain social institutions, places where Communists were the officials.

Bribery was very severely punished. It was considered a high crime, next to spying and treason. There was, of course, ample room for bribery, but, then again bribery is universally practiced everywhere.

17 d. What about hooliganism? Who are they, and what do they want?

Hooliganism is not an invention of the people's democracies. The Kádár-regime, when employing this term, have criminals in mind who were either freed or who have escaped from prison during the Revolution. I did not hear this expression before the Revolution. In Hungary there were innumerable prisons. In these prisons a special lingo was in use, terms which were designed to humiliate the political prisoners, such as "ürge, (hamster), "csibész" (vagabond), "csavargó" (tramp, loafer).

18. Now I should like to talk about friends. Can you think of one of your closest friends in Hungary. When and how did you first meet him (her)?

I have so many good friends and I could tell you so much about them. To satisfy the questionnaire, let me think of only one; I met him in 1942, we were together in a Protestant youth organization. He was a professor in a secondary school and was, also engaged as a researcher in a historical institute. He was four or five years my senior. I was a university freshman at the time.

18 b. Was age and social background the same as yours?

His father was a poor peasant, possessing three holds of land. My father had even less than that.
We both represented first-generation intellectuals.

18 c. What sort of things did you do when you were together?

A scientific undertaking tied us to one another; we investigated the sociological and historical problems facing isolated Hungarian settlements living among people of foreign tongue and culture.

18 d. Did you ever discuss politics?

We discussed politics innumerable times.

18 e. Did your friendship change in any way in the last few years?

Definitely not. We acted together in 1944 and we were arrested and imprisoned at the same time. In 1945, we were members of the same political Party, though our activities were not in the same place. He was arrested in 1947 and I was imprisoned a year later. Between 1948 and 1953 we never met and between 1953 and 1956 only on a few occasions, since I continued to be under police supervision. In 1956 our contacts were much more numerous, we met frequently at the Petőfi Circle and participated in other meetings of political nature. We both participated in the Revolution, though at different parts, and met only again after the government of Imre Nagy wrestled itself free of the domination of the Akadémia-utca. At that time we were again in the same political Party. He left Hungary two weeks ahead of me.

18 f. Are you still friends?

Yes, we are still friends.

g. *What sort of thing do you value most in a friend?*

I assign a great value, first of all, to friendship itself, viewing it as something of great significance. From the point of view of feeling and sentiment, friendship is not as vehement as love, but it does generate a feeling which is at least as deep and enduring, if not longer-lasting. The prerequisite of friendship is an identical point of view and an understanding or agreement in questions of principle. Its essence is trust -- if I learn to know a man and we become friends, I must not make the mistake of looking at him with rigid objectivity. The success of whatever social experiment depends to a degree on mutual appreciation and trust the participants accord to one another. It is naturally understood that this does not exclude the severest criticism of one another, amid discussions, done in an atmosphere of the greatest understanding, of course.

18 h. *Was it easy to make friends?*

Generally speaking, it was not easy to make friends. The possibilities of the present generation were conditioned by those extraordinary situations which, beginning with 1948, followed one another in quick succession, intimately touching our very lives. Hard times usually tend to emphasize much more the dependence of two people on another. Prosperity, in contrast, tends to loosen this feeling of belonging together.

18 i. *How would you describe the circle of friends you had?*

I was a youth leader. My following consisted mostly of peasant boys. I have innumerable friends among them. But I am an intellectual and so are most of my most intimate friends. From the point of view of their age group, they are, I should say, five-six years older or younger than myself. As to their background, most of them are first-generation peasant or worker sons, intellectuals, or such children of the intelligentsia who profess as their own that political and social program for Hungary which was the credo of the populist writers.

This credo included, among others, such principles as the elimination of social inequalities, the just distribution of the means of production, and equitable distribution of the produced consumer goods based on the social standing and education background of people in such a way that those receiving least would be able to lead human lives. We are democrats. Basing ourselves on the opinion of the masses, we formulate our theses accordingly.

18 j. What did it mean to have a friend?

Having a friend meant a great deal, since we found ourselves in such situations where friendship was the only force that kept us going, -- often enough saving our very lives.

18 k. Suppose you had a friend who became a minor Party official. Would this have affected your friendship? Why?

I am unable to answer this question, because a situation like that never occurred. I could base my opinion only on experience, a hypothesis at best represents an uncertainty.

18 l. How many Communists and how many non-Communists were there among your friends?

I had only such Communist friends whose acquaintance I made in prison. Because they, too, were incarcerated, you cannot very well class them Communists. Their number among my friends was insignificant. They all were very decent and honorable men.

RELIGION

19. Do you mind if we talk a little about your religious background? What was your parents' religion?

My father was a Calvinist, my mother was Roman Catholic. My two sisters were Catholics and I am a Calvinist.

19 a. Did all the members of your family have the same attitude toward religion or did some differ from the rest?

In our home there was an absolute peace, understanding, and religious tolerance. Neither of my parents were religious bigots. Both of them were rather liberal. We all received religious instruction, we all went to our respective churches and there was never any attempt by anybody at coercion of prohibition.

19 b. What about yourself?
(What are your personal attitudes in this matter?)

In my early youth I was a member of the KIE (YMCA), spending all my free time there. This was when I was 18-20 years old. I was a devout youth (bibliás faitalember), who often pondered about difficult metaphysical problems. This same could be said of my sisters, who acted similarly in their church organization. Communist rule naturally affected religious life. Communist education is essentially irreligious or a-religious. Communists deny the existence of God. Our calendar begins with Christ, theirs begins with the year zero. After 1948, there was no longer religious instruction in schools. After 1950, religious instruction was made optional, but only if both parents expressed themselves accordingly in writing.

20. *Has Communist rule affected religious life?*

The Communists never proceeded openly and strongly and with determination against religion. Officially, while they did not share the views and beliefs of the faithful, they maintained a religious tolerance. There was an agreement between the state and the various churches after the conclusion of the treason trials. The Communists gave the churches a 25-year tolerance period in which to reorganize themselves within the framework of the new state. They created an ecclesiastical bureau. This bureau functions even today. As I mentioned earlier, they even permitted religious instruction, outside of the school curriculum, but on the school premises, provided both parents requested such instruction in writing.

While giving this permission, they at the same time exerted considerable pressure on the parents not to request it. If one of the requesting parents was a Party member, a direct means was available to discipline him. The Communists thus acted either through the Party machinery or through the so-called democratic organizations in their struggle against religion, but never openly and directly.

A substantial change occurred after 1953. Church-state relations became more liberal. The written request or personal appearance of one of the parents was sufficient to ensure religious instruction of the child and the "quiet terror" was no longer exercised either.

During the Revolution all these restricting directives were annulled. Religion was made part of the curriculum, though not as a required subject. It was up to the parents whether or not a child should receive instruction in it.

After the Revolution the situation reverted to where it was during the early fifties, and the old methods of intimidation are again in use.

20 a. Were all faiths affected equally or not? Why?

Theoretically all faiths were equally affected. In practice, naturally, there were qualitative differences. The most vehement and most determined campaign was waged against the Catholic Church. Next in line were the Protestants: Why? The Catholics were the strongest, theirs was the deepest-rooted tradition, their Masses were the best organized, their organizations were the strongest and they lived a very intensive religious life.

20 b. Do you think the Communists tried to stamp out religion or use it for their own ends? What makes you think so?

The Communists were, in the final analysis, determined to stamp out religion, since religion, as an ideology, is just as total (totális) as is communism. Communism is a religion where there is no God, the center of worship being economic principles. Besides this Stalin, while alive, was shrouded in an air of a fetish. Since Communism is a religion, official pronouncements of its high priests are just as binding and just as infallible as are God's pronouncements to a Christian. It proceeded logically from the very nature of things that Communists opposed and fought against the Churches. Communism, like religion, is a closed ideology, it presumes to answer and reserves to itself the exclusive right to answer, every question pertaining to man and the world and as such cannot tolerate another, rival ideology, desiring to do the same thing.

20 c. What about the "peace priests"? Do you think they were sincere? Who were they?

There was a national peace committee (Országos Békebizottság) in which every denomination and other political personages participated. The National Peace Committee of Catholic Priests was a part, and subdivision of, this organization. This latter group's main purpose was to assist in carrying out the official state policy. The primary purpose of a Church is not, in my opinion, to support the state. These people, however, engaged in activities which at times were decidedly inhuman and employed methods which were clearly violations of the democratic rule of the game. They knew that what they were doing was wrong and with their very activities they sanctioned the system. This, of course, throws some light on their character. They were weak, egotistic, and cowardly. They were prompted or forced to act as they did.

The purpose and task of the Church is not to become a political partner. The strength of the Church lies in the fact that it is able to criticize, from the vantage point of its own moral purity, both the actions of the individuals and of the state. It therefore represents a controlling force; it is able to proclaim to all at all times and in every situation what is the moral, human, or natural point of view. Neither the National Peace Committee, nor the National Peace Committee of Catholic Priests did even attempt to proceed along these lines. With their silence and inaction, these peace priests not only became accomplices of the regime, but were also, to a certain degree, guilty of criminal complicity in the many irregularities and crimes which took place after 1950. If of ten million people one or two enter the Party for the purpose of securing bread thereby, such acts, while regrettable, are also excusable because of the compelling reason behind them. If, however, a person whose very vocation it is to represent divine justice acts similarly, that is an entirely different matter. Such persons ought never to compromise, nor must they fear human consequences, whatever they may be.

Many a priest chose this latter course. Many of them suffered imprisonment or, if they escaped prison, rather than subscribing to the state's desire they accepted the economic and other consequences, but remained with their faithful.

Partly as a result of this heroism of priests, the religious life of the people became deeper between 1948 and 1956. People became more devout than before. A religious reformation took place in the life of many an individual and yet, in the midst and in spite of this spiritual rejuvenation, there were some priests, peace priests so-called, who took upon themselves a task contrary to their vocation.

20 d. What did the Party do to clerics?

The economic status of the priests became insecure -- it is better, I think, if we speak of the Catholic Church, since the others were not in a very good situation even before the war.

Church land and other property was confiscated. Priests were obliged to live on state salaries after 1948. This made them dependent in more than one way on the state. A village priest after 1948 lived in a peculiar, isolated surrounding. He continued to work as before, but most of his doings, except the celebration of the Mass, was considered illegal. The faithful were also acting illegally. Church life, as a result, was practically paralyzed, if not broken, after 1948. The peasants' former practice of going to Mass regularly stopped abruptly. The number of faithful suddenly diminished and it took a certain determination if a person wanted to continue as a publicly practicing member of his Church. To do even more than that, to participate, for instance, in the church's functions and activities, required courage over and above the ordinary. The Church was branded, politically speaking, as the center of reaction. There was some truth in this assertion, though not in the sense in which the Communists understood this.

The clergy belonged, before the war, in a social category of its own and considered itself the possessor of power. They have lost this privileged position after the war. Most clergymen were unable to face this situation, were at a loss explaining the reasons that brought about these tremendous changes and, deep in their hearts, were unwilling to acquiesce in their new lot. The result was that many a priest continued to fight for those privileges which he once possessed, privileges which -- everybody knew -- were things of the past. In a word, the priests were not conscious of the changes which occurred, or were unwilling to take cognizance of them.

Be this as it may, they wanted their old privileges back and viewed with preference such social systems where their desires had better prospects of realization. This, in turn, placed them in a situation where they were ill-equipped to defend themselves against those arguments and accusations which the Communists leveled against them. This attitude of the priests put their followers -- the faithful -- also in a difficult position. Take, for instance, a poor man who received a few holds of land as a result of the land reform, or an industrial laborer who was appointed foreman in a factory. Both the land reform and the bettering of the worker's lot were claimed by the Communists as reforms which they brought about. Both the farmer and the foreman received something and the Party did all it could to persuade them to enter the Party on that account. Knowing as they did their priest's political views and principles with respect to land reform and nationalization, they often wondered whether they really belonged, or ought to belong, to the Church or not. This was the sort of breach or gap which the Communists wanted to effect, and did effect, between the Church and the people. This was not a Communist success, not a victory of their principles, but a psychological battle won by default of the priest who could not, or did not want to, acknowledge and to accept those changes which occurred in the country.

This was characteristic of the times immediately after 1948. It is true, however, that the Communists taught not only the people to better resist the Church, they taught the priests indirectly also, who were gradually awakened and were better able to perform their tasks in the changed milieu. Gradually the people's interest in their Church revived and their religious life deepened, it was warmer and more sincere, and the priests, too, became more natural and more human. This was the positive result of the struggle.

20 f. Could one freely attend church services?

Theoretically, yes. No general prohibition was ever proclaimed. There were no laws against attending church services. The methods used were administrative and social-administrative. The regime did not resort to police methods, people were caught at the very roots and sources of their existence and were made to feel the all-embracing power of the Party. There were certain social methods to which the regime resorted; the organized social events or created occasions, such as festivities or excursions, which coincided in time with the church services. These were temptations for many people. Others, facing the choice of attending church or a factory event, chose the safer way out of the dilemma. The Communists tried to popularize opposition to church-going, often ridiculing those who did go, exerting, at the same time, social pressures. There was, besides this, the so-called cadre policy; a man had to take into account the possibility of his church-going being registered on his cadre-sheet and of being used against him later, not openly, but effectively, in his work-promotion, etc.

20 g. Did any one stay away from church because of fear or because he got into trouble?

There were very many people who did stay away for these very reasons.

20 h. Did you attend church services? How often?

Between 1948 and 1953, I did not attend church services. There was no chapel in the prison, not even priests were given the opportunity of saying Mass. After 1953, I did attend. This, however, is not of interest here, since after 1953 church-going, too, became more free. Actually, I only seldom went to church, being under police supervision I was not permitted to visit public places.

20 i. What sort of people attended church more (less) frequently? Why did people attend church?

Old ladies went to church more often than others. Theirs was the most favorable social position in this respect. And they had a life-long habit behind them. Other than this it is extremely difficult to establish categories. It depended on education, background, and courage. Younger people were more frequent visitors than the middle-aged ones. But this is by no means universally true.

20 j 1. Do you think different faiths adjusted differently to the regime? If so, why?

Yes, there was a certain difference here. These differences stemmed primarily from the actual state of church-state relationships. It all depended on how sharp the disagreements, opposition, or attitude of the various church leaders was towards the political leaders or policy of the state.

The Jews were in an exceptional situation here, and for various reasons; they were persecuted before 1944 and after the war the government made it its program to rehabilitate them and to compensate them. Also, their number was comparatively small and the religious influence of the Israelite Church was restricted to small, local groups, without having a national significance. The influence of the Catholic Church, on the other hand, extended throughout the country; Mindszenty stood up and opposed the state with resolute determination. The Protestant and Jewish priests had a more progressive mentality and outlook than their Catholic counterparts. Neither the Protestant nor the Jewish Churches were ever so within the ruling class as was the Catholic hierarchy, -- who of old possessed immense estates and always was in a privileged position and, therefore, neither of the former two lost half as much as did the Catholics as a result of the change. The change, indeed, produced a very sharp contrast between what the Catholic Church's temporal power and influence was before and after the war.

Generally speaking, people of democratic conviction never did look upon certain members of the Catholic hierarchy with favor. Then came the land reform. The holder of the largest estates was the Catholic Church. It was from her that the largest quantity of land was taken away. Then again the Catholic Church was built constitutionally into the state. Obviously, if changes were to occur, these changes were bound to affect her first and most. Adjustment in her case was naturally more difficult than in the case of the others.

20 j 2. How did people of different denominations get along?

Life under the regime has eliminated denominational problems of all kinds. You no longer have a situation similar to those in my early youth when a Catholic boy often could not marry a Protestant girl because of religious and moral reasons.

20 k. Do you think religion is more or less important to young people than it was to their parents? Why?

You cannot establish categories here. It is my belief that religion means less today than it did before. Church and religion today are no longer a socially accepted and socially sanctioned everyday necessity. It is no longer considered an essential part of good grooming to make the sign of the cross or to attend Mass or service. The people to whom these things do have a meaning, these things do mean a great deal more than they did to their fathers. In former days they used to go to church with the sole object of saving their reputations. The older people are rather more religious (vallásosak), while the youth of today is rather more believing and more devout (hívők). I am definitely on the part of the latter.

20 l. *What part do you think the church played in fostering political opposition in the last five or six years? How? Can you give any examples?*

The Church, as an institution, did not officially play any role in this regard. Individual priests, on the other hand, did play an important role. They were able to take a stand in connection with political developments and thus were able to influence small or larger groups of people. Essentially, however, resistance and opposition did not center around the churches, but rather around other centers of social life.

Going to church necessarily developed a critical stand. Those who did go clearly demonstrated their opposition to the state, at least in so far as the anti-Church policy and tendency of the state was concerned. The priest, if courageous, was able to analyze the events and was able to set in motion the critical judgment of his hearers. These people thus became the small knots in the great Hungarian conspiracy which enveloped and ensnared the whole country.

SOCIAL STRUCTURE AND SOCIAL CHANGE:

21. *Suppose that, while you were still in Hungary, a capable young person whom you knew and trusted had asked your advice on what occupation he should seek. What one occupation would you have told him would be the best to aim at?*

The best-paid occupation is that of a physician, or that of

an engineer with a specialization. I would have told him to try to become a physician.

21 b. *What kind of things would you have told this person were important if he wanted to advance in his line of work?*

I would tell him to become a specialist, say, an excellent surgeon; to become a member of the Party. There were a few physicians who were not Party members. These were the specialists with a well-known reputation. There were others who did not even bother to enter the physician's labor union. For those, however, who started later, Party membership was indispensable. Such membership very often is no more than a nominal one. The situation here is similar to the village physician of older days who, if he really wanted to be popular, had to attend church service regularly.

Worker cadres or poor peasant cadres had the best prospect. Or, if neither of these categories, a good Party cadre of the father was very helpful.

22. *Suppose you were asked to make a list of the groups of people in Hungary whom you regarded as best off and worst off under the Communists. What groups would you name, and in what order would you put them?*

The best off were: the Party, AVH, higher officers of the army. These were best off in both prestige and in monetary rewards. They were also the exposed specialists or expert cadres, (kiemelt szak-káderek), such as the holders of the Kossuth prize (these were mostly writers), scientists, workers, politicians, and other members of the worker-aristocracy. These were holders of technical rather than political jobs. They were good specialists and trusted Party members.

Aside from political considerations, professional competence, knowledge, and technical skill counted most. Thus next in line

I would place the good technicians, scientific personnel and intellectuals. After this came the white-collar workers (tisztviselők) and the so-called free intelligentsia (szabad értelmiség). Next in line were the teachers in secondary and elementary schools. Next came the unskilled workers, peasants (independent peasants and TSzCs members), next came the enemies of the society (this was a heterogenous group, placed there by the state, employable only in certain places and only as menial laborers). This last group had no perspectives whatsoever. They lived in a permanent uncertainty, delivered to the momentary mood and caprice of those in command of the system. The very last and worst off were those in prisons. The number of these was very large between 1948 and 1956.

22 a. Which of these groups would you say you belonged in?

I was in prison.

22 b. Which of these groups would you have liked to belong in?

In those times I felt perfectly well in the group which I was in.

22 c. How did athletes fare? ("sports talents")

Good sports talents had everything they desired. Good pay, good jobs with no work, travels abroad. They could bring into the country certain things and sell them there at good price. Between 1948 and 1956 these sportsmen achieved wonderful results. The Communists spent a great deal of money on them.

22 d. How did artists fare?

Artists were a category by themselves. The Communists were trying to get hold of these people, lured them to their camp and kept them to praise their regime. But willingness to praise was not an absolute requirement in all cases. Zoltan Kodály received everything from them, including a magnificent residence on the Kékestetö without ever having said a pleasant word to them. In fact, Kodály criticized and cursed them openly. He, of course, was an exception. The regime's cultural policy could not afford to lose him. Besides, Kodály's international reputation protected him. His is really a unique case. Writers and poets could not do this. Our greatest writers were condemned to silence. The regime did not fight against them. They were living. They had the material means, too. But every attempt was made to keep them far away from the public. The position of Illyés was similar to that of Kodály. He never said a word of praise, but was recognized, nevertheless, as the greatest living Hungarian poet. And the more down the line you go, the situation is that much more difficult. These writers were obliged to get a job, to earn a living, or else to become members of the Party.

23. *What social classes would you say exist in Hungary today?*

There are three classes in Hungary: workers, peasants, and the intelligentsia. These are the classes we had and we still have them (megvolt és megvan). These three classes are constant factors of any society. Over and above these three classes there emerged a Communist aristocracy. In every society where there is no democracy, an aristocratic layer or stratum necessarily develops, which holds firmly the power in its hands and sits on all positions.

23 a. *How can you tell?*

This aristocratic stratum of Communist Hungary is made up of several factors, such as workers and peasants, its largest single ingredient being the intellectuals, and primarily Jewish intellectuals (and here I enter the slippery and elusive problem of anti-Semitism. I am still accustomed to Hungarian ways where, if you mention the word Jew or Jewish, you are immediately branded an anti-Semite, -- left-over or rudiment of Fascism, after which there is only one more step on this side of the prison, namely, imperialist. If you dare to criticize a person who happens to be a Jew, you immediately have to prove that never in your life were you an anti-Semite) who, after 1919 escaped to Russia. There is also a goodly sprinkling of younger Jewish intellectuals of a later generation among them.

These people lived in a separate world of their own, they came in contact only with their own kind and they based all their actions on one another's opinion. These were the only opinions which counted. These people were and are the possessors of the power. The best proof of how little they knew of the real sentiments of the people is the Revolution itself, the dismissal of Gerő, etc.

23 b. Do you feel that this represents a significant change since the war? If so, due to what?

It certainly represents a significant change, and for two reasons: a) As a result of the change those strata who possessed the power before the war disappeared from the scene. They were not liquidated. The people who held the leading positions in the state machinery and industry were simply relieved and new people, people from different social classes, took over the direction of things. This was a structural change. b) The change was even much deeper than that; the process of democratization of the entire Hungarian population had begun. If this process had not been interrupted and had not been followed by the unfortunate political events of 1948, then it would have brought significant and useful results. During 1945-1948, the differences between classes began to crumble and the age-old distrust between governing and governed began to vanish. While before the war the large masses resented and hated the ruling class, firstly because it was the ruling class and secondly because that ruling class dug too wide and deep a ditch between itself and the rest of the people. After 1945, this gap and the resultant hatred was no more.

Shortly, however, came the Party aristocracy and, if we view things from this angle, then we must say that no change occurred at all. There is again a narrow stratum there, governing above the people and without the people, having only their own interests in mind. This group taught the people anger and hatred only which is not a very fortunate path towards progress in Hungary.

23 c. Is this good or bad?

Yes, and no, depending on the viewpoint.
See above, answer to question 23 b.

23 d. Does class background divide/raise barriers between people?

Your question, I assume, refers to the last twelve years. A differentiation was certainly made between man and man. The narrow ruling circle, utilizing its cadre policy, maintained a thorough and up-to-date record of all the people, carefully noting their class background, and used this information for, or against them on all such occasions when an individual, for whatever reason, had to be classified. A man's class background became an integral part of his qualification.

In social judgments, i.e., when people formed an opinion of a man, the social background of such a man was not a decisive point. The people did not, by any means, reject an individual simply because the Party has judged him an undesirable, or enemy, or what have you.

You can observe a curious phenomenon among American

Hungarians; these people left Hungary a long time ago, but in their eyes Hungary is still the Hungary as they experienced it towards the end of the 19th or at the beginning of the 20th century; even today they have the priests and the magnates and gentlemen (urakat) of all kinds. The picture in Hungary is entirely different. The people do not hate now individuals simply because they may have been their former masters, or because they belonged to the ruling class, their hatred and contempt is directed towards their present-day oppressors whom they despise both as individuals and as a class.

23 e. Do you think people are socially more or less equal than they used to be?

People are socially more equal today, if we disregard the ruling stratum, than they were formerly. In their propaganda and in their declarations of principle, even the members of the ruling circle proclaim equality as their aim and practice, but in reality this is not so. It is precisely on account of this contradiction between the official aim and actual practice that the people no longer believe in the regime's equalitarian pronouncements.

23 f. Is this good or bad?

I am for the fullest social equality possible.

23 g. What about the way people deal with each other: Have there been any changes in manner, attitude, criteria of politeness?

There were many changes in this respect, changes which are many-sided and difficult to pinpoint or define. The youth is more free today than ever before. Regard or respect for authority exists no longer. The old notion of the youth's listening politely to what an elder has to say and of his generally refraining from speaking unless asked to do so is gone and nonexistent. This freedom of the youth has brought with it a certain degree of libertinism (szabadosság), which cannot be approved, of course, since rude and ill-mannered behavior certainly is not a necessary ingredient of freedom. All great changes, however, are accompanied by unpleasant excesses, excesses which no doubt will diminish and wane in the course of time. At the moment they are still very much present and it will probably take a decade or two for their elimination. This is a necessary evil, part and parcel of the change. Individuals are, of course, free to stand up and combat this sort of thing.

Another great change resulted from the mass employment of women after 1948. The living wage was so adjusted that an individual's earnings covered his own maintenance expenses only. Husband and wife and all the children, all went out to work. Very many women traveled on the trolley cars. Males no longer stood up to offer their seats to ladies or to older people, a situation which was inconceivable before the war. With the slogan "now we are all equal", this pre-war custom is completely abandoned. You could, of course, fight against it, and there were some who did abide by the pre-war etiquette. There was even an organized campaign after 1953, admonishing riders to give up their seats to the ladies.

Children began to earn money at a much earlier age now than before. Also a large segment of our youth was automatically precluded from continuing their schooling and were therefore forced to go to work. Here the principle "equal work, equal pay" came into play. Very often a 20-year old son, as a skilled laborer, was able to make 1500-2000 forints, whereas his father, who was on the job for 25-30 years, earned much less. This inequality in pay often caused the young people to overestimate their personal abilities and worth (value) and they demonstrated outwardly their feeling of superiority by ill-bred, rude, and ill-mannered attitude and behavior towards their parents.

This sort of thing was supported by the official policy of the state and was calculated to loosen the ties in the family. It was clearly in the interests of the state to bring about such a situation. In the factories, on production conferences, etc., whenever these things came up for discussion, the Party secretary invariably sided with the youth. Party officials were eager to help them find housing accommodations, so that young people were able to lead an independent life without parental interference or supervision. This again represented a conscious effort on the part of the government; the Party wanted to have and to control the whole man and it is they (the Party) which claimed the exclusive right to answer all the questions pertaining to the young man's life. It is much easier to control and to direct a young man's life if he does not reside in a closed family circle where there is a different, antagonistic air, a unit which formulates and enforces its own laws on its members. This is the reason why the Communists were so eager to create artificial barriers among the family members, this is the explanation of their wage-policies, whereby they forced every able family member to work. While they never dared to openly admit these objectives, i.e., the destruction of the family, they utilized every means at their disposal to bring this about. This is further proved by the repeated official pronouncements of leading Communist theoreticians; Révai repeatedly asserted in Parliament in 1948 that the Communist regime, the workers' rule, will only then be completely established if the Communists succeed in bringing up a generation of fully Communist mentality and action. If this was really so important in theory, the Communists certainly did not overlook its practical implications and consequences.

ANTI-SEMITISM

24. *Do you think any minority groups in Hungary have suffered more than others under Communism? If so, which and why?*

The Communist Party does have a minority program. According to this, minorities enjoy identical status and rights, just as all the rest of the population. The Communists do not recognize any differences between Magyar and minority peoples. This is one instance where they actually acted according to their program. Actually, from the point of view of inter-satellite relations, this was an imperative necessity; all minorities maintained close personal contacts with their relatives in the mother countries and all the mother countries were also people's democracies.

This question, in the form you put it, was nonexistent in Hungary. Nationality and minority problems we did not have. This favorable domestic situation was seized upon by the Communist leaders and used time and again against Western countries. Innumerable accusations were leveled against the United States, where a distinction is made even today between whites and negroes, with ample discrimination against the latter. There may be some reason for this distinction and discrimination of which I am not sure, but to this day I fail to find any justification for it.

24 a. Do you think any minority groups have benefitted more than others under Communism? If so, which and why?

No minority group benefitted more than others in principle, in practice, however, the Hungarian Jewry did derive greater benefits. They benefitted both politically and economically, because many of them turned Communist and those who did not were prepared to cooperate with the regime under certain conditions.

25. How were the Jews affected by the Communist regime? What was the attitude of the Jews toward the regime?

I can say that the Hungarian Jewry, with a little exception, (kevés kivétellel) cooperated in the fullest possible measure with the Communists. Of the exception (those who did not cooperate) very many were imprisoned, others were expatriated (másokat kitelepitettek). It was the Jews who, accepting the conditions set by the Communists, took upon themselves the execution of the various tasks in the political and economic life of the country. These tasks included the organization and direction of the AVH. Very many of the AVH officers were Jews. Jews became the directing forces in the economic life also, and they actively participated in the organization and direction of the Communist Party, Jews occupying the position of Party secretaries in such number which far exceeded their actual numerical proportion in the country. This holds equally true of the highest governmental offices, including the Cabinet itself.

25 c. Did you have any Jewish acquaintances? If so, what was their attitude toward the regime?

I had many Jewish acquaintances. They were with me in the prison.

25 d. How did Jews behave during the Revolt?

This always depended on the individual (Embere vàlogatta). They participated in the Revolution just as I did and as did many others.

Generally speaking, those Jews who opposed the regime were extremely stubborn and determined enemies of the system. This is especially true of the Jewish Social Democrats, who proved to be remarkably courageous and hard fighters.

I had the impression that Jewish intellectuals, in general, have a peculiar aptitude and predisposition towards extremes. Some of them are inclined to easily enter into uncalled-for and unnecessary compromises, while others, who decide to oppose something, are extremely consequential in their opposition.

25 e. What was the general attitude toward the Jews in Hungary?

One can say that the Hungarian nation and the Jews lived well next to one another. In 1944, during the Jewish deportations, the population of the country was on their side, hiding and concealing them, helping and supporting them. In 1944, the Jews reappeared again from various places ... they were an aspersed, tortured, and suffering people. These people came back with a flaming desire of revenge, which first manifested itself clearly during the war-criminal trials and during the liquidation of the nyilas movement. Jews were practically the only government witnesses on these trials. At the same time, Jews also participated in large numbers as members of the people's court councils. Their actions may have been just and right and proper, but these actions certainly did not tend to make the returnees popular in the eyes of the general population.

I knew a Jew, Izador Kner, the owner of a printing institution of European fame. (I always admired their magnificent lithography. There were only two or three such presses in all Europe.) The Kner family lived at Gyoma in Békés County. Gyoma is a small agricultural town, 95 percent of its inhabitants being peasants. The Kners were a highly respected family. In 1944 the entire family was taken away, with only the son, Migor, and his sister returning in 1945. Migor was a young man, of my age, and we were very good friends. They returned to Gyoma, Migor got back his printing presses, and tried to get started in business again. It was hard going, because he was all alone. He tried to engage himself in communal problems, desperately looking for means of forgetting the past.

This young man finally committed suicide in the beginning of 1946. He took his life because he was unable to find and unable to reestablish his former contacts with the people.

How do I explain this? One of the first steps of the returning Jews after 1945 was to enlist in the local and national police forces. The police force of Gyoma also had a fair share of them. These returned Jewish people, now as policemen, very often overstepped not only their functions and authority, but acted in a decidedly tasteless manner, often unable to differentiate right and wrong, guilty and innocent. Kner was looking to the people for justification; he did not emphasize, as did the others, the failure of the peasants to comprehend the grave injustices inflicted upon the Jews -- their lack of feeling of guilt -- instead, he censured and criticized the manner and attitude of his co-religionists. He was bitter and disillusioned. "I cannot creep out of my skin," he used to say, "to disentangle myself from the rest." On the other hand, he understood that the simple peasants, bewildered by the actions of the Jewish policemen, could not distinguish in their minds one Jew from another. The public became reserved and they looked upon all, including my friend, as a potential enemy. Rejected by the peasants he loved, and himself rejecting the actions of the other Jews, he saw no way out but death.

This story clearly shows both the ill-guided actions of many Jews after the war and the failure of many Hungarians to distinguish the "good Jews" from the "bad Jews".

Things quieted down somewhat as time went on; the Jews became sober and they cooled down. But the public retained the ugly memories and people kept on telling one another how many Jews there are in the AVH.

Then came the general persecution; innumerable people were put to jail. The relatives and friends of these imprisoned people constituted a substantial part of the Hungarian population. All these prisoners passed through the AVH and all of them experienced the inhuman brutality and cruel tortures of this infamous institution. Most of these people remained in jail for years, unjustly imprisoned and held without cause in the first place. Both the AVH and the prisons were liberally represented by Jewish officers and guards.

This was the main reason why the Jewish people were so much afraid of anti-Semitic outbreaks during the Revolution. But there were no anti-Semitic outbreaks. The fact that nothing like it occurred only goes to show the Hungarian people's ability to distinguish between Jewish individuals, cruel, unjust, and wicked, and the Jewish population who may have been entirely guiltless. While convinced of the indisputable guilt of some, they did not try to apply the theory of collective guilt at all.

This correct course was so much easier to take as neither the AVH, nor its excesses, nor all the other evils that plagued Hungary were exclusively attributable to the Jews alone. The people were well aware of this. Nevertheless, the fact that nothing happened by way of anti-Semitism must be credited to the mature and sober judgment of Hungary's public opinion and must not be seen as a Hungarian admission that the Jews were not responsible at all.

25 f. Did it change since 1945? Do you think there was more or less anti-Semitism than before the war? Why?

Anti-Semitism in Hungary was always an artificially fabricated movement, nurtured and kept alive by certain interests. The people themselves were never anti-Semitic, just as Hungarians, as people, were always able to freely cooperate with other minorities.

Anti-Semitism, as a European political movement, got well under way only between the world wars, especially after the Anschluss of Austria to Germany. It manifested itself mostly in neighboring states of Germany which had sizeable German minorities, such as in Hungary around Budapest and other places. In Hungary, too, it was among the German minority that the idea of anti-Semitism first began to spread. It was these people who organized and manned the extreme-right Party and propagated anti-Semitism. It was only in 1943 that the Hungarian Parliament, on direct German pressure, passed the first drastic anti-Semitic measures. We did have a Jewish Law as early as 1938, but that was a very mild measure indeed, as compared to similar measures of other countries. It had to do primarily with expulsion of Jews from the economic life of the country, setting at the time some limits to the participation in politics. Administrative measures against the Jews were adopted only in 1944, at the time when Hungary was no longer an independent nation; on March 19, 1944, Sztojay took over the reins in Hungary. This, then, was the situation. The fact is that in the entire German sphere it was Hungary where the Jews received, to the end, the most humanitarian treatment. Many Jews fled to Hungary from Poland, Czechoslovakia, Rumania, and Yugoslavia.

After March 29, 1944, the Jews living in the provinces were deported first. The Hungarian people watched helplessly the nyilas-gendarme terror, condemning it from start to finish.

While unable to resist the armed abductions, those able to do so did hide and conceal many Jews and helped others in every way they could.

The Jews from Budapest were taken away later. Their forced moving into the ghetto only occurred in September 1944, and even in October 1944 we still cooperated with many "illegal" Jewish groups. Of these groups many people knew that they were Jewish and yet only a few people made reports to the police.

From all this we may deduct that the artificially created and nurtured anti-Semitism did not take deeper roots in Hungary. The wide masses were not touched by it at all. And while the role of the Hungarian Jewry after the war was by no means popular, the public opinion always tried to excuse them, constantly referring doubters to their inhuman sufferings; if there had been anti-Semitism in Hungary, then, after all the crimes some Jews committed (in the police, AVH, prisons) after the Second World War, such anti-Semitism would of necessity have come to the surface during October 1956. Such, however, was not the case. This gives an unmistakable answer to your question.

25 h. *What do you think about the future of the Jews in Hungary?*

I am referring here to "minority groups" and I use the term "minority" only in order to be able to intelligibly answer your question. In reality I was never able to distinguish minority groups from people of so-called Hungarian origin. I cannot differentiate between Jews and Hungarians. As to their future in Hungary, it depends entirely on their future attitudes and actions, on how are they going to live and what their relationship to the rest of the nation will be.

There were many (Jewish) writers and newspapermen and other intellectuals who joined the Party in 1945 who later made important contributions to the anti-Stalin and anti-Rákosi struggle. Many of them are now in prison. The people will view and judge these men just as they will view and judge other Hungarians. In determining the future of the Jewish group, the decisive factor will not be the role the Jews played as a group, they will be rather evaluated as individuals, what attitude each and every one of them took and how did they act during Hungary's fateful hour.

GOVERNMENT AND POLITICS

POLITICAL EXPERIENCE AND ATTITUDES

1. *Have you been interested in politics? Why?*

Yes, I was, and still am, interested in politics. I came from a poor peasant family. During the years when I began to acquaint myself with the world's intellectual and spiritual values and phenomena, the question of the peasantry and the question of the poor people was the overriding question of the day.

One of the inevitable parts of every person's development is the fact that every individual begins to think, to a certain extent, through, and in terms of, his own family, and assigns values to many things and ideas by using his father's fate in society as a yardstick. I got extremely interested in the peasants and poor people's problems; the question became my constant preoccupation, an irresistible habit, similar to the drinking habit of an alcoholic. My formative years, the only years when I was really permitted to relate my views, were years saturated with politics. It was in 1938 when I made my first political statements to an audience of six men. Events followed one another in rapid succession, luring me to take a stand and offering ample opportunities at the same time for me to take part more and more in what I thought was decent, good, logical, and beautiful, -- namely combating German anti-Semitism.

In 1945, an opportunity presented itself to reorganize our country according to the wishes and desires of the wide masses of the people. I participated in these development as a youth leader. I was later forced to continue this struggle under the most unfavorable circumstances, against unequaled odds, all the way down to the gates of the concentration camp at Recsk. Developments permitted my release after 1953, and I continued, first in a clandestine fashion and later, during the Revolution, in the open, my struggles for a free and democratic Hungary. In this fashion did I politicize away a large portion of my life.

1 a. Compared with other interests, how important have political developments been to you?

For me, politics was the foundation, the starting point. This was precisely the reason why I chose to become an economist, to enable myself to give expert answers to all the questions. I clearly recognized the great interrelationship between politics and economics; to what great extent the raison d'etre and stability of a political system depends on the economic foundation underlying it and supporting it. I firmly believed that my economic studies would help me most in my determination to assist the people in reorganizing and directing the new Hungary with a view of achieving the maximum good for the wide masses. My primary, though not exclusive, interest centered around the agricultural question; the developing of better production and marketing methods with a view of minimizing, if not eliminating, the costly services of the middle men; how could an agricultural industry be organized which would utilize fully all the fruits of our agriculture giving both security to the farmer and raising the standard of the rest of the population. This is only one of the many examples clearly indicating how decisions in economic questions depend on the political structure of the country, and how the economic life, on the other hand, is capable of either underscoring or undermining political structure and orientation. At first I was interested in political questions only and only later did I recognize the importance of economics.

1 b. Has your interest varied in the course of time?

My interest was fairly stable, constant, and unchanged.

1 c. Have you ever participated in political action of some sort? If so, when (what years) and in what form?

In 1938, I was leader of a local KIE (YMCA) group. In that group others and I analyzed minority questions. We investigated the problems of Germans, Serbians, Slovaks, and other minorities in Hungary, as well as problems of Hungarians living in other lands. We were investigating the possibilities and conditions of cooperation and coexistence of people of different nationality, tongue, and culture.

In 1943 I became a member of the anti-Fascist Liberty Front of Hungarian Students. Towards the end of 1943, I became a member of the executive committee of the Freedom Front of Hungarian Youth, an organization of youths of peasant, workers and intellectual origin. This organization was part of the Independence Front (Függetlenségi Front) in which Communists, Social Democrats, and other parties participated. This Independence Front, working in a clandestine fashion between 1943-45, represented the nucleus of those political forces which took over the direction of Hungary after 1945. I was a representative of the Small Landholders' Party.

In March 1945, we organized a peasant youth movement, under the name of Independent Youth (Független Ifjuság) of which I was elected chairman. The founding meeting took place in the assembly room of the central City Hall of Budapest, under the strict observance of democratic rules and procedures. In May 1945 I was also elected chairman of the National Council of Hungarian Youth (Magyar Ifjuság Országos Tanácsa). This latter was a youth coalition, made up of the Independent Youth, a Small Landholders' Party youth organization, of Social Democrat Youth, of Communist Youth, of the KIE (YMCA), of the KALOT (Catholic), of the MEFESZ (university students) and of the youths of the Communist Party.

On November 4, 1945, the first postwar elections of Hungary

were held. This was a list election, where voters chose between political parties, without voting for individuals. Hungary was divided into electoral districts and the political parties presented a list of nominees in each district. The voters gave their votes for this or that Party's list. The list itself contained the names of Party nominees, set up according to rank. 16,000 votes called for one mandate. (If, for instance, in Szolnok County the Small Landholders' Party received 160,000 votes for their list, then the first ten people whose names appeared on their list were thereby elected members of Parliament.)

From 1945 to 1947 I was Member of Parliament, representing the Small Landholders' Party. Between 1948-1950 I was living under constant police surveillance, at the end I was arrested, and in March 1950 I was already in the Recsk camp. I was permitted to leave the camp in September 1953, being placed under police supervision again.

During the years 1954 and 1955, I succeeded in reestablishing all the contacts with political friends (since I could not leave the village in which I was interned, various people came to me). We continued our discussions of the exciting and interesting political questions of that time, all the way down to the Revolution.

During the Revolution, I was elected member of the Workers' Council of the Pest County brick factories. I was also a member of the executive committee of the Revolutionary Committee of Hungarian Intellectuals, a member of the executive committee of the Petőfi Circle and a member of the executive committee of the resurrected Small Landholders' Party. In my latter capacity, I was chiefly concerned with the organization of the Party in the rural districts. I continued my activities till December 1956, leaving Hungary on December 4.

2. *Can you trace for me, step by step, how you felt about the political system as it emerged after World War II and developed during the following years?*

At the time of Hungary's exit from the Second World War, my place in the political life of the country was already clarified; it was determined by my activities and attitude before and during the war -- my role in the youth movement as well as my illegal anti-German activities.

My first political step on the youth front took place at the beginning of 1945, when, in discussions with leaders of other youth groups with whom we cooperated during the war, we decided to continue to seek ways and means of further discussing and exchanging our views on matters of principle and organization.

It was our sincere endeavor to continue our wartime cooperation with all the other youth groups, including the Communists, and we really believed that such a cooperation would be fruitful and beneficial to all. The idea of cooperation was also imperative in a sense, since on the national level and Cabinet also represented a coalition. The cooperating national parties wanted to see similar cooperation among the youth groups. As a result, partly on initiative from above, partly as a response to Russian desires, we decided to create the MADISZ. The MADISZ, then, was a super-structure, embodying the youth coalition, and serving as a coordinating arm among the various groups which, while sending delegates to the all-Hungarian youth organization, continued their separate existence as before.

The MADISZ coalition lasted only for a few months; we soon became impatient with the domineering tactics of the Communists, who were bent on taking over the direction of everything. The MADISZ presented the same picture which took place in Parliament at the time, since the Communist youth leaders received the very same political instructions which directed the activities of Rákosi and of his group in the national Parliament.

While the coalition of the national parties lasted until 1948, we, in the MADISZ, not affected by those economic forces which kept the parties together, decided to act much earlier; I severed all my connections with the MADISZ at the end of April 1945, and my exit -- I having represented the Independent Small Landholders' Party -- meant the end of cooperation of that Party with the MADISZ. After a few weeks the Social Democrats and the Peasant Party youth also left the MADISZ. Only the Communists remained.

Having left the MADISZ and having completed the organization of the Small Landholders' Party's Independent Youth Movement, I was repeatedly accused of anti-Communist tendencies and was branded an extreme rightist who opposed both the land reform and the Russians. The maneuver did not succeed thanks to the powerful support I received from many quarters. A small residue of anti-Soviet feeling did remain in my views, however, and I was well taken care of on this account during 1948-1956.

The Independent Youth was an organization of peasant youth, a group whose spiritual mentors were the populist writers -- we sympathized particularly with the views of László Németh. We were the so-called Third Road-ists (harmadik utas), desiring to build up Hungary according to the wishes of the people. This political credo placed us against the Germans first and later also against the Russians and Communists, whose basic aims were similar to that of the Germans, even though their tactics and methods were different.

Our decision to leave the MADISZ had great repercussions in the life of the nation. Many articles were written pro and con, and heated polemics continued for some time. At the end the Communists and the Russians, still desiring and insisting on at least a loose cooperation between the various youth groups, after long and protracted negotiations the National Council of Hungarian Youth (Magyar Ifjuság Országos Tanácsa) was brought into being. A committee, made up of delegates of the various groups, held meetings once a week. Actions, if and when agreed upon, were executed by the various groups themselves. I became the chairman of the National Council, at the same time maintaining my chairmanship of the Independent Youth. György Non, the secretary-general of the Communist youth organization, became secretary-general of the National Council also. The work of the Council consisted of the continuous and bitter political duel between Non and me, a struggle in which I lost out in the end, the Communists having succeeded in bringing about a <u>gleichgeschaltet</u> youth organization in 1948.

For the period 1948-1956, I don't have much to say. We could politicize in small communities only. The political fronts reemerged even in the prison camp, only on a much wider scale than in 1945; beginning with the extreme left all the way to the right, every shade of color was amply represented. These colors were, after all, the very reason of their holders' being in prison. In the various prison camps a coalition came into being which later represented the political framework of the Revolution. This coalition embraced all shades from the progressive Christians to the national Communists.

After 1953 (when I was freed and placed under police supervision) and to the beginning of 1956, I was a passive onlooker of the events. I talked politics only among friends. Circumstances changed towards the end of 1955 and towards the beginning of 1956; the Petőfi Circle was in the process of formation. Those young people who ultimately organized it represented, for the most part, the populist colleges, -- a group that grew up on the breasts of the populist literature (a népi irodalom emlöin nevelkedtek föl).

In the formation of the Petőfi Circle and in the development of its guiding principles I also took part, though not publicly (I was still under police supervision), but by means of private conferences and discussions among my friends.

Real political problems came only after the victory of the Revolution, when the political parties reemerged again. I went back to the Small Landholders' Party, became a member of its executive committee, and concerned myself with Party organization for a few days. During these days I had ample opportunity to check and to establish that the generation, torn to pieces and scattered during 1947-1948, did not go under, but survived the storm. That generation reappeared and assembled again; everywhere I met the same people with whom I cooperated in the Independent Youth Movement. Thus the line originating with the 1938 village researchers (falukutatók) is unbroken and uninterrupted all the way up to the Revolution.

This youth attempted its first politicizing in and through the youth movements, limiting itself first to problems affecting the youth alone, taking its place, in 1956, in the life of the entire nation.

2 a. Did you sympathize with any political Party prior to 1948? If so, which and why? If not, why not?

I was a member of the Small Landholders' Party.

2 b. Did your father belong to any political Party?

No, he did not. He was a great admirer of Endre Bajcsy-Zsilinszky, and he had quite a few unpleasant difficulties because of this.

2 c. Did your political views change at all since 1945? If so, in what ways and why?

My views changed since 1945 in so far as I learned a great deal since, and in so far as they were conditioned by later changes in Hungary's status and condition. The basic questions confronting Hungary are the same and my basic principles also remain unaltered.

2 d. What were your feelings about the Communist Party before 1948?

I cannot explain this by giving a static answer. Opinion and feeling is a process which never ceases developing. I have many Communist friends. I always distinguish between Communists and the Communist Party, and especially between these two and the leadership of the Communist Party. This leadership always catered ignominiously and stupidly to all Russian wishes and desires. I could never agree to that.

2 e. What determined your initial attitude toward Communism?

You must, I think, know what my initial attitude towards communism was, before I can intelligently answer your question.

I never approved of communism, viewing it always as incapable of realization, -- as an asocial (nem közösségi) system. For this reason I always opposed it. I have the feeling that communism as a system was based on the criticism of early capitalism and, with the passing of time, and with changes which occurred in the capitalist system, many forceful affirmations and statements of the communist credo have likewise lost their application, usefulness, and ingredients of truth which they initially possessed.

Every person likes to construct his own life, and it is imperative that he is given an opportunity to do so. Leveling, equalization is necessary (nivelláódás kell), but not to the point where each man possesses only one cup. Nor did communism achieve such results; there are social and class differences under communism just like everywhere else. The position of the leaders and of the good cadres is immeasurably better than that of the rest. There is a group of a privileged few under both capitalism and communism, the difference is that the life of those who are not members of the group of the privileged few is incomparably more hopeless under communism than under capitalism. If capitalism oscillates to the detriment of the many, there is always room for slow but orderly and peaceful adjustment. If oscillation of an identical kind occurs under communism, a determined movement towards the caste-system is the result, and the only way for the masses is the way to prison. I value personal freedom above all else and for this reason I oppose communism in principle.

Before and after 1945 I was very often together with individual Communists and I trusted them to a certain extent. Later my attitude became more rigid and rejecting, because I saw that decent Communists don't have much influence in their own camp and that the Communists have put an end even to political freedom and human liberty. This increased even more my opposition to them.

2f. *If you had to choose among the descriptions of your political attitude since 1948, which comes closest to your own case?*

One thing is certain; I always opposed the Communists' efforts. I should perhaps add that I have my own political views which I value and that I was a partner in this political era, but in no way a collaborator.

2g. *Do you think other people felt the same way? Who did? Who did not?*

Very many people felt the way I did. The Independent Youth Movement, starting as it did from scratch, under those political conditions after the war, received its political program from me. And yet the Independent Youth Movement grew to be the largest youth organization of the country. It had almost one million members, -- a phenomenal number, unique in Hungarian political history. I cite this to show that there were many indeed who held the same views as I did. These people were predominantly peasant youths, intellectuals of peasant stock, and children of the intellectuals of the provinces.

2 h. *In spite of their many grievances, just about the whole population obeyed the authorities until October 1956. How do you explain this?*

The explanation is rather simple; there was no freedom in Hungary. The AVH was very well developed, together with the informer system which operated secretly, and the people were afraid to move. Beside these secret institutions you had the Party network, the labor union network, covering every inch of the land and every individual; these two organizations uncovered and disclosed in public every single manifestation or attempt against them.

The entire country lived under constant fear, laws and rights had no validity. There was no possibility for judicial redress, no recourse to the courts. With nobody trusting anybody else, everybody was on his own; there was no way of contact or organization. The automobile stopped in front of the house and a person was taken away; he never came back. Often the whole family was taken away and dispersed in all directions. Under such conditions it is rather difficult to be courageous. A people does not, and cannot, commit suicide. A people cannot live for long in a way which incites its adversary to continuously plague and harass it; what it wants is peace and tranquility. Its object is to survive historical trials and tribulations. In order to do so it is inclined to render to God what is God's and to Caesar what is Caesar's. It does this as it sees fit, as it is possible.

The instinctive judgment is about as follows: there is only one life; and most people (the masses) do not consider themselves responsible for the evils and mistakes emanating from the actions of the regime in power and, considering it an outside factor clearly beyond their competence or duty or power to abrogate it, they accept it and resign themselves to it, forming their lives as best they can.

Hungarians, in this respect, learned very quickly; they only spoke their opinions at home, often keeping their thoughts to themselves even at home.

The basic elements of such behavior are not peculiarly Hungarian, nor are they restricted to their applicability to Hungary. Stemming from the very nature of man, it is universally true. The Hungarian people did not in any way behave peculiarly.

2 i. *What do you know about the use of loyalty dossiers (Káder)? How effective were they in keeping people in line?*

This was a very extensive and very well developed system. The dossiers were very good instruments.

These loyalty dossiers regulated every person's career and everybody tried to do his utmost in his own sphere to reach the best results possible; he either joined the Party or, even if he was not a member, he tried to behave in such a manner as to make it impossible for those in charge to enter on his cadre sheet some such remark which could tend to hinder him later in his possibilities of advancement. Nobody really knew, nor did he have any way of knowing, what incriminating information was held against him. We have seen these dossiers during the Revolution. Many of them contained malevolent and often ridiculous remarks.

For me personally the very life itself was injurious. This was fairly common, I was by no means a unique case in that I spent years in prison and was living later under police supervision; I was not allowed to go to any public places. I could not go legally into movies, to the theater, to the store, to a restaurant, I could not receive visitors, I could not have a radio or a telephone, not to even mention that I had no basic rights whatsoever.

SECTION "G" CURPH #152 Pg. 291

3. *If you think back to day-to-day life in Hungary a few years ago, what were the main grievances you had?*

    (i)   Interference with family life
    (ii)   Interference with religious life
    (iii) Inadequate housing
    (iv) Disagreement with political ideas
    (v)   Inadequate food
    (vi) Fear of arrest and terror
    (vii) Violation of national dignity and traditions
    (viii) Boredom and drabness
    (ix) Interference with civil rights
    (x)   Inadequate opportunity to get ahead
    (xi) Inadequate professional recognition
    (xii) Presence of Soviet troops
    (xiii) Distortion of facts by regime
    (xiv) Over taxation
    (xv) Overwork.

(3 a.) xiii Distortion of facts by regime
    i   Interference with family life
    ix Interference with civil rights

3 b. Which three of these were the least important for you?

(3 b) ii Interference with religious life
    iii Inadequate housing
    vi Fear of arrest and terror

3 c. Which were the most important for the intellectuals?

(3 c) xiii Distortion of facts by regime
    viii Boredom and drabness
    xi Inadequate professional recognition

3 d. *Which for the peasants?*

(3 d)ii Interference with religious life
    xiv Over taxation
    vi Fear of arrest and terror

3 e. *Which for the workers?*

(3 e) xv Overwork
    ii Interference with religious life
    vi Fear of arrest and terror

3 f. *These grievances and complaints—how acutely did one feel them on an average day? Can you give examples?*

At Recsk, on Sundays, we were carrying firewood for the AVH in formations of sixty from 6 a.m. till 3 p.m. I felt very vividly, at every turn, the bleakness, desolation, and utter hopelessness of life as I then knew it. As we kept on going back and forth, carrying our loads, I thought it would never end. Each turn seemed like eternity.

This was about a day. After I was freed, it was not much better or different; getting up in the morning, going to the factory, eight hours work, production conference, explanation and interpretation of the daily press, comments on the press and on the interpretation, remembering Stalin in a few words of praise, going home and on the way home the acute realization that there is no money left at home to buy what I wanted to buy, and that there probably won't be any for a long time, if ever.

3 g. *Did one talk about them with others? If so, with whom? If not, why?*
Did this vary in time?

People very seldom spoke about these things with others who knew them just as well. Weekdays were not discussed, people just lived them. At times people broke out in protest and dissatisfaction, without realizing that the cause of their outburst was the dreariness and hopelessness of their lives.

The impatience of people was rather pronounced and fairly common. The parents were very often angry at one another or at the children.

3 i. *Were there any little annoyances that got on one's nerves? If so, what were they?*

There were innumerable little annoyances, but it is difficult even to reproduce or relate them. A man could only be a truly anti-Communist in Hungary; when the trolley car came and there was no room on it, one usually cursed; and he was cursing the regime. When there was no lard in the store, one got impatient and one cursed the Soviet Union. Such incidents were innumerable.

3 j. *In compensation, what were some things that provided satisfaction, gratification, or relief?*

There were such compensatory things. This again is a universal human ambition to make life more beautiful and more comfortable under whatever conditions. There were really beautiful family lives. These were other occasions. One went to the theater, in spite of the police prohibition. Others drank their three half-deciliters even though the money spent meant no potatoes for tomorrow. Etc., etc.

GOVERNMENT, PARTY AND MASS ORGANIZATIONS

4. *Where was the real power in Hungary?*

The Communist Party had the real power in Hungary.

4 a. What makes you think so?

All legislation stemmed from the Party, all bills introduced in Parliament being Party proposals or recommendations. The Party proposed something or recommended a measure. The Council of Ministers then constructed the Bill and Parliament accepted it. Take the national economy; every essential function was in the hands of trusted Party functionaries; take the AVH, it received its instructions from the top leaders of the Party and was responsible to them and to them only.

4 b. What role did the Council of Ministers play as compared with the Party?

The Council of Ministers executed the Party's commands and acted upon the Party's plans. The Council of Ministers was also manned by the Communists, and the more important posts were held by important members of the Party's Central Committee

4 c. Who ran the government [since 1948]?

Rákosi and a few people around him ran the government after 1948.

4 d. What was the role of parliament?

The Parliament's role was secondary or even tertiary; it provided an aura of constitutionality. Its sessions were very rare. The Presidential Council had the right and power to legislate at such times when Parliament was not in session, i.e., it could proclaim decrees which had the legality and force of law. Between

1948-1956 most laws had the form of Presidential Council decrees. During elections, the Communists were able to get those people elected when they pleased.

4 e. Why did the Communists hold elections?

They held elections because elections were prescribed by, and were part and parcel of, the so-called Constitution. And the regime was using this simple but crude device to legalize itself. Elections are a convenient device to do just that. The regime felt it had to create the appearance of legality to which it could refer occasionally. It could claim to be the legal and desired representative of the people.

4 f. Was there a bureaucracy? How did it compare with pre-1944 Hungary?

Yes, there was a bureaucracy. It was much larger than that before 1944.

4 g. Was there much graft? Why? Can you give examples?

Yes, there was graft. Fear of consequences, however, kept it in check.

4 h. What sort of people went into government service?

Two kinds of people went into the government service: (a) those employees of the old government who were either indispensable or became Party members; (b) worker cadres: these were given quick training courses or evening courses.

4 i. What sort of people became professional army officers? What were the advantages of being one?

Professional army officers represented a privileged stratum. They were a new class. The regime gave them everything. Their pay was very high. They had many advantages and their position carried a high prestige. They had no housing problems.

This class was composed of two elements: worker cadres or poor peasant stock. A determined effort was made to get rid of the remnants of the old officers corps and to replace them with new blood.

4 j. What sort of people became managers?

In Hungary, in filling of all important positions, two principles were operative: (1) to retain of the old personnel those who became Party members as well as those who were both indispensable and docile; (2) to replace all others with new men according to regular cadre procedure. There were a host of worker-directors. The more intelligent workers, if they otherwise qualified, were sent to business administration courses and became plant director.

5. Next I should like to talk about the DISZ [Youth League]. Were there advantages in belonging to it?

Undoubtedly, membership in the DISZ did bring with it certain advantages. In questions of admission to the universities and when the question came up whether a student would, or would not be permitted to continue his university studies, membership in the DISZ, or more precisely, active participation in its affairs, was the basic if not the determining consideration. Such active membership counter-balanced a student's unfavorable social background; if a student came from a family of intellectuals -- a factor ordinarily excluding him from the university -- he was able to continue as a bona fide student if his DISZ activities warranted it.

5 a. *Were there drawbacks?*

One could not very well speak of drawbacks in those days. It was interesting, though, that people were always careful in avoiding too great an involvement lest this be held against them at a future date.

5 b. *Did one have to join?*

Joining was not an obligation. There were campaigns, however, to enlist all the students. In these campaigns joining was declared an obligation and non-members were equated with enemies of the people's democracy. All kinds of methods were used to prompt and to pressure people into joining.

5 c. *What ways were there not to join?*

There were several ways which students and others connected with the universities could use as an excuse not to join the DISZ. One of these was that a person dug himself into some technical or scientific problem or project and said that he was primarily a scientist and that he was not interested in politics. This, of course, was not an adequate defense and in practice everybody was a member of the DISZ, at least nominally; the most that people could do was to refrain from active participation in its affairs.

5 d. *Did you belong?*

I was not a member of the DISZ after 1948. In this connection I should like to say that, in 1945, when the DISZ, or more correctly the MADISZ, was brought into being, I was one of its founding members. The MADISZ, or at least the idea of it, was born before the termination of the Second World War when, in our struggles and battles against the Germans, who were our enemies at the time, we recognized the necessity of creating a common and unified youth front to better serve our purposes. At the time we thought it a good thing to continue our wartime cooperation even after the termination of hostilities and with this view in mind we created the MADISZ (Association of Democratic Hungarian Youth) in January 1945. In this undertaking all youth groups participated, including the scouts and the denominational KIE (Protestant) and KALOT (Catholic), together with the youth groups of the political parties. It soon turned out that this youth coalition or cooperation was unworkable. It did not work out, in my judgment, because the Communists were unable to accommodate themselves to the changed situation and they continued to strive to occupy all positions, a practice which characterized their attitude already during the illegal period. Since the changed situation provided them with even greater possibilities, they naturally took full advantage of it. The result was that the others were forced to assume the defensive and were seeking ways and means to extricate themselves from this uncomfortable and disagreeable situation. The Social Democrats took the exit first, followed by the Small Landholders' Party and others, so that towards the summer of 1945 only the Communists remained in the MADISZ.

5 e. *When and how did you join?*

As I mentioned before, the Freedom Front of Hungarian Youth made the decision as early as 1944 of maintaining a common front even after the termination of hostilities. This common front, as it was later agreed upon, was to take form in the framework of the MADISZ -- an organization created in youth conferences at Szeged and Debrecen, and officially inaugurated in January 1945. I was one of the founding members of this group.

5 f. *What were your duties? Your position?*

I was a member of the MADISZ's executive committee and as such I was the chief of the press section. **Question:** Would you say that there was an essential difference between the DISZ and the MADISZ: **Answer:** There certainly is an essential difference between the MADISZ of 1945 and the DISZ of 1948. The MADISZ was a democratic youth association in which the various groups representing differing views and parties had equal rights and their participation, in principle, was based on equality. That the MADISZ could not satisfy the expectations placed on it was due mainly to the Communists' inability to cooperate. They acted in the same fashion as did the Communist Party of Hungary during 1945 and after. While in big politics people seemed to show more patience and restraint -- the national coalition did last, after all, from 1945 to 1948 -- the coalition of the youth exploded already in May 1945 with all the constituent groups establishing separate organizations.

The MADISZ and later the DISZ became a Communist youth organization. The Communists did not like to talk about this from 1945 to 1948, constantly emphasizing the democratic nature of these organizations which had nothing to do with the Communist Party. In 1948 they openly admitted, however, that the DISZ was a Communist organization under the direction of the Party, its aim being the fostering of Communist education of the youth.

5 g. *Could you describe your work in the DISZ and your attitude toward it?*

I was only a member of the MADISZ, which, as I explained, had no connections whatsoever with the later DISZ. We all cooperated during the war and it was our aim to create a common organization which would permit our young people of different parties and views to grow up together and discuss fully their different aims, methods, and approaches. This seemed to us a worthwhile and useful thing, especially so if we consider that we all considered the Germans to be our only enemies, especially after their forceful intervention in our nation's affairs, which became very pronounced after the beginning of 1944. The presence of the common enemy certainly held us together. Circumstances, however, changed completely after 1945.

In the MADISZ I represented the youth organization of the Small Landholders' Party on the executive committee.

6. *Now about the Party. What did it mean to be a Party member?*

Since I was never a member, I can hardly give an answer to your question.

6 a. *Who had to be a member?*

The Communist Party underwent a change between 1945-1956. It would be best, I think, if we spoke about the most critical period, the years from 1949 to 1953, and tried to give an answer to the question within that period.

Membership in the Party during this period was closely connected with questions of employment opportunities and professional success. Certainly all those people who desired to advance in their fields not only were obliged to become members of the Party, but were also expected to actively participate in the work of the Party. Certain jobs automatically required a Communist Party membership and people desiring to work in intellectual fields were hardly able to do so without it, excepting those, of course, who, because of their outstanding capacity or knowledge, were simply indispensable. In the latter case no pressure was exerted upon the individual to enter the Party. The official Party instructions underlined this; Party secretaries were so advised and they made certain that applicants for certain offices and jobs were Party members.

6 b. Who wanted to be a member?

It is very difficult to answer this question with some degree of precision; all those wanted to become members who desired to advance professionally or who were bent on making a career. These were people who wanted to secure for themselves economic advantages by using their Party membership as a lever. It is hard to guess what the total number of Party members may have been at this time, but estimating it conservatively it must have been well over the million mark. A large number of these people who were looking for economic advantages.

6 c. What are the rights and duties of membership?

I am not familiar with the Communist Party's rules and procedures. At most I can tell you only what I deduced from outward appearances. Speaking of membership rights it is certainly true that Party members were more free to both raise and discuss questions, within and outside of the Party. I never took part in any meetings of the Communist Party, but I was able to observe that on production conferences Party members did raise controversial and delicate questions which another, not a member of the Party, would never have dared to do.

6d. Can you think of some people you knew who joined? If so, when and why did they join?

Of course, I knew a great many of them. I was living in a small town near Budapest and I represented that town in Parliament from 1945 to 1947. I knew a great many people and even more people knew me. It was not an unusual procedure for many of my constituents to come up to me and tell me how they could have this or that job, provided they entered the Communist Party. They wanted to know my opinion and asked me for advice. Giving advice was not an easy thing under such circumstances, but I will tell you frankly that I always told them to enter the Party undisturbed (csak nyugodtan lépjen be a kommunista pártba, etc., etc.). After all, what else could these people have done? Many of them were heads of families, responsible for the rearing of numerous children, who had to make a decision on the spur of the moment. Their decision meant a difference between a well-paid position or going without bread. This, then, was the reason why many people joined the Party. **Question:** Was there any conscious effort made by the leaders of the non-Communist parties, such as yourself or others, to systematically flood the Communist Party with applicants who were not Communists themselves, in order to gain inside information on the one hand and to water down the effectiveness and discipline of the Communists on the other? **Answer:** There were no such things, as least I am not aware of them. There was a sentimental check in that people were not enthusiastic about entering the Party. When a person came to a decision and felt he had to enter, the act of joining caused him a considerable inner disturbance; there was always a feeling of abstention with a residue of fear; people felt that while they may solve their problems, at least momentarily, by joining the Party, their decision to join may later be held against them.

> 6 e. *What did being a member do to people? Do you think some people changed after becoming Party members? If so, in what way? When?*

A great many people changed after becoming Party members. Their situation was similar to that of a person entering a room, the contents of which he does not know; he does not know what awaits him behind the door. Once a person entered the Party, he came under the impact of those forces which were operating there. Various people reacted differently and obeyed the Party in a different manner. The weaker ones succumbed completely and their actions and views, at least in their outward manifestations, suffered an abrupt change from one day to another. Views they held one day they rejected completely on the next, obviously in order to be able to maintain those advantages which they thereby secured to themselves.

6 f. What about Communists who became dissatisfied: on what grounds did they turn "sour"?

The dissatisfaction of Communists had several reasons. When speaking on this question, I should like to restrict myself to a few individuals with whom I was acquainted. Both cases are familiar to me. I could tell you, for instance, about a newspaperman who became a staff member of the Szabad Nép in 1945. The regime gave to this man everything it could offer him, demanding of him, at the same time, everything that a totalitarian regime is capable of demanding. He was expected to write about things and about events which my friend knew quite well were not true. This was a concrete case and the reasons cited were his concrete reasons which caused his gradual disillusionment. When he could not stand it any longer, he gave up his position and all the benefits his position represented to exchange it, after an unsuccessful attempt to cross the frontier in 1948, with imprisonment. This is not a generally known case. There are other, historic examples, the cases of the Hungarian writers, for instance; the question of the writers' rebellion is generally known.

The beginning of this rebellion took place in 1953, after Imre Nagy assumed the premiership, at a time when as a result of certain decrees of the Nagy government, a process of liberalization got under way in the country. In connection with these decrees, the writers visited factories, villages, farms, and cooperatives

(TSzCS's) to acquaint themselves with the real situation. In the course of these visits the writers came to the realization that, while official Hungary praised the success of cooperative farms to high heavens, proclaiming the great advantages these have as against private farms, the members of the cooperatives lived under such miserable economic conditions which were only comparable to those of agricultural laborers (béresek) living on the large estates before the Second World War.

These visits, and what they saw during them, represented the principal cause of the writers' disillusionment. If all this is so bad, they said, and, the nation is systematically deceived about the real situation, there obviously must be something wrong with the top leadership. In innumerable speeches and articles they deplored the situation, but continued to maintain, for a long time, that not the basic principles of the Party were at fault here, blaming the situation on the incompetence of the individuals who put the directives into practice. It was during 1953 that the writers made their second great discovery, finding that the colossal failures cannot be blamed on officials alone and that the very people from whom the directives and principles emanated are basically at fault. The Party and the Party's organization is to be blamed, they asserted. Thus came the following steps, the end conclusions of which was the discovery that the people are led and directed by a stratum which is completely separated from it: a stratum entirely unaware of the condition of the population; a stratum which knows nothing of the problems of the people. The writers took then the next great step and, beginning at the other end of the problem, they endeavored to discover what really were the problems of the people, what were their difficulties, how did the whole system operate. In this fashion they discovered step by step that in Hungary a false economic front was maintained, that the regime speaks about economic prosperity, economic developments at a time when people do not possess the minimum standards of existence. They observed at the same time -- they were in a position to do so -- the striking differences between the standard of living of the large masses and that of the ruling stratum which directed the country's social and economic life; the one group was equipped with television sets and all the modern conveniences, the other had no bread to eat. These, then, were the reasons for the writers' rebellion, during the course of which they discovered the real situation of the country, facts which greatly contributed to the outbreak of the Revolution itself.

6 g. *What sort of position could one attain without being a Party member?*

If I have to categorically answer the question, I must say that without Party membership one could attain no position. This, however, would not be the whole truth. A person's technical knowledge and the employer's actual need of such a person also was a determining factor.

In this connection the basic considerations were the applicant's social background, whether or not a Party member, the contents of his cadre sheet, his relationship to work, and Party activities. These were the determining factors. There were, however, excellent engineers, or agricultural experts who, in their respective fields, were simply indispensable. In situations of this sort, one of two procedures were followed: (1) The indispensable expert was either assigned to work under a less competent man who was a reliable Party member. The expert performed his job, with his superior being credited for it, or (2) the Communist Party and/or the government tried to pay off these people by giving them all kinds of economic benefits. I have in mind here such people as Mr. Wesenmeyer, for instance, an agricultural expert of European reputation, whom the government tried to buy off in this fashion by giving him the Kossuth prize, all kinds of benefits, good dwelling, good pay, freedom to travel in Europe, etc., etc.

6 h. *Were you a member?*

No, I was not a member.

6 p. *Could you have joined?*

I don't really think that I could have joined. Perhaps yes, between 1945 and 1948, and perhaps even between 1948 and 1950. My situation, you must understand, was a peculiar one; I am the son of a poor peasant and my socio-economic condition, as it was termed in Hungary, tended to underline and to strengthen my opinions under certain circumstances. In 1945 I could have joined any Party of my choosing, it certainly would not have been a problem. There were, between 1945 and 1948, a few attempts to enlist me. I met Rákosi a couple of times, who, in a half-jovial manner remarked to me that I am not in that position to which my social origin ought to predetermine me. He continued to say how great a service I could render to my country if I were occupying my proper position. He did not leave any doubt in my mind what he meant by "proper position". There were a few more attempts between 1948 and 1950, the period when I was already in a troubled situation and, being under a strict police supervision, I no longer was a free partner who could freely say yes or no to a question of this sort. The fact that I did say no greatly contributed to my being placed under even more tight conditions.

6 q. *Did non-membership later affect your life or career?*

Non-membership certainly affected both my life and career, though you cannot very well oversimplify matters by considering this factor alone; I would have had a possibility to continue my activities even if I had not become a member of the Communist Party, in the form and fashion which was open to many Small Landholders' Party and Peasant Party representatives. I have in mind here the position of a passive collaborator, who nods approvingly to whatever the Communists do.

6 r. Who ran the Party?

This is a question where there is no room for dispute whatsoever. The Party was run by Rákosi and by a few others of his circle, all the way to somewhere in 1956 (the date escapes me) when Rákosi finally fell.

6 s. What do you think about some of the leaders?

I would have to know who those "some of the leaders" are. **Question:** What do you think about Rákosi, for instance? **Answer:** Regarding Rákosi I am going to cite the opinion of an older friend of mine who played an important role in Hungarian politics and who, in my estimation, possessed a very clear vision. He said of Rákosi at the end of 1947 that Rákosi was a very intelligent rascal (nagyon értelmes csirkefogó).

6 t. Do you think Party policy remained the same or did it change? If the latter, when, how, and under what impetus? What did you think of it?

The policy of the Party undoubtedly changed, since, no matter how programmatical their actions may have been, they could neither disregard nor precisely determine the force-factors which unexpectedly came up as time went on. We can state truthfully, however, that the 1945-1953 developments were exceptionally programmatic, well thought-out, and proceeding as planned. We ought to speak in this connection primarily about agriculture -- it was there that the Communist plans were most conspicuous, -- that agricultural policy which characterized the regime, and which met the stubborn resistance of the peasants between 1945-1953, was definitely a very well developed policy -- though based on theoretical considerations only. Otherwise the population's mood, interests, and points of view would also have been considered, in which case this policy would not have been carried out, or, at least not in the manner we knew it.

The first disturbing moment in the Communists' policy was undoubtedly Stalin's death in 1953, and the various disturbances which took place at different times and locations, shortly after Stalin's death. I have in mind here the East German events which occurred in 1953 as well as the events in other places in the Soviet Union where local uprisings took place. These were isolated events in themselves, but their effect must not be underestimated. These events led the Soviet Union to give certain concessions to the Soviet people and to the satellites.

7. *Did you belong to any other organizations or societies since 1950?*

I was not a member of any Party or society after 1950.

7 g. *What did people think of the mass organizations? Where there any exceptions?*

Membership in the Party as well as membership in the mass organizations fell into almost the same category, it being considered a necessary evil, where one was obliged to be a member, had to perform certain duties in order to maintain his present position or to be entitled to get another.

7 i. *Can you describe the leaders of the organization -- their background, age, education, occupation, motives?*

This, of course, differed with places and people and organizations. I can only tell you of my own little town, where

I was more or less acquainted with the people. There, a variety of types of people participated in the many organizations, the number of convinced Communists being the smallest. Convinced Communists were almost a rarity; I recall one now, the secretary of one of the TSzCs's, who was such a convinced Communist. This man was, I feel, the most pleasant person to deal with in the whole village. I maintained close and friendly relations with him and we were able, even during the toughest times, to discuss all sorts of things in a friendly manner. These were the exceptions. Other types were the opportunists. I certainly consider it a waste of time to deal further with these in greater detail. There was one group which deserves mention; it consisted of people who had reason to fear reprisals, either on account of their pre-World War II activities, or on account of their class origin. The former group consisted of people whose pre-war political or economic activities were irreconcilably opposed to the post-war political and economic picture. The latter group was made up of individuals who, had it not been for their timely decision to enter the Party, would have been considered bad cadres.

In either case they knew that their behavior must be exemplary from every point of view, that they must do according to their best abilities, and even better, whatever task they may be assigned to work on.

In order to cover up their past economic or political "mal-orientation" or their class background, these people, in a constant search of means of compensation, seized every opportunity to prove their loyalty to their superiors by not only reaching, but also exceeding, the "norm" expected of them.

The Communist Party was literally loaded with such people. This was the worst Communist type.

71. *How did the mass organizations function?*

Here I speak of local chapters of mass organizations, the

functioning of their national leadership being an entirely different matter where other principles and points of view came into play.

These local organizations or chapters had their state-affiliated programs. There were several government-sponsored actions, such as the celebrating of May 1, of April 4, in the preparation of which these local groups participated. They also participated in the peace-loan campaigns, in the numerous campaigns for peace and anti-imperialist demonstrations. In a word, these groups took care of such and similar political tasks, being used mostly on such occasions when direct participation of the Communist Party would have been inopportune and disadvantageous.

7 m. How did workers feel about the trade unions?

The workers did not trust the labor unions. Here again I speak only of that period when I myself was a labor union member (1953-1956). I began to work in the fall of 1953 and was employed in a brick factory. I was in the midst of workers, who performed a very heavy physical labor. These laborers were not the best-paid workers in the country. Aside from political slogans, they did not receive much else from the labor union. As a result, the workers considered the union as an adjunct of the Communist Party, an instrument for the execution of certain governmental decrees. They in no way regarded the union as serving to their benefit.

Let me relate to you a small episode which took place in 1954. The labor union conducted a campaign, as usual, that people should read more and should use more fully the factory's library facilities. The workers complained that there were no books available to their liking. A discussion followed in which it became evident that the labor union received each year a fixed amount of money from the factory's budget for library purposes. This money was spent every year on books, the list of titles being compiled by the labor unions, without regard to the taste or interests of the members. A great number of books were available, ostensibly for the education of the workers, which nobody read. The workers did not have even that much influence over their leaders, who in turn were singularly indifferent towards their rank and file.

8. *How many Hungarian Communists do you think really believed in Communism as such -- nearly all, about half, or very few?*

There were very, very few convinced Communists. Those few had a reputation recognized far and wide.

9. *How do you think groups such as the Youth Movement became transformed from a stalwart Communist organization into a center of opposition?*

This is a very involved and complex question, very closely connected with the education of the youth. Révai made a speech in Parliament in 1948, in which he discussed the question of the education of Hungarian youth. Révai stated that the position of the Communist Party will only then become stable in Hungary, if and when the Communists succeed in bringing up a generation whose very first childhood experiences and impressions will be of a type and quality which only a Socialist state is capable of providing.

In line with this view of the chief Communist theoretician, the regime has spent enormous sums for educational purposes. The DISZ, too, it had an enormous budget at its disposal, with the help of which it provided many libraries and entertainment facilities for its members. The fact that in October 1956, besides those who were in their early thirties at the time, the Communist regime's youngest generation proved to be the Revolution's noblest army, only proves how completely the Communists failed in their attempt at Communist education.

This failure became clear only during the Revolution. We, who were released from prison in 1953, were more surprised by this young generation's attitude than anybody else. From 1953 to 1956 we often discussed the youth, and the general consensus was that we might as well forget them entirely, so bad were our impressions of them. We considered them a lost generation, devoid of the very notion of liberty and human freedom.

If we are searching for an explanation of this spectacular transformation from what we honestly thought was a lost generation into a determined army of anti-Communists, the only plausible explanation we can come up with is that, it seems, the family and home had exerted a greater, deeper, and more lasting influence on the youth -- contrary to all superficial appearances -- than did the school and society at large.

The children got used to a peculiar condition, in which they knew they had to speak one language in school and another at home. In the family, a unit of which every child was a member, the mistakes and faults - never touched in schools -- were thoroughly discussed. This critical approach of the family, covering both sides of the coin, exerted a greater influence on their minds, it seems, than other factors.

The fact alone that the family, where everybody worked and yet was unable to get anywhere (mégsem tudott őtröl hatra vergődni); where the child saw his father, laboring for so many years and yet unable to show any results; this and similar facts alone may have convinced the young people, more than any amount of words would, how hopeless their own future appeared to be, all the phrases and promises heard in school and elsewhere notwithstanding. These moments, it seems, were stronger than anything else.

POLICE AND TERROR

10. We have heard a lot about Communist terror. Just how does it manifest itself?

Communist terror was an inseparable ingredient and part of everyday life in Hungary in those times, and I am thoroughly convinced that a person can only be a real anti-Communist in a place like Hungary. There, a mode of thinking, a peculiar reasoning process has become part of the human nature. For every nuisance and difficulty, for shortages and problems, individuals almost involuntarily blamed the leadership of the state, and that part of the state machinery which prevents people from living their lives in their own fashion; which prohibits certain things, holds back some needed supplies, or consumers goods, prevents certain voices and opinions from being heard, etc., etc. If a man in Budapest is waiting for the No. 6 trolley car which is not coming, or, if it finally arrives but is so full of people that he cannot get on it, his first reaction is against the AVH and against the Cabinet, a reaction which is characterized by cursing. Those dirty Communists are responsible for all this. Our man got up early in the morning, gave himself plenty of time, but could not get on the trolley car. He arrives six minutes late in the office and as he enters the building he meets the head of the personnel section. The personnel chief does not say a word, of course, he just views our man from head to foot with a look which makes one shiver in his bones. The next thought is automatic: what is he going to write on my cadre sheet? Our man is not really late, the real work does not start till after four minutes, but he has missed the important "ten-minute movement", during which he was supposed to prepare and set up the day's work. An endless series of such little incidents permeate all people's lives, day after day. This was one face of the terror. The other was even more brutal; between 1948 and 1956, innumerable Hungarians were put to prison. These innumerable people had families and relatives and friends, whose number was many times that of the imprisoned. All these people were affected, some more, some less. These people, whose father or mother or sister or brother or son or daughter was imprisoned, were not permitted to talk about their sufferings, they were expected to conceal this fact, to keep it a veiled secret. If they talked they, too, became enemies of the people's democracy, they were supposed to invent stories, to tell a lie when somebody inquired about the whereabouts of the missing member of the family.

This contradiction, where people could not speak the truth, could not reveal what was on their minds, and beneath the calm and carefree surface their hearts were aching nonetheless, this contradiction was unbearable. When talking about these things, people experienced an intense fear, never knowing with whom they were talking, never being certain who among their acquaintances, relatives, and even among their own family, might be a planted spy or an agent provocateur. They could never tell when their own children might inadvertently reveal a family secret. A husband could never trust his wife in an absolute sense, nor could the wife be entirely certain of her husband. The AVH was all too well known to have turned numerous family members against one another.

The terror, in a word, was everywhere, it was part of the fabric of life, interwoven with whatever a person was engaged in, meeting him on every step from the moment he woke to the time when he fell asleep again. This is the explanation why people went so forcefully and with so much hate against the AVH during the Revolution. And this is precisely what people in the West failed to grasp or understand; why did the Hungarians hang so brutally so many AVH-men (the number was not large, as a matter of fact), why did people set themselves up as arbitrary judges of other men? I will readily admit that the hangings were neither legal nor right or proper, but I also know that underneath the elemental force thus unleashed, the AVH's inhuman and endless terror was the propagating force. The AVH and its associated organizations have managed to penetrate the innermost corners of the human soul, so that a person could not even trust another in bed, not knowing what he or she might do the following morning, whether he will be reported to the AVH or not. This was in rough outlines the great terror, with which a whole nation was held trembling of fear at the mercy of the AVH.

10 b. What do you know of the work of the AVH? Why was it formed? What was its task?

The AVH was organized in the faithful image of the Russian NKVD or MVD. Its purpose and task was the securing of Hungary's transformation into a Communist society. It was supposed to do those cleansing jobs within the country which the Communists considered indispensable before and during the transition.

The AVH was organized after 1945 and from the very beginning it supported the Communist Party, whose creation it really was. It was the center of a very heated struggle of Hungary's post-war politics, because the various administrative heads of the new state, representing as they did the several political parties of the coalition, soon realized that they had no control or influence over the AVH and over its activities. The later political developments in Hungary are generally known.

The repeated efforts to bring the AVH under the jurisdiction of the Council of Ministers remained unsuccessful up until 1948, and after 1948 this jurisdictional question was no longer a problem. Later developments gave the AVH an absolute freedom of action. Between 1948 and 1953 the AVH was responsible for the security and smoothness of that social transformation which took place in the country, which meant in practice an AVH control over the courts (igazságszolgáltatás), over the liquidations, over social activities, and over the political life. It would be more precise to say that these controlling powers belonged to the Executive Committee of the AVH, which in turn was ultimately a political instrument and lever in the hands of those who directed its activities, namely Rákosi and a few others.

10 c. Do you know about any of the departments of the AVH?

The AVH activities were two-fold: (a) Operative activities. Here you had such tasks as liquidation, arrests, interrogation, prisons, etc. (b) Defensive activities. Here you had two divisions. The one was concerned with counter-espionage, the other had in its charge the internal defense and security. This latter supervised the various institutions and organizations. It had sections dealing with the ministries, with the remnants of the post-1948 political parties, with the churches, with the various social institutions, with the youth organizations, with the labor unions, and you could go on enumerating others.

These sections performed their tasks in two ways: (a) They gathered information from the various institutions and organizations by means of planted agents and (b) They built up an extensive network of informers whom they either bribed or blackmailed or forced to spy on individuals, or groups, or both.

The AVH made every attempt, of course, to place its own men into strategic positions everywhere, and in this respect the AVH did have certain constitutional or legal possibilities; thus for instance in the army, beside every commander there was a political officer, representing the AVH, who was not under the jurisdiction and control of the higher military command, and who reported all his observations and data directly to the respective section of the AVH headquarters.

There were, then, two sources of information at the AVH's disposal. The one source was the official source which reached the AVH by regular means, through the defense department. In every ministry, you must know, there was an official AVH representative, and the AVH had the right to interfere in the ministry's work. At the same time the AVH received confidential reports from its political officers who were sitting next to every commander and reported independently. These were situation reports, daily reports, and reports regarding concrete events or situations.

The same was true of every institution, organization, or

association; there were the official reports and the confidential reports made by planted AVH agents. These agents had their own checkers and supervisors, and the supervisors in turn were supervised by others, etc.

At the same time you had the network of informers who reported on concrete events and situations, usually specializing in such phenomena which the regime considered to be of a negative nature.

10 d. Do you know anything about the system of informers, agents, agent provocateurs, pressure methods, and denunciation established by the AVH?

I already said a few words about the informer system. This system represented such channels of intelligence which were beyond the limits of the professional AVH's sphere of activity, and possibility, or effectiveness; people everywhere in the country knew and recognized planted professional AVH agents. Everybody knew, for instance, that the political officer in the army was an AVH-man; that the personnel section chief in an office or factory or TSzCS was an AVH-man, etc., etc. In the presence of these agents the people were more careful and, if one of these agents took part in a meeting, few speeches and no protests of any kind were heard, not even such which otherwise have been voiced.

In order to be able to collect information from these territories also, where the AVH's own men were quite ineffective, the network of informers, the so-called wamser network, was established. For this purpose the AVH, using all sorts of methods, was trying to recruit first of all such people who were wholly beyond possible suspicion. These people had the opportunity to continue to speak freely. If a man spoke too loudly at a meeting and fearlessly denounced Rákosi and Stalin, people immediately knew that he was an informer, a wamser.

The AVH was fond of using methods -- needless to say --

whereby people were made to spy on their friends. They were anxious to collect incriminating personal data, data concerning a family, closely-guarded family secrets, which they used in turn as blackmail material, thereby forcing the victim to supply them with information regarding his own family or others. They searched people's past histories to discover black spots and incriminating evidence, facts which, if used against the victim, would be sufficient reason to imprison him immediately. The AVH did not prosecute these men. They let the person get away with whatever he may have done on condition that he would turn informer and would supply the AVH with desired intelligence.

I can relate to you a concrete case in this connection. During 1948, many of my friends caved in with whom I worked together before and after the war. Towards the end of 1948, one of my friends came up to me. He was very upset and wanted to see me immediately. We went to another room where we were alone and where he told me that he had been arrested three days before, was taken to the AVH headquarters (describing what they did to him, which was not very pleasant). My friend was a family man, had several children, he held a very good job (he was an engineer). In short, he was permitted to leave on the understanding that he would secure certain data concerning two of his friends, one of whom was I.

In view of the beatings received, and because the proposal was presented to him in such a way that would not even think about its implications, he accepted the offer. He went home, etc., etc., finally deciding to contact us. Telling us beforehand what it was all about. I listened to his tale and since I myself was in a very difficult situation, I did not know what to say. Finally I advised him to tell whatever he knew of me, if that would help keep him above water. He left, but people were already waiting for him outside and took him away. Later, in 1950, I was myself arrested and I met him again in prison. Then I learned what he got for not doing his job. My friend was also freed in 1953.

10 e. *How were people recruited into the AVH?*

Regular members of the AVH were recruited on a voluntary basis. These volunteers had to satisfy certain conditions; they had to be members of the Communist Party, their social origin was strictly scrutinized, and they had to be recommended by certain Party organizations or by certain Party functionaries. I must add here that AVH membership meant very many economic privileges and advantages; they were better paid than any other person (an AVH lieutenant received twice the amount of pay of his counterpart in the army). They had many advantages in the purchase of clothing, securing of apartments, etc.

10 f. *What was their social, age, political, religious background?*

It is rather hard for me to give a statistical picture of the AVH, since I have not seen one. I must base what I say on what I observed. AVH members, or more correctly, the privates and lower echelons of the AVH were without question mostly people of worker and peasant origin.

As far as the officers and the entire leadership of the AVH is concerned, -- though it is painful and unpleasant to relate the truth in this situation -- these people were for the most part Jews. The AVH leadership and officers of the AVH, as well as the Jewry of Hungary were, to a certain extent, considered under one hat (egy kalap alá voltak véve) excepting, of course, those honorable Jews who were on the other side of the fence, who, as a matter of fact suffered a great deal exactly for that reason. **Question:** What do you think were the motives of the simple peasants and workers who volunteered for work in the AVH? **Answer:** Material advantages prompted them to volunteer and, on very rare occasions, political beliefs. **Question:** Did the Jews have any special plan or reason when they decided to join to AVH? What prompted them to do so? **Answer:** I do not think that it is proper to speak of Jews as Jews in this connection. As a group I do not think that they had any plans. It is an undeniable fact, however, that the leadership of the Communist Party after 1945 was in the hands of Jewish people or people of Jewish descent. In view of the fact that immediately after 1945 the essential role in the country's economic life was played by the Communists, those people who had been both interested and involved in Hungary's economic life before the Second World War, as well as those, who were either desirous of receiving from the state compensations for suffered losses, or were anxious to play essential parts again in the now socialized sector of the national economy, -- all these categories of people gravitated towards, and actually entered, the ranks of the Communist Party. These categories did not consist of Jewish individuals exclusively. However, since the nation's pre-war economy for the most part was in their hands, Jews did represent the great majority.

As far as the attitude with respect to the AVH is concerned, I feel that there was a basic and -- from the human point of view -- a very legitimate moment, which prompted at least a part of the Jews to enter the AVH. In 1950 I had conversations with people who were Jews and who had been members of the AVH since 1945. I asked them a question similar to your question now. They told me how their families were exterminated before 1945; they told me of the sufferings they themselves went through, -- an explanation which I fully accepted since I myself have seen several atrocities during the war.

Now after 1945 one of the basic aims has been the liquidation of the Fascists in Hungary. In this connection the basic human motive for the Jews was that, as people whom Fascism touched most, as people hardest hit by Fascism in Hungary, they immediately volunteered for this job of liquidation. **Question:** Are you suggesting that the Jews entered the AVH because desirous of revenge? **Answer:** The feeling of revenge undoubtedly played a role in the decisions of many people, a revenge which went over and above the procedure of liquidation itself. People, after all, are not always the same, and they are not always angels. This, of course, was a rather unfortunate thing.

Like every development taking its origin somewhere, after a while oversteps its framework and assumes a life of its own; a Jewish individual became a member of the AVH framework in 1945, -- I assume here that he went there with good intentions, with the intention mainly of liquidating the remnants of Fascism in Hungary. Now after he got in and after he secured for himself a position, the conditions changed, while he retained his position. Under these changed conditions his own relation to the AVH organization necessarily had to change and, since there was no other possibility, he had no choice but to accept the new situation and the new task which went with it.

I consider this whole thing, the AVH and the Jews' participation in it, as rather unfortunate because the population later connected the AVH with the Jews, a procedure which undoubtedly had a solid base. The whole thing resulted in a very determined feeling of resentment towards the Jews, a feeling which practically never entered the hearts of Hungarians before.

10 h. Were they immune from persecution?

Yes, very definitely.

10 i. Can you compare regular AVH personnel and secret informers?

Regular AVH personnel were regular members of this organization. The secret informers were free-lancers, -- to use an American expression.

10 j. What were the relations between the AVH and the police?

There was a very great resentment and distrust between the police and the AVH; the AVH considered the police a bunch of reactionaries, who could not be trusted, whereas the police definitely feared the AVH.

10 k. What were the relations between the AVH and the Party? Who do you think had more authority?

If we look at this question of AVH-Party relationship from a vertical point of view, if we compare the AVH and Party representatives as they existed and functioned in a village or a small town, the AVH there had much greater authority than the Party. Locally, therefore, the AVH was superior. We must not forget, however, that, nationally, the only organization which did exercise control over the AVH was still the central leadership of the Party. The fundamental directives, and principles of procedures, came to the AVH from the Party.

10 l. Did you know any police chiefs? If so, what happened to them?

Yes, I knew Oliver Benjamin, the chief of police of the city of Budapest between 1945 and 1948. He was arrested in 1949, was sentenced and imprisoned. He was freed in 1956.

11. Were you or any close friend of yours ever arrested since 1945?

Most of my friends and I myself were arrested after 1945.

11 a. If so, can you give me some details about the case that produced the greatest impression on you.

This seems to be an extreme question, so I shall try to give you an extreme answer. I knew a young man who was imprisoned together with me. He was a store-clerk (kereskedősegéd) by profession. He used to work in a store on the Baross Street in Budapest. It so happened that his name and the name of somebody else whom the AVH wanted were identical. The AVH picked up this man instead of the other. I don't have to tell you that this poor young boy received a tremendous beating. He simply did not know any of those things for which the AVH possessed proof. And of course he really knew nothing. The mistake was discovered only in 1952.

There was another case; this man was a district veterinarian in the County of Tolna. He, too, was arrested as a result of a name mixup. The other man, whom the AVH really wanted, was a Horthyist army officer who was alleged to have committed various atrocities on the Russian front, including the extermination of a whole village, etc. He was arrested and the AVH asked him the usual questions, where had he been, etc. This poor man denied everything and his denial tended to even more aggravate his prospects. The AVH was unable to get anywhere with him and he was not brought to court as originally planned, but was simply interned. This all took place in 1948. He was later transferred to Kistarcsa and still later to Recsk. At the beginning of 1953, after the death of Stalin, a great rechecking of cases took place at Recsk. Every prisoner was again interrogated and new minutes (protocols) were prepared. When this man's turn came and he dictated his personal data, his mother's name was not the same as the name recorded in the AVH's files. The man was interrogated and beaten again for some three weeks until finally, in 1953, the AVH admitted that a mistake in names was made. An intensive search began for the real criminal, and it was found that he died some 18 months earlier. My friend was informed of all this in March 1953 and he was very happy that he would be freed at last. But he was not freed. They freed him only months later, in October 1953, when by decree of Imre Nagy all forced labor camps and prison camps were liquidated.

I was arrested on March 31, 1950. Three AVH people came to my house during the night and conducted a house search lasting all night. They took me to 60 Andrássy ut, having filled two bags with various books and notes of mine. I was at the Andrássy ut for more than three weeks. At that time, the beginning of 1950, the AVH was in the process of liquidating the remnants of the so-called conspiracy cases, and they made determined efforts to link my case also to one of these cases. They did not succeed in this. They were not able to take a protocol during the almost four-weeks long investigation and finally issued an order of internment (véghatározat) and shipped me to Kistarcsa. Part of the text of this order was as follows: I had to decide as I did because the above-named engaged in anti-democratic activities. No closer reference as to what my alleged anti-democratic activities were given.

During October 1950, I was transferred from Kistarcsa to Recsk, where I remained until the beginning of October 1953.

Let me say a few words now about the methods they used; it was the characteristic feature of my case that I did not have a protocol. Of every man who was sent to a prison camp a protocol was taken, which contained the enumeration and description of the incriminating data or acts which the individual was alleged to have committed, alleged data and/or acts which at the same time represented the basis for the person's arrest and imprisonment. Whether these protocols represented true facts or were only trumped-up charges or forced admissions is of secondary moment now. What I emphasize is that I did not have any protocol at all. They took a protocol of me at the beginning of 1953, during the great re-investigation after Stalin's death, a document which again contained only generalities with no specific and concrete charges against me. Things were relatively fluid by then in Hungary and I decided to sign this document, thinking that the fact of signature would not make much of a difference one way or another. The document called me an admirer and follower of Mindszenty

-- everybody in the country knew that I was not -- I was further called an imperialist spy -- another accusation which no longer had much credence in the eyes of the population. I clearly saw that I would have to sign something in order to be freed, so I did.

I was finally freed at the end of September 1953, with the stipulation that I would be placed under police supervision. This meant in practice that I was permitted to choose a village for my residence -- I chose a village near Budapest where I formerly also resided, a village which I was now not permitted to leave. I could not take a job other than in the village, I had to report to the local police at stated intervals and I had to abide by those rules which are generally applicable for police supervision cases. (I could not go to the movies, public places, I could not receive guests, I could not keep a radio or telephone, etc., etc.) **Question:** Who signed your deportation order? **Answer:** It was signed by Décsi Károly AVH colonel, who was the head of the investigating section of the AVH at the time. This man tumbled down later on, and received some fifteen years. **Question:** I should like to ask you to tell me something of the four weeks during which you were held at 60 Andrássy ut. What did they do to you? **Answer:** This is a rather fantastic episode. I hate to talk about myself, not wishing to put me into too good a light. The questioning started with picture taking and fingerprinting. Thereafter they took me to a questioning room where I met an AVH captain. I don't know his name. He conducted my questioning later on also. He was a very polite and correct man, he personally never beat me, leaving that part to others. He wanted to know essentially two things: (a) of which conspiratorial group was I a member, and (b) which were the imperialist spy organizations with which I was connected and which regularly sent me money and instructions. I could not answer either of these questions in the affirmative -- I was not a member of any conspiracy and, unfortunately, I was not a member of a spy ring either. I would have gladly given them all the information they wanted had I possessed them, because

I would have spared myself a great many things that way. I was forced to "stubbornly deny everything", to use the captain's phrase. The result was that after the end of the questioning session I was not permitted to sit down when I returned to my cell. To the contrary; I was told to stand in perfect attention immediately behind the cell door, about a foot away from the door itself. The guard, obviously following instructions, checked and rechecked me frequently and at varying intervals.

Standing in attention was a rather easy thing at the beginning, becoming more and more difficult and tiring as time went on. It is amazing how a man's power of resistance weakens under such exertions. If you think about this now, you are apt to wonder what there is to it really -- it does not appear to be a dreadful thing -- but if you stand in attention continuously for almost 96 hours, then this sort of thing tends to be an infernal thing, becoming more and more hard and harder to endure. I believe that towards the end of this stretch -- which was interrupted once -- I was no longer in a normal state of mind.

Certain things happened to me which -- even the act of relating them now -- does strain the critical capacities, at least of a normal person.

At about the middle of this long stretch they took me up for questioning and put me in a small room which was facing the room of my questioner. The small room had a sofa, a desk, and a chair. The window was protected by heavy iron bars. They gave me a large stack of paper and told me to write down the story of my life; they advised me to write down honestly and truthfully what I did against the people's democracy, with whom did I conspire, of what spy organizations am I a member, etc. Then they left me alone. While I was trying to think what I should do and how I should do it, my questioner, the captain, came in and took me into his room. As I stepped into the captain's room -- there was a large, deep easy chair next to his desk -- the first thing I notice is that a very close relative of mine is sitting in that chair. Her face is leaning slightly on her hand and her shoes, dress, in a word, everything she had on, I knew and recognized immediately. At that instant, and later on as well, I had no doubt whatsoever in my mind that the person sitting in that chair was she. I wanted to go towards her and to tell her something, but they grabbed me, holding my mouth and hands tight, but permitting me to stay there for a second or two, giving me ample opportunity to view her to make certain that the person sitting in that chair was really she and that no deception occurred and no attempt was made to mislead me. Having accomplished that, they took me back into the small room. There they again told me to sit down and to begin writing my life's story if I wanted to get out of there. They also advised me that, should I refuse to write, the person whom I have just seen would be "well taken care of", and gave me a vivid description of what would happen to her. ***Question:*** You do not consider it important or perhaps you do not wish to further identify the person you have seen? ***Answer:*** She was my wife.

I was again alone in the small room and suddenly I began to write. All things have their psychology and a man is able to exert but a very small resistance under certain circumstances. I began to write and I filled out three pages. Then I stopped; upon deliberating I realized or rather thought that I could not trust these people after all. If I write down all sorts of stupidities, -- such things as they want me to admit -- they will still not keep their word and will not do what they promised to do. Therefore I am not going to write anything at all, I decided. I looked at the three filled pages before me and was trying to decide what to do with them. I took the three pages and ripped them into small bits.

Now the problem was what to do with these bits of paper. No matter what I did with them, if I threw them down on the floor, or into the wastebasket, or if I kept them on my person -- I could not throw them out through the window -- they would no doubt discover them, they would put the bits together, and I would be exactly in the same situation as if I had not ripped up the sheets at

all. A big and daring thought came into my mind; I knocked on the door and when the guard came I asked him to take me to the bathroom. He obliged and I threw the bits of paper into the toilet, flushing them down the drain with the water. I went back to the small room, sat down, and did not write. After about an hour they came for me; so you don't want to write? I don't have anything to write down other than what I have already told you, etc., etc. They took me back to the captain's room and a long questioning followed to discover why I did not want to write, during which time I passively endured those things which they did to me.
Question: Did they beat you? **Answer:** Yes, of course they did.

The most interesting thing in this whole matter was a circumstance which I have completely neglected to consider; namely the fact that they carefully counted the number of sheets of paper before they gave them to me. They immediately discovered that three sheets of paper were missing. The next round of questioning centered around this fact; what did I do with those three sheets, and what did I write on them. Eventually this, too, came to an end and I was taken back to my cell. There I continued standing in attention as before. All my thoughts and energy were geared to discover, somehow, if my wife was still in the building and, if so, what happened to her. I was not able to discover anything of this kind, I was locked in and was surrounded by a system which functioned to perfection.

Towards the end of this 96-hour period -- I shall return to my story later, wishing to complete the story of my standing episode now, -- towards the end of the fourth day -- I of course did not know if it was morning, afternoon, or evening, my cell was way down in the cellar with the electric light constantly on; in a word, I did not know the hour of the day and fact that I had stood in attention for such a long time came to me clear only later, after this episode's termination, when I was transferred to another place on which occasion I was able to determine that four days had passed between two periods, the beginning and end points of which I knew.

It was towards the end of the fourth day when the following things happened to me: two white cats approached my heavily barred window. My cell had an arched ceiling and the ventilation window, its lower end being two and a half meters above the floor, was an arched tubelike opening. The window itself was heavily barred. The two white cats approached this window and one of them grabbed the heavy bars and lifted it out of the wall. I knew precisely that outside on the street a telephone truck was waiting with a heavy cable drum and equipment on it. On the cable drum itself a very heavy type of white cord was rolled on. One of the cats tied a hook on the end of the cord and threw it down to me. I knew that as soon as I grabbed the hook, the apparatus on the truck would set the cable drum in motion, rolling up the cord and pulling me out of my prison cell. The two cats would free me, of that I was absolutely certain. I waited a little while, until the guard would come again and would check my position by opening a little door which was within the cell door itself. He soon came, opened the little door, saw me standing in attention and, closing the door again, he left. At that very moment I grabbed the hook.

From that moment on I don't remember anything at all. The next thing I knew was that the guard was pouring cold water on me and I was lying on the cell floor. As it later turned out, they took me down from the window opening. I climbed up the two and a half meter level wall and was hanging, unconsciously, my hands solidly holding the iron bars. This was the end of the attention-standing episode.

I later was transferred from 60 Andrássy ut and was taken to Kistarcsa, where on two occasions during my stay at the camp the prisoners were permitted to talk for five minutes with their relatives. The conversation itself took place between two barred walls. I was also permitted twice to write a letter to my wife. (I was at Kistarcsa from April to October 1950). On both occasions I wrote to my wife, asking her to visit me and advising her that I had a very important question to ask her, a question to which she must give me a straightforward and unreserved answer. My wife came and I asked her if she had been at 60 Andrássy ut. On both occasions her answer was a definite no. I, of course, did not believe her. I was meanwhile transferred again, this time to the prison camp at Recsk, where I spent some three and a half years. After I was freed and got home to my wife, my first action was to ask her again the above question. My wife was not at 60 Andrássy ut. *Question:* How do you explain this, or rather, what is your explanation for all this? *Answer:* I haven't got the slightest idea. I don't know what they did to me; whether I was in such a condition that I saw those things which they wanted me to see, or whether they placed a person in that chair whose clothes and shoes, etc., were identical or similar to those of my wife's. *Question:* Did you not see her face? *Answer:* Yes, I definitely saw her face. (Wasn't her face practically covered by her hand, which may have prevented you from her full view? *Answer:* Her face, or rather, head, was leaning on one of her hands, but I clearly saw her face, her full face, there is no question about it. To this day I do not really know what happened. This, then, was the psychological result of the four-day long attention standing, beating, and repeated slapping of a person's face are not the only means of punishing a person, there are other means which are even more effective in putting a man in a state of mind where he does not know what he is doing, nor is he responsible for his actions. *Question:* When did the AVH finally give up, during the weeks you spend in 60 Andrássy ut, their attempt to get something out of you? *Answer:* After the guard awakened me with cold water, they frequently interrogated me for several days (two, three times a day), putting me later into another cell, where there was already a prisoner. This young man was a professional prison companion -- as I soon found out -- who, by talking a great deal about himself, is supposed to get certain facts out of you. I was with him for about a week. After this they put me into a solitary room again for another week or so and took me for frequent interrogations again.

This happened for several days. They could not get anything out of me. Later they put me into still another cell, in which there was an elderly man, a former officer of the police. This, however, is rather irrelevant, since they kept me only to see if they could unearth some loose ends or new evidence on which to base renewed assault. In this they obviously did not succeed, as later events definitely proved. Finally they called me in one day and made me sign the order of internment, which I did not sign until years later, at Kistarcsa. I signed another protocol, immediately lodging an appeal, but nothing came of it. **Question:** What sort of place was Kistarcsa? **Answer:** Kistarcsa was an internment camp where only political prisoners were held. The same is true of Recsk. After 1945 we did have several internment camps in Hungary, all of which were liquidated towards the end of 1948 or in the beginning of 1949. Very many people were freed at that time. Those people whom the regime did not want to let go were all transferred to Kistarcsa. During 1950, those inmates of Kistarcsa who were 50 years old or younger were again transferred to Recsk. **Question:** How many people were there at Kistarcsa at the time? **Answer:** Their number was between two and three thousand. There were four regiments, so called, each occupying a building, and a female regiment besides this, women being held separately. We had our regular daily routine; reveille in the morning. Some of the people worked. There were some arts and crafts shops. Most of the prisoners did not work at all, sitting in their rooms all day. At Kistarcsa we had occasional opportunities to write letters and see our relatives, and everybody used his own, civilian clothes, things which we no longer had at Recsk. **Question:** Under whose authority and supervision was the Kistarcsa camp? **Answer:** The camp was under the grey (regular) police up until May 1950, when the AVH took it over. **Question:** What was the difference between Kistarcsa and Recsk? **Answer:** The difference was enormous. We did not like our life at Kistarcsa and later at Recsk we always had a longing for it. At Recsk everybody had to work. We all were employed in a quarry (kőbánya) which we ourselves opened. In short, we came to Recsk in October 1950, cleared a 200-hold forest, then we built barracks, first for the AVH and then for ourselves, then we built a road, to the village, then we cleared the top of the mountain of some 1-5 meter deep humus, then we cut into the side of the mountain, establishing three mining levels. After that we built a 6 km-long funicular railway (kőtélpálya) and at the lower end of it we also built a railway loading platform equipped with nine pairs of tracks.

11 b. Can you give me a brief list of specific arrests you can think of among your circle of acquaintances?

Practically all my acquaintances were arrested.

11 c. Did you know reliably about any physical abuse of anyone arrested? If so, can you tell me about it?

There certainly were many instances of physical abuse. Such abuses were admitted by members of the AVH themselves who, in order to secure some credit to themselves, or in order to prove their personal innocence, freely admitted them during the Revolution.

I myself have seen the effects of such physical abuse in a number of cases. So as not to always speak about myself, let me tell you of a case of a fellow prisoner; with me was an old man in Andrássy út 60, a former police inspector, who served during the Horthy regime. This man has been sitting for more than a year and a half in the Pestvidéki Prison, from where the AVH transported him periodically (bi-monthly, monthly, or even more often) to Andrássy út 60 for further questioning. The time when I met him there -- we were cellmates for a few days -- must have been the most trying period of his life; he became insane. I could not tell you what species of physical abuse was he exposed to because the man never spoke much about these things. What I have seen, however, spoke clearly enough, and told me many things; his face was beaten (this was so natural that it is ever superfluous to talk about it), his entire body, but especially his feet, were covered with wounds and large blue spots, -- obvious evidences of beatings, kickings, and other forms of torture. The very fact that this man has lost his mind while with me in the cell is especially revealing; a man, no matter how weak and how much afraid, does not usually lose his mind overnight. He must have experienced intense fear and torment for a long time, over and above the physical torture, before reaching that condition. He was portraying his own funeral; he played in turn the roles of the cadaver, of his wife, of his children, and of the other crying and lamenting relatives. The sight he presented was both fantastic and unforgettable.

11 d. What sort of people got arrested?

Those people got arrested first of all who actively participated in politics from 1945 to 1948, people whose political viewpoints went contrary to the Communists' real or stated objectives.

Members of the old middle class were also frequently exposed to arrest; this, of course, was an ideological question. As the Communists put it, the old ruling classes had to be liquidated.

Besides those two groups all people ran the risk of being arrested who either said or did something, no matter how minute or insignificant, against the regime, or against the people who represented the regime. Let me give you just one example; the beating up of a member of the AVH was considered a major political offense. With me in Recsk were several people who were imprisoned for many years simply because they happened to have the same girl friends, and quarrels and fights developed over this situation.

11 e. Do you know any cases where the házbizalmi or tömbbizalmi had anything to do with the arrest?

I have no personal knowledge of any concrete case involving the "ház-" or "tömbbizalmi".

There can be no doubt of the fact, however, that these organizations were set up and operated with this purpose in mind. The "házbizalmis" were supposed to observe all people living in a given apartment house; these observations had to do primarily with the surface appearances; that a certain individual is visited by many people, or that he or she has a constant visitor; that a person usually comes home late; that a person repeatedly gets home in a drunken state; the person brings home a package; the person buys furniture; one could go on enumerating God knows how many such facts which the "házbizalmi" from time to time reported to the AVH regarding people under his "care". I must add here that the mere fact of a person's employment at "házbizalmi" did not necessarily mean that such person was also an AVH spy, though this was true in the majority of the cases.

11 f. How could one get in touch with people under arrest?

Getting in touch with arrested people was one of the most difficult things. Once a person was arrested he could not see any of his relatives or friends until such time when he was either tried or sentenced or, failing that, was shipped to one of the numerous internment camps. If relatives of an arrested person happened to inquire and to ask questions about his whereabouts, the authorities simply answered in the negative; they did not know anything about that person.

Once a person was tried and sentenced, he was permitted to have visitors once every half year, bi-monthly, or monthly, depending on the nature of his "crime". A similar schedule of letter-writing was also permitted. This procedure applied for

Kistarcsa, for instance. There were, on the other hand, such forced labor camps where no contacts whatsoever were permitted with the outside world. Nobody knew who or how many people were at such places, there was no visiting and no letter-writing. Such a place, for instance, was Recsk. Relatives learned that a person was at Recsk only after his release.

11 g. Do you know about any prisons, concentration and forced labor camps?

The greatest concentration camp in Hungary was the Pestvidéki Fogház. This installation was used as a military prison during the Second World War. After 1948, it was taken over entirely by the AVH and was used as a detention camp.

All, or practically all, people who were arrested were taken there and were kept there while their case was pending. The interesting feature of this detention camp was that people sat there for years without anything being done in their cases. They would be taken occasionally to 60 Andrássy út for questioning, but that was about all.

The majority of those tried and sentenced were taken to Vác. Vác was the center of convicted political prisoners, where the victims of the recurring arrest waves met one another ever since 1945.

Those arrested individuals who were not convicted or, more precisely, those who, because of lack of evidence were not brought to trial, were usually interned. Kistarcsa was the central internment camp. From here people were sent out to various concentration or hard labor camps, such as Recsk or Kazincz-Barcika, where they spent long years without ever being tried.

There were other hard-labor camps, which were reserved for those Hungarian POW's who were returned from Russia. One such camp was located at Tiszapalkonya, where these former POW's built a great hydro-electric works (dam) of that name. These camps were the most important ones.

11 h. What do you know about forced deportations? What was the fate of the deportees?

Your question, I assume, has to do with deportations which took place before the Revolution.

About those your best possible sources would be such people who were taken to the Soviet Union and who managed, in some miraculous fashion, to get back to Hungary.

The Soviet way of treating prisoners or deportees was about the same as that in use in Hungary. The Hungarians, to be more precise, copied an already tested and well functioning Russian system.

Those who were taken to the Soviet Union could no longer communicate with their relatives in Hungary. This was simply out of the question. What happened to these people once in the Soviet Union? Some of them, no doubt, were better off than others, but none of them could ever hope again to maintain contacts of any kind with their loved ones, once they crossed Hungary's frontiers. **Question:** What would you say was the number of these deportees? **Answer:** Their number was substantial. First of all you had a great number of POW's who were taken out during the war. To this you must add the great number of civilians whom the Russians simply kidnapped and took off the streets of Budapest and other cities after the cessation of hostilities.

From those few deportees who returned we learned the Russian view that, since the Hungarians, fighting on the side of the Germans after 1942, did a lot of damage in Russia, it was reasonable for the Russians to detain POW's and to deport civilians to repair that damage. The trouble was that most of these people never got back. They were used for hazardous jobs, i.e., opening up of mines, etc. The accident and mortality rates were high, food and other supplies were wanting, etc.

12 f. Were you maltreated?

Yes. I find it rather hard and painful to give you statistics in this connection. If at all possible, I'd rather not talk about it.

12 o. *What do you know of health service in prisons?*

Health and sanitary conditions were fairly bad in the prisons, though each prison had a physician. These physicians were usually prisoners themselves, supervised by an AVH sanitary. Very many people contracted TB while in prison, as the result of insufficient food and of inadequate health standards. There was a hospital for prisoners in Budapest, where the serious cases from the many prisons were taken, cases requiring urgent attention. These patients were sent back, if they did get better, to their respective prisons later.

Many people died -- I of course can cite here no figures -- as a result of inadequate or improper medical care. How greatly prison policy determined the state of health services in prisons and to what extent the well-being of inmates was subordinated to other, more important considerations of the AVH or prison management is characteristically illustrated by one of my experiences. In the spring of 1952 I was afflicted with both inflammation of the lungs and pleurisy. After some three days when my temperature ran very high and I was more or less unconscious, they finally took me into the small prison infirmary. The infirmary consisted of three rooms, one used by the doctors, the other two serving as patient rooms. Of these the larger had eight, the smaller four beds. The smaller room was used as an isolation room, mostly for advanced TB patients who awaited their transfer to the prison hospital. Prior to my illness I was in a punish-brigade, strictly segregated from the rest of the prisoners. The doctors did not know what to do with me; according to prison regulations, I was not to communicate with anybody. Now that I got sick they did not know where to put me. Finally they asked the Prison Command for instructions. As a result, I was placed in the smaller room, already occupied by three

TB patients. To this day I don't know how I didn't get TB, most probably because TB-afflicted comrades took good care of me.

13. *If you were asked to advise someone how to steer clear of trouble with the secret police, what would you tell him?*

I find it very hard to give you an answer to this question. Much would depend, no doubt, on whom would I be asked to advise.

There are two ways of steering clear of trouble with the secret police; the one way makes this almost probable; I have in mind joining the Communist Party, and active participation in Party activities, or participation in one of the mass organizations. These are the means a person has of demonstrating his "fidelity" to the "People's Democracy". The other way is simply that you try to remain exceptionally quiet. This latter method, of course, is not a certain guarantee of avoiding trouble. An individual's personal security does not depend solely on his own personal behavior; it depends, among other things, on the turn of day-to-day politics, on such political decisions as a close scrutiny or arrest of a certain group, or of a social stratum. I would, for obvious reasons, recommend the latter method, a method which is not a sure-fire guarantee of longevity in Hungary today.

13 a. *Are there any safe professions?*

No, there is no such thing as a safe profession. There is no such thing simply because the whole life in Hungary is politicized from a point of view which the Communists like to call "dictatorship of the proletariat" or "class-struggle". Whatever your profession, even if you occupy the most insignificant post, in areas far removed from politics and the center of gravity, the work-method is politicized; your relationship to work, i.e., how you perform your job, what your attitude is, how you take orders, etc. These things are not internal organizational questions of a factory, but are political questions of great importance. This makes intelligible enough, I hope, my statement that there simply is no profession which is outside of, and safe from, politics.

13 b. Does it help to be politically active in the Party?

Yes, being politically active in the Party definitely helps. Political activity, participation in Party work, means an improving cadre status. A copy of the cadre sheet is on file in the AVH. If a person participates in Party work and there definitely affirms and approves of those things which are taking place in Hungary, such a person's faults and shortcomings are often overlooked and forgiven. There are many people in Hungary who belonged to the old middle class or to the old bureaucracy, whom the Communists accepted as Party members after 1945, and who continued to keep their old positions.

Being politically active, then, certainly did help, but a status like that, of course, did not represent absolute security or protection; if a person happened to be a Party member and there in the Party committed an "error", he was even more quickly discovered and dealt with than if he had been an outsider.

13 c. Do personal connections help? If so, with whom?

Personal connections are useful everywhere, even in Hungary. In Hungary this sort of thing is called "Socialist connection". Favoritism (protekció) was loudly abolished and something else had to be invented instead; thus "Socialist connection". This meant in practice that certain questions or problems could only be solved through the Party, through the instrumentality of Party leaders. In smaller matters, which were within the jurisdiction of the village or city administration, a word or recommendation from the Party secretary and even from other

Party functionaries very often meant a great deal. When it came to admission to the university, it was extremely important that the applicant be properly recommended by Party functionaries of the school he had last attended. This same applied to cases of job seeking, etc. In a word, recommendations from the Party were the decisive factor in all cases. In certain areas of employment such a recommendation was a basic prerequisite, a sine qua non.

Personal connections were also useful when it came to dealings with the AVH, though in a more restricted sense. The AVH was a closed organization (zárt testület), with its inner laws and regulations; it was impossible for Party secretaries of the lower and middle echelons to intervene in the AVH's work, though the AVH always listened to a Party secretary's opinion, if the exigencies of a case warranted it. When it came to dealings with the AVH, it was the top leaders of the Party only, such as Rákosi and his inner circle, who were able to successfully intervene.

13 d. Does a good class background help? Can you conceal an unfavorable one?

A good class background (népi származás) definitely represented an advantage. This fact was carefully registered on a person's cadre sheet. A cadre sheet showed not only an individual's personal data, but, in the fashion of pre-1944 Semitic Laws, an individual was required to furnish proof regarding his parents' and his grandparent's socio-economic status, and other pertinent information.

If a person concealed his unfavorable class origin, and his true status was later detected, he was liable to immediate dismissal from his job and there was no room for appeal. Persons holding higher positions in the bureaucracy, members of the officers' corps, members of the police force and, of course, the AVH, were also subject to criminal prosecution for failing to reveal their true class origin.

13 e. *Does it help to have money?*

It is quite conceivable that it does help in certain cases. I heard of cases where border guards helped people to cross the border in return for money. My feeling is, however, that money helps only in a few special cases. People are, or rather were, much too afraid of possible consequences to be willing to accept bribes. It was not uncommon for the AVH to have agents do just that, i.e., bribe somebody, and then arrest the recipient. People were much too uncertain, never really knowing who the payoff man might be, a genuine customer or an AVH agent.

13 f. *If one knows how to keep one's mouth shut, is one likely to escape trouble?*

Generally speaking, yes.

13 g. *Are there any religious or national groups who are more likely to court trouble?*

Religious questions were political questions in Hungary. This fact had its necessary political consequences in certain cases. In connection with the Mindszenty trial, very many Catholic priests were arrested. There was, of course, no open religious persecution in Hungary. One could, on the other hand, speak of indirect persecution, one facet of which was exemplified in religious instruction. A 1948 law made religious instruction an elective subject in schools. Administrative interpretation of this law required both parents to request that their children be given religious instruction. Such requests were deposited with the school principal, who forwarded them to higher authorities, who, in turn, turned the information over to the AVH. The AVH used such material right away or kept it as blackmail evidence for future use. The fact is that people holding responsible positions of trust immediately felt the consequences of their action. They were told bluntly that a person holding such a position cannot have his children receive religious instruction. They had to either reverse themselves or give up their jobs. There were, on the other hand, various social pressures exerted against religion, which I explained previously in great detail. Young people were not only discouraged from participating in religious activities, but such participation automatically precluded their acceptance in such organizations as the DISZ, which in turn was a basic prerequisite later for admission to the university.

14. Were there any important fluctuations in the extent and forms of terror?

Yes, there certainly were such fluctuations. After 1948, the terror tended to increase (with a corresponding intensification) and after 1953 the exact opposite was true. There was an attempt to increase and to intensify this terror during 1954-1955, and there was a noticeable increase towards the end of 1955. This again was checked by the pre-Revolution events, and was completely eliminated during the Revolution.

14 a. Were there any waves of purges you can recall?

There were quite a number of such purge-waves. Right after 1945, a system of political classification (bélistázás) was begun. In practice this meant the elimination of anti-Democratic elements from all spheres of activity and their replacement by more trustworthy elements. This was only the beginning and, in view of the war and the changed circumstances, this purge was more or less understandable. After the Communists took over the power in Hungary in 1948, these purges became more numerous. The first step was the re-evaluation of the army officers' corps; the old officers, including those who retained their rank and position after 1945, were either pensioned, downgraded, or transferred to less important non-strategic positions. This process was also characteristic for the entire economic and social life. Everywhere, if at all possible, old people were replaced by new ones. Between 1948-1951, a great many quick-training courses were given, where people were permitted to acquire diplomas or other qualifying certificates within a few months or a year. This meant that people were prepared for such jobs as notaries, teachers, plant directors, administrative heads, etc. All this meant, of course, that the Communists were determined to effect a quick personnel change in the economic, social, and cultural spheres of the country.

Then from time to time the groups which already had been scrutinized were checked and double checked again; after 1949, the Rajkists were done away with. This process continued up until 1956. One group or another was always being checked and personnel was continually being changed -- a process in social systems to control Hungary, was an indispensable necessity. The close and constant supervision, the fact that everybody is constantly checked, everybody has a supervisor whose identity is, of course, not known, -- all this means in practice that reports are being sent in periodically to the center (to the AVH, Cabinet, and the Party). The center, in turn, checked the operation of the state machinery, and discovering some alarming defects in certain territories, strived to eliminate the faults by using the only method it knows: change of personnel.

15. *How important do you think was the Soviet Union in Hungarian affairs?*

The Soviet Union played a very important role in Hungarian affairs. This, of course, is true not only of Hungary, but of all East European states living under the Soviet orbit, -- the so-called people's democracies.

It is my firm belief that the decisions in all important matters affecting these states, including Hungary, were made in Moscow;

Moscow's approval had to be sought and secured in all important matters prior to promulgating and carrying out policy and prior to introducing significant changes.

15 a. What decisions were taken in Moscow, and what in Hungary?

I had no direct contact with Moscow, to be sure, and therefore I did not receive any information from them. On the other hand, the various economic and political methods employed in Hungary clearly demonstrated that this must have been the case. This was underscored, among other things, by the fact that the Hungarian Government was quite willing and prepared to enter into, and to accept, the obviously harmful provisions of foreign trade agreements with the Soviet Union. The Hungarian Government went even further, and publicly praised these agreements as beneficial and very advantageous instruments for Hungary. These foreign trade agreements permitted the Soviet Union to pick and choose what commodities or material she wanted from Hungary. Most important, the Soviet Union set the price, delivery and other conditions, and the Hungarian Government accepted these.

In the final analysis, then, these agreements were not the result of a bilateral understanding, of a mutual give and take, rather they represented unilateral demands and dictates on the part of the Soviet Union. The very fact that the Soviet Union imported raw materials from Hungary and exported in return finished products, only clearly shows Hungary's colonial status.

Over and above the economic sphere, such absurdities are also evident in the political sphere. Look at the October Revolution. Mikoyan, one of the figures of the Soviet leadership, was practically residing in Hungary at the time. As is known, the Hungarian Stalinists did not give up their struggle except on his nodding. Take the case of Rákosi; his position was quite strong, and he did not think of giving up his post until, in June 1956, somebody arrived from Moscow -- in this case Mikoyan again -- and informed him of the Moscow decision that Rákosi must resign and retire. These facts are fair samples of a host of similar other ones and they justify the deduction and generalization that all major decisions having to do with Hungary are made outside of Hungary.

15 d. Did you have any contact with Soviet personnel? If so, tell me about them -- how they behaved, what sort of people they were.

No.

15 e. In what areas of life branches of economy, professions, levels, etc. was Soviet influence most pronounced, in which least?

Soviet influence was most pronounced in the political sphere. Soviet influence was very significant also in the economic area, especially after 1948, exercised through the so-called Soviet-Hungarian enterprises. These enterprises controlled, among other things, the production of oil, the mining of bauxite and aluminum production. Soviet influence here was greatest. Hungary's trade balance, for example, was completely dependent on the Soviet Union. Over 50 percent of all Hungarian exports between 1948-1956 went to the Soviet Union. A similar or higher percentage of all our imports came to us from the Soviet Union.

Where was the Soviet influence least pronounced? Perhaps in the area of education. This does not mean that the Soviets did not make determined efforts in this field, nor does it imply that their influence was not strongly felt -- just look at the introduction of Russian as a compulsory subject in schools. The Soviet efforts, however, were definitely least effective in education.

16. How do people manifest their feelings under the Communists?

Well, now, it all depends on what sort of feelings you have in mind. A man has what I call an official feeling (hivatalos érzület) and also a private opinion, an inner, sentimental conception of things.

There were a great many institutional occasions and events which provided ample opportunity for people to express their devotion and fidelity to the people's democracy. I need only cite the various parades, celebrations, the many factory meetings, the daily <u>Szabad Nép</u> half-hours, weekly labor union meetings. All these were occasions to provoke people to make confessions and/or to declare their allegiance to the people's democracy and to the leaders of the Communist Party. Such declarations were forthcoming, but more and more was demanded, and people had to repeat them time and again.

As far as the manifestation of one's real feelings was concerned, there was practically no opportunity at all. After all, in many instances not even the family was a secure place, since suitable teachers, using the children as their instruments, actually controlled the parents. Such teachers would question their pupils to find out what their parents were talking about at home; what did the parents think about Rákosi, or about this or that political or economic problem or issue. It happened quite frequently that parents, even if they did not suffer more serious consequences, were confronted with compromising statements extracted from their children and were publicly reprimanded for their mistakes or deviations.

16 c. With whom could you be frank, and with whom less so?

I really don't know what to answer you. You are frank with those whom you trust and vice versa. The question is what the yardstick of this trust is. It is a fact that many people paid heavily for this mistaken assumption when they thought they could trust the other person. A case I know is characteristic of conditions in Hungary, respecting trust. There were two brothers, both members of the AVH. Both brothers corresponded with their parents, yet neither of them dared reveal to the other the contents of the letters he received from home. The parents were simple people, living in an obscure village. In their letters they reported this and that, grievances and hardships, not always in conformity with the Party line. The two brothers were afraid of one another, each fearing the other might report him.

16 d. What sort of things would you be more candid about, and about what things least?

Generally speaking, people did not talk freely about political questions. Regarding economic difficulties, the regime was not able to completely silence the people. Such facts as insufficiency of food, the lack of proper clothing, the insufficiency of pay for the feeding and clothing of children, -- these were painful and basic problems, and the regime did not succeed in stopping people to talk about them. These questions were discussed more freely, but only as particular, personal misfortunes, and not as general maladies or grievances. Every generalization meant taking a political stand and that, of course, was extremely dangerous.

17. Are there any ways for a Hungarian citizen to circumvent or ignore official orders?

Naturally, there is always a possibility to do such things, and in Hungary the opinion was prevalent that ignoring or circumventing of official orders did not constitute morally wrong acts. Everybody knew that the promulgated laws did not serve the good of the nation, but were designed for the benefit of only a few, of only one sector of the population.

How did people go about ignoring or circumventing orders? This was a rather difficult and hazardous task. The execution of orders in the villages was supervised partly by the AVH and partly by the regular police. The situation was similar in the cities.

17 b. Can a peasant fail to deliver all he is supposed to? If so, how?

This was simply impossible to do between 1948-1953. The reason is very simple: there were government inspectors at the threshing machines, who supervised the entire operation. The government knew the exact amount of grain a peasant had at his disposal. In most instances the forced delivery quotas were taken out of a peasant's grain right then and there, irrespective of whether the peasant had sufficient amounts for food and seed left. Also, village officials and the police made periodic checks in the house of every peasant. They visited the peasant's house, went down to the cellar, checked his attic, looked into every room and closet, and made sure that the peasant did not conceal anything. Needless to say, the penalties for violations were so draconian that no one tried even as much as think about outwitting the authorities.

18. Well, now, everything considered, what would you say were the strong points and which the weak points of the regime?

The strong points of the regime consisted of the AVH and of the AVH-supervised extensive network of informers. To this you must add the cadre system, the cadre sheets also being at the disposal of the AVH. Hungary was, in essence, a typical police state, where every government order, as well as all cultural, social, and political activities were under a strict police supervision. It was a police state where the laws were characterized by punishing those who failed to do something as well as those who did something. A classical example of this was the failure to report somebody to the police, a law which required the wife to report the husband and vice versa. This perfect police organization was the main strong point of the regime.

What was its weak point? The weakness of the regime lay in that the nation had no faith in it, (nem volt hitele az ország népe szemében). The regime had no credit in the eyes of the population. Those in charge of the regime time and again made statements affirming obvious falsehoods, they were trying to present falsified data as authentic and true, they were trying to present conditions as just when everybody knew full well that they were inhuman. The result of all this was that people simply did not believe any more in official pronouncements and, far from accepting the veracity of the regime's leaders, the population learned to believe in exactly the opposite of what was said.

19. Finally, I want to ask you something about opposition to the regime. What opposition was there, and how was it expressed?

This thing has many facets, and the question is so broad, but let's start out with a concrete example. Let's take an industrial enterprise, a factory, as the basis of our discussion. The factory had its norm system, its organization, the various supervisors, union representatives, informers, and what have you. All these supervisors checked and controlled and supervised every activity from the time the raw material arrived to the time the finished product left the factory gates.

Now the norm system was so tight in most places, and changes in the norm itself were effected with such a complete disregard of the worker, that the workers saw themselves forced to use every opportunity coming their way to circumvent and evade the norm system. Thus the workers did not perform the several work processes according to the prescribed manufacturing manual. When disregarding the provisions of the manual, they were fully aware that the quality of their products will not reach the standard anticipated by the production plan. In spite of that, they consciously continued in this violation. They consciously slowed down their work tempo, they consciously left out some phase of the work process, or altered these steps, or did not put in the necessary material, etc. All these conscious efforts had the same aim: to evade and to weaken that extremely strict and brutal system which weighed so heavily on their lives.

This was much more difficult in the case of the peasant. The industrial laborers had advantages in this respect, their violations could not be detected so easily; it was impossible even in Hungary to place a supervisor behind every single worker to observe the worker's every motion for eight hours a day. The peasantry could not elude the watching eyes of the supervisor, nor was it hard to effectively check agricultural production. All they had to do was to see that the peasant sowed the required amounts and kinds of seed in the spring, and to check the amounts of grain during threshing-time. The peasants, unable to cheat on either of these occasions, tried to use the intervening time to their own advantage. They cut down their wheat while it was still green, for instance, and used it as animal fodder. One could go on enumerating other methods of the peasantry, employed in its resistance to the regime.

An intellectual, always depending on the peculiarities of his profession, tried to find ways and means whereby to weaken, and to make less successful the operation of the state machine.

People did not have a feeling of responsibility towards the regime. To the contrary, people prided themselves if they managed to block the ordinary process here or there, or if they succeeded to negatively influence the outcome of things.

The resistance of the Hungarian people in the period 1948-

1956 must be sought in these little things, in these seemingly insignificant evasions of official rules, laws, and procedures, -- there was no other possibility of resistance.

19 b. What groups were most hostile to the regime? Why?

It is my belief that the industrial workers, as a group, were most hostile to the regime. They were the most vehement opponents. In the peasant class this hostility was less apparent, though the peasants' hostility to the regime had much deeper roots and was instinctive. The industrial workers were the favored group in Hungary and a good skilled worker could talk much more, and more freely, than anybody else. The workers naturally made use of their opportunity.

Why were they opposed to the regime? Their opposition stemmed from a very basic human consideration: the utter helplessness, hopelessness, of their lives; the people felt that their future held nothing in store for them other than the vague assurance that they would have a job somewhere, that they would earn a fixed amount of money every week or month, a sum which would permit them to just about get by, and maybe to buy an occasional piece of clothing, and that they would be permitted to retire at the age of 60 or 65 on a pension that would let them vegetate a little longer. Other than these a person could not hope for, nor could he have any ambition.

I feel that every person has a burning desire in him to construct his own little life in his own peculiar fashion, according to his smaller or greater ambition, and that the hope to be able to do so keeps him going. In Hungary not even the most minimal ambitions had a chance of realization. This was the basic reason of hostility to the regime.

19 c. What groups were least hostile? Why?

There was a special, and rather small group of people, who did not oppose the regime. These were such members of the Party to whom Party membership represented their livelihood. These people were the adherents of the regime. I am not even certain if all within this group were truly faithful admirers of the system. Some of them certainly were, others gave at least the appearance of being such. At any rate, a member of the AVH had a distinct position in Hungary not only socially, but also economically, so that it is hard to conceive an AVH officer as an enemy of the regime. An AVH officer could never have hoped of creating for himself a more advantageous position than the position he already held. The Hungarian Communist leadership intentionally created this situation to secure to itself a highly mobile and faithful control apparatus.

These people were compensated by higher pay, many advantages, and better social status, the value of which, absolutely speaking, was no more than two cups of beans in a prison instead of just one cup. But, if the total population is just about vegetating on a starvation diet, a difference of one cup of beans represents a tremendous value, and is a sufficient inducement for the creation of a small group of adherents.

19 d. Do you think opposition increased or decreased in 1953-55?

Between 1953-55, the opposition did not increase in the sense of an opposition against the regime. What happened was that the activity of the people was greatly augmented and people tried very hard to stabilize and better the situation. People tried to maximize their chances within the broader framework given to them by the Nagy Government. So this was not a resistance pure and simple, but rather a very sharp criticism of the past, a criticism designed and conducted with the view of preventing, as far as possible, the return of that past.

19 e. Do you think it increased or decreased in 1955-56?

In 1955 you had Rákosi's last determined attempt to regain the power, and to bring things back to where they were before 1953. In 1955, however, the resistance was very broad and universal. The criticizing became loud and open in the factories, on the farms and elsewhere. Also, curiously enough, Rákosi's moves in 1955 were not as sure and determined as they were before 1953. He did not order wholesale arrests, though many people were arrested, tried, and imprisoned in 1955. Quite a few people, freed in 1953, got back to prison again.

In 1955, the resistance grew to a loud and open criticizing. Also, you had the rapprochement between the new Soviet leaders and Marshal Tito. Now there was an open, personal, clash between Tito and Rákosi. All these circumstances influenced Moscow to pull Rákosi out of the arena and to experiment with new political tactics.

19 f. Do you think opposition was a personal matter, or were there any organized opposition groups?

My opinion is that the resistance was entirely a personal matter, though you did have smaller organized groups in the Catholic Church who held discussions and considered possible action. On the whole, the resistance was a personal matter, everybody acting individually on personal responsibility and in secret, not informing anybody before or after of his acts. The perfect police supervision rendered concerted conspirative actions dangerous and foolhardy.

19 l. How do you explain the emergence of the Petőfi Circle and of MEFESZ?

The MEFESZ was first organized in 1945. That year saw

the organization of the entire Hungarian youth and it was a necessity that the university youth be also organized. The peculiar feature of the MEFESZ after 1945 was that it did not represent a Party, but functioned as a coalition. Students of differing views and Party associations all participated in its activities. At the time of the Communist advance and seizure of power, the MEFESZ did not prove a suitable instrument either as a group supporting the seizure of power, or as an organization accepting the Communist political line, and was therefore dissolved just as all the other youth organizations, to be replaced by the unitary DISZ.

Now, before the Revolution, the MEFESZ was again called into being, because it had very strong, almost historical traditions, behind it; in the life of the students the MEFESZ always represented a certain degree of freedom, freedom of expression and a possibility of free criticism, which are not the least important values in the eyes of the students. These were the sentimental motives which led the students to reestablish the MEFESZ.

The emergence of the Petőfi Circle had entirely different reasons behind it, though its origins also go back to the DISZ. It was called into being first as the Petőfi Circle of the DISZ. The Government gave its approval to the establishment of this debate forum in the assumption that it would function as an integral part, and within the framework of the DISZ, under the supervision and control of the trusted leaders of that organization. The Government further assumed that the DISZ Petőfi Circle, while becoming a forum of discussion, of debate, and of quarrel, would never really get out of hand; the debaters would find themselves face to face with the Circle's leaders, guardians of the interests of the people's democratic state, the issues raised would be discussed and either solved by means of debate or else troublesome people could simply be silenced.

The Petőfi Circle did not assume the role the Government assigned to it, because from the very outset former and rehabilitated Communists and Rajkists were also admitted as members. Now the Rajkist youth guard -- (actually they were no longer too young at that time) -- had important and close personal contacts, established during the Second World War, with leading members of other disbanded youth organizations; young members of the Györfi Kollegiums, the later Rajkists, fought side by side with other anti-Fascist groups in 1943 and 1944. Close personal contacts and friendships existed, therefore, between the Rajkists and the other dissident groups.

Now the Rajkists were accepted as members of the DISZ Petőfi Circle and were given important assignments there. The Rajkists pulled in with them their personal friends, former wartime anti-Fascist collaborators, who had become leaders and influential members of various youth organizations between 1945-1948, but who now, at the time of the Circle's creation, because of their political status, could not openly participate in the Circle's activities. Many of these people were, like myself, still under police supervision. The result of all this was that the Circle's front became very wide, with a very broad base, encompassing virtually all anti-Stalinist and anti-Rákosi elements. This structural change brought with it a change in the course of the Circle, leading it on its now well-known path. This, then, is the explanation not of the emergence, but of the transformation of the Petőfi Circle. Obviously, the Circle's transformation, not its emergence, is the substantial element in question.

19 m. Did you know of the activities of the intellectuals in 1955-56? What did they have in mind?

Young intellectuals differed in their political intentions according to what their views and opinions were. But they all agreed in one thing; they agreed that what transpired in Hungary after 1948, was bad, and inhuman, and that the most important objective was to correct the abuses and/or to replace existing principles and practices with new and better ones. This view was accepted by all, and this view represented that common denominator which the Petőfi Circle, the Writers' Association, and their camps or followers accepted as a firm base, and point of departure.

The overall views of young intellectuals differed -- which was only natural -- but the majority, be they Communists, or educated under communism, could not even imagine a solution other than improvement of existing conditions, within the existing framework. In this practically all were agreed. One could hardly depend on the West, certainly not on the basis of previous experiences. On the other hand, the proximity of the Soviet Union could hardly be disregarded in Hungary in the past dozen years. All this led people to think in terms of the existing framework; in a state bordering the Soviet Union, therefore, in a Socialist state, we must improve the conditions, and inaugurate a process of development which, while at a later time might undergo changes and suffer corrections, could not reasonably be expected to change then. This is the explanation why these young elements, almost in one voice, demanded new leadership at the top of their respective parties. This was the reason behind the extreme popularity of Imre Nagy. He became so popular precisely because he was a Communist, and being such, seemed to offer an opportunity for improvement within this existing framework. Nobody ever thought in terms of parting with the Soviet Union, or of engineering a political change against the Soviet Union. All people sought was an improvement of existing conditions, a solution with the least number of bad features within the existing framework.

Communications and Propaganda

1. *Where did you get most of your information about what was happening in the world?*

I am going to restrict myself to the 1948-1956 period. The characteristic methods and possibilities for gathering information varied of course from year to year in my case, not only because I was in several places and under different circumstances during these years, but because the government's intentions also showed changes in this period.

Let's start with 1948; the tendency of the government then was to restrict the information media to domestic and Russian sources, which, dealing with the domestic and international issues of the day, naturally gave a characteristically slanted picture.

The government, of course, could not prevent at least a part of the population from somehow controlling this development.

In 1948 the so-called campaign of lies got underway in which both the Soviet center and the people's democracies attempted to show that all things on their side were good and all things on the other side were bad. This brought about a contrary reaction between 1948 and 1953, developing two things in the minds of the people;

a. they did not believe anything at all that reached them through these media,

b. the people quickly learned to read between the lines.

I was in an internment camp from 1948 to 1953, which, especially after 1950, was completely shut off from the outside world. A camp of that size (1200 inmates) cannot, of course, be completely shut off from at least the immediate surroundings, and we in the camp developed an extra sense. From discarded newspaper fragments we were able to put together a reliable mosaic picture, and were always well informed and remarkably up to date. I may truthfully say that though a prisoner, shut off from all ordinary news media, I was better informed regarding both national and international developments between 1950 and 1953 than ever before or after.

I was freed in 1953 and my situation changed. And so did the general situation. Foreign newspapers were gradually coming in, Communist newspapers of course, the French L'Humanite being especially favored.

The L'Humanite was an excellent source for us, since it wrote quite differently than the Pravda or the Szabad Nép. It was, after all, a Western newspaper, which had to treat and to comment on very many things and events, for the sake of its own clientele who were interested, which in Hungary or Russia were either entirely distorted or not even mentioned at all. The L'Humanite was a free press for us, from which, and through which, we could see the world with much less effort than was the case with Pravda or with the Hungarian papers.

After 1953, the situation becoming more free, the people, myself included, felt more free to listen to Western radio broadcasts. I listened to all radio broadcasts, beginning with Free Europe through the BBC and the Hungarian broadcasts of the French radio, listening to every and all stations I could get.

These were essentially the information possibilities which, being fragmentary and incomplete, -- one could not regularly and systematically listen to the radio, nor could one read all the newspapers, -- each person had to use his own innate intelligence to construct the mosaic picture from the available parts and to add, -- usually by deductive methods -- whatever parts were missing.

This led some people, -- especially those who patronized the Radio Free Europe -- to live a life of a happy illusion, particularly with respect to Western assistance to Hungary. How mistaken these people were the Revolution proved beyond doubt, and how ill-advisedly Radio Free Europe acted is impossible to say as yet, since we cannot precisely measure the damage it did, not being able to call to the witness stand the innumerable dead who fought and died as late as November 4, in good faith, not knowing how fallacious their premises were.

1 a. Which of these sources were the most important for you?

L'Humanite.

1 b. Which was the next most important?

Western Hungarian-language radio broadcasts, the most important being Radio Free Europe, giving at times a 24-hour program.

2. Please think of a typical month when you lived in Hungary. During one month, would you read newspapers or magazines?

My answer to this question will be hardly typical, and for obvious reasons; I was imprisoned first (1948-1953), and lived later under police supervision, which, as I already explained previously, meant the imposition of very many restrictions. Just to cite you one example: the police did not mind my subscribing to the Szabad Nép, but I could hardly hope to subscribe to other, say Western, newspapers. Other people, at the same time, did have this opportunity. I read the following domestic papers: Szabad Nép, Magyar Nemzet, Szabad Föld, Csillag (edited by Pál Szabó), Társadalmi Szemle (ideological), Közgazdasági Szemle, and others.

2 g. Did you ever see foreign publications?

L'Humanite, at times I saw The Times and, on a few occasions, The New York Times.

2 j. *Did you ever run across any "illegal" publications? If so, where, and what were they?*

I did run across some leaflets sent to Hungary by means of balloons. Let me use this opportunity to make some comments on this. The leaflet, signed by the Magyar Függetlenségi Mozgalom or some such signature, was what I now know a mimeographed newsletter. I read it, and felt immediately that it was a product of a man who was not living in Hungary. The data it contained were so general, and somehow did not seem to fit into Hungary's life at the time.

3. *During the same average month, would you go to the movies? How often?*

I could not go to the movies because of the police supervision. I could go, nevertheless, occasionally, to Budapest, where I also went to the movies.

3 b. *Were they mostly entertainment, educational, political, or something else?*

I tried very hard not to look at Soviet pictures when I did go.

3 e. *Did you go to the theater?*

I went to the theater four or five times during three years. It was rather risky, in my case, since someone familiar with me or with my case may easily have recognized me.

4. *Did you read any books?*

Yes, I did read books. You must, of course, realize that

I performed heavy physical labor and resting for me was more important than reading of books.

4 e. *Who were your favorite writers (poets, novelists)? Why?*

I was a great collector of books before the Second World War. I had a small library of some 2000 - 2500 books, which, thanks to my family, were preserved while I was in prison. After 1953, when I was home again, I re-read many of these books. Western books were practically impossible to get, excepting such titles as Orwell's *1984*, Hemingway's works, the works of Sinclair Lewis, the works of G. B. Shaw, -- in a word such Western writers were permitted who were either classics or modern authors of a materialistic naturalist complexity and world view.

As far as Hungarian authors went, I read the Hungarian classics Mikszáth, Zsigmond Móricz, Mihály Babits, Dezsö Kosztolányi, Endre Ady, Lörinc Szabó, István Sinka, László Németh, Péter Veres, Gyula Illyés, etc., etc.

5. *Did you listen to the radio?*

Yes, I did listen to the radio. I enjoyed especially radio plays, using them as substitutes to the theater, and I also listened to commentators, always hoping to get some negative information, or rather information in a negative way, thereby.

5 b. *If yes, did you have a set yourself? What kind?*

I had a so-called people's set, a cheap, little set, capable of getting only Budapest I and II, this being the only type permitted in my case.

6. *Did you listen to any foreign stations?*

Yes, but not in my own house. I usually visited friends who had more powerful sets.

6 d. *What about the reliability of foreign broadcasts?*

The BBC's commentaries were the most objective, followed by the Paris radio, and only much behind these the Radio Free Europe.

7. *Did you get any information by word-of-mouth?*

Of course, I lived among people, don't forget, and I had very many friends and acquaintances, not only in Budapest, but in other parts of the country as well. They usually came to see me, in steadily growing numbers, as we approached the Revolution, because I myself was not permitted to travel. This was the basis of my word-of-mouth information. We usually talked about politics and events pertaining to Hungary, and were concerned only secondarily with events of international significance.

8 d. *How could you tell what to believe and what not to believe?*

Digging out the truth, or the possible truth, from a welter of misinformation or slanted reporting is basically a work of the intellect, where the result depends on the person's training, knowledge, and point of view. If you want to get at the truth in a source which you know is slanted, you certainly must have a viewpoint of your own from which to analyze it, to which to compare it. I, too, had such a viewpoint, namely an interest in what goes on in the international scene which might bring about a change in Hungary, or a possible liberalization at least. This was my yardstick, and it is probably excusable that I viewed every international event, -- be it in the Middle or Far East -- from the point of view of Hungary only. Of course, today I am interested in the facts, in what goes on in the United Arab Republic or Jordan, or Yemen. In Hungary, however, we were under an unwanted burden, under a heavy mass, and we could not help viewing whatever occurred through this mass, always acutely aware of its tremendous weight.

8 e. Were some newspapers or some broadcasts considered more trustworthy than others? If so, which?

The English newspapers are well known for their succinctness and objectivity. This goes for the BBC broadcasts also. And in Hungary the English papers were synonymous with the Western press, they being the only ones which were sometimes permitted to enter. American newspapers were excluded.

When it comes to Russia, domestic, and other satellites' news media, the opinion generally held among Hungarians respecting their reliability will be by now clear to you also. If you want to know what my view is, I think exactly the opposite was true of what they said or wrote.

8 f. Did you ever read Irodalmi Ujság? What did you think of it?

I was a subscriber from the very beginning. I had a very high opinion of it: it was a well-written, well-edited paper, it had a beautiful style, it used correct, grammatical Hungarian, a rarity in those days. Its content also was of a kind which commanded everybody's interest at the time. The Irodalmi Ujság was not just a paper, but a spokesman, a sounding board as well. We eagerly awaited its publication days in advance.

9. Do you feel that people tried hard to be well-informed?

If we compare the people's requirements, (igény), needs for information, to that before the war, we see that many more people read papers. People got used to, and were forced to, regularly read the papers and to closely follow the many developments, because their very destiny depended on being well-versed and well informed. People not only read the news, but analyzed the events and the developments, because only by such an analysis of the developments could they form an opinion of what chances they, or Hungary, had for the future.

Since Hungary was oppressed, the people were searching for consolation while following the trend of events, bringing occasionally to their otherwise unenviable situation a ray of hope. Thus the people's need for information tremendously increased, especially after 1948.

10. I'd like you to tell me briefly what you knew before leaving Hungary?

I knew that the dropping of the bombs ended the war against Japan. The signing of the armistice, the coming of the emperor, the former God, to MacArthur on the U.S. battleship made a very deep impression on me.

We viewed the land reform in Japan with great interest, knowing full well it was prepared by United States experts. We are overwhelmed with joy when we saw that the United States had finally made a correct step, has finally decided to throw its support to the democratic elements of a country, a decision almost unique, and totally lacking since then.

The United States, it seems to me, systematically supports the reactionary elements, the narrow oligarchy of the underdeveloped countries, when it comes to economic assistance or commercial agreements, against the truly democratic and wide masses of these countries.

This explains at least partly the events and developments of present-day Asia; when it comes to a movement for freedom or independence in any of these countries, the leaders of such movements have no connections whatsoever to, no relations with, the Western democracies. They obviously have to have relations and connections, after all no man is an island, no country can live alone in the world, somewhere, somehow, they know they must become part of the international community, of international politics; they must oppose certain forces, and must also seek sympathies somewhere. These are nationalist, yet essentially democratic efforts trying to create during their nationalistic upsurge a better situation, better conditions for their country. They are interested in industrial development, in the rising of the standard of living, etc., etc., -- a process which would lead, or could lead eventually, to a process of democratization.

Now those forces who represent this desire, and determination to effect a change, a democratization of their countries, -- be it in Indonesia or elsewhere -- have no connections, no relationships whatsoever with the Western democratic countries, and very often are outright opponents of the West. I am not saying that the way American economic aid is given and is administered is the only factor responsible for the situation, but that it greatly contributed to it is beyond any doubt.

10 b. Who started the Korean War?

The official Hungarian view is well known. The American imperialists started the war, and in the freedom fight of the North Koreans many Hungarians -- notably doctors and engineers -- also participated.

I was not a free man at the outbreak of the Korean war. The news of the outbreak reached us much later, and in meaningless fragments. We in prison regarded the conflict as a conflict between the United States and Soviet Russia, believing at the same time that a world conflict might erupt out of it.

10 c. What about germ warfare in Korea?

I know as much about this as Méray wrote in his articles, no more and no less.

10 d. What about West German re-armament?

A great deal was written and said about this in Hungary. You again had the official opinion. In the opinion of the population, West Germany was regarded as a country which very rapidly recovered economically and reached a very high standard of living -- if not the highest in Europe. Even in the darkest days of the Stalinist oppression, some people did manage to visit West Germany and reported about prices, standard of living, etc.

We knew of the rapid military progress East Germany made under Russian auspices, that its growing army was provided with the most modern Soviet weapons, though newspapers never wrote about this. We were also fully aware of the West German developments, and generally we were in sympathy with them.

10 f. What about the Berlin riots of 1953?

Newspapers reported this event two or three days after, saying that a fascist-imperialist uprising has just been suppressed. Within a few weeks, we knew the precise picture. We knew that the uprising had economic undertones, that economic discontent was behind it.

10 g. What about the "summit meeting" in Geneva?

We viewed with great expectancy the summit meeting. We hoped that some sort of a solution would be arrived at respecting Germany, and, as a result, a situation would come about which would permit a solution of the question of East Central Europe also at a later time.

No one expected the redemption of Hungary as a result of the meeting, though Eisenhower did say that the question of East Central Europe would be put on the agenda. The disappointment was deep and widespread as the question was not even discussed. The United States used it as a tactical weapon to further its sinking prestige in the area. We were not all too enthusiastic about the way the West behaved in Geneva.

10 h. What about émigré activities abroad?

We knew very little about émigré activities. We knew that there was a Hungarian National Council in New York which, in the early 'fifties, repeatedly appeared on the air through the Radio Free Europe, disappearing later completely. We usually learned of its activities in a negative way, when spoken of in official Hungarian and Soviet news media. The émigré groups were never seriously considered and there was no link between the emigrants sitting in New York and receiving pay on the one hand, and those leaders who were in jails at home on the other.

It is interesting to note that during the Revolution certain elements demanded the immediate closure of Hungary's Western borders, -- after they had been just opened -- to prevent the Western emigrants from entering the country. The Revolution wanted to solve its own problems, with no foreign interference. This meant of course that the emigration's ties were completely cut off from Hungary. I don't know what the Council did during the past ten years, the resonance of the thing in Hungary was that nothing was done by the Council which would have facilitated things at home, or would have prepared the way for an eventual liberation.

As a result, the National Council was neither popular nor was it considered a factor. People thought of it as a sort of reactionary group. We just could not imagine how a Kallay or a Bakach-

Bessenyei, -- to cite only a few -- could possibly fit into the Hungarian picture.

Permit me now to draw a parallel between the situation in Asia and that of East Central Europe; a large number of emigrants reside in the West from the latter area, among them Hungarians also. Here again, I must say, the United States had supported the right-wing elements of the emigration. The American foreign policy simply did not recognize that history and developments in East Central Europe have simply left these people far behind. It is my feeling that the United States does not recognize this fact even now. They are trying to support those people in whom they invested money, who have in the course of time established close personal contacts, and there is a growing tendency to discard those elements whose views do not agree with the views of the older emigration.

This will, of course, have its effects later, and these effects will not be advantageous to the United States. Though I do not believe that any Hungarian emigration, -- of whatever variety -- would be able to triumphantly re-enter Hungary, sitting in the saddle of a white horse, that the emigration, myself included, will be received with triumphal arches, though it is also clear that at least some of us will be able to return, if the situation improves somewhat. The emigration will have to account for itself, and certain members of it will be at least in the position to advise, enlighten, and to help the leaders of a future Hungary, -- leaders who definitely will not be emigrants. I would consider it a great misfortune indeed if these returning emigrants would not, or could not, see their way clear to advise a future government to see a Western orientation, and to search in a Western alignment for the future destiny of the country. This danger is clearly a reality, as it is a reality in Asia today.

POLITICAL OPINIONS, ATTITUDES AND IDEOLOGY

1. *Suppose the present system in Hungary were removed. What in the present system would you be sure to change?*

If it is at all possible to speak of a possible removal of the present Hungarian system, the extremely strict state supervision should certainly be changed. Further, all forms and remnants of the even now existing police state should be eliminated. The people ought to be given greater economic freedom. I have in mind here primarily the agriculture, but also the industry. In this latter case (industry), opportunity should be given to the workers to construct and to develop the industry according to their own theory (elképzelés). The direction of industrial development should certainly be changed (which in the Rakosi era overemphasized the heavy industry). Though in 1953 and after the mistake of such a development was clearly recognized, it now seems that Kádár and Munnich gradually revert to it. These are the things which ought to be radically changed.

1 a. What would you want to keep under another regime?

Your questions are very general and I find it difficult to answer them. I would retain all those things which the people consider good and proper. This is my general reply to your general question.

1 b. What features of the present regime would you say are generally accepted?

If we wanted to be precise, then we must say that there is an innovation under the present regime, an innovation brought about by the Revolution which the people generally accept, and which even the Kádár regime did not dare touch thus far. This is the elimination of forced deliveries, and a relatively more normal agricultural policy. They do not as yet force collectivization and they do not employ those methods in general use before the Revolution.

To come back to generally accepted features of the present regime; if the term "present regime" denotes the Communist governments from 1948 on, then I certainly must mention worthy innovations and laws enacted for the benefit of the workers, provisions which were very noteworthy and which represent progress if compared to previous times. To be specific, the insecurity of a worker as regards his employment no longer exists (munkás alkalmaztatásának a bizonytalansága megszünt). A phenomenon so prevalent in the free world, whereby a worker gains employment today and may be laid off two weeks hence or a month hence by, and without any consequences to, the employer, a situation where a worker secures himself a job, but does not know how long his job and pay may last -- this is no longer the case in Hungary. The problem was solved partly by the institution of collective contracts. These contracts laid down the principle that a worker could only be laid off under certain specific conditions. On the other hand, if layoffs were necessary, they could only be effected after the expiration of a "notice period", usually one and a half - two months during which time the worker had ample opportunity to look around for another job, since the collective contract also guarantees him a specified number of hours per day or week, which he could use for job hunting, hours for which he got full pay from his present employer.

The worker then felt more secure. I must add immediately that wages and living standards in Hungary are much lower than those prevailing in the West, and that the condition of the Hungarian worker did not improve phenomenally by the mere addition of this fact of greater security. Greater security in itself certainly did not create a situation deserving praise, nevertheless, the fact that the worker was assured a permanent and stable employment by means of the collective contract is something deserving note and attention.

Another feature I should like to mention is the social insurance, a system also closely connected with the condition of the workers. The problem of social insurance is not really a new question in Hungary, it having been regulated in the 1920s and 1930s, when the OTI (Institute of National Social Insurance) was created. At that time the workers were insured against sickness and all received some money (táppénz) when sick. Employees were obliged to become members of this organization at the time of taking a job. Fifty percent of the premium was borne by the employers, the other half by the employee. This was changed after the Second World War so that the employee bears the entire cost of the insurance now. The insurance coverage, at the same time, is extended to accidents, sickness, it covers medical expenses of the family members and provides free supply of medicaments.

2. *Do you think there should be political parties?*

Yes. There is a need for political parties, since politics without them is scarcely conceivable in a democratic state. The Communists tried to do away with the parties and substituted one Party for the many. In my opinion this represents a dangerous situation. The one Party is necessarily a government Party, with the most important posts relating to the direction of the state being filled by members of this Party. This represents a great temptation both for the Party and for the individuals. It is necessary, therefore, to have a democratic control, i.e., another Party, which brings to light flagrant abuses and opposes obvious injustices, and is able to bring issues to a debate in Parliament, showing incorrect or improper actions or policies on the part of the government.

2 a. *Do you think all people should be free to organize or join political parties as they wish?*

Yes, I believe it is very useful to have a situation where everybody is free to either organize or join a political Party. By everybody I mean all people in full possession of their powers of political judgment. I have in mind here adults and people whose mental powers are not deficient.

2 b. *Would you make any exceptions to this?*

I would not make any exceptions. This is a general rule, applicable to all. The right to freely organize and/or to join political parties is a fundamental human right, stemming from the fundamental right of man to organize for the purpose of achieving a certain aim he considers good or useful. Organizing for the purpose of achieving a certain aim is identical to organizing political parties in the life of a state. Therefore such organizing is everybody's fundamental right and everybody is free to enlist others to create for himself a following for whatever purpose, including the purpose of trying legally to change such things which he considers bad.

3. *Do you think all people should be free to say anything they want, or should there be some limits to it?*

I am for the fullest possible freedom in this question. Freedom of speech, just as the freedom to organize, is a fundamental right. Recognition of these rights and the freedom of fully asserting them are indispensable necessities in the life of a healthy state.

The Western democracies provide a good example for this; insofar as I was able to observe, it is very useful and healthy if a person may express his opinion. The contrary of this I have also observed innumerable times and experienced on my own skin in Communist Hungary.

3 b. *Who should decide what to allow and what not to allow?*

People should not be forbidden to denounce the government. The government, in the final analysis, is not there for its own sake, it is, as Eisenhower aptly pointed out in one of his speeches, the supreme servant of the state. If this be so, then everybody has the right to pass judgment on this servant.

Now, if we take the laws of classical democracy, then the government should always express the opinion of the majority of the population (the opinion of the population should be faithfully represented in the Parliament) and its policy in the political, social, and economic sphere should always be a policy corresponding to the wishes of the population. Thus it is obvious that everybody has the right to pass judgment on the way the government conducts his business, including the right of denouncing the government for what a person thinks was an improper move on the part of the government.

3 d. *Should people be forbidden to say things detrimental to the state?*

I don't know what you mean by the phrase "detrimental to the state". What is it that is detrimental to the state? (Interviewer's reply: The meaning of the phrase is rather clear, I think, as it stands. It is another matter whether you admit or not that it denotes an objective reality. Some people say it does, others deny it. To cite you a recent example from Hungarian history, some contemporaries of Count Károlyi felt that the Count's conduct and activities from 1916 on were detrimental to the Hungarian state. I don't know if this clarifies the point.) Respondent's Answer: I cannot accept the proposition that any government or political tendency is to be equated with the interests of the state. The interest of the state may be, for instance, that the raw materials be not sent out at a low price. If somebody does sell raw materials to foreign states at a low price, such person engages in an activity detrimental to the state. It is also conceivable that the state, in a difficult situation, conducts some sort of a policy, in which case a protest against such a policy again is detrimental to the state. But the determination of whether a citizen's interpellation, or protest, or what have you, is detrimental to the state or not is not possible at the hour the statements are made. Such determination is only possible at a later date. You mentioned Károlyi's anti-war policy from 1916 on. I don't know to this day -- I mean, this is a debatable question - whether Károlyi's policy then was detrimental to the state or if his policy was the policy which represented the true interests of the state at that time. Historical facts seem to show that Hungary would have been better off if she had made her exit as early as 1916, just as another man, Bajcsy-Zsilinszky, was right when in 1935 he demanded that Hungary pull away from Berlin, and immediately. He wanted Hungary to break off all her relations with Germany and to try to realign orientation with the other side. Bajcsy-Zsilinszky's policy was a policy "detrimental to the state" at the time, very many people attacked him, and he was eventually executed -- primarily for this reason -- at Sopronkőhida.

Now that both historical events are years behind us, we must come to the conclusion that in neither case was the interpellation and protest a protest against the state, or detrimental to the state. All we can say is that both men made anti-government statements and speeches.

I could accept the term "detrimental to the state" and all that goes with it only in such a case if it were proven to me beyond any doubt that the person attacking the government or a certain activity of the government, attacked a policy, or activity, or process, which in reality did represent the true wishes or true interests of the people.

4. Do you think that all people should be free to participate in meetings?

Yes. I consider this proper, and base my judgment on the principle that everybody has the right to freely determine his activities and participation in some action or expression of his opinion.

4 b. In what circumstances is an armed uprising against the government justified?

People are always within their rights to change its bad government for a good one. More precisely, a government which does not serve the interests of the people, which disregards the opinion of the majority of the people when it acts and conducts its policy, may always be overthrown and the people are entitled to replace such government with another, which, in the people's opinion, is a better one.

There are legal ways and means to bring this about according to democratic precepts. You have the parliamentary election, on which occasion, the population, if it so desires, simply does not give the majority to the government Party, giving its confidence instead to another Party which, in the opinion of the electorate, has a better program or would pursue a better policy.

Now all those governments which deviate (eltávolodnak) from democracy, try to exclude, to minimize, to reduce, or to completely eliminate this possibility of governmental change -- this means of expression of popular opinion.

History has proven in innumerable instances that a people always try to effect a change in their government by legal means first. This is quite natural, since every action proceeds first in the direction of least resistance, where there is less struggle, less bloodshed, and less risk. In my opinion, however, if there is no other way of effecting a change in the government, i.e., a change in the political leadership, then all people have a legal right to assert and to vindicate its will by the force of arms. This is why, in my opinion, all revolutions express the legal will (törvényes akaratát) of the people, and decrees and decisions which come into being in a revolution obtain their force of law in such cases through the will of the people.

5. *What changes do you think need to be made in the economic system of Hungary?*

This is another of those giant questions. If I am to answer this question, my task will be simplified by the fact that the Revolution has already broken the path before me, and has made certain decisions which were identical then, and are still identical now, with my views and opinions in this question.

In order to answer this question, then, we must analyze first of all the so-called economic demands of the Revolution and those decisions which were made in the Revolution respecting the future economic life of the country.

The most important and fundamental questions in this respect were the land question, and the question of the industrial enterprises. As a result of the land reform and of the nationalization of industry after the Second World War, great ownership changes came about in Hungary. Industrial enterprises became the property of the state, for the most part, and a significant portion of the great estates were parceled out among the poor (nincstelen) peasants. The economic changes and experiments of the 1945-1948 period are extremely important, because the 1956 Revolution sanctioned these changes and experiments or, if you prefer, the Revolution reverted back to them.

The Revolution's most important economic decision was that "we shall not give back the factories to the capitalists, nor the land to the magnates". This decision met practically no resistance or opposition in the country. I don't think I have to go into details as to how this decision was to be practically implemented. A good indication of what would have happened is the well-known fact that over 50 percent of the TSzCs cooperatives established between 1948-1956, were disbanded, and the peasantry went back to that small-scale farming (kisparaszti gazdálkodás) which developed in the 1945-1948 period.

In the factories the situation was somewhat more complicated. Nevertheless, there, too, we can find important initiatives (beginnings -- kezdeményezés) and therefore useful directions. I have in mind here the workers' councils.

These workers' councils played almost exclusively a political role during October-November 1956, and they continued to be almost the only power in the nation's large cities after the Revolution. Actually, the workers' councils were not organized with a political aim in mind. Their role and purpose was to be primarily economic; the organization, direction, and management of factories was to be their main function. One of their first steps in this direction was their preoccupation with affecting new labor union elections.

6. *In some countries, as you know, heavy industry -- such as steel and coal -- is nationalized. Are you in favor of this?*

My affirmative answer to this question would naturally depend on the economic condition of these countries. Generally speaking, I would be in favor of this. However, I am much more in favor of social ownership (társadalmi tulajdon), rather than nationalization. To explain: heavy industry would not be owned by the state, but by the workers. (A dolgozók tulajdonát jelentené.) This was a new experiment and this is what the workers' councils wanted to bring about. In many cases they obtained very good results. The time was short, of course, and their experiments could not ripen, could not show their disadvantages and advantages.

6 b. Should any factories be restored to their former owners? Why?

I don't know of any factory in Hungary, especially a larger factory, where a restoration to the former owners would appear necessary. Why? Because nobody seems to favor a return to the pre-World War II capitalist economy in Hungary.

6 c. Is private profit good or bad?

I would try to answer this question in the negative and would add that I am not in favor of too great differences in the distribution of income. I do not approve of a situation where a few people have very large incomes in a community, and very many people have very little. Social evolution throughout the world, including the United States, clearly shows that economic development invariably brings with it a process leading to equalization of the incomes.

6 e. Should there be any state monopolies?

I am not in favor of any sort of monopoly.

6 g. What about trading monopolies like Közért?

The Közért was not a well functioning, economically solvent, undertaking. First of all it could not satisfy consumer demand; secondly, because of its disorganized administration and direction, it would not effect a normal flow of even those goods it had, shipping to some place too much, to other places too little. Even from a purely economic point of view, the Közért always had a large deficit, and the state had to help it out with tens of millions of forints yearly.

7. *In some countries, as you know, light industry -- such as clothing manufacture -- is nationalized. Are you in favor of this?*

In principle I am in favor, I repeat, not of nationalization, but of social ownership. This ownership would include light industry as well. **Question:** Could you give me a more precise description or definition of "social ownership"? **Answer:** Social ownership differs from private or state ownership in that a factory, for instance, would not be the possession of one or more people, nor would it be owned by the state and directed by an appointed director or commissioner, but the workers, people actually working in the factory, would own that factory. It would be similar to a cooperative (szövetkezet) in that the capital of the factory would be made up of monies contributed by the many workers -- shareholders, and these people would also exercise, as owners, the direction and control over it.

8. *What do you think about government planning?*

Government planning has its advantages and disadvantages. Even here in the United States you have a long-standing debate with some favoring and others opposing it, a debate of free market versus government planning.

The unquestionable advantage of a planning bureau is that it can measure more precisely, and therefore is able to more completely satisfy, consumer demand. Here, of course, you have to distinguish between planning, which takes into account the population's interest and proceeds accordingly, and planned economy where planning is done according to the narrow wishes and interests of the leadership of a state. In this connection Hungary, in the period 1948-1956, presents a classical example. During this period planned economy was based on the proposition that we must develop the heavy industry. All other production, including the production of consumer goods, was subordinated to the overriding determination of bringing into being a heavy industry. This was an example of an improper planning, of what planned economy should not be. I cannot cite you, off hand, an example of good planning, all I can do is to refer to attempts at planning in the underdeveloped regions, where such planning attempts to gauge in a realistic fashion the apparent needs, and then channel the available material and production capacity in that direction.

The real purpose of planning, of course, is the elimination of surpluses in some areas and the prevention of shortages in others; direction of the industrial and agricultural apparatus in such a way that precisely the needed things and amounts are produced, or such amounts as are profitable.

8 b. How has it worked out?

Government planning in Hungary reached a state of complete bankruptcy. The planning bureau degenerated into a bureaucratic state machine -- and the already mentioned undue emphasis on the development of heavy industry largely contributed to this. After all, the country embarked upon this development without possessing the necessary natural resources. Even if the planning bureau had conducted its direction of the economy in the best possible manner, this eventual bankruptcy could not have been avoided.

They were creating such industries between 1948-1956 for which the economic prerequisites simply were not secured. The development and operation of an industry depends on the availability of raw materials, preferably cheap raw materials, and power. There are other prerequisites, but these two are the most important. Now in Hungary they created such heavy industries where neither the raw materials nor the power were inexpensive. Most of these had to be imported in part. And we developed these industries solely for the purpose of being able to tell in our statistics that we had a heavy industry and that we developed it to such and such a degree.

8 c. *Just how far should it go?*

Hungary is also one of the industrially lesser-developed countries and it is necessary that her industrialization be accelerated so that she may reach the level of the more developed Western countries. Because of this, it is imperative that the direction of the country's industrial development be centrally defined. This brings up the question of what industry should be developed. I am in favor of certain branches of the light industry, an area where Hungary has very favorable potentialities, and also the food industry. This would have to be the general direction of development under normal conditions. The Planning Bureau would have to determine the exact ratio of participation by the various industries in the overall production. This should be the outer limit of the bureau's competence beyond which it should not go.

8 d. *Who should decide what to produce and what prices there should be?*

I am not an admirer of state price fixings. This is very inflexible and should be resorted to only if the economy loses its own delicate balance. If you have a balanced economy, the natural interaction of supply and demand determine the price. You must, of course, take into consideration the influence exerted on the price structure by the international demand and supply (i.e., what and how much of it can you buy and sell on the markets abroad?). But given this variable, the price itself is otherwise fixed by the supply and demand.

I am rather in favor of supporting, i.e., protecting certain Hungarian industries. Price fixing by the state in these regions is justifiable and reasonable, I think. I have in mind here industries in the initial stages of development which otherwise have a very good base and prospect of development, but have not yet reached a point where they could successfully compete with similar industries abroad.

9. *In general, are there any areas of human affairs in which the state should not interfere?*

You are using here the term "state", a not easily definable and elusive thing.

If under the term "state" you mean government, and if such a government really represents the interests of the people, if it is a freely elected government, then such government has the right and may interfere (beleszólhat) in questions of principle in any and all areas of human affairs. A government has the right to define and to fix (megszabni) the direction of the nation's political, economic, and cultural development. All this is true only so long as it meets the approval of the people, and not further. The moment this point is reached and overstepped the government becomes illegal (törvénytellenné válik).

10. *Do you feel that a citizen has certain duties toward the state?*

All constitutions define the duties of the citizens toward the state. I can only approve these duties as defined by the constitutions.

10 a. *What about paying taxes? How much should one be taxed?*

This brings up the question of just and unjust taxation, and its seems necessary to state my view of what constitutes just and unjust taxation.

Taxes are levied so that the government may have the means necessary to govern on the one hand, and to pay for other expenditures, -- provided for in the budget - on the other. Under "taxes" I mean total amount of taxes collected, a sum equal to the state's total expenditures. Under normal conditions both the total tax revenue and method, or ways and means, of taxation are determined by elected members of the Parliament. It is quite obvious that all citizens of the state must share the burdens of governmental and national expenditures. Afterall these expenditures are made for the benefit of all, assuming, as always, that both Parliament and government are elected representatives of the people whose acts and decisions meet the approval of the majority of the population.

The partaking in these expenditures, the ratio of taxation, according to which the amount each individual pays in taxes are determined, ought to be based, in my opinion, on the individual's income. Now, -- and here we touch upon just and unjust taxation -- an individual's taxes must never reach a point where they might impede that person's ability to provide for his and his family's basic life's necessities. This would be the yardstick of just taxation. The other important ingredient in taxation is equality. Everybody must be equally obligated to pay his taxes. I don't have equal amounts in mind, all I emphasize is that there ought to be no loopholes, and no exemptions, legally or otherwise, should be permitted. A classical example of this would be the privileged tax-exempt status of the Hungarian nobility in the 19th century. This, of course, is part of history now. What I ought to emphasize is the fact that while everybody was taxed in Hungary, the partaking in this obligation was disproportional, and therefore unjust. State enterprises enjoyed substantial tax privileges while individuals were burdened beyond normal ability to pay.

10 e. Does the government have any duties toward the citizen? If so, what?

I feel that the state or, to be more precise, the government, has definitely more duties toward the state or nation, than it has rights.

Whatever rights a government may have, it gets these from Parliament, and it is the Parliament which determines when and under what conditions acts on the part of the government are justifiable and proper or not. The government's duties, on the other hand, are constitutional obligations. A government is elected by the people for the purpose of assuring peaceful development, of assuring human life; a government is expected to secure and to assure to its citizens those rights and possibilities which constitute prerequisite conditions for a person's normal development and happiness, or at least contentedness.

11. I should like to ask you what has happened in different fields of life in Hungary. Do you feel that medical care in Hungary has improved since the war?

Medical care has not improved much. The number of available hospital beds does not show a substantial increase after the war. The ratio of population and number of physicians -- the number of people falling under one doctor's care also did not decrease substantially, though there is some improvement in both the former and the latter.

On the other hand, there was a substantial increase in the number of such people who now receive regular medical attention, who appear periodically for medical checkups, -- people who, in the old days, were obliged to remain home, and to try to find some remedies -- often unsuccessfully -- for their maladies and illnesses. These people receive regular medical attention and hospital care, if necessary. In spite of this increased demand and opportunity for medical care the pre-war doctor-patient ratio did not substantially change -- not many more patients fall on a physician now than before, because there was a proportionate increase in attending physicians also. In other words, there is a relative increase in both, but the ratio did not get much better. Hungary would have to substantially increase the number of hospital beds on the one hand, and the hospitals should be modernized on the other. Also, the number of physicians should be substantially increased, because all too many people fall on a physician even now.

12. *Does the Hungarian citizen today have more opportunity to go to the movies or attend the theater and concerts than before the war?*

I am not in a position to tell you whether or not individual Hungarian citizens have more opportunities now than before the war to go to the movies, or to attend the theater and concerts. One thing, however, is certain; more people go to these places now than before the war. The increase is not so much an increase of individuals' opportunities of satisfying these cultural needs, -- after all, the standard of living is still lower now than that of 1938, and there was no substantial increase in people's incomes either, -- certainly no increase in their purchasing power. There was a substantial increase in the number of those, however, who take advantage of these cultural opportunities. Thus, if a person went to the movies once a week in 1938, he continues to do so once a week now. But the number of movie-goers increased remarkably.

13. *Does the Hungarian citizen today eat better than before the war?*

One could reply to this question in several ways. After 1945, the food supply in Hungary was extremely scarce. The reason for this was primarily the drought. We had very dry years from 1945 to 1948, with very little rain. The resultant grain yields fell short of the normal. If you add to this the fact that a sizeable portion of these reduced amounts of grain was sent to the Soviet Union as reparation, the emerging picture is obvious; there was less food available, and an individual's share necessarily fell short of his corresponding share of 1938. This situation improved after 1948, more food was available and an increase of the market supply was definitely felt, though the present state still falls short of the pre-world war zenith of 1938.

I should like to mention here an important aspect of this question; people spend relatively more now on food articles -- the percentage of incomes spent on food now is higher than the corresponding spending between the two world wars. The reason behind this is, I believe, primarily psychological; on the one hand, the industrial products, such as clothing, furniture, and household appliances are so expensive now that their purchase is a much more difficult undertaking than say in 1938. Thus, if a person wishes to purchase any of these industrial products, such an act requires much more effort and determination now than was the case in 1938. Now people are rather reluctant to make these increased efforts and, instead of dressing better, they eat better. This psychological moment is, in the final analysis, the explanation for all aspects of Hungarian life from 1948 on to the present; that hopelessness, those hopeless conditions, that aimless life which characterized these years. A family was not able to plan, it could not order its own little existence in a fashion where a continuous year-to-year growth would be noticeable, where the reaching of certain aims could be more or less certainly predicted. People chose instead the day-to-day living which necessarily meant a decision that "we shall eat better, because that is all we have and may indulge in and nothing else".

13 a. *Than in 1946? Than in 1950?*

If we compare 1956 or 1957, to 1946, the result undoubtedly is in 1957 or 1956's favor. If we compared these years to 1950, the result would be the same.

The situation as it exists now (1957 and 1958) has political reasons behind it. The Kádár government was anxious to consolidate the situation and it hopes to achieve this consolidation by securing after the Revolution a relatively great abundance of goods. It made determined attempts to satisfy consumer demand, to make sure that people, at least in this respect, would have no reason to complain or to be dissatisfied. This change is characteristic for the entire industry, with the majority of factories producing consumer goods only, or primarily. This is also clearly evident from Hungary's 1957 trade balance, which shows a large deficit. The government was importing huge quantities of consumer goods (it was the importation of these goods which caused the passive balance), goods which secured a larger and better supply for the population.

14. *Are there great differences in what food is available to different people today? Does the Hungarian citizen today clothe himself better than before the war?*

The answer to this question is rather similar to the one dealing with satisfying cultural needs (12). I have to say again that people do not clothe themselves better, a person has no more suits or dresses now than he or she had in 1938, but many people have better clothing today than was the case in 1938.

14 a. *Than in 1946?*

You had a special situation in Hungary after the war. Most of the industry was at a standstill, beginning to operate in 1946 only. You also had a very large inflation which meant in practice the virtual absence of supply, and a tremendous demand caused the prices to rise. The inflation of 1946 had reached tremendous proportions, when people found it hard enough to satisfy their most basic food requirements. Considerations of clothing were definitely secondary. For this reason you cannot take 1946 as a basis of comparison. If you do compare 1946 to today, the difference you find is tremendous. Thus, the situation is much better than it was either in 1946 or 1950. If you compare today with 1938, then you find that more people have good clothing today, but one person does not possess more now than in 1938.

15. Did industrial production increase in Hungary since 1945?

The answer to this question is a determined yes. Industrial production has increased a great deal, not only as compared to 1950, but also as compared to 1938.

This is quite understandable, and this development in Hungary had ideological, or political causes, especially after 1948. Though the 1945-1948 period also shows a determined industrial development, the substantial tempo in industrialization came after 1948. In the opinion of the Communists, one of the prime requirements of the victory of socialism is the necessity of converting predominately agricultural countries to predominantly industrial states. In the Communists' view, this change-over, this industrialization, is capable of accomplishment only through the emphasized development of the heavy industry. They want to develop a heavy industry capable of securing within the country the needed supply of production machines and equipment. This would be the raison d'être of the heavy industry, over and above its defense and war potential, since, after all, one of the primary purposes of heavy industry everywhere, Hungary included, is to supply the means of war, or of defense.

Now the statistics of industrial development in Hungary shows a tendency of continuous increase from 1948 to 1953, when this tendency stopped. If there is an increase after 1953, such increase is primarily evident in the light industry, emphasizing the production of consumer goods.

15 c. Do you think this is a good or a bad thing for the Hungarian economy?

I don't think the kind of industrial development we had in Hungary was good or advantageous. I don't think the direction this development took was proper because it meant development of such industries, for the operation of which there was no basis in Hungary. Not so long ago, I read that the present regime is further developing the iron works of Stalinváros and that the production capacity of this complex is to be further increased. As I read this article, I dug into this matter and found that the Duna Iron Works was, and still is, operating with a serious deficit. There is a substantial difference between the cost of production and the selling price of the finished product. This difference amounted to a net loss of millions of forints yearly. Identical or similar are the statistics for other heavy industry establishments which were brought into being from 1945 - 1953. This clearly shows that our industrial development occurred in those branches for which the basic requirements are lacking in Hungary.

15 d. Do you think anything should have been done differently about this?

Not only certain things should have been done differently, but the entire industrial development should have been affected in an entirely different fashion. Hungary undoubtedly needed development of its industrial potential. An industrial development was imperative because the land reform could not satisfy the claims of upward of one hundred thousand people. About 52 percent of Hungary's population depended for their livelihood on agriculture. A substantial number of these, while employed in agriculture, were unable to earn enough there to maintain themselves. We always had a large labor surplus. This was the reason behind our earlier attempts at industrialization, and this explains the relatively low wages in industry during the interbellum period. The land reform gave land to a great many people, but it did not provide all land seekers with land. Even after this fundamental reform, we still had several hundred thousand people who represented a surplus in agriculture, and these people necessarily had to gain employment in industries already existing and in those still to be created. This fact alone, aside from any other consideration, would have forced us to industrialize.

Now the prerequisite of any industrialization is the availability of conditions and raw materials necessary for production. Thus we should have directed the development of industry along those lines where the necessary prerequisites for such an expansion were readily available. We should have developed our agricultural industry first, a very neglected field to this day. This, of course, is a political question, just as the question of developing heavy industry is a political question; those countries with which Hungary today maintains commercial relations are also predominately agricultural countries. Thus, if Hungary is to be limited in her trade to these countries with which she actually has trade relations now, then the marketing of her agricultural products will be extremely difficult, if not impossible. The natural outlet for Hungary's agricultural products as well as for her industrial products with an agricultural base would be Europe, or the highly developed industrial states in general.

Agricultural industry (mezögazdasági ipar) has a practically unlimited possibility of expansion in Hungary. Over and above the agricultural industry Hungary also has the necessary conditions and prerequisites for the expansion of certain branches of light industry; I have in mind here primarily factories producing fine mechanical products (electrical motors, precision instruments, gadgets, etc.). These industries would be profitable in Hungary even though some of the raw materials and semi-finished products would necessarily have to be imported. Hungary does have a great number of technicians and skilled workers whose technical abilities would assure these products excellent marketing possibilities even in the highly competitive international markets.

This, then, would have been a proper industrial development in Hungary. Such a development would have assured Hungary the ability to trade not only with Western Europe and with other highly industrialized country, but also with Eastern Europe, -- with countries of predominantly agricultural character. Our primary export to the West would have been agricultural products while the products of our light industry would have easily found ready markets in Eastern Europe.

16. *In factories or work shops, what part do you think workers should play in deciding what is done and how it is done?*

This question is closely connected with the question of social ownership of the means of production. [See question (6) and (7)]. I favor social ownership because the Revolution selected and tried this method, and because I think that the majority of Hungary's population would favor the introduction of this method if it had the opportunity to do so. From this it naturally follows that all industrial establishments, large and small, should be owned by the industrial laborers working in those plants. The workers-- the small man, should own the factory, each according to his ability.

The workers should definitely be given the right to express their opinion in deciding what direction the factory's development should take; they should have a voice in the exact determination of production as well as in questions dealing with investments. This does not mean, of course, that the owners of the plant, -- the workers -- should have the right to force their will in all minute and insignificant questions, on the plant management. The problems of the direction and of the development of the socially-owned factories should be solved in the same democratic manner as is generally customary in democratic countries, i.e., majority opinion should prevail.

16 a. What should be the part of trade unions?

Trade unions in Hungary always played an important role in industry. Though the Hungarian labor movement got started much later than in Western countries, they quickly gained an important voice. Now experience shows that labor unions were strong in those days when membership in them was not compulsory and when the unions were not dependent on the state, were not executive arms of the state.

The Kádár regime time and again voiced its dissatisfaction over the fact that the unions are not sufficiently politicized. This is the best proof that the impact of the Revolution on the unions has not yet died out. (The unions made an attempt to deal with union problems during the revolt.)

16 b. How independent should they be of the government?

I disapprove of the government interfering in labor union affairs, or in the affairs of any social group or movement in a manner decisive for the life of such organization. The disadvantages of a situation where the state interferes in the life of organizations is clearly evident in the case of the labor unions. The unions today are either executors of the state's will, or the defenders of the state's policies and actions, or both. The consequence of this is that though the labor union in Hungary is a very large mass organization, there is no community of interest between it and its members, and the union is generally regarded as a state organization whose main function it is to collect dues.

16 c. How compulsory should membership be?

This boils down to a question whether one, or more than one, person should manage a factory, -- a problem which existed in Hungary under the Communists also. This was also one of the central problems when the Workers' Councils were established. It was decided during the Revolution that the central direction and management of a factory be exercised by the labor unions, a body consisting of eight, twelve, sixteen or twenty-four members.

I personally am in favor of one-man management and personal responsibility, because very often the problem of a factory cannot be solved by eight, ten, or twenty people getting together and discussing the issues. You need one man who is fully competent and responsible, to make decisions and to implement policy.

I would, therefore, combine Workers' Councils with a single manager. There would be a Workers' Council in each factory and a manager, responsible to the Councils, would submit periodically reports to them. The manager would serve as an appointed executive. The manager would either act independently, and on his own responsibility in all matters pertaining to the plant or else would, if this solution be preferred, seek the advice and consent of the Council before major decisions or changes are made.

16 e. To whom should management be responsible?

The manager would naturally be responsible to the Workers' Council. Should the system of social ownership come about, the status of the Workers' Councils would be analogous to the status of the board of directors of a cooperative or of a corporation. Within this framework, the direction of the plant by one man would proceed according to the well known principles of business administration; the board of directors would either name one of its members or an outsider as the plant executive, with the board deciding on major issues from time to time.

17. What do you think of the collective farms?

The question of collective farms (kolhoz) was always a thorny one in Hungary. The peasantry instinctively and jealously protects the principle of private property. This sentiment was particularly developed between 1948-1956, at the time when the Communists used every means at their disposal to forcefully increase the number of collective farms.

Farm cooperatives (termelöszövetkezetek) otherwise are very often justifiable and necessary and proper. In this era of modern agriculture one could not deny the great advantages of large scale production; large scale farming undoubtedly is better equipped and more able to accommodate itself to the ever changing market's requirements. Here again, however, we must go back to previous developments in Hungary, and state that the peasantry was not afraid of the idea of cooperatives as such. We find a large number, and a variety of forms of farmers' cooperatives in Hungary already between the two world wars; you had machine cooperatives, marketing cooperatives, purchasing and investment cooperatives, and a host of similar others. None of these cooperatives touched upon the questions of land ownership. I am not at all convinced of the propriety and expediency of ever raising the questions of land-ownership in Hungary in a manner where you categorically show the way, or lead, or direct the peasantry into a certain path, or force them to accept a solution or the solution. I am convinced that the peasantry would be forced by the sheer force of circumstances to change its face; agricultural competition would be bound to teach the peasantry that in order to better protect its interests it is necessary to adopt some forms of cooperatives. I can very well imagine that some cooperatives would persist in their present form even if you did not have the Communists in power.

The number of such cooperatives would, of course, be very small.

The important thing here is that force and direction from above must never be used; the peasantry itself must come to the realization that in certain situations, in certain branches of agricultural production, cooperatives and cooperation have great advantages.

17 b. What do you think of the state farms?

The institution of state farms, at least in their present form, is completely untenable and improper, and must be abolished. Some of the state farms owe their existence to the fact that certain peasants, wishing to get rid of their holdings, offered their land to the state. The state, accepting these lands, created the state farms in order to secure at least part of the forced delivery quota thereby. The system of the state forms, therefore, is the exclusive creature of the 1948-1953 period, and their creation had political reasons, lacking any economic justification. Some attempts were made from 1945 to 1948 to establish model farms in the various regions of the country. These model farms were to serve as experimental stations, places where specific conditions necessary for modern farming could be discovered, new production methods could be tried out, and the feasibility of introducing new grains or plants could be tested. These and similar objectives are very worthwhile, and experimental stations in this sense were, and still are, fully justifiable. Such model farms would be under the immediate supervision and direction of the Ministry of Agriculture and would serve as examples to the peasant, showing him the way to prosperous and rational agriculture. I can accept the idea of a state farm only in this specific and limited sense.

17 c. What should be done with the collective farms?

The vast majority of the collective farms will disband, or

ought to disband, in Hungary, for two reasons; a) as an economic unit, the collective has either no vitality (nem életképes, not viable) or, b) most of its members are desirous of becoming independent farmers again, not having entered the collectives voluntarily in the first place.

As to the future of the collective farms, i.e., what should be done with them generally, I would leave this decision to the affected farmers themselves. The state should permit the members of the collectives to decide for themselves what they want to do with them.

17 e. Should some or all the land be distributed? If so, to whom?

Since the members themselves are to decide what the future of the collectives should be, it follows that the land, in case of dissolution, would revert to their former owners. By the term "former owners" I mean last owners, people who owned the land after the land reform.

The land reform of 1945, affected about 38 percent of the country's arable land. (The percentage may have been even higher.) The land reform affected large estates of over one thousand holds, peasant holdings over two hundred holds and, at a later time (beginning of 1947), non-peasant holdings of over one hundred holds. These lands were distributed. Both from the point of view of economics, and from the point of view of the interests of Hungary's agricultural population, the land reform was necessary, and the new conditions it created must definitely be maintained.

Now the question of what the peasants want to do with their land, what solution they decide on as regards land ownership on the one hand, and as regards the future disposition of the collectives' present buildings and equipment, tractors and machine stations, etc., on the other -- this is a specific, particular question. It goes without saying that it would be quite improper for a member to carry away one-half, or one-quarter of a tractor; or to dismantle the buildings and distribute the building materials; such absurd solutions would serve no useful purpose and would only disrupt the process of rehabilitation. It is obvious that these properties (i.e., buildings, equipment, machines, etc.) would have to be placed at the disposal of all, by means of a system of cooperatives, or collective ownership. This arrangement would be quite acceptable since cooperatives of this sort flourished in Hungary already in the inter-bellum period.

17 h. Should the land be restored to all kuláks who were expropriated?

Let us start out by saying that the term "Small Landholders' Party" is not at all precise in this connection. Generally speaking, the term "Small Landholders' Party" in Hungary signified a farmer who owned less than one hundred holds of land, and even this category varied in the different parts of the country, depending on the land's quality and yield. These so-called Small Landholders' Party members were not affected by the land reform. After the Communists' advent to power in 1948, decrees were issued which brought about a situation where these Small Landholders' Party members were very anxious to get rid of their holdings; the regime introduced a system of taxation, i.e., it raised the forced delivery quotas, the land tax, and income tax, to a degree where the farmers' income was not sufficient to cover these obligations. As a result, at first the junior members of the Small Landholders' Party family gravitated towards the cities, and became factory workers. Later, the head of the family himself was forced to give up his land, (asking the state to take it away from him) and to find himself another occupation. These abandoned holdings constituted the nucleus of the emerging state farms, appearing in large numbers from 1948 to 1953.

If you have in mind here a settlement and regularization of

land ownership in Hungary, that is a very complicated question; first of all, you had a settlement, a situation, as created by the land reform of 1945. The situation thus created was by no means stable, however, and land ownership and structure was exposed to recurring disturbances ever since 1948, and up to 1956.

The immediate cause of this recurring disturbance was the drive for consolidation (tagositás). In connection with the emergence of state farms and collectives, the government decreed that these be consolidated.

To remain for a moment with the state farms; various Small Landholders' Party members gave up their land to the state for reasons already explained. These holdings were situated in different sections of a village territory, often very far apart. The government, when creating the state farms, decreed that these several holdings be brought together, and be consolidated into one piece. On this one piece of land the government wanted to introduce machines and large scale farming methods, to intensify production, and to raise the yields. The result of this was that the ownership of one particular strip of land was constantly changed; a middle peasant, who from 1945 to 1956 always cultivated his own land, and never joined a collective, saw his property change sites three or four times during this period. His original holdings were taken away from him in the process of consolidation, and he received another strip somewhere else. His new strip was again "consolidated" and he received still another territory. Then came the establishment of the TSzCs's and our farmer again had to move, etc. This constant change of land sites had disastrous consequences, and resulted in a deterioration of production and in falling of yields in both private holdings and state farms. A person was never certain of the geographical location of his property, and he considered it rather unwise to invest in that land, to effect some improvements on it. One of the most important of these investments both from the point of view of upkeep and yield was manuring and the use of chemical fertilizers. Private owners simply refused to manure their lands, and these holdings, as well as the garden plots or small homesteads of TSzCs members on a collective were completely neglected (teljesen kisoványodtak).

You can see from this sketchy exposition some of the complications and the difficulty anyone would have in rearranging land ownership with some degree of fairness and justice. It is obvious that in any future settlement, the 1945 land reform would have to be taken as a basis and point of departure. But even so you would have countless cases where an exception would have to be made; you would have cases where the present owner made substantial investments and effected improvements on a land strip which was not his after the land reform. You would have cases where people planted vineyards or orchards just a few years ago, where the fruits of labor and investment would only begin to show. It would run against the principle of equity if such labors and investments were disregarded.

17 i. Should any estates be returned to their former owners?

> It all depends on who the "former owners" are. If these be the pre-1945 owners, then my answer is no.

17 l. Should the state help agriculture? If so, in what way?

> If we accept, as I do, the proposition that one of the functions of the state is to define the country's economic development and progress, or if, applying this thesis to Hungary, the state is to raise as fast as practicable Hungary's economic standard to the European level, -- and if I therefore accept that the state is to support and protect certain industries and to subsidize others, then I also necessarily accept the proposition that the agriculture, too, be accorded similar qualitative and quantitative treatment.

The development of agriculture in Hungary is a central and

decisive problem. Closely connected with the development of agriculture is the question of developing the agricultural industry, since this industry ought to become our basic industry, the center around which other industries ought to be developed.

The development of agriculture itself may be many-sided, and there are numerous areas where state help may be applied effectively and where such help would stimulate progress and development. I have in mind here primarily capital investments; the purchase of needed machinery, the securing of capital necessary for regular manuring and effective use of fertilizer. All these things could be arranged in the form of a loan, or in the form of a guarantee whereby the state would guarantee that purchases made by individuals or by cooperatives would be paid for within a stated number of years.

17 m. *What would you do with the machine-tractor stations?*

Machine-tractor stations should not be divided among its present users but cooperatives should be established assuring their common and economical use. In this respect the long ago established practice of forming machine-cooperatives clearly shows the path. In olden days members of such cooperatives put up the capital and purchased the machines. In the present instance the state should simply transfer its ownership rights to cooperatives formed expressly for the upkeep and operation of these machines.

18. *What should be the relations between the church and the state?*

I am for the full independence of the church (ES) and I don't think state assistance to them is either necessary or called for. This should apply to all churches without exception. Experience in Europe as well as here in the United States clearly shows that churches are able to exist without support from the state and are able to exercise those functions which clearly are within their sphere.

State assistance to the church only enhances the churches economic power, and together with this increases the political power of the church, -- something which is not always necessary.

There is another consideration which further underlines my stand. If we consider the real reason of the churches existence, which is the propagation of God's word, the conversion of people, and the saving of souls -- the church can much more effectively exercise these functions if it is completely free of the state, and is not bound to it, or dependent on it, in any way.

18 d. Should churches play a part in public education? Just what?

The church in Hungary maintained certain schools with the state's assistance which were church schools. In these schools the church taught according to its own characteristic conceptions. We cannot even say that this teaching was bad or inferior, because highly trained teachers were employed in these schools.

Now if the believers desire that a church school be established, they certainly are able to provide for one out of their own generosity, and I think it proper if the situation is thus solved.

In a word, then, the church shall play such part in education as she is capable to effect through her own schools, supported by her own means. Freedom of education should be guaranteed by the state, and if the church wishes to establish schools and educational institutions of her own, so let it be, let the church bring up and educate students in a spirit she considers proper or expedient as long as she is willing and able to provide for the upkeep of such schools.

18 e. Should the teaching of religion be restored in the schools?

Compulsory teaching of religion in schools is an untenable proposition, I think. I was, and still am, all for religion to be regarded as an elective subject. I maintain this view not because the Communists demonstrated the degree to which religion may be subjugated and abused under such a system, but because I believe that people should have the right to determine what sort of education their children are to get. This is another of those fundamental human rights whereby parents are entitled to themselves give an education to their children. If, therefore, I want my children to be brought up without religion and without God, this is a question of my own conscience. I regard, therefore, compulsory religious instruction in schools to be an interference with the fundamental human rights.

18 f. Would you send your children to public school or denominational school?

I would send my children to a good school, to a school where they would receive all that instruction -- and in the most modern form -- which I consider a necessary basis for their later life and development. Whether or not this would be a public school or a church school, I cannot decide now. Our experience in Hungary showed that church schools gave a better education. Their teachers were more cultured and were more up-to-date, both in their training and methods than the public school teachers. If I had to make a decision, I would naturally want the best and most, like any parent, for my children, whether this be in public school, church school, or private school would really make no difference.

The 1945 land reform is just as applicable to church lands as it is to lands of private proprietors. Since church lands fell in that category which was ordered distributed in 1945, there is no reason whatsoever to treat the church differently in this respect than would one treat anybody else in Hungary. This is one aspect of the question.

As far as church buildings are concerned, and I have school buildings in mind here, I would permit the church to administer these buildings, in conjunction with school instruction, insofar as the church would financially be capable of maintaining them. In cases where the church would be unable to maintain these buildings, such buildings should be sold, and the church equitably compensated.

There were a few, traditional and well-known, church institutions in Hungary, both Catholic and other. These schools had a national reputation and a well developed, long standing tradition. These schools ought to be maintained, perhaps even if their continued existence were not possible without state assistance. These were, after all, outstanding values of the Hungarian culture.

19. *If the present regime were overthrown, what should be done with Party members?*

I don't know what is the number of Party members in Hungary today, if it is three hundred thousand or four hundred thousand. The membership of the MDP (Hungarian Workers' Party) exceeded, I think, one million. I don't think it would be wise and expedient to call such a huge number of people to account, to drag them to court, especially if we consider that a substantial number of these are not convinced Communists, but became members as a result of economic necessity and pressure. From this it obviously follows that a differentiation must be made in evaluating these people. This categorization would have to be made by the Hungary of the future. There are people among these Party members, no doubt, whose trial in court for crimes committed is inevitable. Such people naturally would have to be tried; they knew full well what they were doing when they committed their inhuman acts, when they proceeded according to their own particular interests, flagrantly disregarding and violating the interests of the nation. This would be a limited group. I would not apply this method to the broad masses of the rank and file. At most, the rank and file could be used in the economic reconstruction of the country to which they certainly should contribute with their labors.

19 e. *Youth League members?*

I should like to answer your question by beginning with the other end of the issue; we should start out by saying that in 1953, a very substantial change occurred in the life of the Hungarian nation. In the wake of Imre Nagy's ascendancy a development of liberalization got underway and parallel with this a struggle against the Stalinists began. During the struggle the question of what constituted the real interests of the Hungarian people was fully discussed and determined; all this came to light as it was shown what mistakes the pre-1953 regime had made, what great losses to the nation and to the citizens it had caused, how it denied to the people the exercise of fundamental human rights.

This period served as a watershed, as a dividing line; some people took up their positions on the one side, some others on the other. The role of those Communists who definitely opposed Stalinism and who clearly saw the magnitude of the mistakes of the past was considerable. When judging Communists these people must clearly be distinguished from the rest. A Biblical example comes to my mind, the example of Paul, a Roman soldier who recognized his mistakes and those of his camp, and dramatically changed sides to become an apostle of an entirely different development. We cannot refuse recognition of a similar role played by a Tibor Déry, by a Gyula Hays and by very many others, less known, but not less significant.

I am firmly convinced that these people have become just as rightful and full-fledged citizens of a future democracy as anybody else. After the tremendous trials and tests to which these people were exposed, with many of them paying dearly for their convictions by loss of health, loss of freedom, and of life, -- after all these tribulations the mere fact that they were Communists or even the fact that they catered to the regime, cannot be laid to their account. This, then, must be the basic human consideration in judging the Communists.

I don't consider it a task of a future democratic Hungary to combat Communists with all weapons (tüzzel-vizzel); I don't think it should employ the methods of the Horthy regime, so extensively and brutally used after 1919 when countless people were imprisoned and executed. I don't consider it wise to settle an ideological question by liquidating the exponents of a political movement.

The guilty ones should be punished, yes. But the public must feel, and must be thoroughly convinced that there is a guilt, that the punishment is proper, and just, and legal. People may be condemned for long years in prison, people may even be hanged, but the public must have the certainty that the judgment was proper and the sentence just.

These are the basic considerations which I wanted to mention. This must be the framework when we consider the DISZ.

The DISZ is, over and above this, a separate and distinct problem. After all, it is the organization of the Hungarian youth. It has about 180,000 members today, and includes all university students and even secondary school students who hope to attend the university. The last group is of course keenly aware of the importance DISZ membership plays when it comes to admission to institutions of higher learning; those who are not members cannot hope to continue their studies.

When considering this entire question, you must take into account that a man lives only once, and that a man's years of youth do not return. A young man in Hungary today is hardly responsible for the fact that he is 18 or 20 or 24 years old. He was born into a situation which he neither foresaw nor necessarily desired. Yet, a young man, if bright, wants to get ahead in life. One would like to become a physician, the other an engineer, the third an economist, etc., and circumstances beyond his control limit him so that he may become a doctor, an engineer, or an economist in Hungary only. Obviously he will have to accommodate himself to the existing framework, if he is to get ahead at all. The fact that a person was, or is, a member of the MADISZ, or of the DISZ, cannot under any circumstances be held against him, not be taken as a yardstick in passing judgment over his character or worth. What should be considered is a DISZ member's attitude and actions, and here again the already outlined principles should be operative.

19 f. Members of the AVH?

The judging of the AVH is an entirely different question. Here, too, it must be strongly emphasized that only just sentences, and only lawful punishments should be rendered. It must be said, nonetheless, that the AVH came into being as early as 1945, and that people who did not approve of subsequent developments did not become members of this organization. Thus, while in the case of the other organizations, such as the Communist Party, or of the DISZ, only the striking (kiugró) cases should be examined, the AVH as a whole, and every member of it, should be subjected to a thorough examination.

19 g. Members of the police?

The problem of the police is a much milder one than that of the AVH. Relations between these two always were, and still are, very strained. The police always did look upon the AVH with a feeling of enmity and fear. All this does not mean that the police should not be subjected to a close scrutiny.

20. *Now let us talk about Hungary's past for a minute. What do you think have been some of Hungary's most important contributions to culture and world history?*

The history of Hungary abounds in significant events. We need to consider here only Hungary's role which is not limited to a single historical event but is closely connected with a general historical development, namely her endless and ever recurring battles and struggles in her defense against attacks and invasions from the East. While defending herself, Hungary held up these forces from the East and served as a defense outpost (végvári vitéze) of Europe and of European culture.

Hungarian cultural life generally, and outstanding exponents of this culture in particular, always did try to maintain a cultural level similar to the standards of their contemporaries. During the Middle Ages, as well as at the beginning of the modern era, countless Hungarian students studied abroad. They went to foreign lands to learn what was new and interesting, and to make these their own. While these students of an often embattled and economically poor country did their best to understand Europe and to absorb European culture, we must not lose sight of genuine Hungarian cultural developments and contributions which rightfully belong to, and form an integral and valuable part of, what is known as European culture. I am not restricting myself here to the creations of Hungarian painters and other forms of art which more or less have an international character; perhaps even more important than these are the less cosmopolitan, but typically Hungarian cultural creations, such as the poems of poets, the novels of writers, the writings of statesmen, the politics of politicians, etc.

21. *Do you think there is a Hungarian national character?*

We would, first of all, have to clarify what we mean by

"Hungarian national character". If we consider this question from the point of view of biology, i.e, that the position of a Hungarian's eye, the quality of his hair, etc., are different from those of a German, or of a Frenchman, then we must say that such differences did exist a thousand years ago, rudiments of which are still apparent here and there.

It is very difficult to answer this question with a definite yes or no, since a person's customs, dressing or Weltanschauung (world view) depend, among other things, on his culture. Europeans, be they Germans, Frenchmen, Italians, or Hungarians, cannot be easily distinguished from each other unless you sit next to them and hear them speak.

If we now accept the view that an individual is to a certain extent determined by his environment, (by environment I don't mean physical environment only, though this, too, is included. What I have in mind is the degree of a person's cultural development, that horizon within which he is able to see and to register the various phenomena) then we may say that the more primitive life is, the more typical and characteristic (sajátos) it must be, the more it has retained from those original elements which at one time fully determined a people's world view, customs, dressing, mode of live, beliefs (hiedelmeit) and everything else. Superstition, for example, is still very much alive with the most primitive people, and has adherents even today among those in Hungary who are at the very lowest degree of development on the Hungarian cultural scale. These individuals still continue to believe in certain things as did our ancestors twelve or more generations ago. A fact like this alone definitely leaves its imprint on the individual. In this sense, then, there certainly is a difference between those Hungarians and Germans, for instance, who occupy the lowest level or stratum on their respective cultural scales. Cultural development, or more precisely, the process whereby individuals are becoming more and more cultured (kulturálódás), tends to minimize and to wash away these differences entirely.

21 a. If yes, does it differ from the German?

Since my reply to your previous question (Question 21), though indefinite, was in the negative, here also I can only give you an indefinite "perhaps yes", "perhaps no" answer.

The Hungarian peasantry, the oldest social stratum of the country, definitely did have a peculiar, if not unique, character of its own, exemplified by its own peculiar culture, folk songs, folk dances, customs, dressing, etc. This character, which set the peasantry apart and made it different from the rest of the population, began to decay towards the end of the last century. This decomposition has reached such proportions that today it is practically impossible to speak of a peculiar and typical character.

The urban culture in Hungary, the first to accept, and to assimilate Western and other foreign cultural influences, began to penetrate the village as early as the beginning of the last century. This penetration continued and still continues to this day with a steadily growing intensity, so that the urban culture was, and is breaking up the culture of the village, the village customs, and other village characteristics.

One of the characteristics of the twentieth century, not only as regards Hungary, but respecting other countries as well, is the phenomenon where intellectuals are beginning to try to rediscover their nation's culture -- a culture already doomed, a culture which, unlike in previous centuries when it was transplanted from father to son, is no longer transmitted from generation to generation, a culture which is dying out, a culture forced out of existence by its urban counterpart. These intellectuals have recognized the urgent need of collecting the remaining ruins, in order to save for posterity the characteristic colors of their peasant people.

If we consider your question from this point of view, then we must say that the peasantry undoubtedly possessed characteristic features of its own, some of which I already enumerated, which did set it apart from any and all groups or classes living in

Hungary. Today, however, the folk songs are sung, and the folk dances are danced, not so much by the peasant youth, certainly not by the village folk primarily, -- these peasant characteristics having become the almost exclusive domain and preoccupation of young intellectuals who, searching for solutions to present-day problems go back in a sense to the past for lessons and instructions. These young intellectuals hope to effect a cultural regeneration also through the instrumentality of native, peasant culture.

To return to the peasants; mechanization and other phenomena of urban culture and civilization have completely conquered the villages and there, too, you will find replicas of what obtains in the cities; this superimposed urban culture is diluted, modified, and, generally speaking, of a lower level in the villages than in the cities, but it is essentially the same.

Speaking now of the industrial laborers, I should mention at the outset that in Hungary you did not have as sharp a class distinction between this group and the peasants as say in Germany or even in France, countries whose industrial development occurred at a much earlier date than that of Hungary.

Industrial laborers everywhere were recruited from the surplus peasant population. Technical developments in agriculture having dislocated and transformed former production practices, less and less people are needed for the performance of traditional tasks, and peasants flocked to the cities and found their livelihood in the developing industries. This transformation and the resultant wandering of people from agriculture to industry began in Hungary only after the First World War. If we look at Hungarian statistics, we see that the number of industrial laborers had doubled in the period 1920-1940. The population of the larger cities where the new industries sprang up swelled at the same time, showing an increase of from 50 to 100 percent. A classical example would be Budapest in this respect.

These industrial laborers, coming as they did from the villages, brought with them the villages' customs, the village world view, etc. This separation from the village did not come about in an abrupt and final manner, and significant connections between new and old persisted long after the initial separation; we saw throughout the inter-bellum period how large numbers of the urbanized laborers flocked back to their native villages during the summer to help their brothers or parents perform the tasks of harvesting and threshing during the peak of the agricultural season. This dual residence (kétlaki élet) and the obvious duality that goes with it persisted in steadily diminishing proportions throughout the inter war years, and is a factor even today. The present regime is conducting a vigorous campaign against this practice, especially as it relates to those industrial workers who reside in nearby suburbs and villages. These people still have their own houses and their little vegetable gardens, or orchards, or vineyards, and it is still their standard custom to devote their vacations, or even longer periods to the maintenance of their gardens, to the cultivation of their trees, etc.

The relations between industrial laborers and the village are rather close even today. This means, of course, that the village customs also persisted for a very long time among the workers, and are in evidence to this day. Had these connecting links been severed at an early date, a very great and sharp difference, and conscious class distinction might have developed in both ways of life, thinking, and other respects, between the workers and the peasants. This did not come about and therefore a clear cut distinction between the peasants and the industrial laborers of Hungary cannot be made in the sense of differences and distinctions as evident in the West. These two groups constitute two classes, to be sure, whose interests are not always identical, but in their customs and in their family relations they are so interwoven and essentially so similar that the workers were unable thus far to create a culture of their own which would distinguish them from their ancestors, the peasants.

There is a characteristic and so-called urban culture in Hungary which has been in existence for a number of centuries. The predecessor of this urban culture was the so-called gentry (nemesi) culture. This gentry culture did not have its home in the cities originally -- it actually centered in the provincial gentry strongholds. However, nineteenth-century developments changed all this; the so-called village gentry (falusi nemesség) lost its traditional status, and with it also its characteristics. Some of them withered away (elsorvadtak), some others saw themselves forced to take up residence in the cities, or to accept that culture which was already established and flourished in the cities. This culture, originally under Latin, and later under French influence, had very little in common with the native Hungarian culture. Ever since their emergence (i.e., urban culture, village culture) and throughout their development, these two categories or cultures are clearly recognizable and distinct; the former was originally called gentry culture, which later merged into a new development and became the urban culture. The latter was the native culture, existing in the villages among the peasants. Between these two cultures there is a substantial difference even today, and these two cultures opposed each other (szembeállottak egymással) in the last few decades, particularly in the inter-bellum period.

After the Second World War the native, or so-called populist (népi) culture became predominant, and after the Communists assumed power, the culture of the cities, or urban culture, was definitely regarded as unwelcome. I must of course add that the Communists also tampered with the populist culture, adjusting, transforming, and changing it whenever and wherever they could, in an attempt to relate it to the Marxist-Leninist ideology. It is noteworthy in this connection that only those of the populist writers who were willing to effect the compromises with the Marxist-Leninist ideology were able to make themselves a career.

If we consider this issue today and view the present-day categories in Hungary, then we must say that there is a village culture which has been pretty much confused and mixed up and tainted and infected by the urban culture. When I say that the urban culture has infected the village culture, I mean that it upset and undid those sure judgments and those precisely defined categories which were once the possession of the people and with which the peasant was once able to judge precisely, i.e., if an object, or thing was beautiful, good, or not. The urban culture has cut wide upon the precise boundaries of these categories and has rendered the people's judgment quite uncertain. The people in the villages did not have an education, a training, necessary to judge and to appreciate the influences of the urban culture. They were not able to absorb it, or to create something new out of it. Instead a chaos, and a loss of the ability to certain judgment was the result.

This, then, is the situation in the villages today. This characterization is also applicable to the workers, though the workers were much more exposed to the decaying influences of the city than were the peasants. The peasant and village mode of life, the loneliness and solitariness imposed by their profession, made the peasants more immune and safe.

22. *When in the 20th century did Hungary have the best government?*

Speaking of Hungarian governments in the 20th Century, a natural line of division suggests itself; the dividing line is always a great war, and governments may be grouped in three categories. Before and during the First World War you had the royal and imperialist governments, whose task it was to lead and to administer both Hungary and Austria. After the First World War, Hungary was a kingdom without a king, with a regent at the head of the state. We must say a few words, I think, about these forms of government, before we can arrive at a satisfactory answer to your question. We need not say much about the Austro-

Hungarian governments because post-World War II developments make this period a faraway and anachronistic era. The distance between us and that era is far greater than the actual number of years would indicate. It was an era whose form or content are simply inconceivable as actualities today. Before the First World War, Hungary was a feudal state. Not only was the land in the hands of a few hundred aristocratic families, but with and through the land they also had the state power.

This characteristic feature continued after the First World War also. When I stated that Hungary was a kingdom without a king in the inter-bellum period, I also meant that the state did not change, did not alter its feudal base. Feudalism as such weakened naturally, since almost two-thirds of the country's territory was lost and with this a substantial number of the large landed estates were also detached from Hungary. One of the immediate results of all this was that a large number of formerly rich and powerful landed magnates became impoverished. Thus after the First World War these dispossessed magnates and gentry concentrated all their efforts in securing the continued maintenance of their old rights and privileges. Also, aristocratic and gentry families became more and more interested in securing positions in government offices and other public places.

The cabinets and the government offices were obliged to accept this changing trend, the Hungarian constitution and the all-pervading influence of aristocrats and of the gentry both within and outside of the two Houses of Parliament making this acceptance inevitable. To what extent this situation persisted, how truly Hungary remained the almost only feudal state in Europe is clearly brought out by the determined struggle of the populist writers, who attempted to show how much better it would be if Hungary were a democracy, where all citizens would enjoy equal rights, where all people would participate in the state affairs, instead of only a small group of oligarchies who jealously guarded their ancient privileges. This question has a very extensive literature in Hungary and even today much is written about it.

The governments of the inter-bellum period tried to resist and to combat the growing influence of the populist writers, but the naked facts, the gross social injustice, and the downright misery of a substantial part of the population were all too well known to be concealed or to be treated lightly. The governments were well aware of these conditions and therefore a direct assault against the populist writers was never undertaken. The governments limited themselves to preventing only such developments which tended to directly undermine them, or which were injurious either to them personally or their class. This is the explanation why and how it was possible that the populist literature and the struggle for social justice for the peasants and the workers -- the majority of the population -- could assume such proportions, could fight on such a wide front, could be popularized; books were permitted to be published on the subject, meetings could be organized, conferences could be held, etc. The question was brought up for discussion even in Parliament, especially in the late 'thirties, when the government, to mitigate and to pacify this steadily growing discontent, was forced to offer several minor concessions. The government tried, among other things, to improve the extremely unhealthy and poor housing conditions in the villages through the ONCSA (The National People and Family Protection Fund, abbreviated ONCSA, was a state social organization established for the purpose of supporting large family villagers, increasing the number of births and child protection purposes between 1940 and 1944. Created by an article of law.); the government did not prevent the opposition from periodically lodging a protest in Parliament, etc. In a word, the government tried to maintain an appearance, a facade, of constitutionality in the inter-bellum period and the forces fighting for social justice were using the facade of constitutionality as a sanctuary, as a bridgehead, from behind which they led their attacks.

In the 1930's, the Hungarian governments were gradually going to the right. This tendency had political, geographical, and other causes; the close proximity of Germany and the appearance there of Hitlerism; the sizeable German minority in Hungary; the officials in the state and in the local administrations, who were either of German origin or were related to Germans through marriage, or were simply people who sympathized with national socialism; that drill, those forms and mentality of officialism which were characteristically German in nature (translations or copies of the German original), -- all these factors tended to make the bureaucracy German-oriented and this bureaucracy pressurized the cabinet at the same time when a German political and diplomatic pressure on the part of Hitlerite Germany was also acutely felt. This double pressure, coming both from without and within, made it practically impossible for the government in those days -- given the cultural principles and mentality of government leaders themselves -- to assume an orientation other than gravitation towards Germany.

This policy of the inter-bellum governments was obviously fallacious and wrong, proved sufficiently so by later developments to make it superfluous for me here to substantiate them.

With these observations I have essentially passed judgment on the inter-war governments, convicting (elmarasztaltam) them of having chosen fascism instead of democracy; instead of allowing the people to come within the framework of the constitution, instead of building an economically strong and culturally well-developed nation, they chose to protect their own narrow little rights.

A decisive change occurred after 1945 when, after the termination of the war which changed the destiny of Europe and of the world, Hungary arrived at the threshold of a new development and carried through the land reform, while those forces which already in the inter-bellum period had fought for social justice and social equality have set themselves to the task of establishing democracy in Hungary.

This, in a nutshell, is what I wanted to say. I am now in the position to vote; I consider democracy to be the proper and the best suited social forum for a people to live under, and therefore I affirm a democratic form of government to be my ideal; with all their faults and mistakes, the 1945-1948 governments were Hungary's best governments of this century, because they best served the interests of the entire population or, if you prefer, the interests of the Hungarian nation. ***Question:*** Do you consider the 1945-1948 period as an uninterrupted whole, a continuity, a unit? ***Answer:*** Yes, there was definitely a continuity. The concepts were the same, and while insignificant changes did occur in the cabinets, the governments basic concept, the fundamental endeavor, remained identical. When you look at this period, the fact that Zoltan Tildy or Ferenc Nagy was the Prime Minister is not important. What is important is that Hungary had a Parliament in this period which under the given circumstances -- and these circumstances account for the mistakes and errors -- did attempt to create a state characterized by social equality, where the distribution of wealth and of goods approached that optimum when each and every one was able to bring its hopes to fruition and to prosper. The ingredient necessary for such a development, the intellectual freedom, the freedom of speech, was also fully guaranteed.

22 b. Why did some people then emigrate to the United States and Canada?

Mass emigration from Hungary occurred in the 'nineties of the last century and continued roughly up until the outbreak of the First World War. During this time more than a million people emigrated from Hungary, -- a very impressive figure even if we consider that Hungary in those days had a population of 20 million.

If we look for the causes of this mass emigration we may

explain it in several ways; these explanations are particular in that they vary according to the point of view, and according to the understanding of the viewer. I don't consider it my task to tell you the opinions of others in this question. My own opinion is that the emigration had primarily economic and social causes. The economic causes are to be found in the then prevailing feudalistic society, the system of large landed estates, on which extremely unfair wages and decidedly inhuman treatment combined with a practically inconceivable poverty were the rule.

The village folk and especially the farm laborers living on the large estates not only were not familiar with principles of birth control at the time, but were also utterly ignorant of even the rudiments of hygienic practices; people were dying just as did animals on these estates. In those days the traditions of serfdom were still strongly present generally in Hungary, and particularly on the magnates' estates. Both aristocratic and gentry landowners combined to preserve even at the turn of the 19th Century the medieval idea that serfs -- now called agricultural laborers -- constituted but another kind of good, another sort of property that belonged to the landowner.

These agricultural laborers (cselédek -- servants) usually had very large families, and until such time when their children themselves began to work, -- at a rather young age -- they lived under rather miserable conditions.

Developments taking place at the turn of the century, the introduction of machines not only in the industry but to a certain extent also in agriculture, brought about an agricultural labor surplus, a circumstance which tended to further reduce the already miserable wages of the modern "serfs"; the more Hungarian industry developed, the more miserable did the agricultural workers' situation become.

This explains that state of utter despair in which these simple people, otherwise so tenaciously clinging to their village, to their relatives and friends, people scared of distances, -- most of whom had never left the physical confines of their native village, these people got up and traveled thousands of miles in quest of better opportunities, in the search of a new home. The prime motive behind the large-scale Hungarian emigration to the United States was therefore economic. Another force, also stemming from the economic situation, was the social factor; the roots of this latter are to be found in that decidedly inhuman treatment customarily accorded Hungarian agricultural workers at the time. These people were beaten and punished for a variety of offenses; the landowner continued to retain his feudal judicial right (pallósjog), and though he no longer could order his "serfs" head or hand or nose to be cut off, he could still punish him, he could still bring him to face difficult situations, and he had the connections and the power needed to have his servants imprisoned, even though he himself no longer had the right to imprison them on his own domain. The state and local administration was at the landowner's disposal and did whatever he desired.

22 c. Did Hungary have a feudal society? If so, until when?

Hungary had essentially a feudal society and it persisted till 1945.

22 e. What was the effect of the Communist rule in 1918-19?

It is very difficult to judge Károlyi, difficult even now, after the Revolution of 1956, primarily because Károlyi's endeavors have been left far behind by subsequent events.

I don't doubt for a single moment that Károlyi's endeavors in his own time were modern, proper, and just. The stand he took in connection with the land distribution was a worthy example of how a responsible statesman, a consistent preacher of a principle, ought to behave when it came to the practical implementation of his principle. ***Question:*** Do you have in mind Károlyi's decision to offer one of his own estates for free distribution? ***Answer:*** Yes, that is precisely what I have in mind; when he ordered that large estates be broken up and distributed, he started it with his own property.

Károlyi fought for social justice and for the establishment of democracy in Hungary. But Károlyi, too, had his errors; he proved to be too weak towards the Communists, he proved to be incapable of defending himself in the face of Communist agitation, he permitted a bourgeois revolution to turn into a Communist revolution. I must, of course, add that Károlyi's position was a rather difficult one. It is easy to criticize him now, forty years after the events, and it would have been extremely hard to make decisions if one had been in his shoes. Nevertheless, if we accept that a statesman's, a politician's actions must be judged in the light of subsequent events, then we must say that history did not justify Károlyi these steps.

Question: What do you think of Károlyi's foreign and national policy? ***Answer:*** Károlyi did not have an independent national policy. As to his foreign policy, his possibilities were rather limited and determined, there was not much room for him to pick and choose from. You had a lost war, with Hungary one of the losers, and you had to find a way out. Obviously, he had to seek understanding in the camp of the victors. Károlyi tried to seek this understanding with the French. How far did he succeed is, of course, another question, but I must emphasize again that Károlyi just did not have any other choice.

Károlyi's nationality policy was a characteristic political species, but it was Oszkár Jászi's nationality policy, not Károlyi's. Jászi's nationality policy was a continuation in modernized form, in my opinion, of that political concept which Lajos Kossuth first developed in the years of his exile, in his later years, a concept which I think was proper and humane if considered in the context of those times. We must not lose sight of the fact that with both Kossuth and Jászi we have a Hungary of 20 million inhabitants in mind, a state of 63 counties whose border regions contain sizeable

Romanian, Slovak, Serbian, Croatian, and other minorities. Today the situation is entirely different. If we take Hungary's present borders as our framework, our nationality policy today is no longer the same.

The Kossuth-Jászi concept, however, taking as it does the premise that the Danubian peoples form an economic unit -- this concept continues to be valid and desirable, and a nation which is part of this economic unit obviously must live on very good and friendly terms with its immediate neighbors. After all, not only the other nations of this "unit", but Hungary also is dependent on the others, not only economically, but politically as well, and the cultural interaction among them is unavoidable.

Economic connection and coherence, and the mutual indispensability of the countries of this "unit" makes mutual friendship and cooperation, both political and economic, an indispensable necessity.

I am very close to the United Europe concept, and sympathize with this endeavor. This sympathy of mine is a natural consequence of my hearty approval of the idea of a regional political and economic cooperation.

If we then speak of the political question of the minorities, and if we want to treat it within the above outlined framework, i.e., the close interdependence, both economic and political, of the peoples of the Danube Basin, the close interaction and common growth of their culture, -- if this be our framework, then I, too, do profess the Kossuth-Jászi political principles with respect to the nationalities.

If I am to answer this question succinctly, then I must say that the Communist rule of 1919 gave an ideal opportunity to the later governments to prevent and to frustrate all attempts to bring about social justice. Between 1920 and 1945 all attempts at social reform faltered and failed; the government and the ruling classes successfully opposed, and blocked, any and all innovations, declaring that any social reform necessarily meant a strengthening of the Communist cause. The cabinets and the ruling classes have created a bogeyman (mumus) out of communism, out of the Communist danger, using it as a means of defense for the protection of their own narrow interests.

The 1919 Communist revolution had no other effect between the wars. The 1919 revolution itself was carried by the urban population and by parts of the industrial workers of Budapest. The village remained passive through it all. Thus the newly-emerging intellectual stratum which was recruited primarily from the ranks of educated sons of peasants during the inter-bellum period -- this new generation of intellectuals had no family memories or recollections whatsoever which would tie it to the 1919 events. Take for instance my case; my father was a red soldier. All I know about this question was that my father could not get a job for a very long time. My grandfather was a landless peasant. My father continued in his steps. He pursued fruit growing as a hobby. Now after the First World War there was a limited land distribution, but my father could not get any, because he was part of a category which was excluded: he had been a red soldier. He would have liked to take a job as a gardener, but only trustworthy people could aspire to such a position.

My father was a red soldier; not because he was a convinced Communist. He was brought back from the front and a group of soldiers were simply given new uniforms and became red soldiers. This is all I know about the 1919 events; and this is about the only legacy, the only connection between events of 1919 and later political endeavors. In my case, for instance, all I know is that my father lost ten of his best years; he would have been able to get what he wanted ten years earlier, had he lived in luckier circumstances. My experience permits a safe generalization so that we can truthfully say that the village population had similar, or milder connections to the 1919 events. If the peasant-stock intelligentsia did not have significant, if any, connections, legacies, or experiences regarding the Béla Kun regime, Károlyi's ideas and political endeavors were even less important or enduring; the

Károlyi experience was even more limited in its scope, and was based on an even more narrow stratum, namely on parts of the urban intellectual class.

22 f. Was there much or little social and/or economic inequality in Hungary before 1945?

It would be difficult to answer this question with a definite "yes" or "no". The social and economic status in Hungary constantly changed after 1920. If we want to be more specific then we also must say that significant changes took place in Hungary in the 20th Century. These were sometimes factual changes and, equally important, people thought there were changes.

If we look at the country's political and economic structure before 1945, we must affirm that what we see is a feudal state; the economic structure, the system of land ownership, the possession of political power, -- all these factors contain in themselves those identifying notes which are considered characteristic landmarks of a feudal society. However, by 1945 the ruling stratum, the group which directed the country's economic life, was essentially much smaller than it had been 10, 20, or 30 years before. A development was under way which started right after the First World War and which, if we look for its concrete starting point, (an intellectual movement can hardly be reduced to just one source, but in this case it was the most important and determining source) we find that Dezső Szabó's literary activity was the chief driving force behind it. (Interviewer's note: Dezső Szabó was an outstanding Hungarian novelist of the postwar era, his best known work being the monumental novel <u>Az elsodort falu</u> - The Swept-away Village.)

Dezső Szabó came up with a concept after the First World War, saying that the basis of the country's political and economic life is the peasantry; if Hungary is to achieve a renaissance, if Hungary is to prosper within the framework of the Treaty of Trianon; if Hungary is to assure her long-range healthy development, then the peasantry must be strengthened, and an increasingly important role must be assigned to upcoming intellectuals of peasant stock. This was the only way out according to Dezsö Szabó. This was the beginning of that intellectual movement which, the more we approach the year of change, 1945, became broader and broader. First the writers were the only participants, the writers had a very interesting and very important role in Hungary's history in the last two centuries. During the middle of the 'thirties the writers started the "village explorer" movement, with the aim of rediscovering Hungary. They wanted to present a sociology and sociography of Hungary: what really is what is called Hungary, and what does it look like. How does the peasantry live in the villages; what is the position of the workers; who controls the economic life and the political life; what is the number of the "rulers"; whom do they represent, etc. This was the aim. Not all the parts of this ambitious project were completed. This, then, was the way the sociographic literature began, a literature which was primarily concerned with the conditions of the village peasants, of the landless peasants, and of the agricultural servants.

The picture they presented was an authentic picture, but at the same time an alarming picture. It was discovered that while industrialization went on at a rapid pace, in the cities culture and civilization became more and more universal, while at the same time in the villages, and among the agricultural servants -- the large estates cultural and social life were those of the early years of the 19th Century. This was the picture of the peasants and of the agricultural servants. On the basis of an examination of these findings, and on the basis of a similar research into life patterns of the industrial workers, I can certainly affirm that the differences and inequalities were very great among the several classes in Hungary. The industrial workers were definitely better off than the peasants, especially if we compare their status to those peasants who had only a few holds of land, or landless peasants, or agricultural servants. Nevertheless, even among the workers, the number of those whose cultural level was very low, who were illiterate, was relatively great. The growing industry developed a stratum of unskilled laborers whose wages amounted to little more than the income of the two-three-hold peasants. Neither group could hope to go beyond the basic needs of life, there was no money left for their cultural betterment, and they had no possibility of sending their more promising offspring to schools of higher learning.

22 g. In general, what do you think of the Horthy regime?

I think I already gave you a hint here and there as to what I think of the Horthy regime. To summarize here, the Horthy regime was characterized by a series of men of low caliber who tried desperately to defend their positions.

22 h. Should Hungary have fought in World War II or stayed neutral? Why?

My answer to this question is a definite no. If I have to elaborate, I should like to say that already during the middle 1930s, at a time, therefore, when there was a feverish preparation for war, already in those years it was clearly evident that in the pursuit of that concept which Germany set for herself, she would necessarily reach the state of complete isolation (she would remain alone). Being alone in a world-wide struggle which the Germans precipitated by their aggressive demand for power, necessarily results in defeat. Hungary's leaders, and cabinets, should have thought at least on those historical experiences of expansive European nations who have tried to dominate the continent. These nations finally remained alone, were isolated, and defeated. I have in mind Napoleon at the moment, to cite but one of a series of nations and individuals. Hungary's leaders did not take into account this point of view, and in an unexplainable manner continued to believe that Germany's efforts would be crowned with success. If the danger could not be seen in 1933 or in 1935, it certainly could have been detected in 1942 and later, when Germany fought on two, and sometimes on three, different fronts at the same time. One could certainly have seen the handwriting on the wall when in Italy the first unmistakable signs of political and military uncertainty became evident. In the face of all this, Hungary's supreme leadership -- I mean Horthy and his circle -- continued to maintain that there was no alternative for Hungary but the continuation of the struggle on the side of the Germans. This concept was somewhat modified later, when it was thought that Hungary should minimize her own efforts as much as possible and should refrain from actual participation whenever practicable. This was the time-serving and double-dealing policy of Kállay, which continued till the 19th of March, 1944. This policy had no perspective. From 1935 on this became more and more apparent. It was no more than an aimless and an irrational persistence and devotion to the internal Hungarian status quo which was established in 1920 and continued till 1945.

22 i. How does the period between 1945 and 1948 compare with the years before and after? Explain.

I would devote a separate chapter to the 1945-1948 period in such a study as you are here undertaking. These few years, -- in my opinion at least -- have a very great significance. The 1945-1948 period, in its endeavors, in its structure, in its political content, and in its mechanism differed completely both from earlier and from later years.

The 1945-1948 period also had its characteristic features, lent to it by the Yalta agreement, where the Big Three agreed and divided up the world among themselves, -- in my opinion completely illegally (jogtalanul) and inhumanly, if we accept the premise that every nation has the right to determine its own development and political alignment.

Every nation has the right to select its own style and way of life according to the rules of democracy, and for this very reason the Yalta conference is a very severe indictment of the democratic nations who entered into and concluded the Yalta agreement and accepted its consequences.

But this is not the topic we want to discuss. What we have to say is that the Yalta agreement set the direction of Hungary's development, and delineated that framework within which -- and within which only -- Hungary could move about. This framework, in essence, was that we belong to Russia, and that therefore we must expect the solutions of our questions from the Soviet Union, -- questions, whose solution does not primarily depend on the will of the population. International questions affecting Hungary, therefore, were to be solved by the Soviet Union, we were to petition them with our problems, and we were to entrust ourselves to the desires and wishes of the Soviet Union.

The characteristic feature of 1945 was that those forces assembled in the coalition which, being in the opposition in the interwar period, fought for political, social, and economic development and progress. This former opposition group was much broader in 1945 than in the inter-bellum period because it encompassed all those who opposed the Horthy regime, irrespective of whether they were actually represented by opposition political parties or not. There was in Hungary in the interwar period an intellectual opposition which did not strictly belong to political parties, so that the few pre-war opposition parties do not necessarily represent or delineate the actual, total opposition. The opposition was much broader, much stronger, and much younger, than the opposition parties themselves.

These intellectual forces assembled in 1945, whose aim in the political sphere was democracy with its modern economic and social content. Essentially it supported a just distribution of wealth, and a system of social equality.

These intellectual forces began the laborious task of building up a democratic Hungary. In doing so they had to take into account at the very outset the situation created at Yalta. They had no other alternative but to choose those ways and means which, under the circumstances, were least laden with bad features, and promised the most good.

Under such circumstances democracy made its first steps. In spite of these very severe limitations, which were acutely felt in Hungary, and which forced upon the nation a change in, and postponement and sometimes abandonment of, its economic plans or tendencies, -- in spite of all these limitations, whatever development took place between 1945-1948 had met the unanimous approval of the population. No better proof of this is necessary here than the fact that the 1956 Revolution accepted and approved precisely those economic concepts (economic concepts played a predominant role in the Revolution) which the government tried to put into practice in the 1945-1948 period.

This is the explanation of the fact that in 1956 in its economic blueprints the Revolution did not revert back to another system, but envisaged instead a social ownership of the means of production, securing at the same time opportunities, within limits, for individual initiative and individual undertakings. This was essentially the economic concept of the Revolution, and this was the fundamental concept of the 1945-1948 period also. This was the 1945-1948 concept in that the large industries were nationalized, in that a process already begun before the Second World War was brought to a logical conclusion. (Long before the war the electric power industry was either state- or municipally-owned. So was the bauxite industry, the railroads, the post, telephone and telegraph, and one could enumerate a host of others.) While the 1945-1948 governments favored a large-scale nationalization, they at the same time favored free commerce, -- the gist of the whole concept was to bring about such a system of directed economy which in its content and in its aims best corresponded to the opinions, aims, and interests of the population.

23. *In Hungary's relations with some of the neighboring countries, there used to be some feeling about territorial claims. Do you think borderlines are important?*

Political boundaries always had great significance. If you look at history, it was essentially boundaries and territories on account of which battles were always fought. Boundaries signify the unit within which governments have authority and power, and within which the inhabitants enjoy rights and privileges, freedom of movement, economic well-being, etc.

In Hungary, indeed, very much was said, especially before the Second World War, about the question of Hungary's boundaries. Boundaries were the excuse of governments under Horthy, advanced in opposition to all attempts at bringing about a more proper economic order. All such endeavors were rejected as impracticable, as capable of accomplishment only after a prior correction of Trianon. There was in Hungary a government-supported irredentism in the interwar period, an irredentism which was partly unjust and partly stupid, and in a part definitely insulting. This explains, of course, the unfriendly relations between Hungary and her immediate neighbors.

If I must answer your question as to whether political boundaries are important or not, then I should say that in the final analysis they are not important. They are not important in the sense that the mutual economic dependence, mutual cultural interaction among peoples cannot be limited by political or state boundaries. They develop independently of state boundaries, and adjust themselves rather to natural units and naturally given conditions.

Your question is very tempting and enticing for an irredentist, -- and it is indeed difficult to answer it. He who knows Hungarian history will find answering this question a difficult task, even if he himself is not a Hungarian, and is not bound sentimentally to a characteristical viewpoint of a people, as I am so bound, no doubt.

If I look upon this question from the viewpoint that Hungary's territory is 93,000 km2s, and if I affirm that a just political boundary for a nation must coincide with that nation's ethnographic boundary, -- if we think of Hungary's boundaries not as political but rather as ethnographical dividing lines, then such boundaries no doubt encompass such territories which at the moment are outside of Hungary's territory. To start my enumeration with Czechoslovakia, I have in mind here primarily the Kisalföld, or a part of it; also a significant portion of Transylvania, and a certain portion of the Bácska. (Szabadka and surrounding area.)

The political side of this question is, of course, a different matter. Here the answer is fairly difficult. I would certainly not be prepared to say that the only justice is Transylvania's re-annexation and/or the re-incorporation of those territories into Hungary where Hungarians live at the present time. The final solution of this question can definitely not be imagined on this plane. If a nation is chauvinistically inclined, it only provokes similar attitudes in the ranks of the other, and a state like that could only bring about such results as obtained between the two world wars, when mutual chauvinism impeded and prevented what promised to be fruitful economic developments. For this very reason, to me the idea of a united Europe is a very welcome one.

23 b. Do you think the Hungarian people have a rightful claim to territory beyond the present borders? If yes, to which? Why? Do you think any other people threaten Hungary's territory or part of it?

I don't know of any concrete threats. There were such endeavors in the recent past. I have in mind here German expansionism and threat to Hungary's territory. The Germans were always tempted by the fertility of the Ukrainian soil and by the excellent agricultural opportunities there, which were lacking in Germany. Having realized the impossibility of recreating their colonial empire, the Germans determined to channel their expansionist tendencies towards the East. In their scheme of <u>Drang nach Osten</u>, Hungary, which for centuries was part of the Hapsburg empire, appeared to the Germans as a strategic and convenient springboard; Germany was keenly interested in having Hungary one of her allies and associates in a looser or tighter form. This was a threat to Hungary's territory. At the moment I know of no such threats.

23 d. Do you think there is a natural conflict between Magyars and other people? If yes, which and why?

This question tends to emphasize Hungary's ethnographic loneliness in East Central Europe. Hungary indeed is a unique and lonely nation, surrounded by peoples belonging to unrelated linguistic families; there are the Slavs and the Romanians, the latter trying to propagate herself as being a sister nation of Western Latin nations. Hungary being alone, if we assign great value to linguistic relation and affinity, if we treat linguistic and racial relationship as true and potent realities, -- and Pan-Slavism indeed had great significance in the past -- then there undoubtedly is a natural conflict between Magyar and the surrounding peoples.

I personally consider this conflict an artificial one because friendship or enmity among peoples is based not on linguistics and ancestry, but is rather determined by economic and social identities or similarities, and by mutual interdependence, economic and other.

23 e. How do Magyars and Slovaks get along?

This question is not an important question today for the simple reason that there are very few Slovaks in Hungary today. Similarly, there are not too many Hungarians in Czechoslovakia today either. It is common knowledge that after 1945, a large-scale population exchange took place, an exchange based on an agreement of the Big Three. In respect of the Kisalföld in Czechoslovakia, several hundred thousand Hungarians were uprooted and sent to Hungary, while at the same time similar numbers of Slovaks from the interior of Hungary were sent to Czechoslovakia. Hungarian Germans were at the same time transported into Germany.

In a word, an ordering of the national minorities took place, -- and it is of no significance whether we approve or disapprove of such actions now. Usually it was not up to the affected individuals to decide for themselves whether they wanted to participate in this population exchange or not, the decision was made for them, and independently of them, by others, -- to my mind a decidedly improper and inhuman procedure. All these events have taken place, however, more than a decade ago, and it will be many more years before we can objectively discuss the correctness or incorrectness, the propriety or impropriety of such a large-scale and involuntary exchange. By that time the resultant changes and developments will undoubtedly sanction these decisions, -- these, I must emphasize, inhuman decisions. In Hungary, therefore, this whole question will be bound to lose its importance and significance, since the number of those directly affected is proportionately insignificant.

23 f. How do Magyars and Romanians get along?

This is a similar question, except that no population exchange ever took place between Hungary and Romania. The reason for this is rather obvious; given Hungary's post-Trianon boundaries, only a very small and insignificant number of Romanians lived in Hungary, scattered in villages and cities immediately adjoining the Romanian border, while very many Hungarians continued to live both in Transylvania and in Romania. Bucharest, given the ratio of Hungarians and Romanians living in that city, is, after all, a significant Hungarian city. In Transylvania you have extensive territories where the population is almost entirely Hungarian.

The lot of Hungarians in Transylvania underwent significant changes, -- and though I have no authentic or reliable information regarding their present status, -- the official Communist policy is to grant to each minority autonomy, the right to decide its own questions and issues. To what extent is this an actuality in Transylvania at the moment, I do not know. They do have periodicals, schools, they have their own university in Kolozsvár, etc. What is the degree of intellectual freedom, and to what extent do Hungarians have the right to make decisions in their own affairs, I unfortunately do not know.

23 g. How do Magyars and Austrians get along?

Questions of principle, equally applicable to this question, I have already touched upon before. Austro-Hungarian minority problems are quite insignificant; only a very few Austrians lived within Hungary, along the border, after the border rectification following the Second World War. These few Austrians were either uprooted and scattered throughout Hungary, or, the luckier ones at any rate, escaped and crossed the border into Austria.

24 How do Magyars and Yugoslavs get along? What is the answer to the problems Hungary has to face as a small state?

If I am to answer this question now, and if I am to limit myself to the situation now existing, then the answer is not easy;

I don't know how can a Communist state solve these peculiar problems of a small state. Certain tendencies may be seen from reports coming from Hungary; those definite disadvantages which stem from the fact that Hungary is a small nation, her limited territory being both insufficient and unsuited to satisfy the requirements of an expanding economy and population, are largely offset by attempts to bring about larger economic units. This consideration is the driving force behind the commercial agreements which Hungary concluded with her neighbor satellite countries. At the moment there is talk in Hungary about a broader economic cooperation among the satellites, envisaging a 15-20 year common economic plan. The significance of the plan, in which the Soviet Union also would be partner, lies in its long-range character, permitting meaningful coordination and utilization by all countries of advantageous positions of the several participants.

The basic idea underlying this projected cooperation is not bad, in my opinion. If Hungary were in more free circumstances, though in a different context, under a different formula, but basically the same methods of orientation would have to be employed, and attempts were made already before 1945 in this direction, though generally unsuccessfully.

24 a. It has sometimes been suggested that some sort of regional alliance or federation would be useful. What do you think of that?

I am in favor of regional cooperation.

24 b. If yes, whom should it include, and how should it operate?

The most natural unit would appear to be the one encompassing the countries of the Danube Valley. This is a geographic unit, the states are easily reachable, the raw materials available in these countries generally suffice and can satisfy the requirements of all, thus each nation would be able to develop a special industrial and agricultural form, useful not only to itself but also to the other participating countries. The unit would include besides Hungary, Yugoslavia, Rumania, Czechoslovakia, and Poland. Austria's inclusion is by no means a necessity, though it might be possible to include Austria as well. Austria would certainly be the best market for agricultural products, and the transportation routes to Austria are readily available from all of the above-named countries. Austria's industrial contribution to the other states, especially in a later state of development, would on the other hand be necessarily limited.

Whatever solution we decide on, there are two bases of evaluation; the one is a tight-knit economic cooperation providing an economic autarky or self-sufficiency as a federation, with the economic needs of all well satisfied. The other base would be the political formula where the establishment of a larger unit would appear to be more proper and useful. The unit I have in mind would be Europe, with Poland representing its easternmost part. Russia would be not included, since Russia is primarily an Asiatic state territorially, and since Russia -- whatever combination you may have in mind -- is a political and economic unit unto itself.

24 c. *What should be Hungary's part in it?*

Hungary's part in either a Danubian economic, or European political, federation would have to be commensurate to Hungary's past historic and cultural role, a substantial (hangsúlyos -- accented) role, to be sure.

25. *What do you think about the Russians as a people?*

Let's clarify first what we mean by a Russian. If I think of a Russian as just another man, then, even if I do not accept as binding Christ's command, who created and evaluated all men as equals, but if I vindicate to myself the right of evaluating others, or of considering myself equal to others, I can do this only if I am prepared to accept this very same thing in others.

25 a. Are there different kinds of Russians?

If we look at Russia's territory of today, it is obvious that several peoples inhabit that area. If we accept that in France there are several nationality groups differing from one another, then these differences are much more apparent in Russia.

25 b. Do you think some are good and some are bad?

Which one of these do I consider good and valuable, and which one is bad is a markedly subjective evaluation. I must confess I do not see any difference of value between an intelligent Russian or an intelligent Tartar, with both of whom one can chatter reasonably well. It is a fact, however, that it was the Russians, in their long history, who organized the various nations of the area, who held them together, and served as their leaders. It was the Russians who emerged in literature as representatives of this region. In the course of history, it was these pure Russians, though numerically inferior, who gave the most quality. They obviously must possess intellectual and other powers and abilities to accomplish a thing like that.

Actually, you can never be certain in this respect. There may be other nations, suppressed and silenced, whose sons may be even more talented, whom we do not know and, if we knew them, our opinion of the Russians might change.

25 c. Are they all Communists?

No, they are not.

25 e. What was the feeling toward them when they entered Hungary in 1944?

The Russian troops were not liberators in Hungary, as they indeed were in Bulgaria, where the population received them with joy and obvious sympathy. A great suspicion was felt in Hungary both as regards Soviet troops and Communists, a suspicion kept alive and supported by the 20-years old Horthy propaganda, which steadily emphasized how terrible communism, the Soviet Union, and the Soviet people are. This propaganda, needless to say, was quite misleading, unjust, and malicious. At any rate, the invasion of the Russians was preceded by a widespread fear and anxiety. When the Russians finally arrived in 1945, the erroneousness of the Horthy-propaganda became clear, though it was also immediately evident that at least those Russians who were in Hungary at the time were culturally far inferior to the average Hungarian. The Horthy propaganda appeared to be underscored by the many irregular actions and strange behavior of the Soviet troops, actions and behavior which I think are no different with any other invading force of any other nation, i.e., raping of women, confiscating of property, etc.

26. Now with regard to Marxism, what do you think of it?

I am an economist and when it comes to Marxism, I look primarily for that economic theory in it whose aim it is to establish such an economic system or mechanism under which people may reach their goals, where the economy may develop under prescribed rules, and with which the various economic phenomena may be explained.

Marxism, though it does explain many economic phenomena, its characteristic fashion, nevertheless is not a unitary (egységes) economic system. Marxism is rather a criticism of the developing English capitalistic system of the early 19th Century, and in this category it is a well-written, good, and coherent work. That beginning capitalism was, in final analysis, an unjust economic system, laden with innumerable contradictions. It made all those mistakes and errors which a rapidly developing expanding economy or policy usually makes. I consider it on the other hand a gross exaggeration to build an economic or political system solely on the criticism of early capitalism. In my opinion, Marxism did not come up with either a better or a more coherent economic or social system than provided by democracy which, after all, is one of the oldest forms of government of humankind, and which appears most capable of satisfying those human endeavors which are, so to speak, innate and represent a vital necessity.

Marxism did not give us something else indeed. If a system claims for itself the right to explain everything, and to answer every question, to serve as a substituted new for the old to be discarded, then such a system must of necessity be a whole, unassailable, and capable of answering, explaining, and solving every problem. The bible is capable of such a feat, even if laden with contradictions. Marxism, however, is incapable of achieving a similar result, even in the economic sphere, without encountering gross contradictions, and without exposing itself to clear and easy refutations and denials.

26 e. Was Stalin a good Marxist?

I can hardly answer your question, since my knowledge of Tito, and of Tito's knowledge of, and compliance with, Marxism tenets is insufficient. I myself am not a Marxist, so how could I possibly say if Tito is a good one? My opinion is that Tito is more than a Marxist, even in contemporary interpretation; he has passed the stage, the category of Marxism, if we take Marxism to signify the theory of Marx as corrected by Lenin, with respect to capitalism, imperialism, or respecting the economic order of the state. Tito has tried to do something more in Yugoslavia.

26 f. Are the Hungarian Social-Democrats Marxists?
Do you think one can be a Marxist and a democrat?
What do you think it means to be a democrat?

The Social Democrats were trying to live up to this ideal, to be Marxists and democrats at the same time. I have the feeling that one has to do either the one or the other. Marxism, in the sense as Marx wrote and defined it, or in the sense of later interpretations, be it on the part of the Social Democrats, -- Kautsky and others -- or be it on the part of the Bolsheviks, -- Lenin and company, -- the basis and the foundation of a Marxist society, of Marxian political power, is the dictatorship of the proletariat. Now the dictatorship of the proletariat as a system is not a democracy. The dictatorship of the proletariat denies democracy's basic tenet that each man is equal, it categorized people and declares that society has first class and second class subjects; the first class encompasses Marxists, those whose ancestry is in accord with arbitrary requirements, etc., etc. The second class is the rest of the population, with possibly several sub-groups and sub-categories. This runs counter to democracy, and denies the very basis of democracy, namely the belief that a person is entitled to his opinion and though differing in his opinions, continues to be an equal member of society. Obviously, therefore, one either chooses Marxism or democracy, but not both at the same time. The Social Democrats tried to fuse these two differing things, and unsuccessfully, I think. The more intelligent Social Democrats are more democrats than Marxists, I think.

26 i. When was Hungary a democracy?

Hungary was a democracy from 1945 to 1948.

26 j. Is Tito a Marxist? Is he a democrat?

To be a democrat means to accept those fundamental tenets which democracy considers the chief pillars of human life. Between two limits, life and death, people live one next to the other, and from this living together, mutual interactions and relations come about. This is the basis of society. The life of the society is governed by certain principles, and the society's inner order and mechanism is regulated by those laws which we consider to be the laws of democracy.

If we look at the origin of democracy, democracy means, etymologically, "rule by the people". Rule by the people, therefore majority rule, therefore vindication of the will of the majority. People, in one stage of their development, deciding to accept this term, and deciding to apply its content and meaning, obviously entered into a contract according to which the contracting parties, mindful of the imperative necessity of interdependence, decided to live in common, as a unit, agreeing at the same time to abide by the decisions of the majority in all matters affecting the whole. This majority rule continues to be the basic prerequisite and rule of living together today. To be a democrat, therefore, means to abide by this fundamental rule, and to abide by whatever proceeds from it; if the human society, or a nation, or a tribe, or a city, or a smaller community which is interdependent, which lives in common during a shorter or longer period of time -- if such a unit, in making decisions, takes into account the majority's rules and abides by it, such a unit manifestly leaves it up to its members to form their own opinions, and to take whatever stand they see fit, to vote for whatever proposal they like when it comes to deciding a certain issue. It is manifestly clear, therefore, that acceptance of the majority rule presupposes an absolute freedom on the part of the individual; freedom to determine his own life within the framework of the community, according to the possibilities the community has at its disposal, and according to the ethical concepts and standards of that community. Democracy, therefore, while it does mean compliance and accommodation on the part of the individual to the community, it also means complete personal freedom at the same time. To be a democrat, then, means to abide by this dual law. Such a person is a democrat, he behaves democratically, his community is a democracy, etc. This naturally follows from the fact that the two fundamental rules, i.e., majority rule and personal freedom, are the sources of every particular law, be they of a social, political, or economic nature.

27. *We just talked about Tito. What does the term National Communism mean to you?*

The term "national communism" is a concept of Western origin. It had its inception in the West and only later did it arrive to the satellite countries. It is a propaganda phrase, used to denote a difference which, viewed from the West, appears to be existing between two Communist concepts or viewpoints.

In reality there is essentially no such thing, more precisely, there are certain reform efforts, a search for a new way, for new manners (módozatok), which in the West are identified by the term "national communism".

When Tito attempted to build his own communist state independently of the Soviet Union, he did not have the intention of creating national communism, a Serbian communism, or a Croatian, or a Yugoslav communism if you like, -- what he attempted to do was to organize his state according to the given conditions of his state -- whether considering the people's interests or not is not an issue here -- he tried to organize in a typical fashion (sajátos módon) Yugoslavia's social and economic life according to his own point of view.

This form is not new to Tito, nor was it decided on in Yugoslavia, just as in Poland it was not Gomulka who invented national communism, but the circumstances formed, molded, and brought it about. Gomulka was but a tool, a flag, a symbol for certain efforts, for certain spontaneous efforts which, in certain circumstances, pushed them to the fore. The same holds true, of course, of Tito, and Imre Nagy is also in the same category.

27 a. Do you think there were National Communists in the revolt last October?

If we accept the term "national communism" -- which I personally don't like -- then we must say that those people who were on the side of the Revolution while being Communists, these Communists were national communists. This was the Imre Nagy group in Hungary.

27 b. If yes, who were they? What were they after? What do you think of Gomulka's policy?

Gomulka, as he came to the fore at the time of the process of liberalization, chose from among the many possibilities what I think was best under the given circumstances, a solution which promised to do the most good for the Poles.

If we now relate for a moment Gomulka to the national communist movement -- as is customary in the West to treat Gomulka, Imre Nagy, Tito, and others, under the same common heading -- then we must say that similar efforts exist in every satellite country, in some less developed, in others triumphant. But efforts of this sort everywhere have a common source, the 20th Party Congress of the Soviet Union, when the Soviet Union gave the opportunity to these countries to embark on a limited process of liberalization. This was the process which produced Gomulka and Nagy and a host of lesser individuals in the other countries, who continued to fight in small obscure battles for a freer life. It was this process, this development, which carried on its waves the "leasers", not the other way round.

As to the process of liberalization itself, it is no more than a recognition of the results of past mistakes. Recognizing and acknowledging these, the Communists tried to build up such a Communist state in which the people intensively participate in the various social and political moves and developments. Liberalization is this and no more.

27 d. Is he a Communist?

If I consider this question from a theoretical point of view, my answer is a definite yes.

27 e. Do you think some Communists are Hungarian patriots?

Every theory -- of whatever kind, is compatible, theoretically, with Hungarian patriotism. Whosoever may subscribe to whatever theory and yet, within the framework of that theory, he may desire to find those possibilities and solutions which, in that category, are best for the entire population. A man may believe in communism, in the beauties of the Communist idea, in its goodness, in its applicability, and therefore he may still be a Hungarian patriot.

The question, of course, has a practical side, amply demonstrated by past experiences of Hungarian Communists, when each and every one had reached the point when he realized that he no longer was a Communist or, to be more precise, if he was a Communist, he was a Communist in the then prevailing and accepted category of communism, and therefore no longer a Hungarian patriot, because no longer representing the true interests of the people. Take Tibor Déry and Gyula Hay and countless others. They all clearly reached this point.

28. *Suppose Imre Nagy had stayed in power after the Revolution. Do you think conditions would have changed?*

The victory of the Revolution could not have been identified and equated exclusively with Imre Nagy. Already at the very outset of the Revolution, other forces came to the fore besides the Communists. If we go back a little further we see that the Communists were only the leaders in the pre-revolutionary movement, the rank and file everywhere was made up of non-Communists (pártonkivüliek). This situation would have manifestly had its consequences, had the Revolution been successful to the end. In the very beginning, the idea of a coalition government would have been in the forefront. This, in turn, would have had its effect on practically every sphere of life; a coalition government would have meant in practice that in the various offices, factories, and institutions, in the various parts of the economic and social life, the non-Communist people would have played their role. If we take these changes into account, we must see clearly that under such circumstances the country's life would have been directed from a many-sided point of view. This would have been the formula at the beginning.

What direction this development would have taken is an entirely different question. This direction depends on a person's viewpoint; on where do I sit, and from what vantage point do I view this whole problem. If, assuming that I am a national Communist, my viewpoint is fixed, and what I consider good and proper will be definitely different from what a Christian Democrat might be thinking, who evaluates life's phenomena differently and who thinks in an entirely different category. Manifestly, a democratic struggle would have been the result, a contest for the determination, for the direction of the country's economic, political, and social life. From the intersection of the various forces, a synthesis would have come about which, with its leaders, would have represented Hungary for an indeterminate period.

28 a. *What sort of a system do you think he was aiming at?*

All we have to do here is to refer to Imre Nagy's speeches, which provide a clear answer to this question. Imre Nagy committed himself to the idea of a coalition government, he was committed to holding free elections, and with this he essentially accepted that viewpoint which would have represented the majority of the population in a given situation.

28 b. *Suppose the Russians had not invaded. Do you think he would have remained at the head of the government?*

I can very well imagine that he would have remained at the head of the government, and for two reasons: a) Imre Nagy was an extremely popular figure in Hungary during the Revolution; b) He had a decisive role in those events which brought about the Revolution. It is almost probable that Imre Nagy would have remained at the head of the government until elections were held. What would have been the results of the free elections, I of course do not know, nor am I prepared to enter into predictions. But until the elections, the revolutionary principles would have been decisive.

29. *Now tell me, just in a word, whether each of the following, in your mind, is good or bad:*
   a. -- *Socialism*   (29a) Good.
   b. -- *Colonialism*   (29b) Bad.
   c. -- *Class struggle*   (29c) Bad.
   d. -- *National (Popular) front* (29d) Good.
   e. -- *Imperialism*   (29e) Bad.
   f. -- *Capitalism*   Bad.
   g. -- *Bourgeoisie (Middle class)* (29g) Bad.

h. -- **Peter Veres**	(29h) Bad.
i. -- **Kulák**	(29i) When it comes to personalities, I find it impossible to state just in one word whether a person, and all that he represents, if good or bad.
j. -- **Trotsky**	(29j) The same as "i."
k. -- **Maszaryk**	(29k) The same as above.
l. -- **Chiang Kai-shek**	(29i) The same as above.
m.-- **Anna Kethly**	(29m) The same as above.
n. -- **Mindszenty**	(29n) The same as above.

30. *Today, what Party would win in free elections in Hungary?*

I was a member of the Small Landholders' Party some time ago, and am a Small Landholders' Party members today. Though... This "though" is not intended as a qualification, though I certainly could correct or criticize my own Party as well, let alone the other parties, who would necessarily participate in a free election.

I speak here about "corrections" because there were parties in the coalition of 1945 which were all destroyed in 1948 by the Communists. Most of these parties re-emerged again in 1956, but I cannot tell for sure whether, -- had the population or individuals to decide in 1956 what to demand of these political parties, -- these demands would have corresponded to those platforms which these parties accepted in 1945. You did have a development in Hungary, a change in the people's attitudes, without a corresponding development in the parties, at least in their programs. The parties, after all, could not develop in the last ten years. The only noticeable changes occurred in the views and attitudes of Party leaders, changes brought about by their experiences gained in the last decade. How and to what extent would these changes have been reflected in the parties' programs is impossible to tell, nor is it possible to say what the results would have been. At any rate, one can say that such a Party would have been victorious, or would have secured a relative majority, which was not a Communist, or a Marxist, Party. If we want to be more concrete, we can say that a bourgeois Party would have been victorious. The only question in doubt is the program; namely what program would this Party have had to adopt in order to secure the voters' trust. This bourgeois Party could not possibly have come up with a bourgeois program in the sense of a property-based democratic program. The workers, who were not Communists, who most vehemently opposed communism during the Revolution, gravitated politically, in a very interesting fashion, both in Budapest and in the other large cities, towards the idea of a bourgeois Party. Their orientation was not even in the direction of the Social Democrats.

These workers, while definitely favoring a bourgeois Party, would not have voted under any circumstances for a bourgeois Party program. The workers would never have accepted a correction of the land reform (a correction, I don't have to emphasize, would never have been accepted by the peasants either). Nor would the workers have accepted a program which, in the question of the factories, would have proposed a solution even remotely resembling the pre-World War II patterns. Both workers and peasants would undoubtedly have favored a correction, they would have favored a fair and reasonable settlement, perhaps a constitutional settlement, of this question. They would have voted for a corrected, modified system, for a proposition which would have given the workers the right to partake in the ownership of, and to participate in the direction of, the factories.

This is the hypothesis which, in my opinion, would have secured a majority, or at least a large percentage, of the voters' sympathies.

31. *Sociologists find that often various groups get different rewards from society -- some people get more than they deserve, others get less. I would like to mention some groups to you, and you tell me whether you think, since 1948, these groups have been getting more or*

less than they deserve:

a.	*Workers*	(31a) Less.
b.	*Collective farmers*	(31b) Less.
c.	*Small Landholders' Party*	(31c) Less.
d.	*Kuláks*	(31d) Less.
e.	*Government employees*	Some more, some less.
f.	*Professionals*	

Those who supported the regime, more.

g.	*Party members*	Some more, some less.
h.	*Tradesmen*	There weren't any.
i.	*Artisans*	Less.

32. *As far as you know, which of these groups were better off and which were worse off before 1948?*

In line with the political and economic tendencies, the well-being of individuals was directly proportional with their association with, and active support of, the state power, or of the Party power, which directed the state. The closer people were to these, the better off they were. If we compare the situation of AVH members and, say, of the small artisans, then it is obvious that the situation of the AVH has improved to such a degree that it cannot even be compared to whatever relative improvements there may have been in the lot of the artisans.

If we consider that after 1945 the country was in a desperate economic state, and that because of this the intellectual workers were not always properly compensated immediately after the war, then it will be apparent that such workers as writers, scholars, and artists also experienced a substantial improvement in their economic position after 1948. We should add, naturally, that this category embraced only those who surrendered to, and served the regime, or those whom the regime considered indispensable for whatever reason, irrespective of their political affiliation.

Otherwise a general improvement was noticeable in the life of every member of whatever social group after 1948, as compared to

1945, which is attributable to the very nature of post-war recovery. We should also add that this general relative betterment lasted only until 1950, when the country decided to build a modern heavy industry and the heavy investments began (i.e., Sztálinváros iron works, Budapest subway, etc.)

32 a. Do you approve or disapprove of some of these changes? Which? Do you think that the interests of the following groups in Hungary coincide or conflict: Workers and Peasants? Workers and Intellectuals?

If we assume a democracy, and we accept the definition that the direction or tendency of such a democracy is a compromise of the interests and interaction of its component parts, then the compromise always presupposes the giving up of certain particular interests, in the interests of a large unitary whole. If we accept this, then we must assume that there are certain conflicts of interests among the constituent parts of a society, of any society. It is not in the interests of a man on a Sunday excursion that there should be a rain, when the peasant is probably ardently praying for it.

If we consider that in the evolution of a country's price structure several factors are at work, the resultant price level represents a curtailment of every group's interests. If we considered only the farmers' interests when determining the price of an agricultural product, then we would manifestly assign it a much higher price than is the case in practice. In a free country the basic consideration underlying such a price-determination is the principle that a product's price represents that product's total cost. Here you have again at least an apparent conflict of interest, since people in different occupations may evaluate differently the various cost factors. The value of a service represents one thing to the person rendering it, but is something else to another person, to an observer from another profession. These certainly are conflicts of interest, both between classes and between social groups, which is only natural. If we did not have this, we would not have vital competition, but stagnation. We would not have progress if everyone were satisfied with his present status. **Question**: This conflict being a natural phenomenon, was there in Hungary a conflict of interest among the groups I enumerated, which went over and above this natural phenomenon, or not? **Answer:** Basic conflicts of interest do not develop in a natural way, they do not abide by the laws of natural development, but are influenced by various attitudes and ruling tendencies, which characterize an era or a country. This was so in Hungary also, a formerly feudal country which, after the First World War was transformed into a state that continued to defend feudalism under the guise of a facade of constitutionality. The relatively small ruling class considered it necessary to induce the several classes under it to oppose each other, peasants against the industrial workers, and industrial workers against the intelligentsia.

In the latter combination they were more successful, so that the industrial worker viewed the white-collar person as his personal enemy. This feeling and this attitude of view was a sign of an abnormality which continued to persist, however, even after 1945, becoming very potent again after 1948 when the Communists, reviving and enlarging this semi-dormant feeling of class enmity, attempted to divide the country as a means of securing for themselves the power. After 1948, not only did the industrial workers view the peasants as their enemies, but the several strata of the peasantry were likewise made to face each other. The same was true of the industrial sector; there were the so-called industrial aristocrats, pictured as the friends of capitalism and as enemies of the workers and of the people's democracy. Enmity was also fostered between the workers and intelligentsia. There were the so-called intellectuals loyal to the people (néphez hü -- Volkstreu), an intelligentsia loyal to the workers, while others were branded enemies of the people, enemies of the workers. The post-1948 period may be characterized by an attempt to lift out, to emphasize, the workers, and to govern in their name.

33 g. Prior to 1945, aristocracy and intelligentsia?

I consider it necessary to define the term "aristocracy" and "intelligentsia" before I can answer the question.

The two groups were very often one in Hungary's history, very often they went in different directions, and on occasions they even opposed each other. Opposition was the rule in the later stages of development.

During the beginning stages of Hungary's history, the aristocracy was the intelligentsia. A district group of the intelligentsia appears only as a result of the impoverishment of the lesser nobility (gentry), when a very great difference of wealth separated the leading nobility (magnates) from the gentry. At this time you have the emergence of the so-called gentry intelligentsia (nemesi értelmiség), a group clearly distinct from the aristocracy; the aristocracy, for reasons of wealth, not admitting members of the gentry to its ranks, and not recognizing it as full partners.

This gentry intelligentsia got thoroughly mixed in the 19th Century with the upcoming members of the bourgeois intelligentsia (this mixing went on even much earlier, but reached large proportions only in the 19th Century), and the gentry culture was gradually displaced or absorbed by the new bourgeois culture.

At this stage of the development, aristocracy and intelligentsia were two characteristically differing social groups, no longer bound to each other by those secret ties which persisted at an earlier period between the aristocracy and the gentry.

At this stage the intelligentsia was already demanding, claiming the right to direct things and, as a result, found itself face to face with the aristocracy, which considered government to be its exclusive domain. This struggle became more evident at the beginning of the 20th Century, when the aristocracy was already on the defensive, its intellectual influence suffering a marked decline.

Now after 1920, and throughout the inter-bellum period, workers' and peasants' sons swelled the ranks of the intelligentsia in steadily growing numbers, giving it new life and new impetus, and molding and transforming it at the same time. The numerical ratio and structure of the intelligentsia changed, which meant in practice that the intelligentsia, as a group, began more and more to represent the force of progress.

Now we cannot deny the aristocracy's right to be considered an intelligentsia, a group which, on account of its wealth and political influence commands a distinct position in a country and which, by the very nature of its exclusiveness, represents a distinct, closed stratum in a country.

The numerical and structural changes in the intelligentsia resulted in a direct conflict between the progressive wing of the intelligentsia and the aristocrats. The latter using every means at its disposal to defend both its ancient privileges and positions. This conflict and dispute, prior to 1945, was no longer a dispute between two factions of the same class, nor was it a quarrel between just two classes, but represented, rather, a struggle between proponents of progress on the one hand, and defenders of reaction on the other.

33 h. Prior to 1945, aristocracy and workers? Prior to 1945, landlords and Small Landholders' Party?

The conflicts between land magnates and Small Landholders' Party were primarily of an economic nature and not of a social character. This was a direct result of the fact that about 50 percent of the country's land was in the hands of the magnates, a group representing only about one and a half or two percent of the population, while the other 50 percent of the land was in the possession of some 80 percent of the population. Now if we consider but one factor, namely the natural growth or increase of these two groups, it immediately becomes evident that the proportion of the land falling on any given Small Landholders' Party members were getting less and less.

If we now assume that these Small Landholders' Party members were rational cultivators of their land, and that they were successful in effecting some savings in the course of time, it should also not be too difficult to comprehend that, because of the steadily decreasing amounts of land falling on any one cultivator, the Small Landholders' Party members would have liked to invest their savings into the purchase of additional strips of land, -- if this had been possible. Purchase of land was not possible, however, the available land on sale being far less than the demand. The Small Landholders' Party therefore regarded the entire social system as some sort of a squeeze (szorító), feeling about the same way as you do when you wear very tight shoes. They regarded those who prevented them from purchasing land as more or less personal enemies. This was the economic foundation of the conflict between these two social groups and all other conflicts or conflict categories stemmed from it.

33 j. Prior to 1945, landlords and farm hands (landless peasants)?

There were serious conflicts between these two classes, and of course you will never find a situation where employers and employees would have identical interests.

The magnates' workers were the agricultural servants. The picture was a very dismal one, since you can hardly call these servants' pre-1945 conditions human. I don't remember exactly if it was a statistical report of 1935 or 1937 which gave 25 fillers as the daily compensation of a five-member family of such a servant. This meant that a five-member family's daily wage was 10-12 cents. This was the condition of the agricultural servants and this explains the obvious conflict between him and his master. I have not done any research into this question, so I cannot tell how other Hungarians felt about this. One thing is certain; neither the Revolution, nor the post-1945 leadership of Hungary did ever contemplate an importation or copying of those economic forms which characterize the United States and other Western capitalistic countries. The opinion was generally held that Hungary must maintain a middle stand between two extremes and that the so-called post-1945 achievements (vivmányok) must be maintained and preserved. This does not mean, naturally, any opposition to the United States, nor does it mean an opposition to the Soviet Union, if we view them from an economic point of view.

Hungary would have retained a great many features of the capitalistic economy, borrowing, at the same time, what was thought as good and useful economic patterns from the Soviet Union. In the political sphere, my own view and, I can truthfully say the view of the majority, was based on the principles of Western democracy, both as regards political and social structure. This, I hope, answers your question.

34. *Some people feel that the United States and the Soviet Union are equally dangerous. What were some of the things that concerned you about the United States before you left Hungary? Suppose there were a war in which Hungary was engaged. Who in the population would fight for the present regime?*

It all depends on the circumstances of such a war. In a war between the Soviet Union and the West, Hungary would obviously play a significant role in the Soviet plans. Hungary would not only be occupied by Soviet troops, but the Soviet government and military would no doubt make sure, with or without the consent of the Hungarian government, to safeguard the safe passage of Russian troops through Hungary towards the West. The opinion or sympathies of the population would have very little play in this question and perhaps only at an advanced state would there be some opportunity to act. If the Russians were to draft Hungarian regiments into the struggle, some people no doubt would try to go over to the other side. All this, however, would hardly be considered as of decisive importance.

35 a. Who would fight against it?

It is almost impossible to answer this question, especially to enter into numerical calculations.

In case of a war, the entire nation would be hostile to the regime. The practical implementation of this hostility, however, would not be an easy matter. The Soviet Union, because of strategic reasons, would lend a powerful arm to the regime for the maintenance of an inner stability.

The situation would be similar to that during the Second World War, when, toward the end of that war, very few people indeed favored the continuation of the struggle on Germany's side. Germany, in spite of all this, intervened directly into Hungarian affairs on March 19, 1944, and after, and effectively maintained the strategic lines of communication between Germany and the fronts.

In the case of a future Russian-Western conflict, the same might be true. At a certain stage of the war, if the international situation permitted this, resistance pockets would no doubt spring up throughout Hungary, fighting both the regime and Russia much more effectively and with much more vigor, I think, than was the case of the resistance against the Germans.

36. Do you think your opinion on any of the questions we have discussed today has changed since you left Hungary?

I should like to stress here just one point; my opinion has changed markedly with respect to the policy of the Western nations.

We in Hungary believed, before and after the Revolution, in effective Western political help, if not in the sense and if not to such a degree as Radio Free Europe was trying to persuade us was forthcoming, we at any rate continued to believe that there was such a thing as a "Western foreign policy". A foreign policy encompassing the opinions of the Western powers, a unitary foreign policy, a foreign policy the objects and goals of which are clear and clarified (tisztázottak).

We thought that, just as the Soviet Union possesses a ready plan, a ready answer to whatever eventuality, the West likewise has a workable instrument, perhaps not as dogmatic, and somewhat more loose, nevertheless, capable of dealing with ordinary and extraordinary questions which may arise at any moment.

Traveling from one end of Europe to the other, and finally arriving to the United States, I was nowhere able to find this Western foreign policy, and I am rather uneasy and alarmed because of its absence.

I don't have in mind a cold-war concept, nor do I urge such a concept, believing that we are past that stage when such a concept could be effectively and fruitfully applied.

What I have in mind is a global concept, a set of views, a plan, an instrument, capable of giving a ready answer to whatever phenomenon may arise anywhere in the world, -- since politics, just like religion or philosophy, ought to be able to deal with whatever problem.

What we see instead in the free world is that one big nation takes this stand, and the other power takes that stand, and the stand thus taken is mostly determined by short-range considerations, with a view of one country only. This policy, which has to be fought out first in the Western camp, which has to combat the several national interests first, which has to combat on many occasions the narrow viewpoints, often selfish viewpoints, of the many officials sitting in the various offices and of the administration, this policy, if compared with the policy of the

Soviet Union, which of course is not democratic, but much more definite, firm, and resolute, a policy compulsory on all, so to speak -- this Western policy, we feel, is hardly capable of competing (nem nagyon versenyképes) with that of the Soviet Union. The absence of such a policy in the West disturbs me greatly, and the development of such a policy is urgently needed, I feel.

CONCLUSION

1. ***I have been asking you all sorts of questions. I wonder if you have any questions you want to ask me.***

   I have no questions to ask you.

*1 a. **What do you think about the conversations we had together?***

The interview method seems to be the only possible and meaningful way for the researchers' probing into the essence of the Hungarian Revolution. I don't know what data you have at your disposal, how many people did you ask for their opinions, nor do I think that the opinions thus solicited will be in agreement, or will be unitary. People, after all, do absorb new ideas quickly and their original Hungarian opinions are bound to suffer at least certain minute deviations, without the individuals being aware of the changes themselves.

People arrive in the free world, come under the influence of others who have been here for a long period, and under the impact of these personalities, under the impact of their ideas, change their opinions if ever so slightly, and come to believe that what their present opinion is now, has been their original viewpoint all the time, even while still in Hungary. I don't suppose bad faith or malevolence here, there probably isn't any, but the phenomenon of change is difficult to notice and hard to register.

I made a consistent effort -- and I only hope others did likewise -- to give you the taste of the times under review, to convey the meaning of words, of concepts, which were then authentic. The meaning of concepts today is no longer the same, whether they are related to the entire period under review, or to the Revolution.

It would be best, I think, if those people who will ultimately use the material thus collected, who will try to arrive at scientific conclusions, would follow the same principle; they ought to go beyond the mere meaning of words, beyond the superficial significance of concepts, and try to see them, and to weigh them, in their contemporary setting, in their authentic context, since separation must lead to distortion.

For this very reason I consciously tried throughout to project my answers into the various periods with which they were concerned, so as to provide a fixed point and a background, -- to make you feel as much as possible the contemporary interpretation, the contemporary air, and the importance and significance contemporarily attached to the various issues, movements, and solutions.

Very many books and articles appeared already on the Revolution, most of them describing and analyzing it with praise, in terms of superlatives only. Most of these books and articles contain very few facts and few objective analyses. I am convinced that the true significance of the Revolution will be brought out by this objective analysis for the benefit of those people, -- I should add, who try to deduct from revolutions and freedom aspirations of peoples universally valid pronouncements, or to draw a picture characteristic of an era.

1 b. How much interesting material do you think we will be able to collect through such conversations?
What are some things you would urge us to beware of?

I don't think it is my task to advise you, or that such advice is necessary, -- you see your task and aims very clearly and you have a clear view, I am sure, of the concrete limits and limitations of these aims.

My task was to answer questions, to the best of my ability and recollection. The task of the interview is to give a true picture of an event, of an era, and of the forces which make them and keep them going. But you are just as aware of this as I am, if not even more so.

1 c. Do you think we shall get honest answers or not?

A certain amount of precaution, and a certain percentage of correction is definitely necessary in a project of this kind. The great majority of the answers you get, however, will definitely be in accordance with fact. The questions were either concerned with concrete situations, where concrete data were required, and the other part of the questions was designed to elicit not information, but opinion. With respect to the opinions a certain degree of corrections will be necessary, as I already explained elsewhere. A person's opinion may be influenced by the fact that, living as he does in the United States, he may not wish to say anything which, though is his opinion, may be injurious or insulting to the United States. I may have uttered repeatedly such things, statements which cannot be regarded as all too pleasant or flattering from the American point of view. I did this in an attempt to preserve that validity and force in my statements which they would have had, had I made them in Hungary in response to the same questions. This is, of course, to a certain extent dependent on the interviewee's intellectual ability.

2. Let's see what other things you know about that we have not yet really talked about. Do you ever intend to go back to Hungary?

I would like to go back to Hungary, of course. But I am a realist, and am fully aware that this is not an easy task for me. The task of returning is much easier for most people. I come from a social stratum which -- at least in the present government's interpretation -- is one of those classes which possess the power in Hungary today (workers, poor peasants). For this very reason my past behavior, and my present attitude and activities, are bound to be weighed more precisely and would be judged with greater scrutiny. This renders the road leading back to Hungary now, or later, rather hazardous until such a time, or such a change, in Hungary, which eliminates this roadblock.

I have a long experience of prisons. If one is imprisoned, -- and I don't mean to compare the two situations in any way -- one sooner or later realizes that the best and most sensible thing to do is to settle down in the expectation of a long stay, and to project both his needs and his activities on the basis of a long-range consideration. This is precisely what I am doing now.

3. *You know our aim is to get as much information on Hungary and the Hungarian situation as possible. In this connection, do you have any suggestions for our Project?*

All I can say is that a nation's life is a continuous movement, a development which got under way a long time ago, and is not terminated with an event, however important that event may be, be it even as important as the Hungarian Revolution. The Hungarian nation continues to live in Hungary at this moment.

Now in order to fully understand a historical event, in order to clearly see the intentions of a nation, the stand a nation takes, a full knowledge of the continuous development is necessary. If I may suggest anything to you, I should like to advise you not to disregard this continuity.

You are now analyzing the Revolution and the periods immediately preceding it. But as we have seen with many of these questions, the correct answering, or an approximately balanced answering, made an excursion back to previous times very often necessary. The dynamic forces of a present event are very often buried deep in the past, but they are there, potent and real, nonetheless.

Now there are links not only to the past, but also to the future. If the Hungarian Revolution cannot, and ought not, be separated from the period preceding it, it cannot be separated from the years after it either.

3 a. Any documents (official or other documents, photographs) or other materials that the Project might be interested in having or knowing about?

The Revolution has a very extensive literature, even abroad, written before, during, and after the event itself. I personally have practically no evidence at all in my possession, due to my hasty departure. Attempts are being made in Europe, however, to collect whatever unpublished materials may be available.

3 b. Have you written or do you plan to write any manuscript on the basis of your experiences?

I do plan to write, but have no time at the moment. I do have a large collection of notes, not a real diary, but sketches and annotations which, not being able to relate them to anybody, I nonetheless considered important enough to record and to preserve. From these a book may emerge some day. At the moment I have more serious business to attend to. After all, there are already numerous books on the subject on the market, some are quite good.

I have a pet project which I want to do. I intend to analyze the 1945-1948 economic development in Hungary, a development of a democratic country at times in cooperation with, and at times in opposition to, the Communists, which, in its tendencies and accomplished parts is extremely interesting and modern, later adopted and sanctioned by the Revolution also. These were economic experiments of a democratic country, which were not, however, along the lines of capitalistic economy.

The question I want to treat is specifically an economic question. It is related to both capitalistic theory and practice, as well as to a democratic way of life and democratic form of government.

This economic system was influenced by the pre-World War II Hungarian economy, which was a typically capitalistic economy.

This capitalistic system and the (Hungarian) industrialization was identified in Hungary with that social stratum which was steadily losing ground in the country.

The upsurging democratic forces, when opposing these obstructionist elements who hindered and impeded social progress, (they) saw themselves forced to oppose the capitalistic system as well.

So developed in Hungary an economic system which, if we are to label it correctly, is a mixed economic system.

I am firmly convinced -- and this is why I consider this question so important -- that this mixed system will have distinctive bearings for the future. It is already now being emulated and its principles are being accepted in greater or lesser degree, by the countries in Asia. In this dialectical economic development in which we live, at a time when two great economic concepts, capitalism and socialism, compete with and play against one another, in the oppressed nations and the nations on the threshold of their economic development, a new economic synthesis is developing, which, in the period 1945-1948 has reached a very definitely delineated outline in Hungary, and which, though interrupted and therefore incomplete, is nevertheless gaugeable.

NOTES FROM THE JOURNAL

"The terror, in a word, was everywhere, it was part of the fabric of life"

"A whole nation was held trembling in fear"

MARCH 1953 TO OCTOBER 22, 1956

1953

March 5: Death of Stalin. A major reorganization of the Soviet leadership follows.

March 7: The new Soviet leadership declares an amnesty, promises to give priority to improving living standards, and underlines the importance of collective leadership.

March 8: The Hungarian Parliament passes legislation perpetuating the 'undying memory' of Stalin and orders a national period of mourning.

May 17: Parliamentary elections in Hungary follow the Stalinist pattern.

June 1: Disturbances break out in Czechoslovakia. Workers demonstrating in Plzeò occupy the city hall and display national and US flags. The movement is suppressed by the special police.

June 13-16: Hungary's Party and state leaders are summoned to Moscow. Mátyás Rákosi's monopoly of power is ended. He is instructed to hand over as prime minister to Imre Nagy, but is allowed to remain as head of the Communist Party. The main lines of a new course of policy are drawn up by the Soviets.

June 15: The Soviet Union resumes diplomatic relations with Yugoslavia and with Israel.

June 17-18: A workers' uprising takes place in East Berlin and other cities of the German Democratic Republic (GDR). The military is called in to suppress the insurrection.

June 27-28: The Central Committee of the Hungarian Workers' Party (HWP) convenes to implement Moscow's instructions on the New Course of political and economic reform.

July 4: Prime Minister Imre Nagy, in his programme speech to the new Parliament, outlines the New Course: a new economic policy and a new political line based on legality in government and administrative practice and enhanced sovereignty of the people.

July 7: AVH Lieutenant-General László Piros appointed Minister of the Interior instead Ernő Gerő. Gerő remains a deputy Prime Minister.

July 9: Beria is arrested in Moscow, dismissed from all his positions and excluded from the Party.

July 11: A meeting of Budapest HWP activists is held.

July 21: An interior minister's directive orders the establishment of a unified Ministry of the Interior. The AVH (security police) is reintegrated into the Interior Ministry structure.

July 25: A partial amnesty is declared in Hungary.

July 26: The Council of Ministers (government) passes a resolution ending the practices of internment and internal exile.

July 27: A ceasefire agreement is signed at Panmunjom, ending the Korean War.

August 8: Soviet Prime Minister Georgy Malenkov announces that the first Soviet hydrogen bomb has been tested.

Autumn: Sharp cuts in the size of the Hungarian People's Army begin. By November 15, its strength has been reduced by 150,000 men.

September 6: The government resolves on wide-ranging price reductions.

September 9: Hungary and Yugoslavia resume diplomatic relations.

September 13: Nitika Khrushchev is elected first secretary of the Communist Party of the Soviet Union (CPSU) Central Committee.

October 4: At a camp at Tiszalök, for prisoners of war allowed to return from the Soviet Union, members of Hungary's German minority hold a protest meeting, calling for their release, and try to break out of the camp the same evening.

October 23: A debate is held at the Writer's Union, to discuss a report by a group of writers who have been touring villages in recent weeks.

November 17: Stalin's body is placed in the Lenin Mausoleum in Moscow.

December 1: The US National Security Council re-examines its policy towards Eastern Europe.

December 23: Beria, along with Merkulov, Dekanozov, Goglidze and other senior officials of the Interior Ministry, is condemned to death in Moscow.

1954

January 15: The military high court, chaired by Ferenc Ledényi, passes sentence after an appeal hearing on the prosecution of Gábor Péter, former head of the AVH, and 17 others. They were found guilty by a lower court on December 24, 1953.

April 26-July 21: The Geneva Conference on the Far East recognizes the status quo in Korea and the partition of Vietnam.

Early May: The information Office of the Council of Ministers is formed with Zoltán Szántó as its head and Miklós Vásárhelyi as his deputy.

May 24-30: The Third Congress of the HWP is held amidst political uncertainty and deadlock.

June 2: The freeing of Gyula Oszkó is the first of many releases of Communists imprisoned between 1949 and 1951, who had spent the war in hiding in Hungary or as exiles in the West rather than the Soviet Union.

July 7: AVH Lieutenant-General László Piros is appointed Minister of the Interior instead of Ernő Gerő. Gerő remains a deputy prime minister.

July 28: The Economic Policy Committee is formed, following a resolution by the HWP Political Committee.

August 24: The US Congress declares Communist activity illegal.

September: The Soviet army and navy begin to equip with nuclear weapons.

October 14: The HWP Political Committee passes a resolution supporting the new Soviet policy towards Yugoslavia.

October 20: The central Party daily, the Szabad Nép (Free People), carries an article by Imre Nagy entitled 'After the Meeting of the Central Committee'. This makes it clear there is in-fighting in the HWP and offers the first analysis of the reasons.

October 22, 23 and 25: There is a stormy three-day staff meeting at the Szabad Nép.

October 23-24: The founding congress of the Patriotic People's Front (PPF) elects the writer Pál Szabó as president and the Reformed Church minister Ferenc Jánosi as general secretary. Imre Nagy's speech on national unity led later to charges of nationalism being made against him.

October 23: Full sovereignty is restored to Germany (East and West Germany) through the Federal Republic (FRG). A protocol admitting the FRG to Nato is signed.

November 8: The Soviet-Hungarian joint ventures are transferred to 100 percent Hungarian ownership in a series of economic transactions.

November 14: Control of the daily Magyar Nemzet (Hungarian Nation) is transferred to the Patriotic People's Front, with Iván Boldizsár as editor.

November 21: An article by József Darvas, 'On overbidding', appears in the Szabad Nép. Instigated by Mihály Farkas and Márton Horváth, the article initiates an attack on Imre Nagy's policy line and the reform movement among writers and journalists.

December 1: Rákosi reports to the HWP Political Committee on a message received from the Presidium of the Communist Party of the Soviet Union (CPSU) Central Committee. This begins the process of ousting Imre Nagy from power.

December 15: The HWP Political Committee, continuing along the lines of its December meeting and in Imre Nagy's absence, passes a resolution on the 'right-wing danger' and condemns Nagy's policy. There is a purge among the staff at the Szabad Nép: Péter Kende, Endre Kövesi, Pál Lőcsei and Lajos Szilvási have to leave the paper.

December 21: Parliament meets in Debrecen to mark the 10th anniversary of the convening of the Provisional National Assembly there.

1955

January 8: Following an initiative from the Hungarian side, the Presidium of the CPSU Central Committee in Moscow has discussions with the HWP leaders. The policy of Imre Nagy is strongly criticized, but in a break with Communist tradition, Nagy does not 'exercise self-criticism' (declare himself in the wrong).

January 25: The Supreme Soviet in Moscow issues a decree declaring the state of war between the Soviet Union and Germany (East and West Germany) to be over.

February 1: Imre Nagy falls ill (with high blood pressure, nervous exhaustion and coronary thrombosis). On February 5, the doctors treating him prescribe complete rest, which effectively cuts him off from the political scene.

February 23: Imre Nagy addresses a letter to the HWP Political

Committee protesting against his isolation. He still refuses to exercise self-criticism.

March 2-4: Although the meeting of the HWP Central Committee does not annul the resolution of June 1953, it identifies the 'right-wing, anti-Marxist, anti-Party, opportunist' views represented by Imre Nagy as the main danger.

March 25: The Petőfi Circle is founded at the Kossuth Club, as an adjunct of the Union of Working Youth (DISZ), with Gábor Tánczos as its secretary.

March 28: Imre Nagy tenders his resignation as prime minister, in a letter to István Dobi, the president of the Presidential Council (head of state). Dobi informs Rákosi of this, but no reply is made or action taken.

April 14: A resolution adopted at a meeting of the HWP Central Committee accuses Imre Nagy of anti-Party activity and factionalism. Nagy, who still refuses to express remorse, is removed from the Political Committee and the Central Committee and deprived of all the functions he holds.

April 15: Rákosi informs Dobi in writing of the HWP Central Committee's proposal that Nagy be dismissed, arguing that 'he has not fulfilled satisfactorily the office of chairman of the Council of Ministers'.

April 18: Dobi, as head of state, appoints Adrás Hegedüs prime minister, as proposed by Rákosi.

April 29: Following a demand by the HWP Political Committee, Imre Nagy resigns his seats in Parliament and on Budapest City Council, his vice-chairmanship of the Patriotic

People's Front, his membership of the Hungarian Academy of Sciences, and his post as professor at the University of Economics.

May 5: The HWP Political Committee bans Nagy's published works.

May 9: The Federal Republic of Germany (East and West Germany) is admitted to Nato, as the Paris treaties come into force.

May 11-15: At a conference of Soviet-bloc countries in Warsaw, Albania, Bulgaria, Czechoslovakia, the GDR, Hungary, Poland, Romania and the Soviet Union sign a treaty of friendship, cooperation and mutual assistance, in response to the military cooperation established in Western Europe. The Warsaw Pact countries are to follow an agreed foreign policy and form a military alliance. The seat of the military high command is to be in Moscow.

May 15: The signing of the Austrian State Treaty turns Austria into an independent, democratic, neutral country.

May 26-June 2: A delegation led by Khrushchev, Bulganin, Mikoyan and Shepilov visits Belgrade. Relations between the Soviet Union and Yugoslavia are normalized.

July 17: Cardinal József Mindszenty, primate of the Catholic Church, is moved from prison to house arrest in Felsőpetény, Nógrád County.

July 18: An article in the Szabad Nép blames Gábor Péter and his 'gang' for the deterioration in Yugoslav-Hungarian relations.

July 18-23: A summit meeting of the Soviet Union, the United

States, Britain and France is held in Geneva.

September: The strength of the Hungarian People's Army is reduced by a further 20,000 men.

September 9-13: German-Soviet negotiations are held in Moscow, with Federal Chancellor Konrad Adenauer taking part.

October 14: József Grösz, archbishop of Kalocsa, is released from prison and placed under house arrest.

October 18: Communist writers and artists draft a memorandum addressed to the HWP Central Committee.

November 2-4: Zoltán Zelk presents the Writers' Memorandum at a Party meeting in the Writers' Union. It is passed on to the HWP Central Committee, with the support of the vast majority of members.

November 11: The heads of the Interior Ministry meet to discuss a report by the Ministry and the Chief Public Prosecutor's Department on the activity of the AVH, in which countless illegal acts are cited.

November 20 and 22: Two groups of about 1200 political prisoners return from the Soviet Union. Among them is Béla Kovács, former general secretary of the Small Landholders' Party (FkgP).

December 14: Sixteen new members are admitted to the United Nations, including Hungary, Bulgaria and Romania.

December 24: Reprisals are taken against the signatories of the Writers' memorandum, causing most of them to withdraw their signatures.

1956

January 1: A big reduction is made in the strength of the AVH.

January 23: Nikolai Bulganin, the Soviet Prime Minister, proposes in a letter to US President Eisenhower, that their two countries conclude a friendship and mutual non-aggression treaty.

February 14-25: The 20th Congress of the CPSU marks a turning point in the policy and ideology of the Soviet Party and of the international communist movement. The resolution breaks with the dogma that a third world war is inevitable and proclaims 'peaceful coexistence' between the two world systems. Khrushchev denounces Stalin's crimes in a four-hour speech to a closed session.

March 8: The Hungarian government abolishes the restricted border zone and the technical equipment sealing the Hungarian-Yugoslav border.

March 12-13: Rákosi reports on the 20th Congress to the HWP Central Committee. He states that the HWP has already been working along such lines.

March 17: The Petőfi Circle holds its first major event: an informal meeting at the Kossuth Club of former leaders of MEFESZ (the Hungarian Association of University and College Unions).

March 19-May 3: A disarmament conference of UN member-states is held in London.

March 27: Speaking at a meeting of Party activists in Heves County, Rákosi admits that the 1949 treason trial of László Rajk was a show trial.

April 7: The Information Bureau of Communist and Workers' Parties (Cominform) is disbanded.

April 10: Poland rehabilitates Wladyslaw Gomulka, former general secretary of the communist Party, who was convicted in 1951.

April 18-27: Khrushchev, first secretary of the CPSU Central Committee, and Prime Minister Bulganin visit London.

April 27: The guidelines for Hungary's Second Five-Year Plan are put forward for public discussion.

May 9 and 22: The Petőfi Circle holds an economic debate entitled 'Current Questions of Marxist Political Economy and the Guidelines of the 2nd Five-Year Plan'.

May 12: József Grösz, archbishop of Kalacsa, is released from house arrest.

May 18: Mátyás Rákosi makes what is to be his final public appearance, at a meeting of Budapest HWP activists in the Sports Hall.

May 28: The new leadership of the Petőfi Circle, which has been operating for two months, is formally convened. The secretary is Gábor Tánczos, with András B. Hegedüs, Balázs Nagy and Kálmán Pécsi as deputies.

May 30-June 1: The Petőfi Circle holds a historians' debate entitled 'Current Questions in Marxist Historical Studies'.

June 1: Vyacheslav Molotov, one of the main opponents of reconciliation with Yugoslavia, is dismissed as Soviet foreign minister and replaced by Shepilov.

June 6: A celebration is held at Imre Nagy's house in Orsó utca (2nd District), to mark his 60th birthday.

June 6-14: The Soviet politician Mikhail Suslov has talks in Budapest with the members of the HWP leadership and with János Kádár and Imre Nagy.

June 9: The Petőfi Circle holds a reunion of students of people's colleges, to rehabilitate Nékosz (the National Association of People's Colleges).

June 14: The HWP Central Committee passes a resolution on policy towards the intelligentsia. The Petőfi Circle holds a philosophers' debate entitled 'Current Problems in Marxist Philosophy'.

June 16: Communist propaganda receives criticism in the Irodalmi Újság (Literary Gazette) (Writers' Union), in an article by Tibor Tardos entitled 'Seawater is Salty'.

June 18: The Petőfi Circle holds an informal meeting of former wartime partisans and underground Communist-Party workers with young members of the Budapest intelligentsia, in the Central Officers' Hall in downtown Váci utca.

June 20: A Petőfi Circle debate takes place on 'Exploiting This Country's Natural and Economic Endowments in Planning the People's Economy'.

June 22-23: Leaders of the Soviet-bloc countries meet in Moscow to discuss the rapprochement with Yugoslavia

June 27: There is a Petőfi Circle debate on aspects of the press and information, held at the Central Officer's Hall.

June 28: In Poznań (Poznań workers' uprising), Poland, 100,000 workers take to the streets, calling for improvements in living and working conditions and free elections. The security forces use arms to break up the crowds. There are about 100 deaths and several hundred wounded. About 600 demonstrators are arrested.

June 30: The HWP Central Committee, in a resolution, condemns the anti-Party manifestations apparent in the Petőfi Circle.

July 2: The Pál Vasvári Circle in Szombathely, with teacher Miklós Horn as secretary, holds a debate of intellectuals, patterned on the Petőfi Circle events in Budapest.

July 3: The June 30 resolution of the CPSU Central Committee, on the cult of personality, appears in the Szabad Nép (Free People).

July 10: Speakers at a Party meeting in the Writers' Union criticize the June 30 resolution of the HWP Central Committee.

July 12: The US National Security Council issues a document on American policy towards the Eastern European countries.

July 13: A Malév Hungarian Airlines flight from Budapest to Szombathely is diverted to West Germany by armed hijackers.

July 17: Soviet politician Anastas Mikoyan arrives unexpectedly in Budapest and announces that Mátyás Rákosi is to be dismissed.

July 18-21: Rákosi announces his resignation as first secretary of the HWP, to a meeting of the Central Committee, citing his 'state of health'. His successor is Ernő Gerő. Rákosi leaves for exile in the Soviet Union, never to return. András Hegedüs remains as prime minister.

After July 21: The HWP Central Committee reports to the Party membership on the rehabilitations. The vast majority of these have been completed, with 474 cases being reviewed.

July 30: The government is reshuffled.

August 1: The government resolves to cut the strength of the army by 15,000.

September: Residents displaced from the Hungarian-Yugoslav border zone are allowed to return to their homes.

September 1: The Presidential Council rehabilitates 50 previously convicted social democrats.

September 2: A resolution of the HWP Central Committee proposes that streets may no longer be renamed after living persons.

September 14: A secret Soviet decree grants an amnesty to political prisoners with non-Soviet citizenship.

September 17: The General Assembly of the Writers' Union demonstrates in support of Imre Nagy.

September 19-27: Khrushcev pays a private visit to Yugoslavia, where he has talks with Tito on the Yugoslav island of Brioni.

September 19: The Petőfi Circle debates resume after a politically imposed break of two-and-a-half months. The first autumn event is entitled 'The Educational Experiences of the People's Colleges'. Removal of the technical equipment sealing the Hungarian-Austrian border is completed.

September 26: The Petőfi Circle holds a debate entitled 'Questions of Economic Leadership'.

September 28: A resolution of the HWP Political Committee orders the reburial of László Rajk, György Pálffy, Tibor Szőnyi and András Szalai, in a ceremony on October 6 with full military honors.

September 28 and October 12: The Petőfi Circle holds a debate entitled 'Questions of Hungarian Educational Affairs'.

September 30: Tito and Gerő meet in the Kremlin. Gerő reports on their discussions at the HWP Political Committee meeting on October 8.

October: Troop reductions in the Hungarian People's Army continue. The strength of the army at the outbreak of the Revolution is 120,000 - 130,000 men.

Early October: A Petőfi Circle of local intellectuals is founded in Békéscsaba. In Veszprém, the Batsányi Circle is formed according to the same pattern, with Árpád Brusznyai, a grammar-school teacher, at its head.

October 1: The main speaker at a several-day mass assembly at the College of Dramatic and Cinematic Art in Budapest is the writer István Csurka.

October 2: The government transfers control over the prisons from the Interior Ministry to the Justice Ministry.

October 4: Imre Nagy, based on a compromise formula, makes an application by letter for his HWP membership to be restored.

The Soviet government complies with a request from the Hungarian government for a loan of 100 million roubles for 1957.

October 5: The Presidential Council calls a meeting of Parliament for October 22.

The Supreme Court discharges Bishop Lajos Ordass of the Evangelical (Lutheran) Church, who was illegally convicted in 1948. The AVH officers Vladimir Farkas, Ervin Faludi, György Szendi, György Szántó and Ferenc Toldi are arrested.

October 6: The reburial of László Rajk, György Pálffy, Tibor Szönyi and András Szalai takes place at Budapest's Kerepesi út cemetery (8th District). The Szabad Nép carries on its front page a long article entitled 'Never Again', about the Communists executed seven years before. A crowd of 100,000 carrying no political slogans, attends the funeral.

After the funeral, there is a demonstration mainly of arts undergraduates, most of them members of the Kolkhoz Circle, at the Stalin Statue, before the Yugoslav Embassy and before the AVH headquarters at Andrássy út 60 (6th District), carrying slogans against Stalinism and the AVH and in praise of Yugoslavia.

The HWP Political Committee resolves to arrest Mihály Farkas, formerly the defense minister. Stricter military service is introduced at the Defense Ministry. The Attila Józsep Theatre in Budapest shows József Gáli's play Liberty Hill. University students in Szeged call for an end to compulsory teaching of the Russian language.

October 8: Imre Nagy has his final discussion with Ernő Gerő about the former's return to the Party.

The newspaper Hétfői Hirlap (Monday News) appears, with Iván Boldizsár as editor. This is the first example of a more relaxed style of newspaper to appear since the papers supporting the non-communist coalition parties were closed or taken over after 1948. (The daily papers do not appear on Mondays in this period.)

October 10: The Petőfi Circle holds a debate on 'Technical Development and the Problems of the Young Technical Intelligentsia'.

October 11: A local Petőfi Circle is founded in Pécs.

October 12: Mihály Farkas is arrested on the orders of the Chief Public Prosecutor's Department.

October 13: The HWP Political Committee passes a resolution readmitting Imre Nagy into the Party. The Kossuth Circle holds its first debate in the Old County Hall in Debrecen.

October 15: A Party and government delegation, consisting of Ernő Gerő, Antal Apró, András Hegedüs, János Kádár and István Kovács, leaves for a week's visit to Belgrade.

A literary and political debating society called the Bocskai Circle is founded in Hajdúnánás.

The United States suspends its deliveries of aid to Yugoslavia, due to the conspicuous improvement in Soviet-Yugoslav relations.

October 16: A meeting of about 1600 undergraduates in Szeged founds MEFESZ (the Hungarian Association of University and College Unions), a students' organization independent of DISZ (the Union of Working Youth) and the HWP.

October 17: The Petőfi Circle holds a debate on Gábor Pap's article 'Garden Hungary'.

October 18: The Presidential Council postpones until October 29 the session of Parliament scheduled for October 22.

A parliament of secondary-school students is held at the Party Instructors' House.

October 19: A students' assembly at the Budapest Technical University hostel in Hess András tér (1st District) sums up its demands in a 15-point resolution.

Soviet troops stationed in Hungary are placed on alert.

The Attila József Circle in Szeged arranges a debate on the position of the intelligentsia.

Gyula (Julius) Hay holds a writer's evening in Györ.

The 8th Plenary Session of the Polish United Workers' Party Central Committee coopts Wladyslaw Gomulka. This prompts a visit to Warsaw by CPSU Central Committee members Khrushchev, Lazar Kaganovich, Molotov and Mikoyan, along with Defense Minister Georgy Zhukov and Marshal Konev, Warsaw Pact commander-in-chief. Soviet forces and some Polish units move towards the Polish capital on the pretext of holding military exercises.

October 20: The Petőfi Circle debates the problems of the applied arts.

The Hajnóczy Circle is founded at the law faculty of Budapest's Loránd Eötvös University and the Széchényi Circle at the University of Economics. The universities also found the Vasvári Circle as a joint forum for debate.

A mass meeting is held at the Budapest Technical University on the current problems of the students and the technical intelligentsia.

The József Katona Theatre presents László Németh's play Galilei.

MEFESZ holds a mass meeting at the Szeged University of Sciences, chaired by Professor József Perbirö.

The HWP branch at the Lajos Kossuth University of Sciences in Debrecen holds an open day.

Agreement on reforms is reached early in the morning in Warsaw. The Soviet leaders accept the personnel changes in the Polish United Workers' Party and fly home. Anti-Soviet assemblies take place in almost every Polish town, culminating in demonstrations in some cases.

October 21: The Kossuth Circle is founded at the Eger teachers' training college and affiliates to MEFESZ.

Student delegations arrive in Budapest from Debrecen and Szeged for the national student parliament. The Szeged delegation also has talks with leaders of the Petőfi Circle.

In Warsaw, Wladyslaw Gomulka is elected first secretary of the Polish United Workers' Party Central Committee.

October 22: Commanders of units of regiment size and higher, along with their political deputies, are summoned for a meeting at the Defense Ministry on October 24.

A meeting of the DISZ (Union of Working Youth) Central Committee is called for the following day.

Also represented at an afternoon assembly at the Budapest Technical University are the Construction and Transport University, the Agricultural Engineering College, the Physical Education College, the College of Horticulture and Viticulture, the Military Engineering College, the Petőfi Academy, and the Máté Zalka Barracks. The meeting debates the demands put forward by the MEFESZ delegates from Szeged.

There are meetings at several other Budapest institutes of higher education during the afternoon, concurrently with the assembly at the Technical University. They include the University of Economics, the Budapest Medical University, the Drama College, the College of Horticulture and Viticulture, and Gödöllö Agricultural University.

The committee of the Petőfi Circle meets in the evening.

An assembly of students from the medical and legal university and of students and teachers from the teachers' training college begins at 3 p.m. at Pécs Central University.

The workers at the Dimávag engineering factory in Miskolc, led by Gyula Turbök and Károly Bogár, begin on October 15 and organize a Party open day, to clarify the problems. By October 22 they have collected 2000 signatures in the factory for this.

The students of the Miskoic Technical University affiliate to MEFESZ.

Students of the Forestry Engineering University and the Technical University for Heavy Industry hold a joint students' parliament in Sopron.

A branch of MEFESZ is formed at the Benczúr utca students' hostel, Debrecen.

Behind the remarkable memories and details he reports there is a highly refined analysis. He stressed critical thinking as an essential skill in life, and he demonstrates his own excellence in the answers to the questions.

I can "hear" Senator John F. Kennedy's words

Four thousand four hundred and six miles from here there lies tonight a captive city. While we who are free salute at festive banquets her noble fight for freedom, she weeps for the freedom—and the sons and daughters—that she has lost. While we who acted not deplore the frailties that held us back, she guards the graves of those who gave the last full measure of devotion. While we who only watched and waited seek loudly now to fix the blame and point with shame, she silently waits with ever dimming hope and strength for the keys to her prison door.

This is October 23, 1957— the first anniversary if a day that shook the world—a day that will forever live in the annals of free men and free nations—a day of courage and of conscience and of triumph. No other day since nations were first instituted among men had shown more conclusively, to oppressed and oppressor alike, the utter, inevitable futility of despotic rule. No other day has shown more clearly the eternal unquenchability of man's desire to be free whatever the odds against success, whatever the sacrifice required of him.

István B'Rácz rejected the Nazis, rejected the Communists, and experienced the inhuman treatment and serious flaws in the actions of those governments. The withering pain of the losses he saw when the world did not come to help Hungary be free stayed with him all of his life, and lays a sadness on my own for what they endured.

He brings forward a familiar reality that updates as "…because I am involved in mankind…send not to know for whom the bell tolls; it tolls for thee."

B.Gail Addis
Burning Bush Press of Asheville
2021

www.ingramcontent.com/pod-product-compliance
Lightning Source LLC
Chambersburg PA
CBHW032022290426
44110CB00012B/628